Understanding and Teaching Contemporary US History since Reagan

Edited by

KIMBER M. QUINNEY AND
AMY L. SAYWARD

The University of Wisconsin Press

The University of Wisconsin Press
728 State Street, Suite 443
Madison, Wisconsin 53706
uwpress.wisc.edu

Gray's Inn House, 127 Clerkenwell Road
London EC1R 5DB, United Kingdom
eurospanbookstore.com

Printed in the United States of America

This book may be available in a digital edition.

Library of Congress Cataloging-in-Publication Data
Names: Quinney, Kimber Marie, editor. | Sayward, Amy L., 1969–
    editor.
Title: Understanding and teaching contemporary US history since
    Reagan / edited by Kimber M. Quinney and Amy L. Sayward.
Other titles: Harvey Goldberg series for understanding and teaching
    history.
Description: Madison, Wisconsin : The University of Wisconsin Press,
    [2022] | Series: The Harvey Goldberg series for understanding and
    teaching history | Includes bibliographical references and index.
Identifiers: LCCN 2022013226 | ISBN 9780299339500 (hardcover)
Subjects: LCSH: United States—History—20th century—Study and
    teaching. | United States—History—21st century—Study and
    teaching.
Classification: LCC E175.8 .U53 2022 | DDC 973.9071—dc23/
    eng/20220603
LC record available at https://lccn.loc.gov/2022013226

To all the teachers and students who worked so diligently to teach and to learn during the pandemic

Contents

Contents

*Understanding and Teaching
Contemporary US History
since Reagan*

Introduction

Teaching Contemporary History
since Reagan

AMY L. SAYWARD AND
KIMBER M. QUINNEY

It is not easy to teach the history of contemporary American history in the best of times, but it would seem that today the study and teaching of US history is undergoing a dramatic, if not historic, evolution. We seem to be experiencing a critical moment in the history of history education. Increasingly loud and often partisan debates between academics, politicians, journalists, and media personalities question what American history *is*, what the purpose of learning history is, who gets to decide what is taught, how to reconcile our lives today in this country with the realities of our nation's history, and therefore how we should be teaching history, whether we are in a K–12 classroom or in a college.

As we were preparing this manuscript in 2021–22, the American Historical Association (AHA), the American Association of University Professors, the Association of American Colleges and Universities, and 147 other historical organizations had just issued a statement of "firm opposition" to legislation introduced in some twenty state legislatures that sought to outlaw the teaching of "divisive concepts," including "critical race theory." The primary objections listed by these historical organizations were that "these bills risk infringing on the right of faculty to teach and of students to learn" and that such legislation could hinder "students' ability to learn and engage in critical thinking across

3

differences and disagreements." The AHA statement identified such legislation as targeting "academic lessons, presentations, and discussions of racism and related issues in American history in schools, colleges, and universities."[1] Indeed, such legislation passed during the 2021–22 legislative session in Tennessee and Oklahoma (as well as Idaho), where protests connected to the Black Lives Matter movement intersected with public battles over the historical memory and commemoration, respectively, of Nathan Bedford Forrest (Confederate cavalry general and founder of the Ku Klux Klan) and the centennial of the 1921 destruction of the "Black Wall Street" Greenwood district of Tulsa and the massacre of Black residents there.[2] Another part of the context of such legislation was the *New York Times'* 1619 Project's efforts to identify and publicize the pervasive influence of race-based chattel slavery on the development of the American colonies and nation on the quadricentennial of its introduction—as well as its subsequent curriculum project.[3] Finally, since all three state bills passed on strictly party lines (with all but two Republicans in three states voting in favor and no Democrats), there clearly seems to be a political agenda at play that rightfully concerns educators.[4]

However, looking closely at the passed legislation (which is virtually identical state-to-state), few educators would argue that the goal of their instruction is that "an individual should feel discomfort, guilt, anguish, or another form of psychological distress solely because of the individual's race or sex," although discomfort is often a natural by-product of confronting difficult histories from the past, especially in one's home country. Additionally, the Oklahoma legislation stated that the new law "shall not prohibit the teaching of concepts that align to the Oklahoma Academic Standards," and the Tennessee legislation specifically enumerated that the law does not prohibit teaching "the history of an ethnic group," "the impartial discussion of controversial aspects of history," "the impartial instruction on the historical oppression of a particular group of people based on race, ethnicity, class, nationality, religion, or geographic region," or "historical documents" that cover these issues.[5] Of course, defining "impartial" is certainly open to interpretation—especially given the partisan nature of this legislation as well as the promotion of "patriotic education" by President Donald Trump's 1776 Commission (which did not include any historians studying or teaching US history and which directly sought to refute the 1619 Project's focus).[6] Most ominously, it is clear that the bills are already having a chilling effect on history educators who take race seriously.[7] Nonetheless, as a number of legislators, educators, historians, and commentators have noted, such legislation seems largely unconnected to the realities of classroom teaching in the United States, where education and critical thinking rather than indoctrination are the goal. Indeed, Oklahoma City School Superintendent Sean McDaniel called his state's legislation a "solution looking for a problem which does not exist," and even a Republican legislator acknowledged that the bill he was voting for "does not indicate that we've got some rampant problem in Idaho, but we don't want to get one."[8]

Such controversies over how history should be taught and the purpose of education in broader society are anything but new. Although many other states and communities did not share the Puritans' religious ideology, passage of the 1647 "Old Deluder Satan" law in Massachusetts set the pattern and example for publicly provided elementary education that has largely shaped the nation. Debates in the nineteenth century, ranging from John Dewey and George Washington Carver to the new land-grant colleges, argued that education needed a new direction, shifting away from a focus on classics and theology and toward the skills needed to compete in an increasingly globalized industrial and agricultural marketplace. At the dawn of the twentieth century, urban communities worked to acculturate an influx of immigrants and their children, while rural communities pushed against compulsory education and textbooks that seemed to idealize the modern experience of city dwellers. Fights over school textbooks have continued, largely unabated since that time. The federal government increasingly intervened in education starting with the Cold War's emphasis on math and science education as a matter of national defense. Since then, federal funding for education has frequently served as the lever that Washington, DC, uses to bring about change at the state level, ranging from promoting racial integration to standardized testing and accountability. The National History Standards debate of the 1990s put history education front and center in the nation's "culture wars." Nonetheless, through all of this and more, teachers have persisted in providing the best preparation they could for their students to become tomorrow's citizens, entrepreneurs, artists, parents, and more.[9]

As others have argued, it is important—even essential—that we, as history educators, engage with controversial issues and teach our students to critically read and think about such problems and to debate them in a thoughtful and civil manner.[10] So this book does not shy away from controversial issues, whether they are questions of voter suppression, LGBTQ+ rights, immigration over the southern border, climate change, or the different scrutiny that female appointees to the US Supreme Court have experienced. However, we also know that few educators enjoy the full legal protections of tenure and academic freedom, so in these pages we provide teachers with a variety of topics and lesson-plan approaches from which they can pick and choose. But at its heart, each chapter seeks to equip teachers to tackle any and all of these issues by empowering students to learn from the primary sources of the time, to think critically about them, and to develop their own interpretations about what happened in the recent past. After all, these are the key skills of the historical profession and of the future of our democracy in the twenty-first century.

Why Teach Contemporary History?

Contemporary history—the history that has happened within the lifetime of the instructor and/or the students—can be problematic first and foremost because the same chronological span of even twenty years, for example, is experienced so very differently by teachers and students. Our memories of and teaching about September 11, 2001, provides an excellent case in point. For the more seasoned instructor familiar with the history leading up to the event, the "recent" history of 9/11 may be viewed as a longer history, a continuation of the less recent history of the Cold War or even longer history of imperialism and colonization in the Middle East; for those who directly experienced the events related to 9/11, especially as children or young adults, their historical recollections of the event presumably may have an entirely different, personal impact; and for our students, even if they were not yet born, 9/11 marks a moment that defined their youth, their world, and perhaps their worldview as well—but sometimes in ways that are not evident to the student because their world has always had a Department of Homeland Security, for example. The value, then, in teaching contemporary history can be found in encouraging students to recognize that the same historical time period or event is experienced differently by different people, even when those people occupy the same generation.

Moreover, recent history often garners very little time and attention in our classrooms, whether we are teaching at the high school or college level. First, it frequently comes at the end of the semester or school year, when the cumulative effect of all of the schedule changes of the term come to bear, whether they were snow days or those class periods when you decided that students needed an extra period to grasp a particularly challenging assignment or concept. Second, the closer we get to the present, the more opinionated our students become, whether based on their own experience or what their parents or grandparents have shared with them about their own lives. Sometimes our natural response can be to shy away from these increasingly partisan and divisive issues.

Finally, the more contemporary a historical issue is, traditionally the less inclined are historical thinkers to want to weigh in. Implicit in our thinking as historians is the *past*; so, if we are asked to debate events of last year, or five years ago, or even ten years ago, we sometimes wonder, is that really *history*? For example, diplomatic historians are leery about drawing conclusions about a president's foreign policy before most of the documents related to that decision-making have been declassified (a process that starts after twenty-three years). And it takes even longer for historians to understand whether a particular event represents a fundamental change or illustrates the greater strength of the forces of continuity in history. Most of us can recall, for example, the election of US President Barack Obama in 2008 and the sense at the time that racial issues in the country might have fundamentally changed—that if a majority of the electorate could vote for and then reelect in 2012 the country's first Black president, then maybe some fundamental watershed had been reached. However, events since that historic election have called this tentative conclusion into question. For all of these reasons, state standards also grow sketchier the closer we get to the present, and even textbook authors can seem far more hesitant and even reluctant to draw conclusions in their analyses of contemporary events. Therefore, it may be hard for classroom teachers to judge and teach such things. As a result, the historical period closest to the present can seem the most daunting to teach.

There are, however, compelling reasons to give significant time and attention to the most recent periods of history when teaching the modern US history survey. For many—if not most—of our students, the history we will teach them about the United States will be the last formal instruction they will receive on the topic. For today's students—who generally lack personal recollections about the 9/11 terrorist attacks on the World Trade Center and the Pentagon in 2001 even if it is a formative event in

7

shaping the world in which they live—it can be confounding to understand why US troops in Afghanistan were only recently withdrawn and why there are still prisoners being held at Guantánamo Bay Detention Camp. And when President Donald J. Trump faced impeachment in December 2019 and the news media contextualized the proceedings by citing earlier inquiries into presidents Bill Clinton and Richard Nixon, it can be difficult for students to understand the present situation when they lack formal instruction in recent American history.

In order to appreciate how we got to the present historical moment, we are absolutely convinced that we need to look behind us to trace our steps, to analyze the events and decisions that were made around those events. Students need historical understanding to help them contextualize the present. Additionally, historians in the present seem increasingly willing to bring their historical training and expertise to bear on the present. The *Washington Post*'s "Made by History" series features exactly this and can be a rich resource for the teacher wanting to see how history is informing the present moment—with the website featuring both the most recent columns and the most read ones.[11] So we invite teachers to go boldly into the recent past in their teaching, drawing on the resources of engaged historians and on this volume.

Why Teach Historical Thinking?

If our students today are to be the informed citizens of tomorrow, we need to teach them how to understand the present through the prism of the past. Additionally, most of us who teach history believe and state—either explicitly or implicitly—that learning US history is a cornerstone for civic engagement among our students, which in turn is key to the future of a healthy, functioning democratic republic that relies on an electorate that is knowledgeable, motivated, and able to think critically about the issues and candidates of the day. Our students and electorate have to do this within a different media landscape as well. The decline of many traditional news outlets (especially newspapers) and the fact that both foreign and domestic influences try to shape US public opinion through "fake news" on a variety of topics has fostered a growing emphasis on media literacy in US society. In our classrooms, we can help students learn how to identify legitimate sources of information and to better identify the perspective of the author writing a piece.[12] In light of these important goals that transcend the classroom and the semester, teaching contemporary history—and teaching it well—seems all the more important.

Since you picked up this book and have read this far, you likely want to teach contemporary US history well, but you may be wondering how to do this. A foundational assertion of this volume is that teaching history means teaching students how to think historically—for example, teaching students how to "source" a document and understand how the perspective of the author and the historical context influenced what they wrote, how to understand the forces of change and continuity in history, how to understand the importance of chronology and cause-and-effect relationships, how to develop historical empathy (be able to think yourself into a historical actor's shoes), and how to understand that there are always multiple perspectives on the same historical event that can complicate and deepen our understanding of what happened.[13] Another essential historical thinking skill that we emphasize when we teach contemporary history is the notion of critically examining historical issues through the lens of *analysis and decision-making*. According to the American Historical Association,

> One should examine the events of the past and think about what led up to them. What might have been done differently to resolve problems? What alternative actions might have been taken? What can we learn about how people made decisions to do the things they did? To answer these questions, [students] should be able to evaluate the implementation of a decision by analyzing the interests it served; by estimating the position, power, and priorities of each actor involved; by assessing the ethical dimensions of the decision; and by evaluating its costs and benefits from a variety of perspectives.[14]

If you are new to teaching or new to the idea that your goal is to teach historical thinking (rather than simply covering historical content), we hope that you will find the lesson plans in this volume provide you with good and useful examples of how to structure such a lesson and to help your students develop and hone these key critical thinking skills. In fact, we asked each of the authors not simply to talk about how to teach these topics, but to include specific lesson plans or recommendations so that you (the reader/teacher) can potentially pull this book off the shelf and teach the lessons included with little additional work. But given that class periods vary in length, that students are different from

9

one year to the next and one institution to the next, and that you have been developing particular themes, ideas, and skills all semester that might change in the next, we decided that yet more flexibility and additional teaching options would be especially helpful. So, we have also provided a companion website (http://GoldbergSeries.org/UTContem poraryUSHistory) where you will be able to access additional teaching materials—worksheets as well as primary-source documents—that you can edit to fit your needs. We have also made a commitment to keep the links active and potentially to update the materials over time, so feel free to email us to provide any input, suggestions, or ideas on how we might make these materials even better. Our contact information can be found at the website.

The chapters and lesson plans in this volume are far from uniform, a testament to the reality that we all think differently about history and that we all teach—and think about how to teach—in our own ways. Rather than create a uniform template, we have instead welcomed diversity to meet the needs of our diverse group of readers and learners. Additionally, our authors teach and have taught at a variety of types of educational institutions, ranging from K–12 public schools to community colleges and universities around the country. We are very proud of the great group of authors who agreed to join this project and to share their expertise and their passions to help the broad community of educators better teach the history of the recent past.

Why Teach Primary Sources?

If we agree that teaching historical thinking skills is important—even vital—then we need to bring students to the study of primary sources, the raw material of all historical inquiry. Primary sources range widely in their variety, from written documents, archaeological excavations, material culture, and photographs to maps, charts, music, bumper stickers, and political cartoons, among others. Think of these lessons as laboratories in which your students will work with the same materials and practice the same procedures that you yourself have done in your own historical research and writing (including, whenever possible, researching and identifying the sources themselves). Students will be reading the sources, understanding the perspective of the author who wrote them (their time, location, background, perspective, etc.), perhaps examining the same event from multiple perspectives, trying to understand the intention of the author or the order of events, or discerning how or whether there was more change or continuity in policy across presidential administrations. More significant still, through close reading and analysis of primary sources, students will be invited to draw their own conclusions about big, open-ended questions that historians today (and in the future, most likely) ask: What have been the key factors driving climate change? Has there been more change or continuity in US foreign policy over the past forty years? And what about other policies related to education, drugs, and homeland security? Were the actions of protesters important in advancing nuclear arms control? Have race relations in the United States improved over the past forty years? Is voting primarily a right or a responsibility? Have the lives of LGBTQ+ Americans improved? Has US immigration policy had a negative or positive effect on the country? How could two primary or secondary sources reporting on the same event reach such different conclusions? How have women leaders and feminist social movements changed the nation over the past four decades? And how have the major political ideologies— liberalism, conservatism, radicalism, and populism—affected the way Americans live their lives?

Not only are teaching historical thinking skills and having students engage in historical laboratories with primary sources good activities in themselves, but such a framework also provides a way to unravel the partisanship and tension that have been so prevalent in the last forty years. The aim is not for students to reach consensus around these contentious events, but rather for students to appreciate, in the words of historian James Loewen, that "history is furious debate informed by evidence and reason."[15] Rather than the instructor drawing their own conclusions and sharing those in a lecture format with students, these lessons—grounded in primary-source exercises and supported by historical context through secondary sources—ask students to draw their own conclusions based on the words of the key historical actors at the time. What did Americans say about the first woman to be nominated to sit on the US Supreme Court? How did Ronald Reagan's characterization of the Soviet Union change from the beginning of his presidency to the end of his second term? How have Mexican migrants described their experiences of crossing the border and living in the United States?

A helpful question or intervention in the classroom discussions built into these lessons, especially when students fall back on language about "my opinion," is to ask, what in the text(s) that you read supports this point of view? Placing the onus on students to conduct their own analysis and interpretation of the document has several potential benefits: It helps establish or reinforce that history is a discipline that relies on what is in the historical record. It helps students examine their previous mindsets about historical issues and people in light of new information and to potentially change or alter their opinions.[16] This questioning strategy also has the potential to prompt students to do additional research to find sources that might support their own views, which could lead to a deeper and richer discussion about how historians put different sources into conversation with one another. Finally, this approach can help democratize historical inquiry, positioning the teacher and the student as seekers on a more equal footing in the texts and empowering the student to reach their own informed, historical conclusion (far better than an opinion!).[17]

In sum, we have created this volume to help our colleagues who are teachers to better handle the crucial yet daunting history of our own lifetimes in an effective way that helps students think more critically and more historically about the world around them. We hope students will act from this historical knowledge in a way that helps build a better nation and a better world in the future. In essence, through the lens of the wide-ranging historical issues covered in this book, our hope is that teachers and their students engage in conversations about the recent history of the United States that facilitate their crafting of a future better than our own contemporary history.

NOTES

1. "Joint Statement on Legislative Efforts to Restrict Education about Racism in American History (June 2021)," American Historical Association, June 16, 2021, https://www.historians.org/divisive-concepts-statement. For a summary of state legislation, see "Map: Where Critical Race Theory Is under Attack," *EducationWeek*, updated July 30, 2021, https://www.edweek.org/policy-politics/map-where-critical-race-theory-is-under-attack/2021/06.

2. See, for example, Johnny Diaz, "Bust of Klan Leader Removed from Tennessee State Capitol," *New York Times*, July 23, 2021, https://www.nytimes.com/2021/07/23/us/nathan-bedford-forrest-bust.html; Associated Press, "Oklahoma Governor Booted from Tulsa Race Massacre Commission," *U.S. News & World Report*, May 14, 2021, https://www.usnews.com/news/politics/articles/2021-05-14/oklahoma-governor-booted-from-tulsa-race-massacre-commission.

3. The 1619 Project, *New York Times Magazine*, August 14, 2019, https://www.nytimes.com/interactive/2019/08/14/magazine/1619-america-slavery.html; "The 1619 Project Curriculum," Pulitzer Center, https://pulitzercenter.org/lesson-plan-grouping/1619-project-curriculum (accessed August 7, 2021).

4. For voting on these bills see Matt Trotter, "House Holds Do-Over Vote on Critical Race Theory Ban over 'Voting Anomaly,'" Public Radio Tulsa, May 3, 2021, https://www.publicradiotulsa.org/post/house-holds-do-over-vote-critical-race-theory-ban-over-voting-anomaly#stream/0; Ray Carter, "Senate Advances Ban on Critical Race Theory," Oklahoma Council of Public Affairs, April 22, 2021, https://www.ocpathink.org/post/senate-advances-ban-on-critical-race-theory; Marta W. Aldrich, "Tennessee Governor Signs Bill Restricting How Race and Bias Can Be Taught in Schools," [Nashville] *Tennessean*, May 25, 2021, https://www.tennessean.com/story/news/education/2021/05/25/tennessee-critical-race-theory-governor-signs-bill-restricting-how-race-and-bias-can-taught-schools/7427131002/; "Roll Call: ID H0377, 2021: Votes," LegiScan, https://legiscan.com/ID/rollcall/H0377/id/1062907.

5. Oklahoma State Legislature, "Enrolled [final version] House Bill No. 1775," http://webserver1.lsb.state.ok.us/cf_pdf/2021-22%20ENR/hB/HB1775%20ENR.PDF, specifically Section 1(b); Tennessee State Legislature, "Conference Committee Report on House Bill No. 580 / Senate Bill No. 623," https://www.capitol.tn.gov/Bills/112/CCRReports/CC0003.pdf, specifically Section 51. See also "Bill Text: ID H0377, 2021, Regular Session, Introduced: Texts," LegiScan, April 29, 2021, https://legiscan.com/ID/text/H0377/2021.

6. The President's Advisory 1776 Commission, *The 1776 Report*, January 2021, https://trumpwhitehouse.archives.gov/wp-content/uploads/2021/01/The-Presidents-Advisory-1776-Commission-Final-Report.pdf; American Historical Association, "AHA Condemns Report of Advisory 1776 Commission (January 2021)," January 20, 2021, https://www.historians.org/news-and-advocacy/aha-advocacy/aha-statement-condemning-report-of-advisory-1776-commission-(january-2021).

7. Hannah Knowles, "Critical Race Theory Ban Leads Oklahoma College to Cancel Class That Taught 'White Privilege,'" *Washington Post*, May 29, 2021, https://www.washingtonpost.com/education/2021/05/29/oklahoma-critical-race-theory-ban/.

8. Oklahoma State Legislature, "Enrolled [final version] House Bill No. 1775," specifically Section 1(b); Tennessee State Legislature, "Conference Committee Report on House Bill No. 580 / Senate Bill No. 623," specifically Section 51. See also "Bill Text: ID H0377, 2021, Regular Session, Introduced: Texts."

9. Wayne J. Urban, Jennings L. Wagoner Jr., and Milton Gaither, *American Education: A History*, 6th ed. (New York: Routledge, 2019); Sarah Curran Bernard and Sarah Mondale, eds., *School: The Story of American Public Education* (Boston: Beacon Books, 2002); Oriana Bandiera, Myra Mohnen, Imran Rasul, and Martina Viarengo, "Nation-Building through Compulsory Schooling during the Age of

Mass Migration," *Economic Journal* 129, no. 617 (January 2019): 62–109, https://doi.org/10.1111/ecoj.12624; Kyle Ward, *Not Written in Stone: Learning and Unlearning U.S. History through 200 Years of Textbooks* (New York: New Press, 2010); Marilyn Irvin Holt, *Cold War Kids: Politics and Childhood in Postwar America, 1945–1960* (Lawrence: University Press of Kansas, 2014); Gary Nash, "Reflections on the National History Standards," *National Forum* (Summer 1997), http://www-personal.umich.edu/~mlassite/discussions261/nash.html; Olivia B. Waxman, "Trump's Threat to Pull Funding from Schools over How They Teach Slavery Is Part of a Long History of Politicizing American History Class," *Time*, last updated September 17, 2020, https://time.com/5889051/history-curriculum-politics/.

10. Jonathan Zimmerman and Emily Robertson, *The Case for Contention: Teaching Controversial Issues in American Schools*, 2nd ed. (Chicago: University of Chicago Press, 2017).

11. "Made by History," *Washington Post*, https://www.washingtonpost.com/made-by-history/ (accessed August 6, 2021).

12. Sam Wineburg, *Why Learn History (When It's Already on Your Phone)* (Chicago: University of Chicago Press, 2018). See also Sam Wineburg and A. Reisman, "Disciplinary Literacy in History: A Toolkit for Digital Citizenship," *Journal of Adolescent and Adult Literacy* 58, no. 8 (2015): 636–39; S. McGrew, J. Breakstone, T. Ortega, M. Smith, and Sam Wineburg, "Can Students Evaluate Online Sources? Learning from Assessments of Civic Online Reasoning," *Theory and Research in Social Education* 46, no. 2 (2018): 165–93.

13. Bruce Lesh, *"Why Won't You Tell Us the Answer?" Teaching Historical Thinking in Grades 7–12* (Portsmouth, NH: Stenhouse, 2010); University of Maryland—Baltimore County Center for History Education, "History Labs: A Guided Approach to Historical Inquiry in the K–12 Classroom," UMBC, https://www.umbc.edu/che/historylabs/ (accessed July 16, 2020); Bruce Lesh, "Social Studies Labs with Bruce Lesh," Thinking Like a Historian Social Studies Video Series, Georgia Department of Education, https://www.georgiastandards.org/Georgia-Standards/Pages/Thinking-Like-a-Historian-Social-Studies-Video-Series.aspx (accessed July 16, 2020); Historical Thinking Matters, https://historicalthinkingmatters.org/ (accessed July 16, 2020).

14. American Historical Association, "Historical Thinking Skills: What Skills Should You Have When You Leave a History Class?," https://www.historians.org/teaching-and-learning/teaching-resources-for-historians/teaching-and-learning-in-the-digital-age/the-history-of-the-americas/the-conquest-of-mexico/for-teachers/setting-up-the-project/historical-thinking-skills#5 (accessed August 9, 2021).

15. James W. Loewen, *Lies My Teacher Told Me: Everything Your American History Textbook Got Wrong* (New York: New Press, 1995), 8. See also James M. Banner Jr., *The Ever-Changing Past: Why All History Is Revisionist History* (New Haven, CT: Yale University Press, 2021).

16. Sam Wineburg, *Historical Thinking and Other Unnatural Acts: Charting the Future of Teaching the Past* (Philadelphia: Temple University Press, 2001); Carol S. Dweck, "The Power of Believing That You Can Improve," December 2014 TED talk, TED, https://www.ted.com/talks/carol_dweck_the_power_of_belie ving_that_you_can_improve (accessed July 16, 2020); Carol Dweck, *Mindset* (New York: Random House, 2006).

17. Great Books Foundation, "What Is Shared Inquiry?," https://www .greatbooks.org/nonprofit-organization/what-is-shared-inquiry/ (accessed July 16, 2020).

PART ONE

Within the Borders of the United States

"Life, Liberty, or Property"

Analyzing American Identity through Open Resources

Monica L. Butler

Why Teach This Lesson?

This lesson explores what it means to be an American. It is a topic many educators struggle with or simply avoid due to its pliable and contentious nature. It is ironic that we approach this topic with hesitancy, given that educators possess a unique set of skills and knowledge to help students understand the relevance and complexity of American identity. This lesson aims to alleviate some of our shared reluctance by scrutinizing primary source documents and assessing students' competency in key historical thinking skills: identifying historical concepts, analyzing sources and context, historical reasoning, and developing an argument.[1]

When teaching this topic, it is essential for educators to provide students with a framework for understanding American identity and to engage authoritative voices from the historical record. The lesson presented in this chapter requires students to engage presidential policy regarding the Due Process Clause. Given America's origins as a patriarchal, slaveholding colony, American identity is not tied to citizenship but rather the relentless pursuit of equality under the law. Integral to the history of the United States of America, the Due Process Clause affirms that no one can deny another's right to "life, liberty, or property without due process of law."[2] For over two hundred years, institutions and individuals in the United States have promised to maintain these freedoms. Yet the nation's history of uprisings, court battles, and other sociopolitical conflicts demonstrates that the quest for equal access to life, liberty, and property is ongoing and violently competitive. In an effort to understand the application of due process over time, this lesson requires students to investigate the policies of modern presidents. While the perspectives of the American people in general are supremely valuable, executive policies dictate the parameters of due process at a given moment in history.

Focusing on presidential policies and legal concepts does not prevent us from embracing diversity in the classroom or fostering an inclusive environment. As a history professor at an open access institution, I aim to provide students with the analytical skills and historical knowledge necessary for civic engagement and professional success. I neither discourage nor promote patriotism. My teaching philosophy acknowledges the varied experiences that shape student perceptions of history. This informs my choice of teaching strategies, as I strive to make course goals accessible and relevant while exploring the dynamics of American identity and access to justice. Using a summative assessment as an example, this chapter demonstrates the utility of Universal Design to engage students in historical thinking about American identity and due process.

Universal Design

Training students to understand the meaning of these constitutional promises at the open access or community college level creates unique challenges and opportunities. Instructors often teach overloads of general education courses with limited resources while accommodating students' varied academic backgrounds.[3] My effort to fit within the parameters of open access education has led me toward Universal Design (UD) to ensure collective access to materials and diverse ways of expressing historical knowledge. As explained by educator Sheryl E. Burgstahler, "UD promotes an expanded goal to make products and environments welcoming and useful to groups that are diverse in many dimensions, including gender, race, ethnicity, age, socioeconomic status, ability, veteran status, disability, and learning style."[4] Providing accessible online materials, adaptable open educational resources (OER), and an inclusive classroom environment places value on the diverse experiences of students, which, in turn, enhances engagement.

A universal or *democratized* approach to teaching and learning mirrors the historical content students explore in a United States history survey course. In keeping with UD, I assign free, peer-reviewed, OER materials, as well as open access podcasts, films, and contemporary art relevant to course content.[5] Therefore, all course materials are available free, online, and in formats accessible to students of varying abilities. Yet the classroom environment must also be accommodating to employ UD genuinely. This is not only done by simply following the guidelines of our disability services departments but rather by making sure students feel seen and heard as individuals in the classroom. We can foster diversity, equity, and inclusion through the content we choose, the way we facilitate discussion, and the assignments we create. These are all reflections of what we value as educators. Throughout the modern US history survey, I introduce students to debates on American identity over time so that we can see the evolution, and lack thereof, in the collective quest for liberty.

Students have a personal investment in this historical narrative. Therefore, as a final summative assessment, I require students to demonstrate historical knowledge and critical thinking by constructing their own analyses of contemporary policies regarding American identity. This final lesson plan requires students to demonstrate new skills and knowledge by interpreting assigned presidential policies on religious freedom, marriage equality, and other issues Americans have identified as inalienable rights. Analysis of policies since 1980 tells us a recognizable story of expanding and contracting access to due process of law.

Primary Sources

The first source assigned for this project is Ronald Reagan's opposition to the Civil Rights Restoration Act of 1987 (CRRA), which serves as a transition to modern presidential policy. Congress developed the law in response to the case of *Grove City v. Bell*, which limited federal enforcement of civil rights to federally funded programs.[6] The CRRA sought to eliminate ongoing discrimination in all private institutions and businesses accepting federal funds. In Reagan's remarks on the proposed legislation (freely available online), he both revived segregationist arguments from America's past while also appealing to his New Right base in ways that would become familiar in the coming decades. Interrogation of this document helps students understand Reagan's legacy on due process and his relationship with America, as Congress overrode his veto by a wide margin.

Reagan's objections to the CRRA presented a religious freedom argument that both harkened back to previous and helped craft future rhetoric. Characterizing the Civil Rights Restoration Act of 1987, Reagan stated,

> The bill presented to me would diminish substantially the freedom and independence of religious institutions in our society. The bill would seriously impinge upon religious liberty because of its unprecedented and pervasive coverage of churches and synagogues based on receipt of even a small amount of Federal aid for just one activity; its unprecedented coverage of entire religious elementary and secondary school systems when only a single school in such a system receives Federal aid; and its failure to protect, under Title IX of the Education Amendments of 1972, the religious freedom of private schools that are closely identified with the religious tenets of, but not controlled by, a religious organization.[7]

Students recognize the "religious freedom" argument from our interrogation of the 1950s' Massive Resistance movement against civil rights and desegregation. As historian Jane Dailey explains in "The Theology of Massive Resistance," white segregationists in the South often argued that interracial socialization was sinful and an affront to their interpretations of Christianity.[8] Reagan's opposition to the CRRA illustrates a revival of this perspective to impede contemporary movements toward equal access. Following Reagan's lead, the New Right has continued to employ this concept of religious freedom into the twenty-first century. Subsequently, Reagan's interpretation of civil liberties warrants comparison with that of his vice president and successor, George H. W. Bush.

Although Reagan and Bush were ideologically similar, their legacies diverge. Bush echoed Reagan's opposition to affirmative action and women's reproductive rights and likewise vetoed legislation to expand American liberties during his own administration. Bush also planted himself firmly at an intersection of race and sex by nominating conservative Clarence Thomas for Justice Thurgood Marshall's vacancy on the US Supreme Court. Much of this stands in contrast to Bush's enthusiasm for the Americans with Disabilities Act (ADA). Bush stated,

> For too many Americans, the blessings of liberty have been limited or even denied. The Civil Rights Act of '64 took a bold step towards righting that wrong. But the stark fact remained that people with disabilities

were still victims of segregation and discrimination, and this was intolerable. Today's legislation brings us closer to that day when no Americans will ever again be deprived of their basic guarantee of life, liberty, and the pursuit of happiness.[9]

While Bush proudly supported expansion of due process to include Americans with disabilities, his final sentence here acknowledges that America has yet to fulfill its founding promises. Like the Reagan document, Bush's remarks are freely available online. Yet students can also watch or listen to Bush deliver this speech through the Miller Center at the University of Virginia or on C-SPAN, which further enhances their learning experience.

In keeping with UD, I aim to assign primary sources that are available in multiple formats. However, while it may be ideal to use film or audio for all modern primary sources, I also want students to interact with rarely utilized documents. This does not require abandoning the open access model but rather choosing equally accessible alternative texts. This is the case with Bill Clinton's legacy on due process.

Unlike the previous decade of conservatism, President Bill Clinton promised to expand civil liberties and equal access to opportunities. As a presidential candidate, Clinton pledged to end the military's long history of discrimination against LGBTQ+ service members. Yet barriers to equal opportunity define his legacy on due process, given his endorsement of the "Don't Ask, Don't Tell" (DADT) policy. Presented as a "compromise" between the liberal administration and military leaders, DADT largely reinforced existing regulations that discriminated based on sexual orientation. The policy states, "Homosexual conduct is grounds for barring entry into the Armed Forces, except as otherwise provided in this section. Homosexual conduct is a homosexual act, a statement by the applicant that demonstrates a propensity or intent to engage in homosexual acts, or a homosexual marriage or attempted marriage."[10] While Clinton's remarks on DADT are available in audiovisual format, the LGBTQ+ community broadly criticized him for misrepresenting this policy.[11] Therefore, I require students to study the DADT policy itself, Department of Defense Directive Number 1304.26. While this policy is available freely online and is accessible to students using document readers, it is not multimediated.

This choice in documents extends to George W. Bush's presidency as well. During his first address to Congress in February 2001, Bush expressed an indistinct policy on racial profiling. He indicated, "Earlier today, I asked John Ashcroft, the attorney general, to develop specific recommendations to end racial profiling. It's wrong, and we will end it in America. In so doing, we will not hinder the work of our nation's brave police officers. They protect us every day, often at great risk. But by stopping the abuses of a few, we will add to the public confidence our police officers earn and deserve."[12] These remarks are widely available online but do not clearly or genuinely capture the president's legacy of due process. The Bush administration inextricably linked the practice of racial profiling to its domestic War on Terror, which began several months after this widely publicized speech.

Therefore, I have students study the Department of Justice (DOJ) "Fact Sheet: Racial Profiling," which was made public in 2003. Examination of this document reveals that while the DOJ collected data on racial profiling and condemned the practice, it failed to offer any solutions.[13] Moreover, this document was a response to mounting criticism of the 2001 U.S. Patriot Act, which codified racial profiling of foreign nationals for the sake of national security.[14] The "Fact Sheet" acknowledged ties between racial profiling and the War on Terror in stating, "The racial profiling guidance recognizes that race and ethnicity may be used in terrorist identification, but only to the extent permitted by the nation's laws and the Constitution. The policy guidance emphasizes that, even in the national security context, the constitutional restriction on use of generalized stereotypes remains." Therefore, this document confirms the centrality of racial profiling to Bush's legacy on due process.[15]

Finding documents that definitively express Barack Obama's policies regarding due process is equally challenging. Despite being America's first president of African American heritage, or arguably because of this, he carefully maneuvered around issues of social justice. An arguable exception is Obama's legacy on indigenous rights. He actively campaigned in Indian Country and articulated an understanding of tribal self-determination. As president, he seemingly upheld his commitments by signing the United Nations Declaration on the Rights of Indigenous People while also repatriating lands and resources to several tribal nations. Moreover, his administration signaled support for the Standing Rock Sioux Tribe in blocking the construction of the Dakota Access Pipeline.[16] While several Obama proclamations reinforce this legacy, his 2015 Presidential Proclamation on Asian American and Pacific

Islander (AAPI) Heritage Month complicates his policies toward indigenous peoples and challenges students to demonstrate key historical thinking skills.

Obama's adherence to AAPI as a demographic undermines his legacy on indigenous rights and reveals significant nuances in our understanding of American identity. While indigenous Pacific Islanders have political and cultural histories distinct from mainland tribal nations, they share the same rights as outlined by the United Nations. Assimilating indigenous Pacific Islanders into a demographic with non-indigenous, immigrant populations serves as a form of cultural erasure and obscures the realities of settler colonialism.[17] While this 2015 proclamation recognizes America's history of imperialism, it falls short of recognizing indigenous Pacific Islanders' struggles for resources and sovereignty. Instead, Obama's remarks often shifted toward multiculturalism, which he credited for shaping his perspective on American identity.

Obama's conflation of diverse immigrant and indigenous communities and his emphasis on due process reinforce his policy of multiculturalism. The proclamation offers a condensed history of Chinese American labor, Native Hawaiian cultural resilience, Japanese American internment, and discriminatory military policies. The president then summarized existing limitations to equality under the law by stating,

> We must also acknowledge the many struggles AAPIs continue to experience in the face of persistent inequality and bigotry, including barriers to equal access to education, employment, and health care. South Asian Americans—especially those who are Muslim, Hindu, or Sikh—too often face senseless violence and harassment due only to the color of their skin or the tenets of their faith. And to this day, many AAPIs continue to live in the shadows and are separated from their families due to our broken immigration system.[18]

Despite this insight, Obama neglected to acknowledge contemporary struggles for sovereignty, as they conflicted with this message of multicultural access to due process. He subsequently shifted focus to increases in federal programs and his restoration of the White House Initiative and President's Advisory Commission on Asian Americans and Pacific Islanders. It is this federal intervention that highlights the unique status of indigenous Pacific Islanders and distinctions within the AAPI demographic.

While many AAPI communities welcomed the administration's efforts, federal intervention held separate meaning and consequences for indigenous Pacific Islanders, specifically Native Hawaiians.[19] In the months following this proclamation, the Department of Interior (DOI) announced a Notice of Proposed Rulemaking initiating a government-to-government trust relationship with Native Hawaiians. The DOI argued this status would "provide the community with greater flexibility to preserve its distinct culture and traditions and special status under Federal law that enables the community to exercise powers of self-government over many issues directly impacting community members."[20] Subsequently, this rule has highlighted the complexity of Hawaiian politics by eliciting competing responses from Native Hawaiian leadership and sparking non-indigenous debate of due process.[21] Overall, Obama's proclamation encourages students to critically evaluate the meaning of citizenship within a settler colonial context. Doing so also inspires informed discussion of how multiculturalism conceals indigenous rights and disguises systemic inequalities.

Subsequently, the media has littered the internet with sound bites and video of President Donald Trump expressing his views on equal rights, or lack thereof. Despite the wealth of public statements made by President Trump, it is challenging to identify a single coherent document for academic analysis. In keeping with the course theme on due process, I selected the president's 2019 remarks on the United States census. Trump had ordered the Department of Commerce to inquire about citizenship status on the 2020 census. While the courts upheld the administration's right to do so, all courts agreed that the president's expressed goal of penalizing undocumented workers denied them rights of due process.[22]

Trump's response to the US Supreme Court's ruling reiterates views expressed throughout his campaign and tenure in office. He stated, "Now they're trying to erase the very existence of a very important word and a very important thing: citizenship. They're even coming after the Pledge of Allegiance in Minnesota. I'm proud to be a citizen. You're proud to be a citizen. The only people who are not proud to be citizens are the ones who are fighting us all the way about the word, 'citizen.'"[23] Based on previous interrogation of primary sources, I press students to identify key individuals and institutions discussed in the historical record. Here, it appears that the "they" Trump refers to are the federal courts. Unlike Obama, who handed off responsibility to co-branches of government, President Trump seized power as executive to circumvent undesirable results from the judicial system. He settled on a strategy for achieving his goals by proclaiming: "Today, I will be issuing an executive order to put this very plan into effect immediately. I'm hereby ordering every department and agency in the federal government to provide the Department of Commerce with all requested records regarding the number of citizens and non-citizens in our country. They must furnish all legally accessible records in their possession immediately."[24] Therefore, rather than operating within the constitutional parameters established by federal courts, the Trump administration wielded its power of executive order to potentially limit the rights of American residents.

As with other assigned documents, Trump's remarks are available in multimedia format online. I not only chose these primary sources for their accessibility but also for the way these documents have come to define each executive's stance on life, liberty, and property. Moreover, each document requires students to draw on their knowledge from the course as a whole in understanding the barriers of due process and historical trends in presidential domestic policy. As evidenced by the resources I select for this assignment, modern presidents have adopted dissimilar approaches to due process while grappling with the boundaries of American identity. Ultimately, this summative assessment allows me to measure the analytical skills and historical awareness of students while engaging them in concepts that have a direct impact on their lives.

Lesson Plan

As previously noted, this is a summative lesson. Throughout a fifteen-week semester, students learn the differences between primary and secondary sources and the utility of both in developing a historical awareness. Lecture and OER textbook readings provide the foundational knowledge necessary to understand assigned primary sources. I assign brief writing assignments and class discussions to help students develop communication skills necessary to articulate an informed historical perspective. Therefore, students have acquired the expertise for this assignment throughout the course.

Given the chronological scope and complexity of the assignment, I have found it imperative to devote class time to guiding students through construction of this final project. This takes a single class day or, in the case of online courses, a half-hour video lecture. Since I created this lesson for an open access classroom of learners, I provide strict parameters to guide students through the process of research. In addition to assigning six primary sources, I also require students to review Miller Center articles regarding each president's domestic policies, so the class has a developed historical context. In keeping with UD, this final assignment includes a creative component allowing students to use other skills or knowledge they believe will enhance their ability to communicate a historical argument. However, I am also compelled to ensure students have the writing skills consistent with undergraduate degree requirements. Therefore, this assignment includes an essay in which students describe and analyze basic elements of the secondary source they have created. I scaffold the assignment by requiring students to submit portions of their work over the course of several weeks so that I may intervene in the creative/writing process if necessary.

Learning Objectives

This lesson will help students learn to

- Contextualize presidential policies from 1980 to the present.
- Create and communicate a historical argument to a general audience.
- Evaluate primary and secondary sources as supporting evidence.
- Reconcile prior knowledge with interpretations of new evidence.
- Identify and analyze evidence of varying historical interpretations.

Lesson Outline

Project: Using assigned materials, students create a secondary source for a general audience that analyzes American identity through the lens of presidential policies since 1980.

Each project must make an argument (thesis statement). The thesis may identify and explain one of the following:

- What was each president's legacy regarding American identity?
- How do presidents' policies expand or limit the application of due process?
- What are the successes or failures in applying due process over time?

Considerations

Projects may be any type of secondary source (e.g., presentation, film, podcast, painting, cartoon, song). This assignment fosters engagement by encouraging students to apply existing experience, skills, and creative interests to their subject. I evaluate student success based on established learning outcomes for the course, such as analyzing historical issues and utilizing primary sources to support an argument.

Essay: Students analyze the structure, thesis, arguments, motives, and primary sources of their project using the following prompts.[25]

- Structure
  - How did you organize information from assigned sources?
  - Why did you choose to organize it this way?
  - In what way is this structure helpful in communicating your thesis?
- Thesis
  - Summarize your thesis in one or two sentences.
  - How did you express your thesis statement?
- Arguments
  - What arguments supported your thesis?
  - Is there any evidence that challenges your thesis?
- Motive: your motive is not "because the professor told me to" or "because I want a grade." You are creating a source for a general audience (family, friends, coworkers).
  - Why did you create this type of source?
  - Why did you choose this thesis and arguments?
  - What impact do you hope this source will have on a general audience?
- Primary Sources
  - How do the primary sources shape your thesis and arguments?
  - How do the primary sources shape your structure and motive?
  - Based on assigned readings, are there other primary sources that would be helpful?

Assessment (Rubric)

Modifications/Expansion

Instructors can easily adapt this assignment to their teaching environment. However, educators may want to allow students to conduct their own research into presidential policy. The Miller Center is a tremendously helpful resource for students seeking primary sources on presidential policy. While scaffolding can be effective, classrooms with a stronger set of writers may choose to forego these steps. Brief formative writing assignments or discussions can replace the summative project and essay. This approach would allow for greater intervention in writing or communication of facts. Analysis of these documents also lends itself well to group projects or peer review. Some instructors may also choose alternative primary or secondary sources for analysis of contemporary interpretations of due process. I have endeavored to demonstrate what resources are readily available in multiple formats online.

Project Grading Rubric	*Points*
Objectives:	25
Contextualize presidential policies from 1980 to present.	
Create and communicate a historical argument to a general audience.	
Evaluate primary and secondary sources as supporting evidence.	
Reconcile prior knowledge with interpretations of new evidence.	
Identify and analyze evidence of varying historical interpretations.	
Project Style:	25
Presents information in an original or unique style.	
Identifies the original source of all quoted and paraphrased material.	
Sets a professional tone to maintain credibility.	
Essay Format:	25
Structure, Thesis, Arguments, Motives, Primary sources	
Essay Style:	25
Spelling, Grammar, Clarity	
Complete paragraphs, Topic sentences	
Accurate quotation, Accurate citation	
Total	100

Reflection

Overall, this assignment has given my students and me a significant sense of fulfillment. Students continue to surprise me with their creativity by submitting songs, magazines, mixed media art, podcasts, and hilarious reenactment videos, just to name a few examples. While the assignment required substantial time and effort, students have thanked me for providing the opportunity to express themselves and have indicated that this method enhanced their understanding of material. This is apparent in the written portion of the assessment, as those who embrace the spirit of the assignment are better prepared to analyze the construction of their project. Of course, some students choose to use this project as an opportunity to promote their favorite political figure or champion a particular cause. This is why I find scaffolding and grading rubrics to be essential, as they establish clear benchmarks for progress, allow for intervention in the writing process, and provide transparency in assessing student work.

While I make every effort to accommodate the evolving and diverse needs of students, the biggest obstacle with this lesson plan is one at the center of the conversation about due process: equal access. As the COVID-19 pandemic has taught us, many underprivileged and rural students do not have reliable access to electronic devices and the internet off campus.[26] Therefore, this lesson plan requires effort up front to ensure that students who need printed materials are able to obtain them at no personal cost. In the absence of a global pandemic, I suggest consulting the college or university foundation for potential scholarships or contacting student affairs to assist students with these needs.

NOTES

1. This list of skills is adapted from *AP U.S. History: Course and Exam Description* (New York: College Board, Advanced Placement, 2020), 15–17, https://apcentral.collegeboard.org/pdf/ap-us-history-course-and-exam-description.pdf.
2. US Constitution, amend. 5, sec. 1; US Constitution, amend. 14, sec. 1. The Due Process Clause extends to noncitizens as well. See, for example, Daniel Fisher, "Does the Constitution Protect Non-Citizens? Judges Say Yes," *Forbes*, January 30, 2017, https://www.forbes.com/sites/danielfisher/2017/01/30/does-the-constitution-protect-non-citizens-judges-say-yes/#31adba044f1d.
3. See, for example, Rajiv Jhangiani and Robert Biswas-Diener, eds., *Open: The Philosophy and Practices That Are Revolutionizing Education and Science* (Berkeley, CA: Ubiquity Press, 2017); John S. Levin and Susan T. Kater, eds., *Understanding Community Colleges* (New York: Routledge, 2012); Suzanne K. McCormack, "Teaching History Online to Today's Community College Students," *Journal of American History* 101, no. 4 (March 2015):1215–21, https://doi.org/10.1093/jahist/jav100; Peter Suber, *Knowledge Unbound: Selected Writings on Open Access, 2002–2011* (Cambridge, MA: MIT Press, 2016).

4. Sheryl E. Burgstahler, ed., *Universal Design in Higher Education: From Principles to Practice* (Cambridge, MA: Harvard Education Press, 2015), 3. See also Alexa Darby, "Understanding Universal Design in the Classroom," *National Education Association: Higher Education Best Practices* (Washington, DC: NEA, 2019).

5. Abbey K. Elder, *The OER Starter Kit* (Ames: Iowa State University Digital Press, 2019), https://iastate.pressbooks.pub/oerstarterkit/ (accessed August 13, 2021).

6. Byron Raymond White and Supreme Court of the United States, *U.S. Reports: Grove City College v. Bell*, 465 U.S. 555, 1983, https://www.loc.gov/item/usrep465555/.

7. Ronald Reagan, "Message to the Senate Returning without Approval the Civil Rights Restoration Act of 1987 and Transmitting Alternative Legislation," March 16, 1988, President Reagan's Public Speeches and Statements, 1981–1989, Ronald Reagan Presidential Library, https://www.reaganlibrary.gov/research/speeches/031688e (accessed August 13, 2021).

8. Jane Dailey, "The Theology of Massive Resistance: Sex, Segregation, and the Sacred after Brown," in *Massive Resistance: Southern Opposition to the Second Reconstruction*, ed. Clive Webb (Oxford: Oxford University Press, 2005), 151–80.

9. George H. W. Bush, "Remarks by the President during Ceremony for the Signing of the Americans with Disabilities Act of 1990," National Archives, July 26, 1990, https://www.archives.gov/research/americans-with-disabilities/transcriptions/naid-6037492-remarks-by-the-president-during-ceremony-for-the-signing-of-the-americans-with-disabilities-act-of-1990.html (accessed August 13, 2021); George H. W. Bush, "July 26, 1990: Remarks on the Signing of the Americans with Disabilities Act," Presidential Speeches: George H. W. Bush Presidency, Miller Center, University of Virginia, https://millercenter.org/the-presidency/presidential-speeches/july-26-1990-remarks-signing-americans-disabilities-act. See also "Americans with Disabilities Act Signing," C-SPAN, July 26, 1990, https://www.c-span.org/video/?13297-1/americans-disabilities-act-signing.

10. "Department of Defense Directive Number 1304.26, December 21, 1993," Edward P. Richards, The Climate Change and Public Health Law Site, LSU Law Center, Louisiana State University, https://biotech.law.lsu.edu/blaw/dodd/corres/pdf/d130426wch1_122193/d130426p.pdf. See also Bill Clinton, "January 29, 1993: Press Conference on 'Gays in the Military,'" Presidential Speeches: Bill Clinton Presidency, Miller Center, University of Virginia, https://millercenter.org/the-presidency/presidential-speeches/january-29-1993-press-conference-gays-military.

11. Alejandro de la Garza, "'Don't Ask, Don't Tell' Was a Complicated Turning Point for Gay Rights: 25 Years Later, Many of the Same Issues Remain," *Time*, July 19, 2018, https://time.com/5339634/dont-ask-dont-tell-25-year-anniversary/.

12. "George W. Bush on Racial Profiling," C-SPAN, https://www.c-span .org/video/?c4524225/user-clip-george-w-bush-racial-profiling (accessed August 13, 2021).

13. Department of Justice, "Fact Sheet: Racial Profiling," USDOJ: Archives, June 17, 2003, https://www.justice.gov/archive/opa/pr/2003/June/racial_profil ing_fact_sheet.pdf.

14. Neal Kumar Katyal, "Equality in the War on Terror," *Stanford Law Review* 59, no. 5 (2007): 1365–95.

15. Department of Justice, "Fact Sheet: Racial Profiling."

16. For analysis of Obama's legacy, see Alysa Landry, "Barack Obama: 'Emotionally and Intellectually Committed to Indian Country,'" *Indian Country Today*, November 1, 2016, https://indiancountrytoday.com/archive/barack-obama -emotionally-and-intellectually-committed-to-indian-country.

17. See, for example, Vicente M. Diaz, "'To 'P' or Not to 'P'? Marking the Territory between Pacific Islander and Asian American Studies," *Journal of Asian American Studies* 7, no. 3 (October 2004): 183–208; Lisa Kahale'ole Hall, "Which of These Things Is Not Like the Other: Hawaiians and Other Pacific Islanders Are Not Asian Americans, and All Pacific Islanders Are Not Hawaiian," *American Quarterly* 67, no. 3 (September 2015): 727–47; Stephanie Nohelani and Maile Arvin, "Decolonizing API: Centering Indigenous Pacific Islander Feminism," in *Asian American Feminisms and Women of Color Politics*, ed. Lynn Fujiwara and Shireen Roshanravan (Seattle: University of Washington Press, 2018), 107–37.

18. Barack Obama, "Presidential Proclamation—Asian American and Pacific Islander Heritage Month, 2015," White House: Office of the Press Secretary, April 30, 2015, https://obamawhitehouse.archives.gov/the-press-office/2015/04/ 30/presidential-proclamation-asian-american-and-pacific-islander-heritage-m.

19. For praise of Obama's attention to the non-Native Hawaiian commu- nity, see, for example, Melanie Yamaguchi, "As Hawaii's First President, Obama Put Spotlight on Islands," *Hawaii News Now*, January 17, 2017, https://www .hawaiinewsnow.com/story/34280872/as-his-presidency-ends-many-reflect-on -obamas-legacy-in-islands/.

20. Jessica Kershaw, "Interior Proposes Path for Re-Establishing Govern- ment-to-Government Relationship with Native Hawaiian Community," U.S. Department of the Interior, September 29, 2015, https://www.doi.gov/press releases/interior-department-proposes-pathway-re-establishing-government -government.

21. For context and critique of DOI rules, see, for example, Troy J. H. Andrade, "Legacy in Paradise: Analyzing the Obama Administration's Efforts of Reconciliation with Native Hawaiians," *Michigan Journal of Race and Law* 22, no. 2 (2017): 273–326; Chad Blair, "Obama 'Spat' on Hawaiians," *Honolulu Civil Beat*, September 23, 2016, https://www.civilbeat.org/2016/09/obama-spat-on -hawaiians/.

22. Department of Commerce et al. v. New York et al., No. 18–966, 588 U.S. (2019), https://www.supremecourt.gov/opinions/18pdf/18-966_bq7c.pdf.

23. Donald J. Trump, "Remarks on Citizenship and the Census," White House: President Donald J. Trump, July 11, 2019, https://trumpwhitehouse .archives.gov/briefings-statements/remarks-president-trump-citizenship-cen sus/. See also Donald Trump, "President Trump Remarks on Census Citizenship Question," C-SPAN, July 11, 2019, https://www.c-span.org/video/?462535 -1/trump-administration-longer-pursue-citizenship-question-2020-census.

24. Ibid.

25. Adapted from Patrick Rael, "Reading, Writing, and Researching for History: A Guide for College Students" (Brunswick, ME: Bowdoin College, 2004), https://courses.bowdoin.edu/writing-guides/ (accessed August 13, 2021).

26. Jonathan Custodio, "Disabled Students Already Faced Learning Barriers: Then Coronavirus Forced an Abrupt Shift to Online Classes," *Chronicle of Higher Education*, April 7, 2020, https://www.chronicle.com/article/Disabled-Stu dents-Already/248444; Edward J. Maloney and Joshua Kim, "The Challenge of Equity in Higher Education under COVID-19," *Inside Higher Ed*, May 21, 2020, https://www.insidehighered.com/blogs/learning-innovation/challenge-equi ty-higher-education-under-covid-19.

FOR FURTHER READING

Carter, Dan T. *From George Wallace to Newt Gingrich: Race in the Conservative Counterrevolution, 1963–1994*. Baton Rouge: Louisiana State University Press, 1996.

Jeffries, Hasan Kwame, ed. *Understanding and Teaching the Civil Rights Movement*. Madison: University of Wisconsin Press, 2019.

Locke, Joseph L., and Ben Wright, eds. *The American Yawp: A Massively Collaborative Open U.S. History Textbook*, vol. 2, *After 1877*. Stanford, CA: Stanford University Press, 2019. http://www.americanyawp.com/.

Patterson, James T. *Restless Giant: The United States from Watergate to "Bush v. Gore."* New York: Oxford University Press, 2005.

Shull, Steven A. *American Civil Rights Policy from Truman to Clinton: The Role of Presidential Leadership*. Armonk, NY: M. E. Sharpe, 1999.

PRIMARY SOURCES (IN CHRONOLOGICAL ORDER)

Reagan, Ronald. "Message to the Senate Returning without Approval the Civil Rights Restoration Act of 1987 and Transmitting Alternative Legislation." March 16, 1988. Ronald Reagan Presidential Library, President Reagan's Public Speeches and Statements, 1981–1989. https://www.reaganlibrary.gov/ research/speeches/031688e.

Bush, George H. W. "Transcript of Remarks by the President during Ceremony for the Signing of the Americans with Disabilities Act of 1990." National Archives. https://www.archives.gov/research/americans-with-disabilities/transcriptions/naid-6037492-remarks-by-the-president-during-ceremony-for-the-signing-of-the-americans-with-disabilities-act-of-1990.html.

Bush, George H. W. "July 26, 1990: Remarks on the Signing of the Americans with Disabilities Act." Video. Presidential Speeches, Miller Center, University of Virginia. https://millercenter.org/the-presidency/presidential-speeches/july-26-1990-remarks-signing-americans-disabilities-act.

Clinton, Bill. "January 29, 1993: Press Conference on 'Gays in the Military.'" Video. Presidential Speeches: Bill Clinton Presidency, Miller Center, University of Virginia. https://millercenter.org/the-presidency/presidential-speeches/january-29-1993-press-conference-gays-military.

"Department of Defense Directive Number 1304.26, December 21, 1993." Edward P. Richards, The Climate Change and Public Health Law Site, LSU Law Center, Louisiana State University. https://biotech.law.lsu.edu/blaw/dodd/corres/pdf/d130426wch1_122193/d130426p.pdf.

Department of Justice. "Fact Sheet: Racial Profiling." June 17, 2003. US Department of Justice Archives. https://www.justice.gov/archive/opa/pr/2003/June/racial_profiling_fact_sheet.pdf.

Bush, George W. "George W. Bush on Racial Profiling." February 28, 2001. Video. C-SPAN. https://www.c-span.org/video/?c4524225/user-clip-george-w-bush-racial-profiling.

Obama, Barack. "Presidential Proclamation—Asian American and Pacific Islander Heritage Month, 2015." April 30, 2015. The White House: Office of the Press Secretary. https://obamawhitehouse.archives.gov/the-press-office/2015/04/30/presidential-proclamation-asian-american-and-pacific-islander-heritage-m.

Trump, Donald. "Remarks on Citizenship and the Census." July 11, 2019. The White House: Donald J. Trump. https://trumpwhitehouse.archives.gov/briefings-statements/remarks-president-trump-citizenship-census/.

Trump, Donald. "President Trump Remarks on Census Citizenship Question." July 11, 2019. Video. C-Span. https://www.c-span.org/video/?462535-1/trump-administration-longer-pursue-citizenship-question-2020-census.

SECONDARY SOURCES

Calmes, Jackie. "Donald Trump: Domestic Affairs." U.S. Presidents: Donald Trump, Miller Center, University of Virginia, 2019. https://millercenter.org/president/trump/domestic-affairs.

Cannon, Lou. "Ronald Reagan: Domestic Affairs." U. S. Presidents: Ronald Reagan. Miller Center, University of Virginia, 2019. https://millercenter.org/president/reagan/domestic-affairs.

Gregg, Gary L., II "George W. Bush: Domestic Affairs." U.S. Presidents: George W. Bush. Miller Center, University of Virginia, 2019. https://millercenter.org/president/gwbush/domestic-affairs.

Knott, Stephen. "George H. W. Bush: Domestic Affairs." U.S. Presidents: George H. W. Bush. Miller Center, University of Virginia, 2019. https://millercenter.org/president/bush/domestic-affairs.

Nelson, Michael. "Barack Obama: Domestic Affairs." U.S. Presidents: Barack Obama. Miller Center, University of Virginia, 2019. https://millercenter.org/president/obama/domestic-affairs.

Riley, Russell L. "Bill Clinton: Domestic Affairs." U.S. Presidents: Bill Clinton. Miller Center, University of Virginia, 2019. https://millercenter.org/president/clinton/domestic-affairs.

Examining African American Voter Suppression, from Reagan to Trump

AARON TREADWELL

Why Teach This Lesson?

Civil law is the foundation on which American liberty is both defined and appropriated. America's representative democracy provides citizens the right to vote, and elections have given those who govern an opportunity to punish and reward. The power of the ballot cannot be understated; prison reform, wealth reform, education reform, and even healthcare reform rise and fall based on the general public's access to the polls. Certainly, voting is a significant issue for all political ideologies within the United States, including those individuals who chose violence in the 2021 attack on the US Capitol to stop the official certification of electoral college votes.

The central purpose of this lesson is to analyze primary documents concerning Black Americans' ability to vote. This lesson also covers issues that tap into the rollback of Reconstruction-era protections and ongoing battles for civil and human rights. Additionally, for teachers trying to improve their students' ability to think critically about the causality of equal voting rights, there is a suggested activity at the end of the lesson plan to encourage classroom dialogue.

Introduction

When teaching early America history, I always begin the semester by asking students to define the concept of chattel slavery and to compare it to the twenty-first-century perception of sex slavery. Simple logic will point out that the former practice was a legalized form of bondage that the state and national governments protected, whereas the latter is illegal without exception. The end result of this particular lesson is twofold: First, it helps define fundamental terms such as "slavery" and emphasize why historians must avoid the practice of equating hardships with bondage—this includes the practice of misappropriating concepts outside of their historical and fundamental realities. For example, describing the experiences of indentured servants as "slave-like" is a slippery slope for budding historians. Second, this exercise introduces the complexity of American politics and exposes students to the reality that the United States of America has a history of reforming and sometimes resurrecting constitutional ills. Any close study of the Constitution's impact on minorities will require students to move beyond the practice of patriotic hagiography and instead to employ a method of critical examination.

Ethical adjudicating of American constitutional history has also been a fluid process. At times, hard-fought constitutional reforms have lapsed. For example, following the Civil War, Black men received the right to vote from the Fifteenth Amendment to the Constitution, but this legal protection dissolved in subsequent decades. The restoration of that right, achieved through the Voting Rights Act of 1965, has been consistently challenged. In 2021 alone, more than twenty laws have created restrictive voting regulations across the nation that are contrary to the spirit of the Voting Rights Act.[1]

Two prominent arguments in support of strict voting regulation are that most people are not sufficiently informed to vote well and that efforts to enhance voter registration produces mass fraud. These arguments continue to be used in twenty-first-century legislation in order to suppress the vote of Black Americans.[2] These policies also have significant impacts on poor and young voters, beyond the racial impact. This chapter examines the contemporary efforts to suppress Black voters in order to properly highlight the United States' history of minority voting battles. By so doing, this chapter argues that the privileges gained by voting inequality have created a social and political disadvantage for Black Americans. To justify disenfranchisement, proponents of stricter voting access have declared that Black voters are misinformed and that broader access to the vote is antithetical to the customs of this country, but both assertions contradict the theory of *liberty and justice for all.*

The first section of this chapter analyzes the historical precedents of Black voter suppression up to the signing of the Civil Rights Act of 1964 (which outlawed racial segregation) and the Voting Rights Act of 1965 (which put states with a historical record of voter suppression under federal control and supervision). The second section analyzes the conditions and consequences of the Voting Rights Act, focusing on efforts to constrict and expand voting rights. Overall, this essay highlights voter suppression as the fulcrum of social and political oppression in the United States, cementing this concept as paramount for teaching American history.

The History of Black Voter Suppression

In the US Constitution, voting is neither mandated nor deemed a legal right for all people. In response, many have used this omission to depict voting as a privilege, putting the onus on the citizen to appreciate whatever opportunity they may have to participate. For a long period in American history, stringent rules and social precepts have dictated people's ability to vote, although many of the intricacies within this process have been overlooked.

Early Black (Negro) voting suppression in the United States began with the three-fifths ratio proposal of James Madison at the Constitutional Convention. The intent of this legislation was to address southern state tax obligations, real estate holdings, and electoral representation, whereas additional study exposed that this document also legalized the status of bonded African people within the country.[3] Soon after, Article I of the US Constitution adopted the aforementioned proposal and titled it the "Three-fifths Compromise," which legalized the disinheritance of enslaved people in America. Simply put, this law aided the identification of who would receive the rights of full citizenship. Simply put, this law established a political stance concerning the enslaved populations and their access to full citizenship, making this population non-citizen and non-American.

The constitutional revision to the three-fifths compromise can be found in the Thirteenth, Fourteenth, and Fifteenth Amendments to the Constitution, which happened in 1865, 1868, and 1870, respectively. The Thirteenth Amendment meant to curtail state practices such as the doctrine of *partus sequitur ventrem* dating back to 1662 Colonial Virginia, which legalized the enslavement of all persons born to a mother in bondage. This amendment also constituted a federal decree against chattel slavery nationwide, unlike the Emancipation Proclamation. Additional revisions to the three-fifths compromise included the Fourteenth and Fifteenth Amendments' stance legally granting Black Americans their alienable rights, as the latter declared "The right of citizens of the United States to vote shall not be denied or abridged by the United States or by any State on account of race, color, or previous condition of servitude."[4]

If you have not already discussed the Fourteenth and Fifteenth Amendments in class, students are highly encouraged to read and assess them prior to this lesson plan.[5] Many national leaders expressed animosity toward these amendments. Some of the legislation's adversaries included persons who were simultaneously fighting for women's suffrage. Advocates Elizabeth Cady Stanton and George Francis Train warned that the expansion of Black male voting rights could cheapen the national ballot. Lori Ginzberg, in her biographical work on Stanton, described her as making "ugly, conscious, and unforgivable appeals to nativist and racist sentiments." George Francis Train was said to be a racist who "attacked the intelligence and integrity of black people," which included him "offering women's votes as a weapon to be used against the specter of black supremacy."[6] Even the suffrage activist Susan B. Anthony argued that although Black men deserved the right to vote, this opportunity should not happen prior to women's suffrage. In response to the discussion over the eventual Fourteenth Amendment, Anthony would argue that "she would sooner cut off her right hand than ask the ballot for the black man and not for woman."[7]

Political leaders who detested these amendments led rank-and-file cohorts to protest, as the southern states regressed back into institutionalized disenfranchisement of Black males with methods of extreme voter suppression. Justification for these acts rested on claims of white supremacy, often using eugenics to claim that Black Americans were unable to make the informed decisions required to vote and govern. Students should observe and recognize how the *myth of rational voting* is still preserved and disseminated in twenty-first-century American politics, which can include a close examination of the electoral college's role in recent elections.[8]

Methods of voter suppression in the nineteenth century have received their fair share of study, given their explicit practice across the country. *Poll bullying* was one particular method of suppression, which required voters to carry oversized tickets with their candidate's name in bold for all to see. This exposure identified voters supporting the opposition and exposed them to harassment, unemployment, and other forms of intimidation.[9] *Poll watchers* also intimidated voters, as they had the authority to question all persons "deemed suspect."[10] In addition to intimidation at the polls, states erected a variety of institutional obstacles to target Blacks. The *poll tax* was a voting fee that was due at the county assessor's office ahead of the election; both the amount of money and the process of paying the fee at this local office were obstacles to voters.[11] The *grandfather clause* was an ancestral method of exclusion, limiting voting opportunities to those who had a family history of voting—something most African Americans were without in the nineteenth century.[12]

Literacy tests were another method used to exclude black voters. On its face, making voters prove their literacy satisfied the "rational voter" theory—that those who are illiterate are unable to make informed decisions on their government, but registrars often administered these tests in a discriminatory manner, which is clearly evident in the results. According to historian Laughlin McDonald, Blacks often failed, whereas no white was ever recorded as failing.[13] Similarly, the *secret-ballot practice* often tricked persons out of the ability to vote coherently. Sometimes the "secret-ballot" included a long list of varying names without any identification of office or party.[14] A variation on this "secret-ballot" practice was the *eight-box law*, which placed eight possible submission boxes on a table and required voters to be able to read and interpret the directions; if you put your ballot in the wrong box, it was disqualified.[15] If you want to emphasize how one of these practices functioned and how it could be used to discriminate against voters well into the twentieth century, have students take a voter literacy test from Alabama[16] or Louisiana.[17]

These practices achieved their desired outcome of disenfranchising Black voters, replacing Republican rule with Democratic rule in the southeastern states, and ending efforts to change the status quo of white supremacy. According to one Reconstruction-era Alabama legislator, the state's "secret-ballot" process promised to "restore the Democratic party in Alabama."[18] In Tennessee, eight-box laws were only applied in the state's larger urban areas, which had larger Black populations. The result was that by 1890, Black voting turnout in the state had fallen 50 percent in a decade.[19] The end of the nineteenth century saw Alabama only having 1.3 percent of its Black population registered to vote, and in Louisiana and South Carolina, voting dropped to 1.1 percent and 3.8 percent, respectively. J. Morgan Kousser attributes these trends directly to the secret ballot, poll taxes, various types of literacy tests, and stringent registration procedures noted above.[20]

Despite its success, voter suppression tactics had to adapt in the early twentieth century. Some counties in southern states lamented that poll tax policies were negatively impacting poor whites.[21] Additional pressures to evolve the tactics of voting suppression came from the federal government. In the 1944 case *Smith v. Allwright*, the US Supreme Court struck down the Texas Democratic Party's effort to require all voters in primary elections to be white.[22] The Civil Rights Act of 1964 and the Voting Rights Act of 1965 also provided additional federal protections against explicit voting suppression. In response to such federal protections, many southeastern politicians developed less explicit methods to maintain their voting hegemony. This evolutionary tactic of institutionalizing oppression has erroneously caused students to overlook the continued acts of suppression well beyond the civil rights era. To help students understand that voter suppression has persisted, this chapter helps students see the goals of voter suppression and therefore understand that new, nuanced strategies have the same intent and purpose.[23]

The civil rights legislation of 1964 and 1965 precipitated a great spike in Black suffrage—a considerable change. According to the United States Commission on Civil Rights, the period from 1965 to 1967 saw 556,767 new Black voters register.[24] In this same period, the commission's analysis saw the percentage of Blacks in Mississippi who registered to vote go from 6.7 percent to 59.8 percent; in Alabama from 19.3 percent to 51.6 percent; in Georgia from 27.4 percent to 52.6 percent; in Louisiana from 31.6 percent to 58.9 percent; and in South Carolina from 37.3 percent to 51.2 percent.[25] The 1966 election resulted in 159 Black elected officials in the eleven southern states targeted by the Voting Rights Act of 1965, and voters the next year elected more than 200 Black officials—a 200 percent increase over a three-year span.[26] What these numbers indicate is the electoral power that African Americans possess when given the opportunity to freely exercise their right to vote. By the 1980s, this freedom had resulted in a 59 percent growth in Black voter registration, which facilitated more than 2,042 Blacks serving as public officers in the Southeast.[27] This information highlights the important role that voter suppression has played in American history.

Disenfranchisement Policies from Reagan to Trump

President Ronald Reagan's landslide victory in 1984 exposed three major truths in this new era of American politics: First, a majority of white southern voters, for the first time, had turned to the Republican Party, largely abandoning the Democratic Party. Second, a party-line stance on voting legislation made it easier to "cage" (or isolate) and challenge minority voters, creating a system of party-line voter suppression. And third, decisions from the highest courts frequently proved they were unwilling to fully protect Black suffrage in response to the systematic shifts taking place—in part due to the simultaneous growth in the politicization of judicial appointments.[28] So while the first document in the lesson plan below—a 1981 report by the US Civil Rights Commission—shows an underlying optimism that there are some elements of the 1965 Voting Rights Act that simply need refining, what we see below are a series of methods that have been used in the post–civil rights movement period to suppress voting rights among Black American citizens.

Caging is a practice of voter intimidation and interrogation reminiscent of the poll bullying and poll watching of the nineteenth century that allows citizens to challenge the registration status of other citizens at the polls. Done in the name of preventing voter fraud, caging became quite popular during the 1964 presidential election when Republican Barry Goldwater ran against incumbent Lyndon B. Johnson for the presidency. The Republican Party launched "Operation Eagle Eye," whose stated goal was to "frighten off Democratic wrongdoers" by challenging these voters' eligibility to vote.[29] Not only did this discourage voters in general, but by the 1980s it had evolved into an overt strategy to slow voting lines, increase wait times, and further discourage voting. In a 1986 interview, Supreme Court Justice William Rehnquist acknowledged that in Los Angeles there was a strategy to "clog the voting polls in heavily minority Democratic precincts," which supports the reality that institutionalized voter suppression continued to impact voting rights.[30]

Evolved caging turned into a system of *mail denial*, which is a practice that purges voters from the rolls ahead of time in order to deny voters at the polls. For example, in 1981, the New Jersey Republican Party created a "Ballot Security Force" that mailed out 200,000 letters to predominantly African American, Democratic neighborhoods. When

45,000 letters were returned as "undeliverable," the security force brought these returned letters to the courts and demanded these voters be purged from the voter rolls. In response, the courts found that the Republicans had violated both the Fourteenth and Fifteenth Amendments, resulting in a consent decree requiring them to discontinue this practice.[31] Similar mail fraud schemes took place in Louisiana, Indiana, Pennsylvania, and Missouri in 1986, and all were condemned by the courts.[32] In 1990, North Carolina exploited mail denial by sending 150,000 postcards with misinformation to African American, Democratic communities, and another example from 2019 in Georgia is presented in Document 4 of the lesson plan below. These statewide acts of voter suppression demonstrate new efforts to put obstacles in the way of voters who wish to retain their registration and exercise the right to vote that harken back to earlier practices of poll taxes and literacy tests.[33]

In the face of these efforts to contract and limit suffrage, Democrats and others have sought to expand the voting population by minimizing obstacles to registration and voting; Republican opponents have often characterized these efforts as promoting voter fraud. We see this dynamic specifically in connection to the National Voter Registration Act (NVRA), which started to gain support from the Democratic Party in the wake of Reagan's dominant reelection in 1984. Also known as the *motor voter law*, this act sought to create accessible registration avenues, by allowing people to register at their local department of motor vehicles, at public assistance agencies, and by mail.[34] The "motor voter law" grew legs as the 1992 National Voter Registration Commission found that over 70 million people had not voted in the previous election, and the majority had lower incomes and less education than the regional average. Although the bill passed the House and Senate, Republican president George H. W. Bush vetoed it, and the Senate failed to override that veto (62–38, five votes short of the two-thirds vote required to override).[35] Motor voter passed the next year when Democrats controlled the White House and both houses of Congress, but these 1993 debates show what became the predominant discourse about voter registration, which we see in Document 2 in the lesson below. On the one side, Republicans such as US Representative David Dreier from California called the NVRA "the National Voter Fraud Act" and believed that the lack of address verification would allow citizens and noncitizens alike to vote.[36] And Representative Spencer Bachus III

(R-AL) used language reminiscent of President Reagan, warning that the act would register "millions of welfare recipients, illegal aliens, and taxpayer funded entitlement recipients." On the other hand, Democrats talked about making it easier for all eligible Americans to vote while maintaining the integrity of the voting system.[37]

The fight against motor voter continued even after it became the law of the land; attempts to repeal, make its stipulations voluntary, and delay implementation were all techniques used to stall voting progress.[38] In 1995, seven states sued to prevent implementation on the bases that it would promote voter fraud and increase the states' financial costs. This effort failed, as courts found "no single party was able to show mass corruption."[39] This is indeed a testament to the law's significant safeguards against corruption, given that more than two million voters registered under the law's provisions in the first three months and more than eleven million within the first year. Interestingly enough, more Republicans utilized NVRA for registration than Democrats.[40] Perhaps recognizing this fact, the next decade's key electoral reform legislation, the "Help Americans Vote Act," which became law in 2002, was signed by President George W. Bush following the controversial 2000 election that brought him to power. This is Document 3 in the lesson plan below.

When discussing "new era" voter suppression and its disproportionate impact on Black Americans, we cannot ignore felon disenfranchisement. The Sentencing Project found that over five million African Americans were barred from casting a ballot in the United States in 2012 under these provisions. This number equates to 13 percent of the African American male population, a number that could surely swing elections nationwide.[41] This is especially significant, as historians Jeff Manza and Christopher Uggen have found that over 73 percent of registered felons identify as Democrat.[42] When Florida voters in 2018 supported—exceeding the required 60 percent approval rate—a referendum to amend its constitution to automatically restore the voting rights of most former felons who had fully completed their sentences (including probation and parole), its political drama became national news.[43] While Republican governor Ron DeSantis said that the state's legislature would have to create enabling legislation to implement this action, the amendment's proponents argued that its provisions were self-executing. When subsequent developments called for felons to re-register and make a taxable payment to retain their rights, even the governor thought that this was too reminiscent of the poll taxes of an earlier era.[44]

When covering the issue of felon disenfranchisement in the classroom and potentially in one of the expansions of the lesson plan below, it is important to examine several interconnected issues. As previously mentioned, many Black convicted felons identify as Democrats. Therefore, states that have large Black populations—such as Florida and Alabama—have historically suppressed a large number of Democratic votes. These states also have African American imprisonment rates of 30 percent, which is far above the national average of 2.4 percent.[45]

Looking at these rates in a classroom, one must ask complicated questions that go beyond the stereotypical morality myths of Black criminality. For example, it is important to point out that over 60 percent of convicted (and therefore often disenfranchised) African American felons are no longer serving a sentence. This ratio of potential voters becomes vital in determining the election of future candidates. For students who need additional information to supplement this argument, there are valuable resources that focus on predatory arrest strategies and the history of the *prison-industrial complex* in American history. The conceptual idea of predatory racial arrest helps explain why so many Black males have historically been arrested, convicted, and given longer sentences compared to their white counterparts.[46] In simple terms, African American males are being held to higher standards than their white counterparts in courts of law.[47] The systemic impact of this trend means far more than jail time for Blacks. Considering the methods used by prior generations to eliminate the Black vote, one should seek to understand how Black felonies could serve as a tool of disenfranchisement, and as this chapter argues, losing votes can dramatically change the landscape of a community, state, and nation.[48]

Conclusion

Ongoing battles for full civil and human rights will continue to pinpoint voter suppression as a major systematic issue. The 2020 national election has provided future generations an example of the importance of voting and the lengths some people will go to in order to maintain social privilege. The overwhelming success of the Fair Fight national voting rights organization in Georgia has often been used as an example of this nation's progressiveness, although this interpretation is far too simplistic. Instead, the unmitigated determination to fight against voting "mismanagement, irregularities, unbelievably long lines and more" arguably exposes what is required to achieve basic voter opportunity for African Americans.[49] Fair Fight, Fair Vote, and Civicus are among numerous awareness campaigns supporting election reform, but the most vital tool for advancing full voting rights is a citizen's political education. For example, ethical voting training and its historical context should be taught in the classroom for the sake of basic awareness. College campuses all share the unique experience of educating future state election managers and future election officials, who will eventually have the judicial power to end voter suppression. By properly educating students on the unconstitutional measures laid out in this essay, academia can play a part in defeating suffrage inequality for good.

Lesson Plan: Voting Past and Present

Bellwork/Initial Prompt

As students enter the room, have them write reasons for and against this prompt: *Should all eligible Americans vote in elections?*

Follow-up Question

After everyone has had an opportunity to jot down at least a couple of ideas, ask the class—*Who is eligible to vote in elections in the United States?* Student responses should point out that

- you have to be at least 18 years old (as a result of the Twenty-Sixth Amendment),
- you have to be a citizen of the United States,
- you have to be a resident of the area where you are voting,
- you generally have to register ahead of time to vote,
- you cannot have been convicted of a felony (in many states), and
- you have to present a current, valid, state-issued form of identification with a photograph at the polling station (in many states).

Students might also—or you might want to—point out some of the changes in voting that you have covered this semester:

- That Black Americans can vote as a result of the Reconstruction era's Fourteenth and Fifteenth Amendments plus the civil rights movement (especially the Voting Rights Act of 1965),
- That women gained the right to vote in national elections as a result of the Nineteenth Amendment in 1920,
- And that those aged 18–20 were given the right to vote by the Twenty-Sixth Amendment.

Segue

To segue into the next topic (and circle back to the initial prompt), ask students if they think that there should be any additional requirements to vote. Alternatively, do they think that some of the extant requirements should be repealed? After a short discussion, explain that in this lesson we examine how these different philosophies have played out in recent history:

- Expansionists: Those who have sought to expand the pool of eligible voters and to increase the number of people voting in each election. Members of this group are more likely to describe voting as a "right" and to stress that it is more "democratic" to have most or all Americans voting for the people who will represent them at all levels of government and on issues of interest to them.
- Contractionists: Those who have sought to limit or contract the pool of eligible voters and to decrease the number of people voting in each election. Members of this group are more likely to describe voting as a "privilege" or "responsibility"; to be very concerned that voter fraud will result from making it easier to register and vote; and to be critical of "misinformed" or "irrational" voters.

Explain that some arguments and people may include elements of both philosophies.

Primary Source Exercise

Next students examine a set of primary sources that are listed below; Word versions of each are provided on the companion website (http://GoldbergSeries.org/UTContemporaryUSHistory). There are a number of ways that you can do this, but I outline a suggested procedure below the list of documents:

- Document 1: Excerpt from United States Civil Rights Commission, *The Voting Rights Act: Unfulfilled Goals* (Washington, DC: US Government Printing Office, September 1981), 89–92.
- Document 2: Excerpts from the contributions of Nydia M. Velázquez (D-NY) and Robert H. Michel (R-IL) to the debate on H.R. 2 (the National Voter Registration Act) on the floor of the US House of Representatives on February 4, 1993, *Congressional Digest* 72, no. 3 (March 1993): 80, 82, 87, 89.
- Document 3: Excerpt from US Congress, "H.R. 3295—Help America Vote Act of 2002: 107th Congress (2001–2002)," Congress.gov, https://www.congress.gov/bill/107th-congress/house-bill/3295.
- Document 4: Excerpt from *Fair Fight v. Raffensperger*, challenging the legality of Georgia voting practices in February 2019. "Second Amended Complaint for Declaratory and Injunctive Relief," in the United States District Court for the Northern District of Georgia, Atlanta Division, Case 1:18-cv-05391-SCJ, filed December 3, 2020, https://fairfight.com/wp-content/uploads/2021/05/Second-Amended -Complaint.pdf.

Divide students into four groups (or eight groups if the class is larger) by having them count off 1–4. Give each group copies of one document to read (give Group 1 copies of Document 1, etc.) and the worksheet (see questions below and Word version on companion website [http://GoldbergSeries.org/UTContemporaryUSHistory]). Each document is from a different decade in order to illustrate change and continuity in the debates—as well as addressing some of the major pieces of federal legislation related to voting and registering to vote from the period. Students may read the document individually or together in the group before answering the questions on the worksheet (available in Word format from the companion website [http://GoldbergSeries.org/UTCon temporaryUSHistory]), which asks the following questions:

- Who wrote this document? If you're not familiar with the organization, you might want to Google it or ask your teacher to learn more.
- When was it written?

- What kind of document is it?
- How might the "who," "when," and "what" answered above affect the tone of the document and its recommendations?
- What voting practices/legislation does the document discuss?
- What group(s) does it identify as needing additional help in order to more fully exercise their right to vote? Or what groups does it identify as potentially taking advantage of easier voting/registration processes to perpetrate fraud?
- What remedy or remedies does it identify to the problem identified?
- Does the document have an expansionist or contractionist philosophy on voting? Circle words, phrases, or sentences in your document that support your conclusion, and explain your views below.
- Be prepared to summarize your document, its contents, and its philosophy and share it with the other groups.

Whole-Group Discussion/Wrap-up

You will want to check in with the groups and their progress but also be prepared at the end of their reading and discussion to summarize key points of their work on the board as they report out to the class. You can ask clarifying questions during this reporting out as well. To wind up the discussion, ask students what elements of change they see across these four documents and decades and what elements of continuity they see.

Handling the Discussion

The purpose of this lesson plan is to expose students to the systematic implementation of voting restrictions and why this process is inherently volatile. If students are in favor of repressing votes, the professor might readdress the importance of equity in a federal constitutional republic. A quick and easy exercise that can be used in a classroom to introduce voting inequality is a "paper to trash" test. The teacher places a trash can in front of the class and asks students from the front to rear to shoot a balled-up piece of paper into the trash can. When students in the rear complain, the teacher can contextualize the similarities this process has with voting restrictions. To ramp up the exercise, tell students that those who make the shot will receive a higher grade. This exercise shows students that by putting barriers in the way, their opportunity to be graded fairly becomes nonexistent. Therefore, the inequality within this experiment has cheapened, if not ruined, the integrity of what a true class assessment should be—an equal opportunity for all to succeed. Some teachers have altered this test by labeling the papers handed out to students in order to personalize the conditions of their row; this includes worsening their wealth and education row by row. Finally, ask students how to alter this test to make it a fair assessment. If students can take the conversation deeper and expose implicit advantages beyond seat placement, all the better.

Assessment

If you are looking for a formal assessment of the learning in this lesson, you can provide each student with a packet containing all four documents and an assessment prompt such as, "Write a short essay explaining whether there was more change or continuity in voting practices from 1981 to 2019, using specific historical examples from the documents we examined in class."

Additional Activities or
Expansion of the Lesson Plan

If you have a longer class period or are looking for an additional activity for students, you might have them chart voter turnout in the federal election years from 1982 to 2018. The Federal Election Commission reports on these election years when there are candidates for federal office—the House of Representatives, the Senate, or the president: https://www.fec.gov/introduction-campaign-finance/election-and-voting-information/. Then have students add to the time line the key pieces of voting legislation passed during this period that were discussed in this lesson. See if they can identify any correlation between the legislation and voting turnout. Have them also brainstorm about other factors that might have impacted voter turnout beyond federal legislation. This exercise and discussion will help students as they develop the historical thinking skill of identifying causality.

If you want students to further examine expansionist and contractionist voting philosophies as they apply to the issue of felon enfranchisement and disenfranchisement, start with the question, "Should people convicted of felonies be allowed to vote?" Have students write down reasons for and against this proposition. You might want to point out that the states that make up the United States have not been able to agree on this issue: a few states never take voting rights from felons; some states automatically restore voting rights after incarceration; some states automatically restore voting rights after probation, parole, and court fees have all been fulfilled; and some states suspend voting rights indefinitely. Information on this division of opinion as well as links to each state's statute are available from the National Conference of State Legislatures, "Felon Voting Rights," January 8, 2021, https://www .ncsl.org/research/elections-and-campaigns/felon-voting-rights.aspx. After identifying when your state passed its statute, you might have students research the public positions on the issue taken by different legislators or organizations during the year before this legislation was passed.

NOTES

1. Brennan Center for Justice, "Voting Laws Roundup: July 2021," July 22, 2021, https://www.brennancenter.org/our-work/research-reports/voting-laws roundup-july-2021.

2. Bryan Caplan, *The Myth of the Rational Voter: Why Democracies Choose Bad Policies* (Princeton, NJ: Princeton University Press, 2008).

3. Garry Wills, *Negro President* (Boston: Houghton Mifflin, 2005), xii, 242.

4. US Constitution, Article XV, §1.

5. "United States of America's Constitution of 1789 with Amendments through 1992," last updated June 28, 2021, https://www.constituteproject.org/ constitution/United_States_of_America_1992.pdf?lang=en.

6. Lori D. Ginzberg, *Elizabeth Cady Stanton* (New York: Hill and Wang, 2010), 121; Ellen Carol DuBois, *Feminism and Suffrage* (Ithaca, NY: Cornell University Press, 1999), 93.

7. Eleanor Flexner and Ellen F. Fitzpatrick, *Century of Struggle: The Woman's Rights Movement in the United States* (Cambridge, MA: Belknap Press of Harvard University Press), 137–38.

8. For more historical research undermining the myth of rational voting, see Edward L. Ayers, *The Promise of the New South* (Oxford: Oxford University Press, 2007); Mary Frances Berry, *Black Resistance, White Law: A History of Constitutional Racism in America* (New York: Penguin Press, 1994); Dwight B. Billings, *Planters and the Making of a "New South": Class Politics and Development in North Carolina* (Chapel Hill: University of North Carolina Press, 1979); and Jeff Strickland, *Unequal Freedoms: Ethnicity, Race, and White Supremacy in Civil War-Era Charleston* (Gainesville: University Press of Florida, 2015), 83–117.

9. Richard Franklin Bensel, *The American Ballot Box in the Mid-Nineteenth Century* (New York: Cambridge University Press, 2004), 36–38.

10. Spencer v. Blackwell, United States District Court, Southern District of Ohio, Western Division, complaint, case number 1:04CV738, October 27, 2004.

11. The amount of the taxes varied. In Tennessee, Article 2, Section 28 of the state constitution did not specify the amount of the tax on polls but provided that the tax should not be less than fifty cents nor more than one dollar a year (Frank B. Williams Jr., "The Poll Tax as a Suffrage Requirement in the South, 1870–1901," *Journal of Southern History* 18, no. 4 [November 1952]: n22). In South Carolina, the 1895 constitution put the poll tax at one dollar for males between the ages of twenty-one and sixty (Herbert Aptheker, "South Carolina Poll Tax, 1737–1895," *Journal of Negro History* 31, no. 2 [April 1946]: 139).

12. Steven F. Lawson, *Black Ballots: Voting Rights in the South, 1944–1969* (New York: Lexington Books, 1999), 12–13; Huey Perry and Wayne Parent, *Blacks and the American Political System* (Gainesville: University Press of Florida, 2005), 4.

13. Laughlin McDonald, *A Voting Rights Odyssey: Black Enfranchisement in Georgia* (New York: Cambridge University Press, 2003), 46.

14. J. Morgan Kousser, *The Shaping of Southern Politics: Suffrage Restriction and the Establishment of the One-Party South, 1880–1910* (New Haven, CT: Yale Historical Publications, 1974), 134.

15. Ibid., 110.

16. "1965 Alabama Literacy Test," https://www.thirteen.org/wnet/jimcrow/literacy_popup.html, webpage embedded in "The Rise and Fall of Jim Crow: Tools and Activities," 2002, PBS, https://www.thirteen.org/wnet/jimcrow/tools_voting.html.

17. "The State of Louisiana Literacy Test," Tennessee State Library and Archive, https://sharetngov.tnsosfiles.com/tsla/exhibits/aale/pdfs/Voter%20Test%20LA.pdf.

18. Kousser, *Shaping of Southern Politics*, 134.

19. Ibid., 116.

20. Ibid., 61.

21. Alexander Keyssar, *The Right to Vote: The Contested History of Democracy in the United States* (New York: Basic Books, 2000), 180.

22. "Smith v. Allwright," Oyez, https://www.oyez.org/cases/1940-1955/321us649 (accessed January 18, 2021).

23. "Civil Rights Act (1964)," US National Archives, https://www.ourdocuments.gov/doc.php?flash=false&doc=97 (accessed August 17, 2021); "Voting Rights Act (1965)," US National Archives, https://www.ourdocuments.gov/doc.php?flash=false&doc=100.

24. United States Commission on Civil Rights, *Political Participation* (Washington, DC: US Commission on Civil Rights, May 1968), https://www.crmvet.org/docs/ccr_voting_south_6805.pdf.

25. Jay Barth, "Democratic Party," in *The Encyclopedia of Arkansas History and Culture*, ed. Central Arkansas Library System, last updated December 1, 2016, http://www.encyclopediaofarkansas.net/encyclopedia/entry-detail.aspx?entryID=593.

26. US Commission on Civil Rights, *Political Participation*.

27. United States Commission on Civil Rights, *The Voting Rights Act: Unfulfilled Goals* (Washington, DC: US Government Printing Office, September 1981).

28. Ibid., 27.

29. As quoted in Tova Wang, *The Politics of Voter Suppression: Defending and Expanding Americans' Right to Vote* (Ithaca, NY: Cornell University Press, 2012), 167n7.

30. As quoted in Wang, *Politics of Voter Suppression*, 46.

31. For the practice generally, see Joseph P. Harris, *Registration of Voters in the United States* (Washington, DC: Brookings Institution, 1929), 231–32; and Justin Levitt and Andrew Allison, *A Guide to Voter Caging* (New York University School of Law: Brennan Center for Justice, June 2007). For New Jersey specifically, see Democratic National Committee v. Republican National Committee, Civil Action 81–3876 (D.N.J. 1981), https://www.govinfo.gov/content/pkg/US COURTS-njd-2_81-cv-03876/pdf/USCOURTS-njd-2_81-cv-03876-0.pdf.

32. Laughlin McDonald, "The New Poll Tax," *American Prospect: Ideas, Politics & Power*, December 6, 2002, https://prospect.org/features/new-poll-tax/.

33. Chandler Davidson, Tanya Dunlap, Gale Kenny, and Benjamin Wise, "Vote Caging as a Republican Ballot Security Technique," *William Mitchell Law Review* 34, no. 2 (2008): 533–62, https://open.mitchellhamline.edu/cgi/viewcontent.cgi?article=1239&context=wmlr.

34. "A Summary of the National Voter Registration Act," Project Vote, February 19, 2006, http://www.projectvote.org/wp-content/uploads/Summary-of-the-NVRA.pdf.

35. "H.R. 2—National Voter Registration Act of 1993," 103rd Congress (1993–1994), https://www.congress.gov/bill/103rd-congress/house-bill/2/text.

36. As quoted in Clifford Krauss, "The 1992 Campaign; Bill to Simplify Voter Registration Clears House and Pressures Bush," *New York Times*, June 17, 1992, https://www.nytimes.com/1992/06/17/us/1992-campaign-bill-simplify-voter-registration-clears-house-pressures-bush.html.

37. As quoted in Tova Wang, "9 Ways Voting Is Suppressed in America," Century Foundation, August 17, 2012, https://tcf.org/content/commentary/9-ways-voting-is-suppressed-in-america/?session=1.

38. Jonathan E. Davis, "The National Voter Registration Act of 1993: Debunking States' Rights Resistance and the Pretense of Voter Fraud," *Temple Political and Civil Rights Law Review* 6 (Fall 1996/Spring 1997): 117–37.

39. US Federal Election Commission, "Executive Summary," *The Impact of the National Voter Registration Act of 1993 on the Administration of Federal Elections*, June

1997, https://www.fec.gov/about/reports-about-fec/agency-operations/impact
-national-voter-registration-act-1993-administration-federal-elections-html/.

40. Ibid.

41. "Voting Rights in the Era of Mass Incarceration: A Primer," Sentencing
Project, July 28, 2021, https://www.sentencingproject.org/publications/felony
-disenfranchisement-a-primer/.

42. Jeff Manza and Christopher Uggen, "Punishment and Democracy: Disenfranchisement of Nonincarcerated Felons in the United States," *Perspectives
on Politics* 2, no. 3 (September 2004): 497.

43. Florida Amendment 4: Voting Rights Restoration for Felons Initiative,
2018, Ballotpedia, https://ballotpedia.org/Florida_Amendment_4,_Voting_Rights
_Restoration_for_Felons_Initiative_(2018).

44. Ibid.

45. Morgan McLeod, "Expanding the Vote: Two Decades of Felony Disenfranchisement Reforms," Sentencing Project, October 17, 2018, https://www
.sentencingproject.org/publications/expanding-vote-two-decades-felony-dis
enfranchisement-reforms/.

46. Brennan Center for Justice, "An 'Unhealthy Democracy,'" Editorial
Memorandum, July 2, 2002, https://www.brennancenter.org/sites/default/files/
legal-work/download_file_10042.pdf.

47. For sources concerning African American policing and the prison-indus
trial complex, see Douglas A. Blackmon, *Slavery by Another Name* (Norcross, GA:
Printing Trade Company, 2012); Daniel Mark Larson, "Killing Democracy; or,
How the Drug War Drives the Prison-Industrial Complex," in *Challenging the
Prison-Industrial Complex: Activism, Arts, and Educational Alternatives*, ed. Stephen
John Hartnett (Urbana: University of Illinois Press, 2011), 73–104; Joshua Reeves,
"Recognize, Resist, Report: D.A.R.E. America and the Kid Police," in *Citizen
Spies: The Long Rise of America's Surveillance Society* (New York: New York Univer-
sity Press, 2017), 109–36; "White v. Pauly," Oyez, https://www.oyez.org/cases/
2016/16-67 (accessed August 17, 2021).

48. Pippa Holloway, *Living in Infamy: Felon Disfranchisement and the History
of American Citizenship* (Oxford: Oxford University Press, 2013).

49. "About Fair Fight Action," Fair Fight, https://fairfight.com/about-fair
-fight/.

"Work Does Not Stop with This March on Washington"

LGBTQ+ National Mobilizations, 1979–2009

JOSH CERRETTI

Why Teach This Lesson?

The struggle for justice by LGBTQ+ people is undoubtedly one of the most significant social movements of the twentieth century, and the impacts of both its successes and failures are only beginning to manifest as we close out the second decade of the twenty-first century. This lesson helps students appreciate that the LGBTQ+ struggle must never be understood as a solitary, monolithic, or completely unified one. Rather, LGBTQ+ communities, and as a result LGBTQ+ struggles, have always been multiple, plural, and contested both within the movement and outside of the movement. A deeper engagement with primary source documents allows students to better understand the polyvocality composing LGBTQ+ histories and to more confidently use those histories to shape more just futures.

Introduction

Few social movements in US history have experienced such a rapid move from lows to highs as LGBTQ+ organizing around the turn of the twenty-first century. Looking backward from the year 2000, one is confronted with the massive political defeats of the Defense of Marriage Act (1996), the Don't Ask, Don't Tell policy (1993), the US Supreme Court decision in *Bowers v. Hardwick* (1987), and citizens' initiatives to roll back antidiscrimination ordinances across the country.

56

Pessimists can be forgiven, then, for failing to anticipate the subsequent string of victories manifest in *Lawrence v. Texas* (2003), the end of Don't Ask, Don't Tell (2011), the overturning of the Defense of Marriage Act (2014), and many other legislative and judicial wins for LGBTQ+ communities. These contestations are best understood not only in reference to the policies enacted by predominantly cisgender and heterosexual officials but also in reference to the LGBTQ+ movements that pushed from margin to center over the course of the late twentieth century.

In order to better historicize the changes in LGBTQ+ politics from the late 1970s to today, this chapter provides an examination of the platforms embraced by a series of national mobilizations to Washington, DC, that shaped and conditioned the course of these movements. Students can gain enormous insight by comparing and contrasting the 1979 National March on Washington for Lesbian and Gay Rights, the 1987 Second National March, the 1993 March on Washington for Lesbian, Gay and Bi Equal Rights and Liberation, the 2000 Millennium March on Washington, and the 2009 National Equality March. I both discuss the distinct naming conventions of these events and group them together under the label "March on Washington" (MOW). Here, I guide readers through the historical context and documentary content of each of these events, providing an outline for discussion and activities in order to bring these major activist moments into a range of educational settings.

I begin with an overview and comparative analysis of the five events in reference to conflicts both between the heteronormative public and LGBTQ+ movements as well as those within linked but distinct LGBTQ+ communities. Throughout, I present pieces of key documents from the organizers of these marches in order to best assess these events through the lenses of those who made them happen. After that, I provide a framework for bringing these sources to life through interactive engagement and historically informed discussion. Finally, I summarize the demands made during each of the five events discussed, which can serve as the focus for group activities within the classroom.

Before going any further, a quick note on language is necessary. As we will see, how one chooses to refer to communities that exist beyond the limitations imposed by conventional, binary heterosexuality is an important political choice that encodes a great deal of power. A full accounting for the evolution of terms such as "gay," "queer," and "trans" is beyond the scope of this chapter, but one should not proceed into discussions of these issues without an awareness of the thorny and

contested politics of naming genders and sexualities.[1] Here, I carefully
and intentionally make the sweeping and inclusive gesture of using an
acronym for lesbian, gay, bisexual, transgender, and queer people that
ends with a plus sign, signaling the open-ended inclusion of many who
are part of this coalition without having their identity specified by the
previous terms (for example, people who are asexual, Two-Spirit, pan-
sexual, nonbinary, and many more). Where I do not include a letter or
term that otherwise appears in this list, it is intentional, as not all statements that apply to some underneath the LGBTQ+ umbrella apply to
all. At the same time, it is important to recognize that, for many, identity
is a moving target in that it is subject to the same sorts of changes that
language undergoes over time and that LGBTQ+ identities are always
crosscut by a variety of intersecting oppressions and privileges that can
be, for many people in many cases, more relevant than a fixed sense of
belonging within the community.

1979 National March on Washington for Lesbian and Gay Rights

The National March on Washington for Lesbian and Gay
Rights was the first national mass mobilization of lesbian and gay political power and set the standard by which future marches were mea-
sured. Many participants in gay liberation organizations that had sprung
up in the aftermath of the 1969 Stonewall Riots in Greenwich Village
sought to organize national networks, but several tentative steps fal-
tered. The nascent gay liberation movement's earliest gains at the local
level provoked a backlash through which avowedly heterosexist movements emerged during the late 1970s.[2] The combination of widespread
antigay campaigns targeting municipal antidiscrimination ordinances
made famous by Anita Bryant, the mollifying effect of San Francisco
mayor Harvey Milk's assassination, and the lack of an effective government response to it, as well as the ten-year anniversary of Stonewall, all
created the conditions of possibility for thousands to gather in DC in
October 1979.

The march was scheduled to coincide with the first National Third
World Lesbian/Gay Conference, which over three days sought to establish networks for and address oppression "among, by and against" queer
people of color. The promotional pamphlet invited "women, Third
World people, the labor movement, and other progressive groups" to

join "young and old . . . poor and affluent . . . the disabled . . . and trans-people" in "lay[ing] the foundation for" a "genuine national movement for lesbian and gay rights."[3] Tens of thousands attended the march with a contingent of Third World women leading, and they did lay such a foundation on a cool Sunday afternoon.

Newspaper coverage of the event belies the accuracy of any single report of the event. The *Washington Post* claimed the crowd "appeared to include more women than men," whereas the *Los Angeles Times* averred, "Most marchers were young, white, and male."[4] As with many other public mobilizations, attendance was one of the most sharply debated figures. The *New York Times* described "an enthusiastic crowd of at least 75,000 people," whereas the *Washington Post* headline identified only 25,000 attendees.[5] The subsequent outpouring of criticism drove the *Post* to publish three critical letters of their coverage of the MOW the following week.[6] Many lesbian and gay publications estimated the crowd to be 100,000 or even 500,000 and indicated homophobic publishers' vested interest in minimizing the power of their constituency.[7]

Iconic Black lesbian feminist Audre Lorde, still known primarily as a poet, oriented her Saturday evening keynote address toward memories of DC ranging from the Jim Crow discrimination she experienced as a child to her attendance at the celebrated 1963 March on Washington for Jobs and Freedom. Taking center stage at this event in the fullness of all her identities allowed Lorde to address the intersectionality of seemingly separate axes of oppression as well as how movements against a single oppression may easily replicate others. She ended by stressing that "work does not stop with this march on Washington, each has a responsibility to take this struggle back to her and his community translated into daily action."[8]

1987 Second National March on Washington for Lesbian and Gay Rights

That struggle continued throughout the 1980s under increasingly challenging conditions, as right-wing backlash against sexual liberalism and the growing HIV/AIDS crisis encouraged a variety of attacks on the community. Planning for the second national mobilization discussed here, the 1987 Second National March on Washington for Lesbian and Gay Rights, occurred within a bleak and even desperate context when compared to its predecessor. Not only had tens of thousands of LGBTQ+ people already died from a disease for which there were not yet any effective treatments, but the *Bowers v. Hardwick* US Supreme Court decision had validated legal homophobia and proved that not only the executive branch but also the judicial branch of the US government was hostile toward the community. Consequently, the movement's demands refocused on the potential for legislative action and more substantially addressed the intersecting oppressions of heteropatriarchy and white supremacy in the United States and abroad.

Although participants at the Second March enjoyed cool weather similar to the first march, they experienced an increasingly bifurcated world of lesbian and gay organizing. The coalition behind lesbian and gay civil rights had grown dramatically, with labor (Cesar Chavez, Service Employees International Union President John Sweeney), celebrities (Whoopi Goldberg, Robert Blake), and politicians both straight and gay (Jesse Jackson, Barney Frank) prominently in attendance. A mass marriage in protest of restrictions on same-sex marriage and a veterans' ceremony at the Tomb of the Unknown Soldier portended issues that soon came into dedicated focus for the national movement. At the same time, the People with AIDS contingent that led the march and the highly visible presence of AIDS Coalition to Unleash Power (ACT UP) imagery throughout the march dramatized the urgency of a moment in which many had died and so many more were dying.[9] On the Tuesday after the march, on the steps of the Supreme Court, six hundred marchers were arrested during civil disobedience against the *Bowers v. Hardwick* decision that had rendered their right to privacy void and their sexual lives illegitimate in the eyes of the law.[10] Whereas the 1979 March demonstrated the strength of the LGBTQ+ community through its diversity, the 1987 March demonstrated that some members of the community could successfully court mainstream acceptance, while others sought radical confrontation with those same institutions.

Like eight years earlier, LGBTQ+ organizers were disappointed in the media response to the event, especially around the question of attendance, but this time organizers had prepared a more concerted campaign in response. A month after the event, the March on Washington Committee sent a mailer lamenting the lack of coverage in national magazines such as *Time* and *Newsweek*. It asserted, "Given the objective enormity of the Washington events we find this omission unconscionable," and it went on to encourage people to speak back to the media and "consider how you might make a statement with your money."[11] The dearth of attention given to the Second March ultimately failed to constrain its legacy, however, as two aspects of the event grew into beacons of LGBTQ+ organizing bright enough to often eclipse their origins. First appearing on the National Mall during the MOW, the NAMES Project AIDS Memorial Quilt—a massive stitching together of fabric representative of the lives lost to the epidemic—subsequently toured the country, was viewed by millions, and was eventually nominated for a Nobel Prize. Furthermore, as any survey of contemporary social media will attest, October 11 has evolved into the annual National Coming Out Day in which new generations of LGBTQ+ people, wittingly or not, carry on the slogan of the Second March to "come out, come out, wherever you are!"

1993 March on Washington for Lesbian, Gay, and Bi Equal Rights and Liberation

LGBTQ+ politics had truly "come out" into the national political discourse during and in the wake of the 1992 presidential elections, which in many ways set the context for the Lesbian, Gay, and Bisexual March for Equal Rights and Liberation in 1993. Leadership struck an optimistic tone in promoting the event, writing, "The election and inauguration are over, the new Congress is in session, and George Bush is in Houston . . . we have changed the question from '*Will* Congress pass a federal civil rights bill?' to '*When* will Congress pass the bill?'"[12] The 1993 March broke with the October tradition in order to schedule it fewer than one hundred days after President Bill Clinton took office. However, organizers placed this move within the genealogy of past marches, claiming, "The last Washington march, in 1987, did more for our movement than 100 Clintons."[13] One could again see space open up between those in the LGBTQ+ community who could comfortably integrate into the raced, classed, and gendered orthodoxies of US society were it not for discrimination on the basis of sexual orientation and those who oriented their struggle against the very idea of "normal."

The Lesbian, Gay, and Bisexual March for Equal Rights and Liberation was particularly notable for elevating bisexual people into the name of the march while opting to exclude the word "transgender" from it, despite significant participation by trans people. Bisexual organizer Lani Ka'ahumanu, an attendee in 1979 and 1987, took the stage to say, "Bisexuals are here, and we're queer. . . . Our visibility is a sign of revolt." Building off her concerns about tokenism and the "gayristrocracy," Ka'ahumanu, who is cisgender, went on to criticize the lack of "a sincere effort to confront biphobia and transphobia."[14] Early versions of the march's name and many related materials include the word "transgender" at the end of "Lesbian, Gay, Bisexual," but at least one source put it first. *The Nun Issue*, a broadside issued by the gender-queering Sisters of Perpetual Indulgence "For Transgender, Lesbian, Gay, and Bi Rights," questioned, "If we create a conformist, heterosexist image and try to fit all gays, lesbians, bisexuals, and transgender people into it, what have we gained? Are we not back in the same closets we were in before Drag Queens of color had the balls to face down the police at the Stonewall Drag Riots of 1969?"[15]

Despite these unanswered questions and divisions, many regarded the march as a significant success. As Urvashi Vaid said in her speech, broadcast nationally on C-Span, "This day marks the return from exile of the gay and lesbian people. We are banished no more, we wander the wilderness of despair no more, we are afraid no more."[16] Organizers paid special attention to setting the tone of media coverage in advance, writing before the march, "We were disappointed in 1979 and 1987 — let's work to succeed now in 1993."[17] Wary of the impact of low attendance estimates, the organizers created numbered rainbow wristbands for attendees so, as the march pamphlet said, "The park service can't lie this time."[18] *Washington Post* coverage, for example, identified "hundreds of thousands of marchers" and called it "A Day of Joy, Anger, Learning and Solidarity."[19] At the same time, editors interspersed these mostly positive assessments of the event with a homophobic article from Malcolm Gladwell that asked, if queerness isn't "a moral weakness, a criminal act or an illness . . . then, what is it?"[20] That is to say, in spite of progress, much work remained to be done.

2000 Millennium March on Washington

The 2000 Millennium March on Washington took up this work at the dawn of a new century but was mired in controversy long before it even began. In October 1998, the Ad Hoc Committee for an Open Process called for a national meeting to address "the top down and closed-door process which continues to be used by the organizers of so-called 'Millennium March'" and "the increasingly conservative direction of much of the national leadership of the l/b/g/t movement."[21] Following this meeting, the group marshaled the history of the event, writing, "The marches on Washington strengthened our movement largely because they were democratically run grassroots efforts on a massive scale. . . . Now, as a fourth march on Washington is being proposed, we must summon the legacy of the previous three."[22] As this was the first MOW to take place during a presidential election year, many organizers were concerned about the event turning into "Gays for Gore," even though the Clinton-Gore administration had followed through on few of its promises to the community during its years in office. These fears were justified by the eventual declarations of the organizers that the event sought to "empower and inspire voters for the 2000 elections," with the executive director of the Human Rights Campaign declaring, "We must elect Al Gore the president of the United States" from the stage, and a video message from the candidate himself shared with the assembled marchers.[23]

The 2000 March innovated in many ways; it was the first to make extensive use of the internet in organization, promotion, and documentation, in part due to the influence of primary sponsor PlanetOut, one of the first online media corporations to target the LGBT demographic. The prominent inclusion of other corporate sponsors with limited connections to the community such as United Airlines and the Showtime television network followed a long-growing trend in Pride Parades but was a first for a MOW, which had tended to aim for a somewhat less festive and more socially conscious tone. Another significant departure was the lack of a formal platform of demands. Although organizers had identified eight "Priority Issues" in 1999 that could have evolved into the specific planks articulated at the three previous marches, they found the process too contentious and fraught to complete, highlighting a focus on electoral politics as the only avenue for change authorized by certain movement leaders. Finally, the Millennium March on Washington most visibly broke with previous MOWs by avoiding any direct reference to the LGBTQ+ people in the name, dodging some debates about language choices while seemingly bowing to assimilationist critiques of visibility.

Regardless of significant internal dissent, the Millennium March had some external success. The organizers pointed to over eight hundred thousand attendees as the clearest proof, an estimate that went uncontested because "the United States Park Police no longer issues crowd estimates, which had become an unending source of debate with the organizers of various marches."[24] Many participants visibly celebrated Vermont's recent passage of a same-sex civil union law, the movement for which faced stiff headwinds in the 1990s but spread rapidly following Massachusetts' legalization of same-sex marriage in 2004. On stage, the families of recently slain Matthew Shepard and James Byrd Jr. united publicly in a speech that portended the 2009 passage of the Matthew Shepard–James Byrd Jr. Hate Crimes Protection Act. In her report back from the march, Dorie Clark, a political consultant and lesbian, trumpeted "the gay movement's growing political sophistication and success over the past seven years at breaking into mainstream American life" while expressing her hopeful anticipation of the impending "point where we can stay home, confident of our place in the social fabric."[25]

2009 National Equality March

Given the electoral defeat of the Millennium March's candidate and subsequent years of increased scapegoating of LGBTQ+ people by right-wing forces, paired with little reform at the federal level, that point had clearly not come when planning began for the 2009 National Equality March. The organizers of the final MOW addressed here attempted to seize the reins of LGBTQ+ history but ultimately were unable to execute an event as historic as those in past decades. Cleve Jones, the force behind the AIDS Memorial Quilt, called for a mobilization to hold recently inaugurated President Barack Obama accountable for his promises to LGBTQ+ constituencies earlier in 2009, but he faced an even steeper uphill climb than past organizers. Familiar divides over whether the event should be serious or celebratory, locally or nationally focused, and led by grassroots organizers or nonprofit professionals opened up alongside concerns about focus, language, tactics, and equity in the composition of the leadership.[26] Well-organized constituencies long excluded from speaking on behalf of an imagined monolithic "gay community" were able to use the more direct forms of engaging media and the public offered by the internet to air their concerns earlier in ways that made the event less appealing to many. Simultaneously, the passage of same-sex marriage legislation at the state level had already demobilized some who saw that as their primary issue, and increasingly cozy relationships between some mainstream same-sex marriage advocates and politicians made others wary of confrontational protest.

Thus, the 2009 National Equality March has, for the time being, ended the tradition of the queer MOW with more of a whimper than a bang. The estimated two hundred thousand attendees were by no means insignificant but were only a fraction of those who showed up in 2000, 1993, and 1987—perhaps even fewer than were present in 1979. Lower attendance was, of course, not a true measure of the power of the communities under the LGBTQ+ umbrella but a reflection of limitations in the event's organization, the general slump in progressive protest during the Obama administration, and the multiplication of other avenues of political and cultural engagement outside of major marches for LGBTQ+ people. That a more modest crowd gathered in 2009 than previous years did not seem to hold back the 2011 repeal of the Don't Ask, Don't Tell policy or the 2014 and 2015 US Supreme Court decisions validating marriage equality in all fifty states. While the National Equality March's single demand of full equality in all civil matters is yet to come to fruition, arguably we won more advancements in LGBTQ+ rights at the federal level in the half-decade following this march than we had in the previous four decades.

Looking across this era, from the 1979 MOW on the cusp of the "Reagan Revolution" to the 2009 National Equality March at the dawn of Obama's historic presidency, we can trace continuities across these distinct moments. Rather than casting these developments as a two-dimensional struggle between pro-gay and antigay forces, an approach that honors the multidimensional nature of LGBTQ+ struggle can better support those interrelated struggles without flattening the distinctions between them. Such an approach, which draws connections rather than either equivalences or distinctions, can also be useful for contextualizing LGBTQ+ Marches on Washington in relation to many other mobilizations focused on the nation's capital. A deeper engagement with the documents produced within these moments, rather than a simplified narrative that draws a direct path from the Stonewall Riots to the creation of the Stonewall National Historic Site, allows us to better understand the polyvocality composing LGBTQ+ histories and to more confidently use those histories to shape more just futures.[27]

Classroom Discussion

Building off the above background and making use of the documents below, groups can discuss the broad sweep of LGBTQ+

history from the late 1970s to the early 2010s as well as the particular moments in which each of these events occurred. This is structured as a "snowball" discussion in which you can begin with individuals or pairs, combine those into small groups for intermediate activities, and eventually culminate with a large group discussion.

First, provide each group or individual with one of the lists below (also included as Word documents on the companion website [http:// GoldbergSeries.org/UTContemporaryUSHistory]) from a particular MOW. The group should review the language and first discuss anything that is not clear so that they can begin from common ground. Then students address the following questions: What do these demands tell us about LGBTQ+ life in the era that they are from? What insight do they give us on everyday concerns as well as the big picture of LGBTQ+ politics? What other things were happening at the same time that might have intersected with or had some bearing on these demands and whether they were met? How have things changed or not changed since then? Which demands are still relevant and which have been addressed to one degree or another?

Second, have the groups share their findings or pair up with another group to begin a comparative discussion. The group should review both documents and reflect on the similarities and differences between two different MOWs. Then they address the following questions: How do the demands resemble each other and how do they contrast? Whose concerns get more attention in one set than another? Can you point to events or shifts that occurred in between these two documents being written that might explain some of the changes? Can you point to events or shifts that might have occurred afterward because of the changes you see in the later document? Which demands (individually or overall) seem more or less relevant today?

For the third part of the lesson, reorganize the participants by either breaking up and recombining small groups or simply dividing them all into two groups. The next activity is to create a time line or other graphic representation of change over time from the 1979 MOW to the 2009 iteration. Participants might chart the rise and fall of a particular issue, examine a formal issue such as the number of demands, or evaluate whatever aspect interests them most. This is an opportunity for more open-ended exploration, practicing the skill of converting textual information into visuals, and practicing the historical skill of chronological thinking.

Finally, all participants can work together on a final activity: drawing up a set of prospective demands for the next LGBTQ+ March on Washington. Given that no more than nine years had elapsed between these five previous MOWs, we became overdue for another massive mobilization and display of LGBTQ+ communities' power by 2019. You can provide a structure for a formally organized process such as *Robert's Rules of Order*, an open process of suggestions followed by votes to adopt a limited number, or more of a consensus-based process in which stock is taken and proposals are modified through extensive discussion— whatever style best fits the group and your facilitation style. Whatever approach you use, it is wise to put a time limit on this activity in order to simulate the pressure organizers are under to summarize the vastness of a complex and diverse set of communities into a simple list of demands.

Lists of Demands

Demands from the 1979 March

1. Repeal all anti-lesbian/gay laws.
2. Issue a presidential executive order banning discrimination based on sexual orientation in the Federal Government, the military and federally contracted private employment.
3. End discrimination in lesbian mother and gay father custody cases.
4. Protect lesbian and gay youth from any laws which are used to discriminate against, oppress and/or harass them in their homes, schools, jobs and social environments.[28]

Demands from the 1987 March

1. Passage of the congressional lesbian and gay civil rights bill.
2. An end to discrimination against people with AIDS . . . Money for AIDS, not for war.
3. The repeal of all laws that make sodomy between consenting adults a crime.
4. A presidential order banning anti-gay discrimination by the federal government.
5. Legal recognition of lesbian and gay relationships.

6. Reproductive freedom, the right to control our own bodies, and an end to sexist oppression.
7. An end to racism in this country and apartheid in South Africa.[29]

Demands from the 1993 March

1. Passage of a Lesbian, Gay, Bisexual, and Transgender civil rights bill and . . . repeal of . . . laws that criminalize private sexual expression between consenting adults.
2. Massive increase in funding for AIDS education, research, and patient care; universal access to health care . . . and an end to sexism in medical research and health care.
3. Legislation to prevent discrimination . . . in the areas of family diversity, custody, adoption and foster care and . . . include the full diversity of all family structures.
4. Full and equal inclusion of Lesbians, Gays, Bisexuals, and Transgendered people in the educational system, and . . . multicultural curricula.
5. The right to reproductive freedom and choice, to control our own bodies, and an end to sexist discrimination.
6. An end to racial and ethnic discrimination in all forms.
7. An end to discrimination and violent oppression based on actual or perceived sexual orientation/identification, race, religion, identity, sex and gender expression, disability, age, class, AIDS/HIV infection.[30]

Priority Issues from the 2000 March

1. Hate crimes legislative protections.
2. Ending GLBT discrimination in the workplace.
3. Racial justice.
4. GLBT family values, including marriage and partner rights, equality of adoption laws, and child custody protections.
5. GLBTQ health care issues.
6. Legal protections for GLBT youth.
7. Overturning anti-gay initiatives and laws on both the federal and state levels.
8. Privacy rights.[31]

Demands from the 2009 March

1. Our One Single Demand: Equal protection in all matters governed by civil law in all 50 states.
2. Our philosophy: As members of every race, class, faith, and community, we see the struggle for LGBT equality as part of a larger movement for peace and social justice.
3. Our strategy: Decentralized organizing for this march in every one of the 435 Congressional districts will build a network to continue organizing beyond October.[32]

NOTES

1. For a practical primer, see Alex Kapitan, "The Radical Copyeditor's Style Guide for Writing about Transgender People," https://radicalcopyeditor.com/2017/08/31/transgender-style-guide/ (accessed August 20, 2021).

2. For more on these movements, see Emily Johnson, "God, Country, and Anita Bryant: Women's Leadership and the Politics of the New Christian Right," *Religion and American Culture* 28, no. 2 (2018): 238–68.

3. "National March on Washington for Lesbian and Gay Rights" pamphlet, Lesbian Herstory Archives [accessed through Gale *Archives of Gender and Sexuality* in June 2020, https://www.gale.com/primary-sources/archives-of-sexuality-and-gender], National March on Washington (October 14–November 6, 1979) collection, MS Folder No. 09540.

4. Courtland Milloy and Loretta Tofani, "25,000 Attend Gay Rights Rally at the Monument," *Washington Post*, October 15, 1979, p. A1; Times Wire Services, "Thousands Attend Rally in Capital for Gay Rights," *Los Angeles Times*, October 15, 1979, p. B4.

5. Jo Thomas, "75,000 March in Capital to Support Homosexuals," *New York Times*, October 15, 1979, p. A14.

6. "The Post's Coverage of the Gay Rights March," *Washington Post*, October 23, 1979, p. A16.

7. Wende Persons, "Media's Message," *Empty Closet* 99 (November 1979): 1; Janet Sergi, "We Marched on Washington," *Big Mama Rag* 7, no. 10 (November 1979): 6; Brian McNaught, "Reflections on the March," *GPU News* 9 no. 3 (November 1979): 21–22, all available through the Lesbian Herstory Archives; Gerry Hunt, "March on Washington, October 14, 1979," *GO Info/Update* 6, no. 5 (November 1979): 5, International Gay and Lesbian Periodicals and Newsletters, https://link.gale.com/apps/doc/NAVMJF120864383/AHSI?u=wwu_wilson&sid=bookmark-AHSI&xid=0ff72f7a.

8. Audre Lorde, "Audre Lorde Speaks! March for Lesbian and Gay Rights, Washington, D.C., 1979," May 25, 2015, https://www.youtube.com/watch?v=bQK8yawGQXE&t=126s.

9. "Press Release: March on Washington for Lesbian and Gay Rights Draws Record Crowd," October 11, 1987, Lesbian Herstory Archives, National March on Washington for Lesbian and Gay Rights (October 2–13, 1987) collection, Folder No. 09570.

10. "Lesbian/Gay Rights March Scores Political Triumph," *National NOW Times* 10, no. 4 (September/October/November 1987): 1, 6.

11. "Some Suggestions for Individual Action," November 24, 1987, Lesbian Herstory Archives, Marches on Washington: Millennium (November 24, 1987–March, 2000 and undated) collection, TS Folder No. 08590.

12. Committee for the March on Washington Inc., *Our Time Has Come: Federal Civil Rights Now!*, p. 1, New York Public Library [accessed June 2020 via Gale *Archives of Sexuality and Gender*], March on Washington (1993) collection, TS Box 96, Folder 11: ACT UP: The AIDS Coalition to Unleash Power: Series VIII.

13. Donna Minkowitz, "Forward, March!" from *Our Time Has Come: Federal Civil Rights Now!*, 3.

14. Lani Ka'ahumanu, "User Clip: Lani Ka'ahumanu 1993 March on Washington," C-SPAN, April 25, 1993, https://www.c-span.org/video/?c4792729/user-clip-lani-kaahumanu-1993-march-washington.

15. Xena Philia, "Dragphobia," *The Nun Issue* 1 (1993): 2, Lesbian Herstory Archives, Marches on Washington (1979–June 26, 1994), MS Folder No. 08600.

16. Urvashi Vaid, "1993 March on Washington Speech," C-SPAN, April 25, 1993, https://www.c-span.org/video/?c4443798/user-clip-urvashi-vaid-1993-mow-speech.

17. Committee for the March on Washington Inc., *Our Time Has Come*, 2.

18. Ibid., 7.

19. Rene Sanchez and Kunda Wheeler, "Gays Demands Rights in 6 Hour March," *Washington Post*, April 26, 1993, p. A1; "The Gay Rights March on Washington: A Day of Joy, Anger, Learning and Solidarity," *Washington Post*, April 26, 1993, p. A8.

20. Malcolm Gladwell, "Studies Underscore Ambiguity about Nature of Homosexuality," *Washington Post*, April 26, 1993, p. A11.

21. "Controversy over 'Millennium March' Sparks National L/G/B/T meeting in Pittsburgh," October 16, 1998, Lesbian Herstory Archives, Marches on Washington (Millennium, November 24, 1987–March 2000, and undated) collection, TS Folder No. 08590.

22. "Proposal to the June Meeting from the Ad Hoc Committee for an Open Process," Lesbian Herstory Archives, Marches on Washington (Millennium, November 24, 1987–March 2000, and undated) collection, Folder No. 08590.

23. Millennium March on Washington for Equality, "About the March," https://web.archive.org/web/20020101203802/http://www.planetout.com/mmow/about/; Robin Toner, "A Gay Rights Rally over Gains and Goals," *New York Times*, May 1, 2000, p. A14.

24. Toner, "Gay Rights Rally."

25. Dorie Clark, "All Grown Up," *Boston Phoenix*, May 8, 2000, http://weeklywire.com/ww/05-08-00/boston_feature_1.html.

26. Shauna Miller, "Controversy Brews around National Equality March," *Atlantic*, September 28, 2009, https://www.theatlantic.com/politics/archive/2009/09/controversy-brews-around-national-equality-march/27343/.

27. For a more detailed engagement with the first four marches discussed here, see Amin Ghaziani, *The Dividends of Dissent: How Conflict and Culture Work in Lesbian and Gay Marches on Washington* (Chicago: University of Chicago Press, 2008).

28. Derived from "National March on Washington for Lesbian and Gay Rights: Official Souvenir Program 1979," Houston LGBT History, http://www.houstonlgbthistory.org/Houston80s/TWT/1979/MOWprogram1979.compressed.pdf.

29. Derived from "List of Demands," National March on Washington for Lesbian and Gay Rights, October 2–13, 1987, TS Folder No. 09570, Lesbian Herstory Archives. See also "Our Demands: March on Washington for Lesbian and Gay Rights," October 11, 1987, One Archives Foundation, http://www.onearchives.org/wp-content/uploads/2015/02/Our-Demands-March-on-Washington-for-Lesbian-and-Gay-Rights-Oct-11-1987.pdf.

30. Derived from Committee for the March on Washington Inc., *Our Time Has Come*, 3. See also "Platform of the 1993 March on Washington for Lesbian, Gay, and Bi Equal Rights and Liberation," Queer Resources Director, http://www.qrd.org/qrd/events/mow/mow-full.platform (accessed June 20, 2020).

31. Derived from Millennium March on Washington for Equality, "Press Release: Flurry of Activity, Accomplishments Marks Millennium March on Washington Board Meeting," December 8, 1999, https://web.archive.org/web/20050125083859/http://www.planetout.com/mmow/about/press/december/19991208.html.

32. Derived from Equality across America, homepage, 2010, https://web.archive.org/web/20100722063551/http://nationalequalitymarch.org/.

Studying Recent US Supreme Court Nominations

Examining Public Debate and Citizen Participation

Leah Vallely

Why Teach This Lesson?

Today's students may well think that presidential appointments to the US Supreme Court have always been divisive, widely broadcast, politically charged events in American history. Therefore, they may be surprised to learn that this is—historically speaking—a relatively recent development. The Supreme Court and its justices are often in the news, and they play a crucial role in balancing power between the three branches of the federal government under the Constitution. Therefore, the institution is clearly important, and students' knowledge of its work is important to their ability to be responsible US citizens. This lesson specifically focuses on both citizens' engagement with their democracy through the nomination and confirmation process of Supreme Court justices as well as how this process has changed over time, helping students learn and hone the historical thinking skill of recognizing change and continuity over time.

Introduction

This lesson invites students to explore how the nomination and confirmation process for US Supreme Court nominees has changed over time and to consider how and to what extent these changes reflect ways in which American democracy has been a process of citizen participation, debate, and compromise between government and the people. The impetus for the creation of this lesson stems from the recent nominations and confirmations of Amy Coney Barrett and Ketanji Brown Jackson to the Supreme Court. Trump nominated Barrett in 2020 to fill the vacancy left by the death of Justice Ruth Bader Ginsburg, and in 2022 Biden nominated Jackson to succeed Justice Stephen Breyer upon his retirement. Trump's nomination of Barrett and Biden's nomination of Jackson generated impassioned commentary from myriad sectors of the American public and further polarized an already partisan Senate. In the case of Barrett, after a speedy confirmation process, a bitterly divided Senate voted 51–48 (strictly along party lines) to confirm Barrett's nomination to the bench—the first time since the nineteenth century that a nominee was confirmed without a single vote from the opposing political party. Eighteen months later, the Senate, still sharply divided, confirmed Jackson with a near party line vote of 53–47.[1]

The nomination and confirmation of both Barrett and Jackson brought to mind the nomination and confirmation of Sandra Day O'Connor—the first woman nominated (by President Ronald Reagan) and confirmed to the United States Supreme Court—which, like Barrett's and Jackson's, produced a flurry of public reaction and response about her suitability for the high court. Despite the historical nature of O'Connor's nomination and the depth and breadth of her judicial credentials, not all supported her nomination. But unlike the partisan vote that characterized both Barrett's and Jackson's confirmations, the Senate voted unanimously to confirm O'Connor. While much of the general public marveled over the perceived speed of the nomination and confirmation processes of Barrett and Jackson, what is ultimately more interesting is the degree of public discussion and deliberation about their nominations and confirmations juxtaposed with the actual Constitutional process for appointing justices to the Supreme Court. In this regard, all three women's nominations and confirmations were remarkably similar in generating wide public debate not only about their judicial philosophies but about how their gender might reflect on their qualifications for the court.

The aim of this lesson is for students (1) to identify the nomination and confirmation process for Supreme Court justices as delineated by the US Constitution, (2) to assess how this process has changed over time, (3) to examine various primary sources related to the nomination and confirmation of former Justice Sandra Day O'Connor, and (4) to evaluate how these sources demonstrate citizen participation, debate, and compromise. Moreover, these sources provide a window through which students can discern issues in contemporary American political culture and society. Given that there are myriad primary and secondary source documents for each of the Supreme Court candidates nominated since the first Reagan administration, this lesson specifically focuses on the records related to the nomination process and confirmation hearings for Sandra Day O'Connor. This lesson can easily be adapted and modified to include any or all of the justices nominated since.

Background Information

The process of appointing justices to the Supreme Court has changed over time since the nomination and confirmation of the first justice in 1789, but the most basic features of the process have remained the same—the president must nominate a candidate, and that candidate must be confirmed by the United States Senate by a simple majority. The specific procedure for appointing a justice is provided for by the Constitution under Article II, Section 2, clause 2, which states that the president "shall nominate, and by and with the Advice and Consent of the Senate, shall appoint . . . Judges of the supreme Court." The process purposefully prevented the general public from directly choosing members of the Supreme Court, reflecting the founders' anxiety about unbridled democracy. Though the founders may have successfully prevented *"we the people"* from directly nominating and confirming Supreme Court nominees, American citizens, over time, have found ways to influence and change the nomination, selection, and confirmation process since the creation of the court in 1789.

Originally, Supreme Court nominations were not subject to committee examination nor to public scrutiny. The first public hearings on a nominee did not take place until 1916—some 127 years after the creation of the Supreme Court—and even then, the nominee, Louis D. Brandeis, did not appear in person. Brandeis's nomination by President Woodrow Wilson was controversial because he was the first Jewish nominee, but more importantly he had earned a reputation as a pioneering reformer who sought to use the legal process to address the pressing social justice questions of the day, including workplace safety and monopolies. In this case, the senators sought a public outlet to express their reservations about Wilson's nomination. But it was not until 1939 that a nominee, Felix Frankfurter (a Jew born in Vienna, Austria), first appeared before the Senate Judiciary Committee in a public session. Since 1955, every Supreme Court nominee has participated in public confirmation hearings (except those whose nominations were withdrawn by the president), and beginning with Sandra Day O'Connor's 1981 hearing, all Supreme Court nomination hearings have been nationally televised. Though there is nothing in the Constitution that stipulates such hearings, the American public has become accustomed to "the modern confirmation hearing—public, extensive, and with testimony by proponents and opponents."[2] As a result, "they have become an important forum for democratic engagement," deemed "essential to our system of self-government."[3]

Contemporary nominations of Supreme Court justices continue to follow the process outlined by the Constitution, but now include these additional stages—and at each stage nominees can stumble:

1. The president usually will seek and consider suggestions for a potential nominee. These suggestions may come from various senators, advisers within the president's administration, political party leaders, and interest groups. After Reagan nominee Douglas Ginsberg was announced as the administration's nominee but before the confirmation process had started, news of his marijuana use became public and led him to withdraw in 1987 (following the unsuccessful nomination of Robert Bork earlier that year).

2. The president then sends his nomination to the Senate Judiciary Committee for consideration. Toward the end of President Barack Obama's second administration (March 2016), the Republican-controlled Senate refused to consider Obama's nomination of Merrick Garland, arguing that the Supreme Court justice should be chosen by the next president elected by the American people in the upcoming presidential election in November 2016.

3. The Senate Judiciary Committee then initiates an investigation into the nominee's background. When President George W. Bush nominated Harriet Miers, White House counsel to the Bush administration, to replace Sandra Day O'Connor, a request from the Senate Judiciary Committee for internal White House documents that the administration insisted were protected by executive privilege prompted withdrawal of the nomination, though other issues were likely more pressing.

4. The Senate Judiciary Committee's public hearings feature witnesses who both support and oppose the nomination, the nominee's

presentation of their own views, and questions from committee members about the nominee's qualifications, judgment, and judicial philosophy. In 1991, committee hearings were reopened and televised nationally when Anita Hill, professor of law at the University of Oklahoma, made allegations of sexual harassment against Clarence Thomas, President George Bush's nominee to replace Justice Thurgood Marshall. Nonetheless, Thomas received a majority vote in both the committee and the full Senate, and he was still serving on the nation's highest court at the time of this writing.

5. The Judiciary Committee then votes on the nomination and sends its recommendation to the full Senate. The last time that the committee did not move a candidate forward came in 1954 when Eisenhower's nomination of John Marshall Harlan II was not reported out; but Harlan was renominated and confirmed a year later.

6. The full Senate debates the nomination and then votes on it. A simple majority of the senators present and voting is required for the judicial nominee to be confirmed. If there is a tie, the vice president, who also presides over the Senate, casts the deciding vote. In 1987, Robert Bork's nomination was the last time the Senate failed to confirm a nominee (42–58).

Lesson Plan

This lesson would be most useful after students have had the opportunity to survey and discuss the domestic context of the Reagan administrations or as a stand-alone lesson used in conjunction with a thematic unit on American democracy. Additionally, this lesson is best suited for students who have experience with the Think-Pair-Share reading strategy and familiarity with sourcing, contextualizing, close reading, and corroborating documents from their work earlier in the semester.[4]

Learning Objectives

By the end of this lesson, students will be able to

- source, contextualize, close read, and corroborate various sources,
- identify changes and continuities among the nomination process and confirmation hearings of Supreme Court justices,

- evaluate changes over time (public debate and hearings) to the US Supreme Court nomination and confirmation process as an expansion of American democracy.

Materials

The graphic organizer appears at the end of this chapter; Word versions of the documents, graphic organizer, and lesson variations are also available from the companion website (http://GoldbergSeries.org/UTContemporaryUSHistory).

Copies of Documents A–G

- *Document A*: US Constitution, Article II, Sec. 2, Clause 2, https:// constitutioncenter.org/interactive-constitution/article/article-ii.
- *Document B*: Lori Ringhand and Paul Collins, Scotus Blog post, "Legal Scholarship Highlight: The Evolution of Supreme Court Confirmation Hearings," March 25, 2016, https://www.scotusblog.com/2016/03/legal -scholarship-highlight-the-evolution-of-supreme-court-confirmation -hearings/.
- *Document C*: Letter from Marie Craven, a Chicago resident, to President Reagan, July 7, 1981, https://artsandculture.google.com/ asset/marie-craven-letter-typed-page-01/YQHaRfJMszIYJg?hl=en.
- *Document D*: Memo from Marileee Melvin, White House staff, to Ed Thomas, deputy to White House Counsel Ed Meese, July 6, 1981, https://artsandculture.google.com/asset/_/SAFb-4fh1 E_yGg.
- *Document E*: Letter from US Senator Strom Thurmond (R-SC) to President Reagan, July 7, 1981, https://artsandculture.google.com/ exhibit/sandra-day-o-connor-u-s-national-archives/pQICl_trUHo_ Iw?hl=en.
- *Document F*: Letter from Iris Mitgang, Chair, National Women's Political Caucus, to President Reagan, June 18, 1981, https:// artsandculture.google.com/asset/_/BAGzOy3xkgZmDQ.
- *Document G*: Table of contents from the hearings before the Committee on the Judiciary, United States Senate, on the nomination of Judge Sandra Day O'Connor (pp. 1–6), September 9–11, 1981, https://www .loc.gov/law/find/nominations/oconnor/hearing.pdf.
- Copies of Graphic Organizer.

Plan of Instruction

I. *Introduction*
   A. Provide students with copies of the Graphic Organizer and Documents A and B.
   B. Tell students that they will be examining a series of documents in order to
      1. identify changes and continuities among the nomination process and confirmation hearings of US Supreme Court justices, and
      2. evaluate the relationship between public engagement and debate about Supreme Court nominees and the expansion of American democracy.
   C. Assess Prior Knowledge: Ask students what they know about the nomination selection and confirmation process for justices to the Supreme Court.
      • *Note:* This informal prior knowledge check can be done while the Graphic Organizer and Documents A and B are being provided to students.
   D. Ask students to read Document A and to summarize to what extent the US Constitution invites public debate and deliberation about Supreme Court nominees. Have students record their summary on the Graphic Organizer.

II. *Identifying Change and Continuity*
   A. Ask students to read Document B and then use the Think-Pair-Share (TPS) strategy to summarize examples noted by the authors of how the process for nominating and confirming Supreme Court nominees has changed over time.
      • *Note:* TPS is a collaborative learning strategy where students work together to answer a question about an assigned reading. This strategy requires students to think individually about a topic or answer to a question, share ideas with a partner, and then expand the shared information to a whole-group discussion.

III. *Whole-Group Discussion of Documents A and B*
   A. Clarify the ways in which the constitutional process for nominating and confirming a candidate to the US Supreme Court has changed over time.
   B. Clarify the creation and changing role of the Senate Judiciary Committee relative to the confirmation process.

    C. Clarify how and why public engagement and debate with the nomination and confirmation process has changed over time.

    D. Ask students to comment on the extent to which this process reflects American ideals about democracy.

IV. *Transition*

    A. Tell students that they will be examining various documents related to the nomination and confirmation of Sandra Day O'Connor to the US Supreme Court.

    B. Briefly review the basic historical thinking skills students should rely upon to critically examine documents (Sourcing, Contextualizing, Close Reading, and Corroborating).

V. *Think-Pair-Share*

    A. Have students think about what they have read, pair with a partner, and share what they think in order to develop the best possible answer.

    B. After passing out Documents C–G, ask students to work in pairs to complete the Graphic Organizer using the provided documents.

VI. *Closure / Whole-Group Discussion*

    A. Ask students to summarize their discussion to answer the following questions:

        1. How and to what extent do these documents provide a glimpse into both the changes and continuities of the nomination and confirmation processes for candidates selected to serve on the US Supreme Court?

        2. How and to what extent has public engagement and debate about a nominee's suitability become a forum for citizen participation within the American democratic tradition?

        3. How and to what extent do the changes to the nomination and confirmation process reflect the notion that American democracy is dynamic rather than static?

Graphic Organizer

Document A: According to the Constitution, what is the process for nominating and confirming a candidate to the U.S. Supreme Court? (*Close Reading*)

_____

_____

_____

Document B: What kind of document is this? Who created this source? Is this document reliable? According to this document, what are three examples of how the nomination and confirmation process of Supreme Court justices has changed since 1789? (*Sourcing and Close Reading*)

_____

_____

_____

Document C: What kind of document is this? Who created this document and for what purpose? What concerns does Marie Craven express to President Reagan? How does this document reflect citizens' engagement and debate about President Reagan's nomination of Sandra Day O'Connor to the Supreme Court? (*Sourcing and Close Reading*)

_____

_____

_____

Document D: What kind of document is this? Who is Harold O. J. Brown? What concerns does Brown have about President Reagan's nomination of Sandra Day O'Connor? How does this document reflect citizens' engagement and debate? How is the document similar to or different from Document C? (*Sourcing, Close Reading, and Corroboration*)

_____

_____

_____

_____

Document E: Who created this document and for what purpose? What concerns are reflected in this document? How does this document reflect citizens' engagement and debate about President Reagan's nomination of Sandra Day O'Connor to the Supreme Court? How is this document similar or different from Documents C and D? (*Sourcing, Close Reading, and Corroboration*)

_____

_____

_____

Document F: Who created this document and for what purpose? How does this document reflect citizens' engagement and debate about President Reagan's nomination of Sandra Day O'Connor to the Supreme Court? How is this document similar to or different from Documents C, D, and E? (*Sourcing, Close Reading, and Corroboration*)

_____

_____

_____

Document G: What kind of document is this? What is the purpose of this document? How does this document reflect citizens' engagement and debate about President Reagan's nomination of Sandra Day O'Connor to the Supreme Court? How is this document similar or different from Documents C, D, E, and F? (*Sourcing, Close Reading, and Corroboration*)

_____

_____

_____

_____

NOTES

1. Jennifer Haberkorn, "Amy Coney Barrett Confirmed to Supreme Court by GOP Senators," *Los Angeles Times*, October 26, 2020, https://www.latimes.com/politics/story/2020-10-26/democrats-ask-pence-skip-barrett-confirmation-vote-coronavirus; US Senate Committee on the Judiciary, "Judge Ketanji Brown Jackson: Nominee to Become the 116th Associate Justice of the United

States Supreme Court," https://www.judiciary.senate.gov/judge-ketanji-brown -jackson (accessed May 31, 2022).

2. William Fassuliotis, "Brandeis in Brief: The First Public Confirmation Hearing," *Virginia Law Weekly*, September 26, 2018, https://www.lawweekly.org/col/2018/9/26/brandeis-in-brief-the-first-public-confirmation-hearing.

3. Lori Ringhand and Paul Collins, "Legal Scholarship Highlight: The Evolution of Supreme Court Confirmation Hearings," SCOTUSblog, March 25, 2016, https://www.scotusblog.com/2016/03/legal-scholarship-highlight-the-evolution-of-supreme-court-confirmation-hearings/.

4. Historical Thinking Matters, http://historicalthinkingmatters.org/how/.

The Drug War Era

From the Crack Epidemic to the Opioid Crisis

KATHRYN MCLAIN AND

MATTHEW R. PEMBLETON

Why Teach This Lesson?

The War on Drugs is one of the longest and most costly policy campaigns in US history. Modern observers agree that the drug war has failed to prevent the illicit use of drugs, and yet it continues and exerts a profound influence on American policing, foreign policy, and political culture. The opening essay provides the instructor with an introduction to major federal initiatives in drug policy since the Reagan administration, with a clear mapping of how the War on Drugs developed and persisted. The narrative shows how political, economic, social, and cultural factors in the United States converge to shape federal drug policies, which in turn shape US society.

The lesson plan asks students to consider their own ideas about the issue of drugs in the United States, the messaging of a variety of federal antidrug initiatives, and the change in public policy and public opinion over time. The question for students through the lesson is this: after reading through different leadership approaches to drug policy, what approaches do you find effective and what approaches do you think should be pursued in the future and why?

Introduction

On the evening of September 5, 1989, viewers across the nation tuned in to watch Republican President George H. W. Bush's first Oval Office address—and it was a memorable one. Looking squarely into the camera, Bush got right to the point: "The gravest domestic threat facing our nation today is drugs." One drug, in particular, he asserted, was stretching the country's legal system "to the breaking point" and "sapping our strength as a nation." That drug was crack cocaine, an inexpensive derivative of powdered cocaine that had first appeared on US streets some three to four years previous. Brandishing an evidence bag stuffed with crystalized rocks he claimed were seized "just across the street from the White House," the president paused briefly and, with a strange smile, remarked, "It's as innocent-looking as candy, but it's turning our cities into battle zones, and it's murdering our children."[1]

Over the next twenty-five minutes, President Bush laid out a new national strategy for winning the nation's War on Drugs. As vice president under Ronald Reagan, Bush had played a key role in leading the previous administration's response to the drug problem, popularized by the slogan "Just Say No." Now he proposed to go bigger. The solution, he argued, was to get tougher, and that meant more policing at home—"more prisons, more jails, more courts, more prosecutors"—and a greater role for the US military abroad. Over the course of the speech, Bush announced a $1.5 billion increase in federal drug enforcement spending, a $2 billion initiative to counter Colombian drug cartels, a $1 billion public-private partnership for antidrug messaging, and a $321 million increase in federal spending on drug treatment.[2]

Minutes later, Senator Joe Biden offered the Democrats' rebuttal, which largely reiterated the president's message. Calling drugs the "number one threat to our national security," Biden described a nation "under attack" by a well-financed and well-armed enemy. "We are fighting and losing the war on our own soil," he argued, because Republican policies were too timid. Democrats in Congress, he said, would support Bush's strategy but thought it was "not tough enough, not bold enough, not imaginative enough." Nevertheless, in the weeks that followed, the Democratic-led Congress approved each of Bush's funding requests. All in all, the bill represented the single greatest budget increase in the history of US drug enforcement.[3] The legislation was a revealing moment in the long history of America's drug war, a conflict that arguably stretches back over a century with strong bipartisan support. Both Bush's and Biden's speeches reflected profound frustration with the country's inability to make progress on a distressing social problem— as well as policymakers' stubborn insistence on seeing drugs as a problem of crime, foreign policy, and national security.

Left unsaid in Bush's and Biden's speeches was the central importance of race, a theme that emerged more clearly a few weeks later
when the story of a Washington, DC, high school student named Keith
Jackson became public. Deciding they needed a visceral prop for the
president's speech, Bush's aides directed the US Drug Enforcement
Administration (DEA) to provide crack seized near the White House.
The DEA, in turn, lured Jackson, a high school senior from the predominantly Black Anacostia neighborhood, to Lafayette Park in order to make
the bust—and even had to give him directions (twice) to the location. An
obvious setup, the case was thrown out by two different juries before
a judge gave Jackson a mandatory ten-year sentence for selling to an
undercover agent prior to his September arrest, despite having no prior
criminal history.[4] Jackson's experience was far from unique. Between
1991 and 1993, Black Americans made up 40 percent of those arrested
nationally on drug charges (mostly drug possession—64 percent or
more—rather than drug sales), while their proportion in the general
population and drug-using population was approximately 13 percent.[5]

Drugs have always been a challenging policy issue for the United
States, and this especially pointed tale is but one in the long and complex history of drugs in America. At the heart of that story lies the
drug war. Most observers root the War on Drugs in the presidencies of
Richard Nixon and Ronald Reagan, making the conflict forty to fifty
years old. But historians are increasingly realizing that as a system of
ideas, assumptions, and policies, the "long drug war" stretches back
over a century.[6] The dynamics that shape the War on Drugs today were
present in the first control laws passed in the early twentieth century,
sharpened by the experiment with banning alcohol during Prohibition,
fed into the obsession with national security and social order at midcentury, and further intensified in the late twentieth century, as Nixon
drew the issue firmly into the national spotlight. For a summary of this
earlier history prior to the Reagan administration, please see our introductory essay on the companion website (http://GoldbergSeries.org/
UTContemporaryUSHistory).

Research into this earlier history reveals a predictable pattern of drug
crises in US history—a cycle of panic and prohibition in which initial
social enthusiasm for novel iterations of various drugs (most apparent
with opiates and cocaine but also discernible with alcohol, tobacco,
marijuana, and psychiatric drugs) is followed by caution, fear, and prohibition as use of that drug is taken up by poor and marginalized
communities. Likewise, as the failures of prohibition become obvious,

antidrug attitudes soften, taboos weaken, drug use proliferates, and the pattern repeats.[7] For example, when cocaine returned to the American drug scene in the 1970s after a roughly fifty-year absence, the public response was muted so long as the drug was confined to elites. However, attitudes shifted as cocaine again slipped down the socioeconomic ladder and indelibly shaped the drug war of the 1980s and 1990s.[8] Together with a host of structural factors, including racism and inequality, that cycle drives the various iterations of the drug war that we see from the Reagan administration to the present.

At the national level, US drug policy has focused almost exclusively on illicit production, trafficking, and distribution. This focus comes from a recognition that the most successful drug products are typically global commodities—a fact that applies equally to illicit drugs such as heroin and cocaine, licit pharmaceuticals, and legal intoxicants such as alcohol and tobacco. Most drugs travel a long journey before they reach their ultimate user. Each of those stages is subject to global market forces and has its own nexus of actors and influences for both policymakers and historians to consider. As any organic drug moves through these stages its intoxicating, addictive, and disruptive potential grows exponentially, as with the coca leaf's transformation to cocaine and crack. So, too, does its cost. However, generations of US drug warriors have had little success in curbing overseas production or eliminating illicit markets within the country's own borders. Nonetheless, the damage wrought by the drug war can be clearly seen in the many crises that beset the country, including the opioid crisis, profound health inequities, mass incarceration, the failures of American policing, and a state of perpetual war at home and around the world. All of these shortcomings have wrought significant and costly damage, which falls disproportionately on poor, disadvantaged, and minority groups. For example, from 1980 to 2008—the height of the War on Drugs—the US incarceration rate grew from 220 per every 100,000 residents to 756, the highest proportion of incarcerated population in the world.[9]

"Just Say No"

In the public mind, no president is as closely associated with the drug war as Ronald Reagan—and, indeed, Reagan did more than any other president to elevate the (lowercase) drug war to the (uppercase) War on Drugs. The core of Reagan's electoral campaign, and the larger political realignment of the Reagan Revolution, was the marriage of corporate capitalism with a new suburban conservatism that repudiated the social policies of the 1960s and 1970s and their focus on alleviating drastic racial and economic inequality through government action. As antidrug attitudes hardened in the suburbs, Reagan revived the war on crime rhetoric of the Nixon years to attack the political consensus underwriting US social policy. At a September 1981 gathering of police chiefs, Reagan described crime as "an American epidemic" driven by narcotics, a flourishing criminal subculture, and permissive social norms, and he explicitly rejected the idea that government spending could address social problems. "The truth is that today's criminals, for the most part, are not desperate people seeking bread for their families," he argued; "crime is the way they've chosen to live."[10]

This rhetorical focus on crime and on individual choice was a way for Reagan to reassert the idea that people were ultimately responsible for their own individual circumstances, regardless of the larger structural forces at play. The government therefore had no duty to redress the enduring inequalities in American life, which could all be explained away as the result of poor decisions—and drugs quickly became one of the centerpieces of this governing philosophy. The only duty the government did have under this philosophy was to tackle drugs at their source and on the streets. One veteran Republican policymaker later summarized the significance of these intertwined economic, social, political, and rhetorical changes: "Between 1977 and 1992 a conservative cultural revolution occurred in America. It was called the drug war."[11]

The Reagan White House quickly identified major metropolitan centers as problem areas in need of greater police intervention—essentially ignoring a spiraling urban crisis that Reagan's supply-side economic policies and corporate tax cuts did little to address. In Miami, for example, the murder rate tripled in only a few years, as the city became a central point of origin for the illicit drug trade.[12] In January 1982, the White House responded by creating the South Florida Drug Task Force, led by Vice President Bush, bringing several federal law enforcement agencies together with local jurisdictions. In June, Reagan created the new Drug Abuse Policy Office and installed Carlton Turner, a staunch social conservative, as the new drug czar. In October, Reagan announced the addition of several other drug task forces around the nation and delivered lines he had rehearsed all summer. "Drugs are bad, and we're going after them," he declared. "We've taken down the surrender flag and run up the battle flag. And we're going to win the war on drugs." Reagan had used the battle flag line back in June, but this was the first time he publicly uttered the phrase "war on drugs."[13]

The arrival of the crack epidemic in late 1985—three years *after* Reagan's declaration of war—played directly into conservative narratives about the ultimate causes of enduring poverty and urban decline.[14] In pharmacological terms, cocaine and crack are essentially the same. Their only real distinction is in their mode of consumption; cocaine is absorbed through the mucus membrane of the nose, whereas crack is absorbed through the lungs—a more direct pathway to the brain, speeding onset of the drug.[15] In sociological terms, crack represented the democratization of cocaine and the arrival of cheap, small doses available to the masses. As in previous cycles of the long drug war, the movement of a novel drug down the socioeconomic ladder to already marginalized groups prompted a vicious backlash.

The crack epidemic turbocharged Reagan's punitive approach at home and abroad, turning 1986 into another major milestone in the evolution of the drug war. Pointing to regional instability in Central America and the participation of leftist guerillas in the cocaine trade, Reagan's National Security Council formally designated the illicit drug trade a threat to US national security in April.[16] In June, University of Maryland basketball star Len Bias fatally overdosed on cocaine shortly after he was drafted into the National Basketball Association (NBA), prompting a major public outcry and further galvanizing public sentiment against drugs. In September, Ron and Nancy invited the American public into their West Wing living room to deliver their famous "Just Say No" speech. The essential message was total abstinence; there was no such thing as casual or moderate drug use. "There's no moral middle ground," Nancy remarked at her husband's side. "Indifference is not an option." A few years later, she elaborated: "The casual user cannot morally escape responsibility for the action of drug traffickers and dealings. I'm saying that if you're a casual drug user you're an accomplice to murder."[17] This messaging from the White House sought to simplify the public discourse around drugs to a fundamental choice between good and evil. The rhetoric was followed by a nationwide campaign led by the First Lady and sweeping legislation.

In October, Congress passed the Anti-Drug Abuse Act of 1986 with overwhelming bipartisan support, including from Black leaders; this law and its successor—the 1988 Anti-Drug Abuse Act—became central pillars of the carceral state. Legislators overwhelmingly felt compelled to respond to a growing urban crisis in which crack seemed the most obvious culprit. The 1986 law specifically targeted crack offenders, re-introducing mandatory minimum sentencing and levying the same five-year sentence for the possession of five grams of crack or five hundred grams of cocaine. The impact of the law was disproportionately felt by communities of color and explicitly racist in outcome.[18] The 1988 act codified the official policy of a "drug-free America" and created the Office of National Drug Control Policy (ONDCP)—a.k.a. the office of the "drug czar"—to coordinate a series of public-private partnerships and education campaigns that became infamous for their hyperbole and reductive simplicity. One of the most famous examples was the Drug Abuse Resistance Education (D.A.R.E.) program, created in 1983 by Los Angeles Police Department Chief Daryl Gates. The effectiveness of the D.A.R.E. program has since been thoroughly discredited, but at the time it was a perfect emblem of the era's messaging and scare tactics. In 1990, Gates told senators that casual drug users "ought to be taken out and shot," echoing Nancy Reagan's language of drug users being moral accomplices of drug traffickers.[19] Although this style of messaging and zero-tolerance approach almost certainly did not aid the country's struggle with potentially harmful drugs, the "tough on crime" posturing at the heart of the drug war was essential for bolstering government power and, increasingly, a robust and interventionist foreign policy.

The foreign policy side of the administration's efforts became increasingly central as the decade wore on, as US law enforcement and military forces actively worked to disrupt trafficking networks and bolster security forces throughout the hemisphere. One consequence of US interdiction, however, was to shift much of the cocaine traffic from the sea and air routes leading to Miami to the overland route running through Central America and Mexico. In time, that led to the rise of the Mexican cartels, whose growing influence and violence were foreshadowed by the gruesome murder of DEA agent Enrique "Kiki" Camarena in early 1985.[20]

By the end of Reagan's term, the drug war had been thoroughly integrated into American life and cast as a stark emblem of the country's identity. Seated in his West Wing living room in his 1986 "Just Say No" speech, Reagan framed the drug war as a "national crusade" on par with other historic turning points such as the Civil War and Normandy invasion. "Drugs are menacing our society," Reagan warned.

"They're threatening our values and undercutting our institutions. They're killing our children."[21] Such a threat clearly seemed to call for drastic action.

Incarceration Nation

George H. W. Bush came into the White House ready to follow Reagan's lead and make the War on Drugs a central policy initiative. Bush expanded the federal drug control budget during his administration from around $5 billion per year to over $12 billion by 1993. This was the sharpest escalation in the history of the drug war.[22] Bush also continued and expanded the international dynamics of Reagan's policy. Over the twelve years of the Reagan and Bush administrations, the Pentagon's annual counter-narcotic budget ballooned from around $1 million to $1.2 billion—an increase of over 100,000 percent.[23] In 1989, Bush ordered the invasion of Panama to arrest dictator Manuel Noriega on drug charges issued in Miami.[24] Colombia, however, was the focal point. The country's role in drug production shifted from marijuana cultivation in the 1970s to cocaine in the 1980s under powerful groups such as the Medellín and Cali cartels. Under a project called the "Andean Initiative," President Bush pledged an estimated US $2.2 billion in economic, military, and law enforcement assistance in counter-narcotics operations to Colombia and other Andean countries over four years, orchestrating a paramilitary campaign against Pablo Escobar and the Cali Cartel. That was a major victory in the DEA's "kingpin strategy" of targeting drug cartel leadership, but the vacuum left by the end of the major cartels resulted in smaller organizations stepping in and no reduction in the overall volume of the drug trade. Cocaine production in fact went up in Colombia the decade following the breakup of these major cartels.[25]

Back on US soil, the Bush-era ONDCP was headed by former secretary of education William Bennett. An ardent social conservative, Bennett continued the Reagans' sharply moral approach to the drug war, describing drugs as "the enemy within" and encouraging a zero-tolerance attitude among the American public—all while privately battling a compulsive gambling habit.[26] Bennett also took a special interest in escalating the drug war in the nation's capital as an example to the rest of the country. Only a few months after Bush's televised address on crack, federal agents orchestrated the arrest of Washington, DC, mayor Marion Barry on charges of cocaine possession after recruiting a former girlfriend to lure him into an undercover sting operation.[27] The District of Columbia was, indisputably, in the midst of a profound drug crisis; but arresting an emblem of the Black political class also had clear racial overtones, and Barry's legal and political troubles quickly became part of White House messaging about the failure of local leaders in America's cities to control the drug problem. While Blacks and whites across the country engaged in drug offenses—both possession and sales—at roughly comparable rates at the time, arrests and incarceration fell disproportionately on Black men and women. As Human Rights Watch reported, "in every year from 1980 to 2007, blacks were arrested nationwide on drug charges at rates relative to population that were 2.8 to 5.5 times higher than white arrest rates."[28] By the end of Bush's presidency, the drug war had become even more inextricably woven into the structure of American policing, driving the politics of mass incarceration, bringing many US cities to the boiling point (illustrated by the explosion of the Los Angeles riots in the spring of 1992), and effectively becoming a war on the poor and racial minorities.[29]

Many observers believed that the election of former Arkansas governor Bill Clinton as president in 1992 would bring a change in direction for US drug policy, given his relative youth and sympathy for the plight of those same communities. Clinton instead presided over a period of sustained escalation in the drug war, seemingly trying to demonstrate that Democrats could be as "tough on crime" as Republicans. Total federal drug spending increased every year of the Clinton presidency, going from $12.1 billion in 1993 to $19.2 billion in 2000, with the majority of funding going toward the criminal justice system and supply-reduction programs.[30] Hardline sentencing from the Reagan/Bush era was also solidified and expanded under Clinton in the Violent Crime Control and Law Enforcement Act (1994), the largest crime bill in the history of the country. The "three strikes" statute under this law provides for mandatory life imprisonment if a convicted felon has a severe violent felony and two or more previous convictions in federal or state court. Although the long-term consequences of this bill were still unclear, strong antidrug public sentiment made it popular, even as the number of people held in state and federal prisons for drug-law violations grew from fewer than 25,000 in 1980 to nearly 300,000 by 2018.[31] This wave of incarceration (also fueled by new arrests for methamphetamine[32]) and the new "three strike" law disproportionately affected African American defendants, and President Clinton rejected a 1995

91

recommendation from the US Sentencing Commission to eliminate the disparity between crack and powder cocaine sentences, despite the demonstrated racial impact. Clinton assured Americans that during his presidency, he would not "let anyone who peddles drugs get the idea that the cost of doing business is going down."[33]

While political parties turned over when George W. Bush took over the Oval Office from Clinton, there was little change in the approach to drugs until the terrorist attacks of September 11, 2001, which refocused US national security and intelligence priorities from Colombia to Afghanistan and Iraq.[34] The Clinton administration had launched "Plan Colombia" as a six-year program to increase the Colombian government's capacity to fight narcotics trafficking. The United States ultimately poured over $10 billion in foreign assistance into Colombia and created a substantial US military presence there, including a sizeable contingent of marines that remains to this day. In fact, on September 10, 2001, the biggest and most active CIA station in the world was in Bogota, Colombia's capital. In 2007, Bush launched the smaller Mérida Initiative, a similar foreign aid program designed to promote US-Mexican cooperation to combat transnational crime and improve security and the rule of law in Mexico. Despite the layered domestic and international efforts to stop the drug trade and drug consumption that marked the administrations from Reagan through George W. Bush, rates of addiction and incarceration continued to climb as a new drug crisis began.

America's Newest Drug Epidemic

Barack Obama was elected by an American public that was tired of war. While President Obama worked to abandon the rhetoric of the Global War on Terrorism and the Global War on Drugs, his policies were slower to follow, as his administration faced the new international threat of the Islamic State and the new drug threat of opioids. An increase in use of opioids for pain management in the first decade of the 2000s resulted in a drug trend that came in three waves starting with legal opioids in the form of pain medication such as oxycodone and hydrocodone.[35] A second wave arose as federal authorities belatedly sought to reduce the supply of prescription opioids, leading to an increase in fatal heroin overdoses. The third wave came in the use of fentanyl, a synthetic drug similar to morphine but a hundred times more potent. Just as crack cocaine caused public panic in the 1980s, so too did opioids in the 2010s. Before the COVID-19 pandemic, opioid use was the major public health threat facing the nation. In 2020, the country recorded the highest number of fatal drug overdoses in US history, with a 30 percent increase over 2019.[36] Combined, the pandemic and overdose deaths decreased the average life expectancy in the United States by one full year.[37]

While much of the language on drug policy under both George W. Bush and Obama touted a more comprehensive approach focusing on prevention, treatment, and enforcement, the reality in federal drug control is that dollars played out in favor of law enforcement and supply reduction. The FY2015 drug control budget released by the ONDCP showed that approximately 60 percent of all federal drug control spending was dedicated to supply reduction and around 37 percent of the total drug control budget for domestic law enforcement. Nonetheless, the Obama and Trump years saw a shift in treating drugs more as a public health issue than a punitive criminal justice undertaking. As many states legalized marijuana, the White House did not act, and these presidents pushed through executive efforts to undo harsh sentences against nonviolent drug offenders.[38] In late 2018, President Trump signed into law the First Step Act, a bipartisan effort to improve criminal justice outcomes, as well as to reduce the size of the federal prison population. The act builds on what Obama did by making the 2010 reform to crack sentencing laws retroactive but goes beyond that by shortening mandatory minimum sentences across the board for nonviolent drug offenses at the federal level.

The role of the ONDCP also shifted during this time, with the ONDCP director losing cabinet-rank status during the Obama presidency. Demoting the national agency meant to provide a whole-of-government response to drug policy both at home and abroad in the midst of the deadliest drug epidemic in US history was a policy that prompted questions. The ONDCP continued to wan in influence under President Trump. It failed to publish a national strategy for two years (2017–18) and lacked a permanent director until mid-2018.[39]

Meanwhile, the wheels of the drug war continued to turn—especially in neighboring Mexico, where drug trafficking–related violence rose to record numbers in the 2010s. US engagement through the Merida Initiative included law enforcement training and equipment purchases for Mexican agencies. Foreign assistance in this capacity was diplomatically challenging but also technically complicated given the layers of corruption and violence woven into the criminal organizations of the region. One disastrous example occurred with a DEA-supported Special Investigations Unit (SIU) in 2011. When members of the Zetas cartel learned that someone had divulged intelligence to the DEA, cartel members responded by killing more than three hundred people in the town of Allende, Coahuila, as well as destroying homes and businesses.[40] Violence and rising homicide rates in neighboring Mexico stoked fear in US voters, pushing many to demand stronger border security and tougher immigration requirements. Another result was Donald J. Trump starting his presidential campaign with a rallying cry against illegal drugs coming into the United States from Mexico. He promised his supporters he would build a wall to keep out illegal immigrants whom he characterized as drug traffickers, rapists, and killers of American jobs. In office, President Trump redirected the focus of both Homeland Security and foreign aid to border enforcement and migration prevention and away from counter-narcotic and violence prevention.

During both the Obama and Trump presidencies, the opioid crisis accelerated demands for effective, accessible treatment, as more punitive methods were increasingly seen as ineffective and costly public policies.[41] Public health increasingly became the ostensible focal point of drug policy during these years, including calls to end the stigma that prevents people struggling with addiction from seeking or receiving treatment.[42] In October of his first year in office, President Trump declared a public health emergency: "No part of our society—not young or old, rich or poor, urban or rural—has been spared this plague."[43] The few faltering public health initiatives launched by the Trump administration, however, were quickly lost in the global crisis of the COVID-19 pandemic. It remains to be seen what approach the Biden administration may take to America's ongoing drug crises.

Conclusion: Drug Policy in Perspective

Despite a global war on drugs that has persisted for decades, the United States continues to experience some of the highest levels of drug consumption in the world.[44] This brief history of the modern drug war reveals how consistently US policymakers have preferred to respond to drugs as a law enforcement and national security challenge rather than a problem of public health. That tendency helps explain some of the drug war's stubborn longevity and how the trappings of the drug war outlive specific drug crises. Reagan's War on Drugs, for example, continued to escalate dramatically over the presidencies of George H. W. Bush and Bill Clinton, even well after the crack epidemic had burned out. Fighting drugs has become a way to assert a particular brand of American values and morality while offering a powerful rationale for robust security capabilities at home and around the world.[45]

This approach to better understanding the government's characterization of drug use and abuse in the United States should remind us that drug use is not a recent phenomenon in US society, nor are the underlying issues around trafficking, use, and addiction. One sees a perpetual feedback loop; the social impacts of criminalizing drugs challenges government officials as they try to manage domestic drug control and foreign policy, struggling to balance both security and drug supply.[46] The War on Drugs redirected public and political attention away from systemic, structural problems in American life, while increasing the power of the federal government.

Lesson Plan

The following lesson is estimated to take place in a one-hour time period in the classroom. The core of the lesson has students analyze textual and visual primary source material related to presidential responses to drug use in the United States, either in class or as homework ahead of or following the class meeting. They then analyze the different approaches and themes highlighted in the materials. An expanded lesson plan is offered as well in which students can explore a broader range of materials or develop a briefing for their governor or an incoming US president.

Student Learning Objectives

1. Examine textual and visual primary sources using analytical skills to determine audience and thesis.
2. Enhance ability to think historically about US public policies related to drug policy, crime, and public health.
3. Synthesize different kinds of information to provide analysis of a public policy issue.

Resources Needed for the Lesson

Copies of the texts below are available as Word documents on the companion website, which also includes links to the video resources (http://GoldbergSeries.org/UTContemporaryUSHistory).

1. George H. W. Bush Speech, September 5, 1989, "Address to the Nation on the National Drug Control Strategy."[47]
2. Donald Trump Speech, October 26, 2017, "President Trump Remarks on Opioid Crisis."[48]

Lesson Outline

Introduction: Prior to the class, have the students watch or read the September 5, 1989, speech by George Bush titled "Address to the Nation on the National Drug Control Strategy" and come to class ready to incorporate it into the discussion. During class, start by having students identify what they think is the key drug-related issue facing the nation or your city, region, or state and why this is such an important issue (there is a sample worksheet on the website that teachers can use/adapt [http://GoldbergSeries.org/UTContemporaryUSHistory]).

As students are completing this task, tell them that you will circle back to this at the end of the lesson and that this lesson will help them understand how the federal government has defined and addressed some key drug-related issues in the past.

Primary-source analysis: At the start of class ask students to discuss the reading they did or video they watched of President Bush's speech in small groups. Explain that their job is to identify the audience that the speaker is addressing, to identify the problem they are proposing to address, and to identify the ways they propose to do this. You might also ask them to jot down key phrases and adjectives that the speaker used to describe the problem. Then have students watch a portion (starting at minute 8:30 and ending at minute 21) of the October 26, 2017, briefing by President Trump titled "President Trump Remarks on Opioid Crisis."

Conclusion: Point out that Bush was speaking about a different drug issue than Trump. But ask students if they saw similarities in how drugs in general were approached and discussed. Then ask students if they saw significant differences in how each administration approached drug use. To solicit other student ideas, ask what other themes they heard about public health and safety. Finally, depending on the themes that you have developed during the semester or year, you might tell students the backstory about the bag of crack that Bush used in his speech and share the different incarceration rates for various groups in the United States discussed earlier in this chapter; this could open up a discussion of the impact of racism on policing and imprisonment as well as the corresponding effect on communities of color. Alternatively, you might want to end this lesson by discussing the expanded lesson plan below and preparing students to do that work.

Expanded Lesson Plan

A lesson with an expanded time frame could review media messaging related to drug-use prevention over these decades. These examples widen the set of approaches to this issue beyond the White House and help students see more clearly how messaging about drugs changed over time.

Resources needed for expanded lesson: Copies of the texts below are available as Word documents on the companion website, which also includes links to the video resources (http://GoldbergSeries.org/UTContemporaryUSHistory). Please note the Montana Meth Project video ads are disturbing and might be triggering for some people. We have cited the print ads in the links below but also recommend you warn students about the subject matter and content.

1. Video of Nancy Reagan's "Just Say No" Campaign, September 1986.[49]
2. Video ads from the Partnership for Drug-Free America, "This is Your Brain on Drugs," released in 1987, and "From You,"[50] as well as a remake of "This Is Your Brain on Drugs" from 1997.[51]
3. Montana Meth Project Print Ads.[52]
4. National Safety Council's exhibit titled "Prescribed to Death" and embedded video titled "Louie's Story" (2 minutes).[53]

Ideas for Expanded Lesson Plan: Just as in the earlier lesson, where students identified the audience that the speaker in the video is addressing, students identify the problem they are proposing to address and identify the ways they suggest to do this. Start by having students watch Nancy Reagan's address to the nation in September 1986 that kicked off the "Just Say No" campaign (5 minutes). Follow with the three different media campaigns aimed at prevention efforts. Students then meet in small groups to answer the following questions:

- What things stood out to you from the examples?
- What similarities did you see in the media campaigns? What differences?
- Describe how the ads frame drugs and drug use—as a public health issue, a criminal justice issue, a family issue, etc.—and how that may influence your response to the ad.

Students then return to the larger group to share what they discussed. Did they find these ads convincing? Dated? Still relevant? Ask them to brainstorm some ideas of how they would create an ad for today. Ask them to consider the most engaging format, framing, and representation and write some of their ideas on the board.

Finally, as an assessment of students' historical and critical thinking, you could ask them (either individually or in small groups) to develop a briefing (written or oral) for an incoming president, governor, or mayor identifying the key drug-related problem facing their administration (which they identified at the beginning of the lesson) and how they might address it. Encourage them—in line with the historical content they have examined and analyzed—to consider how to frame the issue (for example, as a public health issue, as a crime or law enforcement issue, as an international issue, etc.), how to best communicate their message to the public and other key stakeholders, what partners (local, national, and international) they need to recruit, and what existing resources (including budget and personnel) might be reallocated. This assessment could be used for either the expanded or the shorter lesson plan listed above. Depending on your location, the level of the students, and the receptivity of lawmakers, you might consider having students present their ideas to local governmental leadership or local representatives to the state or national legislative branches.

NOTES

1. George H. W. Bush, "Address to the Nation on the National Drug Control Strategy," September 5, 1989, American Presidency Project, University of

California, Santa Barbara, https://www.presidency.ucsb.edu/documents/address
-the-nation-the-national-drug-control-strategy. See also Bush, "Presidential
Address on National Drug Policy," C-SPAN, September 5, 1989, https://www.c
-span.org/video/?8921-1/president-bush-address-national-drug-policy.

2. Bush, "Address to the Nation."

3. Joe Biden, "Democratic Response to Drug Policy Address," C-SPAN, September 5, 1989,https://www.c-span.org/video/?8997-1/democratic-response-drug
-policy-address.

4. Maureen Dowd, "White House Set Up Drug Buy in the Park for Bush TV
Speech," *New York Times*, September 23, 1989; Tracy Thompson and Michael
Isikoff, "Lafayette Square Drug Suspect Indicted," *Washington Post*, September
27, 1989; Tracy Thompson, "Drug Purchase for Bush Speech like Keystone
Kops," *Washington Post*, December 15, 1989; Tracy Thompson, "D.C. Student Is
Given 10 Years in Drug Case," *Washington Post*, November 1, 1990.

5. Patrick A. Langan, "Racial Disparity in U.S. Drug Arrests," Bureau of
Justice Statistics, October 1995, https://bjs.ojp.gov/library/publications/racial-dis
parity-us-drug-arrests.

6. Anne L. Foster, "The Long War on Drugs," in *Oxford Research Encyclope-
dias: American History*, ed. Jon Butler, June 28, 2017, https://doi.org/10.1093/acre
fore/9780199329175.013.402.

7. David F. Musto, *The American Disease: Origins of Narcotic Control*, 3rd ed.
(Oxford: Oxford University Press, 1999), vii–xvi, 294–300.

8. Richard Steel, Susan Agrest, Sylvester Monroe, Paul Brinkley Rogers,
and Stephan Lesher, "The Cocaine Scene," *Newsweek*, May 30, 1977.

9. "Incarceration Rate in the United States, 1960–2012," Hamilton Project,
May 1, 2014, https://www.hamiltonproject.org/charts/incarceration_rate_in_
the_united_states_1960-2012; "U.S. Incarcerates a Larger Share of Its Population than Any Other Country," Pew Research Center, May 1, 2018, https://www
.pewresearch.org/fact-tank/2018/05/02/americas-incarceration-rate-is-at-a-two
-decade-low/ft_18-04-27_incarcerationrate_map/.

10. Ronald Reagan, "Remarks in New Orleans, Louisiana, at the Annual
Meeting of the International Association of Chiefs of Police," September 28,
1981, American Presidency Project, University of California, Santa Barbara,
https://www.presidency.ucsb.edu/documents/remarks-new-orleans-louisi
ana-the-annual-meeting-the-international-association-chiefs. See also Lisa
McGirr, *Suburban Warriors: The Origins of the New American Right* (Princeton, NJ:
Princeton University Press, 2001); Emily Dufton, *Grass Roots: The Rise and Fall
and Rise of Marijuana in America* (New York: Basic Books, 2017). See also Marsha
Manatt, *Parents, Peers, and Pot* (National Institute on Drug Abuse, 1979), https://
wellcomelibrary.org/item/b18034718#?c=0&m=0&s=0&cv=0&z=-1.1709%2C
-0.0845%2C3.3417%2C1.6908.

11. John P. Walters, former director of the Office of National Drug Control Policy (2001–2009), as quoted in Dan Baum, *Smoke and Mirrors: The War on Drugs and the Politics of Failure* (Boston: Back Bay Books, 1997), 104.

12. James Kelly, "Trouble in Paradise," *Time*, November 23, 1981; June Preston, "New York, Miami Area Had Record Number of Murders in 1981," UPI, January 1, 1982.

13. Herbert H. Denton, "President Forms Drug Abuse Task Force," *Washington Post*, June 25, 1982; "Reagan Vows War on Dope Trade," *Washington Post*, October 3, 1982; Ronald Reagan, "Radio Address to the Nation on Federal Drug Policy," October 2, 1982, American Presidency Project, University of California, Santa Barbara, https://www.presidency.ucsb.edu/documents/radio-address-the -nation-federal-drug-policy; Ronald Reagan, "Remarks Announcing Federal Initiatives against Drug Trafficking and Organized Crime," October 14, 1982, American Presidency Project, University of California, Santa Barbara, https:// www.presidency.ucsb.edu/documents/remarks-announcing-federal-initia tives-against-drug-trafficking-and-organized-crime.

14. Jane Gross, "A New, Purified Form of Cocaine Causes Alarm as Abuse Increases," *New York Times*, November 29, 1985; Peter Kerr, "Drug Treatment in City Is Strained by Crack, a Potent New Cocaine," *New York Times*, May 16, 1986; "New York Police Fight 'Crack' Epidemic," *Baltimore Afro-American*, May 31, 1986; Peter Kerr, "Crack Addiction Spreads among the Middle Class," *New York Times*, June 8, 1986; John J. Goldman, "New York City Being Swamped by 'Crack,'" *Los Angeles Times*, August 1, 1986; "Crack Wars," *Baltimore Afro-American*, August 30, 1986.

15. John Strang and Griffith Edwards, "Cocaine and Crack: The Drug and the Hype Are Both Dangerous," *BMJ: British Medical Journal* 299, no. 6695 (1989): 337–38.

16. National Security Council, "National Security Decision Directive Number 221: Narcotics and National Security," Federation of American Scientists, April 8, 1986, https://fas.org/irp/offdocs/nsdd/nsdd-221.htm.

17. Nancy Reagan in Ronald Reagan, "Address to the Nation on the Campaign against Drug Abuse," September 14, 1986, American Presidency Project, University of California, Santa Barbara, https://www.presidency.ucsb.edu/doc uments/address-the-nation-the-campaign-against-drug-abuse; Nancy Reagan in Ronald Reagan, "Remarks at a Meeting of the White House Conference for a Drug Free America," February 29, 1988, American Presidency Project, University of California, Santa Barbara, https://www.presidency.ucsb.edu/documents/ remarks-meeting-the-white-house-conference-for-drug-free-america.

18. Michelle Alexander, *The New Jim Crow: Mass Incarceration in the Age of Colorblindness* (New York: New Press, 2012); James Forman Jr., *Locking Up Our Own: Crime and Punishment in Black America* (New York: Farrar, Straus and Giroux, 2017).

19. Ronald J. Ostrow, "Casual Drug Users Should Be Shot, Gates Says," *Los Angeles Times*, September 6, 1990.

20. Richard J. Meislin, "Body of U.S. Drug Agent Believed Found in Mexico," *New York Times*, March 7, 1985.

21. Reagan, "Address to the Nation."

22. Matthew R. Pembleton, "George H. W. Bush's Biggest Failure? The War on Drugs," *Washington Post*, December 6, 2018, https://www.washingtonpost.com/outlook/2018/12/06/george-hw-bushs-biggest-failure-war-drugs/.

23. Bill Billiter, "Military to Get into War on Drugs," *Los Angeles Times*, February 14, 1982; Baum, *Smoke and Mirrors*, 168; Peter Zirnite, "Reluctant Recruits: The US Military and the War on Drugs," Washington Office on Latin America, TNI (Transnational Institute), August 1997, https://www.tni.org/en/report/reluctant-recruits-us-military-and-war-drugs.

24. Ronnie Ramos, David Lyons, and Martin Merzer, "He Was U.S. Prisoner #41586: How Noriega Landed in a Miami Jail after Invasion," *Miami Herald*, May 30, 2017.

25. United Nations Office on Drugs and Crime, "Coca Cultivation in the Andean Region: A Survey of Bolivia, Columbia and Peru," June 2006, https://www.unodc.org/pdf/andean/Andean_full_report.pdf.

26. Howard Kohn, "Cowboy in the Capital: Drug Czar Bill Bennett," *Rolling Stone*, November 2, 1989; David G. Savage, "Bennett, First U.S. Drug Czar, Quits," *Los Angeles Times*, November 9, 1990; Katherine Q. Seelye, "Relentless Moral Crusader Is Relentless Gambler, Too," *New York Times*, May 3, 2003.

27. Sharon LaFraniere, "Barry Arrested on Cocaine Charges in Undercover FBI, Police Operation," *Washington Post*, January 19, 1990; Michael Massing, "D.C.'s War on Drugs: Why Bennett Is Losing," *New York Times*, September 23, 1990.

28. Human Rights Watch, "Decades of Disparity, Drug Arrests and Race in the United States," March 2009, https://www.hrw.org/report/2009/03/02/decades-disparity/drug-arrests-and-race-united-states#.

29. Patrick A. Langan, "Racial Disparity in U.S. Drug Arrests," Bureau of Justice Statistics, October 1995, https://bjs.ojp.gov/library/publications/racial-disparity-us-drug-arrests; "Drug Arrests for Sales and Possession," Bureau of Justice Statistics, June 2021, https://bjs.ojp.gov/drugs-and-crime-facts/enforcement/arrtot-table.

30. Michael Walther, "Insanity: Four Decades of U.S. Counterdrug Strategy," Carlisle Papers, Strategic Studies Institute, U.S. Army War College, December 2012, https://publications.armywarcollege.edu/pubs/2215.pdf, p. 12.

31. "More Imprisonment Does Not Reduce State Drug Problems," Pew Charitable Trusts, March 8, 2018, https://www.pewtrusts.org/en/research-and-analysis/issue-briefs/2018/03/more-imprisonment-does-not-reduce-state-drug-problems.

32. PBS *Frontline* has a timeline that shows the rise of meth and the impact on communities: https://www.pbs.org/wgbh/pages/frontline/meth/etc/cron.html, last updated May 16, 2011. See also Dana Hunt, Sarah Kuck, and Linda Truitt, "Methamphetamine Use: Lessons Learned," National Criminal Justice Reference Service, February 2006, https://www.ncjrs.gov/pdffiles1/nij/grants/209730.pdf.

33. Elsa Y. Chen, "The Liberation Hypothesis and Racial and Ethnic Disparities in the Application of California's Three Strikes Law," *Journal of Ethnicity in Criminal Justice* 6, no. 2 (2008): 83–102; Ann Devroy, "Clinton Retains Tough Law on Crack Cocaine," *Washington Post*, October 31, 1995, https://www.washingtonpost.com/archive/politics/1995/10/31/clinton-retains-tough-law-on-crack-cocaine/0f435210-4bfd-45b5-b1ab-3f95b65a0e68/.

34. Robert S. Leiken, "Border Colleagues: On Migration, Bush and Fox Belong on the Same Side," Brookings Institution, September 2, 2001, https://www.brookings.edu/opinions/border-colleagues-on-migration-bush-and-fox-belong-on-the-same-side/.

35. Daniel Ciccarone, "The Triple Wave Epidemic: Supply and Demand Drivers of the US Opioid Overdose Crisis," *International Journal of Drug Policy* 71 (September 2019): 183–88, https://www.doi.org/10.1016/j.drugpo.2019.01.010; "Understanding the Epidemic," Centers for Disease Control and Prevention, updated March 19, 2020, https://www.cdc.gov/drugoverdose/epidemic/index.html.

36. Bill Chappell, "Drug Overdoses Killed a Record Number of Americans in 2020, Jumping by Nearly 30 Percent," National Public Radio, July 14, 2021, https://www.npr.org/2021/07/14/1016029270/drug-overdoses-killed-a-record-number-of-americans-in-2020-jumping-by-nearly-30.

37. Steven Ross Johnson, "CDC: Nearly 92,000 Drug Overdose Deaths in 2020," *U.S. News and World Report*, December 30, 2021; Laurel Wamsley, "American Life Expectancy Dropped by a Full Year in 1st Half of 2020," National Public Radio, February 18, 2021, https://www.npr.org/2021/02/18/968791431/american-life-expectancy-dropped-by-a-full-year-in-the-first-half-of-2020.

38. Kevin Liptak, "Obama Cuts Sentences for Hundreds of Drug Offenders," CNN, January 17, 2017, https://www.cnn.com/2017/01/17/politics/obama-cuts-sentences-of-hundreds-of-drug-offenders/index.html.

39. Office of National Drug Control Policy, "Budget, Performance, and Data," https://trumpwhitehouse.archives.gov/ondcp/about/budget-performance-data/; Dan Diamond, "Trump Budget Would Effectively Kill Drug Control Office," Politico, May 5, 2017, https://www.politico.com/story/2017/05/05/trump-budget-drug-control-office-238035.

40. Justice in Mexico, "Remembering the Allende Massacre," https://justiceinmexico.org/remembering-allende-massacre/ (accessed July 13, 2021).

41. *Report of the Western Hemisphere Drug Policy Commission, December 2020*, https://foreignaffairs.house.gov/_cache/files/a/5/a51ee680-e339-4a1b-933f-b15e

535fa103/AA2A3440265DDE42367A79D4BCBC9AA1.whdpc-final-report-2020
-11.30.pdf.

42. Michael P. Botticelli and Howard K. Koh, "Changing the Language of Addiction," *JAMA: Journal of the American Medical Association* 316, no. 13 (October 4, 2016): 1361–62, https://www.doi.org/10.1001/jama.2016.11874; Chris Christie, Chair of the President's Commission on Combating Drug Addiction and the Opioid Crisis, in his letter presenting the Commission's Final Report, November 2017, https://trumpwhitehouse.archives.gov/sites/whitehouse.gov/files/images/Final_Report_Draft_11-15-2017.pdf, pp. 5–11.

43. "Remarks by President Trump on Combatting Drug Demand and the Opioid Crisis," October 26, 2017, https://trumpwhitehouse.archives.gov/brief ings-statements/remarks-president-trump-combatting-drug-demand-opioid -crisis/.

44. Louisa Degenhardt, Harvey A. Whiteford, Alize J. Ferrari, Amanda J. Baxter, Fiona J. Charlson, Wayne D. Hall, Greg Freedman, Roy Burstein, Nicole Johns, Rebecca E. Engell, Abraham Flaxman, Christopher J. L. Murray, and Theo Vos, "Global Burden of Disease Attributable to Illicit Drug Use and Dependence: Findings from the Global Burden of Disease Study 2010," *Lancet* (British edition) 382, no. 9904 (2013): 1564–74.

45. Many states across the United States are taking drug policy measures into their own hands. In the 2020 election, Oregon became the first state to decriminalize possession of all illicit drugs (including heroin, cocaine, and meth) and to legalize the use of psilocybin (found in hallucinogenic mushrooms) for mental health treatment. As of January 2021, thirty-five states now allow medicinal use of cannabis, and fifteen permit recreational use.

46. Lisa N. Sacco, Congressional Research Service, "Drug Enforcement in the United States: History, Policy, and Trends," October 2, 2014, https://fas.org/sgp/crs/misc/R43749.pdf.

47. George H. W. Bush, "Address to the Nation on the National Drug Control Strategy," September 5, 1989, American Presidency Project, University of California, Santa Barbara, https://www.presidency.ucsb.edu/documents/address-the-nation-the-national-drug-control-strategy. See also Bush, "Presidential Address on National Drug Policy," C-SPAN, September 5, 1989, https://www.c-span.org/video/?8921-1/president-bush-address-national-drug-policy.

48. "President Trump Remarks on Opioid Crisis," CNN, October 26, 2017, https://www.c-span.org/video/?436363-1/president-trump-declares-public -health-emergency-opioid-epidemic.

49. "Nancy Reagan's 'Just Say No' Campaign," CNN, 1986, https://www .youtube.com/watch?v=lQXgVM3omIY.

50. Two 1987 Partnership for a Drug-Free America ads, "This Is Your Brain on Drugs" and "From You," are found together in this link: https://www.youtube .com/watch?v=LSFaDeRpSHA.

51. "The Original Rachael Leigh Cook Brain on Drugs," https://www.you tube.com/watch?v=dAHoxaphbEs. If time allows you could show students the Drug Policy Alliance's remake of the video with the original actress criticizing the war on drugs. Tony Newman, "Remake of Classic 'Your Brain on Drugs' Ad Slams Disastrous Drug War," April 19, 2017, https://drugpolicy.org/blog/remake-classic-your-brain-drugs-ad-slams-disastrous-drug-war.

52. Montana Meth Project, "Meth Project Ads: Print," https://www.montana meth.org/our-work/#ads (accessed July 17, 2021). There are eight ads on its website, and we recommend the two titled "Brain" and "Looks" to go along with the lesson.

53. National Safety Council, "Facing an Everyday Killer," https://www.nsc .org/home-safety/get-involved/prescribed-to-death-memorial, and embedded video from that page titled "Louie's Story," November 1, 2019, https://www .youtube.com/watch?v=TSopSysOKXE.

A Difficult Balance

National Security and Democracy from Reagan to Trump

KIMBER M. QUINNEY

Why Teach This Lesson?

This lesson will help students discover how US foreign policy is closely linked to domestic policy, especially when national security collides with civil rights. Students will learn more about the history of government policies toward domestic threats to national security from the Reagan era to the present and, in the process, weigh security priorities against constitutional rights. The historical thinking skills that are emphasized include patterns of continuity and change over time as well as corroboration and comparison of documents by relying on primary source analysis. One of the historical thinking skills that matters most in this lesson, however, is the capacity for analysis and critique of historical decision-making. According to the American Historical Association, the capacity "to identify issues and problems in the past and to analyze the interests, values, perspectives, and points of view of all of those involved" is an invaluable skill. This lesson encourages students to ask, What might have been done differently to resolve problems? What alternative actions might have been taken? What can we learn about how people made decisions to do the things they did?[1] Ideally, students will become aware of the ways in which the history detailed in this lesson affects their lives today—in more ways than they might appreciate.

Introduction

America's self-declared "mission" to democratize the world has long been vigorously debated by historians, but scholars have paid less attention to a related but very different debate: the extent to which democracy should be subordinated to national security *within the United States itself*.[2] The relationship between national security and civil liberties is often contradictory. As sociologist David Segal wrote in 1994, when he helped shape the Clinton administration's decision to invade Haiti to restore its democratic system, "The values of national security and democracy are sometimes necessarily in conflict, and one may be compromised in defense of the other."[3]

This lesson asks students to think about the history of the relationship between national security (and, after 9/11, *homeland security*) and democracy at home. Protecting national security and ensuring constitutional rights in a democracy is a balancing act.[4] As the history shows, when American presidents and lawmakers—or, for that matter, the American media and public—give too much weight to one consideration, the other is in danger of being treated too lightly and either neglected or deliberately abused.

Since 1980, this balance has tipped in favor of national security. Presidents have paid lip service to the need to defend democratic principles and practices at home, but the tendency to prioritize national security has prevailed. Furthermore, this period has witnessed a technological revolution that has only accentuated the inclination—and the motivation and the ability—to infringe on the privacy of US citizens: namely, the advent of digital technology. Email, cellphones, websites, social media, online forums, and other digital innovations have been a boon to spies and terrorists, but they have also been a godsend for governments and their spymasters.

Trust, Allegiance, and the Social Contract

An effective way to open the dialogue with students is to begin with a contemporary case, such as that involving Elizabeth Jo Shirley, a forty-seven-year-old mother from Hedgesville, West Virginia. In July 2020, Shirley pleaded guilty to unlawfully retaining a national security document that "outlined intelligence information regarding a foreign government's military and political issues."[5] Shirley, who had been granted high-level security clearance while serving in the US Air Force, was arrested in Mexico when she attempted to offer classified information to the Russian government. For her crime, she faced up to ten years in prison and a fine of up to $250,000.

Students can be asked to read the Department of Justice press release describing Shirley's apprehension and arrest, as well as a brief report in the *Washington Post*.[6] In both summaries of the case, the word "trust" is repeated by the authorities interviewed about the case. The *Washington Post* article quotes Michael Christmas, the FBI special agent in charge of the case: "Ms. Shirley had a duty to safeguard classified information. Instead, she chose to break the law and *trust* [my emphasis] placed in her and made plans to pass national defense information to Russian officials, which could have put our citizens at risk."[7]

After a close reading and comparison of both documents, students can then be invited to respond to questions:

- What was Shirley's crime?
- Are there any benefits from sharing secret information with the public?
- Are trust and loyalty necessary for national security?
- Are trust and loyalty necessary for democracy?

Students may be interested to learn that this is just one of hundreds of cases since the 1970s of American citizens found guilty of espionage.[8] Clearly, Washington has reason to worry about protecting its secrets—about individual Americans betraying the nation's trust. But it is important to pause to help students think more deeply about the role that trust and loyalty play in the relationship between government and citizenry.[9] The government demands loyalty from its citizens, but loyalty to *what*, exactly? When American citizens are asked to pledge allegiance to the flag of the United States, what are we really pledging their allegiance to?

Students may be surprised to learn that when immigrants become US citizens, they are required to take a public oath of allegiance not to the president of the United States or even to the United States itself, but to the Constitution.[10] In doing so, they are effectively signing America's version of the unwritten "social contract."[11] The essence of the social contract, a concept that was much discussed by eighteenth-century philosophers and embraced by the Founding Fathers, is that individuals agree to give up some of their freedoms and submit to the authority of the state (or the rule of law) in exchange for the state maintaining social order and protecting their rights. The US Constitution itself is a social contract, and the Bill of Rights elaborates on the government's obligations to the contract and the American people.

Did Shirley break the social contract by betraying the trust *of* her government? If students decide she did, then teachers can ask them about the government's contractual obligations. What should the state do to deserve citizens' trust *in* government? Protect national security? Protect the rights laid out in the Constitution? Can it do both at the same time? What does history tell us about its ability to balance democracy and national security? With these questions in mind, it is time to turn to the heart of the entire lesson: how, since the 1980s, successive administrations have struggled to strike a balance between national security and democracy, and more particularly between intelligence gathering and respect for constitutionally guaranteed civil liberties.

From a Wartime Exception to a Peacetime Practice

National security and individual freedoms guaranteed in the Bill of Rights—including especially free speech, freedom of religion, freedom of the press, freedom to assemble, and privacy—are often in tension, but most especially during wartime or the threat of war. Throughout its history, the United States has shown a readiness to curb constitutionally guaranteed civil liberties during wartime or the prelude to war. Among the many examples that could be cited are President John Adams's Alien and Sedition Acts of 1798 during the Quasi-War with France, which severely curtailed freedoms of speech and the press; and President Abraham Lincoln's suspending of the writ of habeus corpus during the Civil War. President Woodrow Wilson introduced the Espionage and Sedition Acts during World War I, which made it a criminal offense to criticize the government during the war; and in World War II, President Roosevelt signed Executive Order 9066, designating Americans of Japanese descent as enemy aliens and establishing internment camps.

World War II also saw the Roosevelt administration begin to routinely intercept all telegrams sent from or to the United States. The information was handed to the Armed Forces Security Agency, the precursor to what would become the US government's most important agency for spying on Americans, the National Security Agency (NSA).

108

The codename for this national security effort was Project Shamrock. In 1947, with the Cold War intensifying and the threat of communism escalating, the Truman administration demanded government and public employees sign an oath of loyalty to the government.[12] Five years later, with the United States gripped by the anticommunist witch-hunting of McCarthyism and by headlines about the arrest—and, in some cases, the execution—of Soviet spies, the Truman administration established the NSA to monitor, collect, and process information pertaining to the security of the nation.[13] The "watch list" of Americans identified as potential threats to national security would later be expanded by the Johnson and Nixon administrations to include anti–Vietnam War activists and even two US senators.

As a consequence of the Watergate scandal that led to the resignation of President Richard Nixon, the extent of this domestic surveillance finally came to light in 1974. Investigative journalist Seymour Hersh published a front-page article in the *New York Times* titled "Huge C.I.A. Operation Reported in U.S. against Anti-War Forces, Other Dissidents in Nixon Years."[14] Hersh's lengthy article presented evidence that various government intelligence agencies, including the NSA, the FBI and the CIA, had been spying on antiwar activists and others the government considered "dissidents" because they criticized US foreign and domestic policies. Hersh's article is an excellent primary source for students to consider, given the popular and congressional governmental response that followed its publication.

In response to the article, both the White House and Congress expressed dismay about—and ignorance of—intelligence-gathering activities on Americans. Several Senate and House committees were created to investigate, including one that came to be known as the Church Committee, named after its chair, Senator Frank Church, who had himself been under surveillance by the CIA. The committee's investigations in 1975–76 confirmed that the US government was collecting data on American citizens. Voicing the concerns of many in Congress and throughout the country, Senator Walter Mondale warned that the NSA "could be used by President 'A' in the future to spy upon the American people, to chill and interrupt political dissent."[15]

The final Church Committee report was published in April 1976 in six separate books.[16] Students would benefit from reading the first twenty pages of book 2, *Intelligence Activities and the Rights of Americans*.[17] The following excerpt is worthy of inclusion here because it explicitly lays out the tensions between maintaining national security and the violation of civil liberties, as discovered by the Church Committee's investigation:

> Americans have rightfully been concerned since before World War II about the dangers of hostile foreign agents likely to commit acts of espionage. Similarly, the violent acts of political terrorists can seriously endanger the rights of Americans. Carefully focused intelligence investigations can help prevent such acts.
>
> But too often intelligence has lost this focus and domestic intelligence activities have invaded individual privacy and violated the rights of lawful assembly and political expression. Unless new and tighter controls are established by legislation, domestic intelligence activities threaten to undermine our democratic society and fundamentally alter its nature. . . .
>
> A tension between order and liberty is inevitable in any society. A Government must protect its citizens from those bent on engaging in violence and criminal behavior, or in espionage and other hostile foreign intelligence activity. . . .
>
> But, intelligence activity in the past decades has, all too often, exceeded the restraints on the exercise of governmental power which are imposed by our country's Constitution, laws, and traditions.[18]

In response to both congressional and public concerns that were aired by the Church Committee's findings, presidents Gerald Ford and Jimmy Carter issued executive orders. Ford's EO 11905 was fairly restrictive and reflected the public distrust of the intelligence agencies, but Carter's order was much more so. In January 1978, Carter issued EO 12036, which required that intelligence gathering be "conducted in a manner that preserves and respects established concepts of privacy and civil liberties" and which stipulated that the CIA refrain from "engag[ing] in any electronic surveillance within the United States."[19] Whereas most executive orders run to between 20 and 40 pages, Carter's was 236 pages.

President Carter also signed into legislation the Foreign Intelligence Surveillance Act (FISA) in 1978, establishing guidelines for government collection of foreign intelligence. In the same way that the Fourth Amendment demands a warrant to search, FISA requires that government agencies "seek a FISA order to engage in surveillance or conduct physical searches for purposes of collecting foreign intelligence." FISA thus created the Foreign Intelligence Surveillance Court (FISC) to vet requests for government surveillance efforts. As stipulated by the FISC, the court is responsible for reviewing applications made by the US government "for approval of electronic surveillance, physical search, and certain other forms of investigative actions for foreign intelligence purposes."[20]

Although primary sources related to FISA and FISC are less accessible to students because of the heavy legal jargon, it is important to make them aware of the government institutions that were created specifically to protect Americans from unconstitutional intelligence gathering. However, as this lesson reveals, since FISA was enacted, various amendments to the law have made Americans more vulnerable—not less—to warrantless surveillance.

Reagan Tips the Balance Back

Carter's successor in the White House, Ronald Reagan, had a very different conception of what the balance between civil liberties and security should be. He tipped that balance firmly back toward the latter, and all presidents since Reagan have left it there, albeit sometimes for different reasons. This is not to say that Reagan did not care about democratic rights. To the contrary, he is seen by many historians— although certainly not all—as a champion of global democracy.[21] And, of course, Reagan is often credited with piloting the United States to victory over the Soviet Union, thereby ending the Cold War and destroying the undemocratic forces of Soviet-style communism throughout the world.

Yet, unlike Carter, Reagan does not seem to have been overly worried that freedom at home might be eroded by domestic intelligence gathering. In the first year of his presidency, on December 4, 1981, Reagan signed Executive Order 12333 (commonly referred to as "twelve triple three"), which was intended to replace Carter's EO 12036.[22] An important historical thinking skill for students at this point is to corroborate sources—to compare sections of the two documents to reveal distinctions in tone and substance. For example, Section 2 of EO 12036 is titled "Restrictions on Intelligence Activities"; the same section in EO 12333 is titled "Conduct of Intelligence Activities." Students could be asked what this seemingly minor change in wording might indicate about the Reagan administration's view of intelligence gathering.

In contrast to Carter's emphasis on protecting constitutional rights, Reagan emphasizes the importance of intelligence to national security. EO 12333 asserts, "Timely and accurate information about the activities, capabilities, plans, and intentions of foreign powers, organizations, and persons, and their agents, is essential to the national security of the United States. All reasonable and lawful means must be used to ensure that the United States will receive the best intelligence available."[23]

The order made major institutional changes to the national security apparatus that have endured to this day. In particular, EO 12333 established the US Intelligence Community (IC). The IC has since grown to become a federation of seventeen distinct government intelligence agencies that work both separately and together to conduct intelligence activities to support US foreign policy and national security. Member organizations of the IC include intelligence agencies, military intelligence, and civilian intelligence and analysis offices within federal executive departments. Today, the IC is overseen by the Office of the Director of National Intelligence (ODNI), which is headed by the director of national intelligence (DNI). The position and influence of the DNI has grown significantly in recent decades, as this lesson reveals.

New Threats, New Technologies

Among his many accomplishments, Reagan's successor, George H. W. Bush, had been head of the CIA for a year in the mid-1970s. It was not surprising, therefore, that he continued Reagan's policy of giving the intelligence agencies significant leeway in gathering intelligence at home. But he had other reasons, too, for not keeping the intelligence community on a tight leash. The Soviet threat was rapidly diminishing when Bush entered office in 1989, and it disappeared entirely when the Soviet Union dissolved itself in 1991, but other threats to national security were fast emerging.

One of the greatest dangers was perceived to be drug trafficking. Bush's attorney general from 1991 to 1993 was William Barr (a role he later reprised in the Trump administration), and in response to the drug menace, Barr authorized the Justice Department and the Drug Enforcement Administration (DEA) to collect data of telephone calls from the United States to various nations suspected of drug trafficking. Carried out by the DEA's intelligence arm under Barr's watch, this effort set a precedent for the phone record collection program under the USA Patriot Act of 2001 (see below). According to one report, the DEA program became "the first known effort to gather data on Americans in bulk, sweeping up records of telephone calls made by millions of US citizens regardless of whether they were suspected of a crime."[24]

The Clinton administration, no less concerned than the Bush administration about drug trafficking and conscious of the growing threat of terrorism, was equally robust in its efforts to protect national security by collecting intelligence data on American citizens. Announced in 1993, the Clipper chip was an encryption device to be installed on telephones, with the government holding a decryption "key." The device is a seemingly innocuous chip. But its purpose provoked controversy among computer geeks—dubbed "cyberpunks"—of the 1990s.[25] The idea was to give the government a technological tool that would it allow it to override conversations between parties that may have posed a national security threat. The concept was known as "key escrow." Created at the time when the cell phone equipment itself was manufactured, an additional key (Clipper) would be held by the government "in escrow." According to the 1994 *New York Times Magazine* report, "With a court-approved wiretap, an agency like the F.B.I. could listen in. By adding Clipper chips to telephones, we could have a system that assures communications will be private—from everybody but the Government."[26] In addition to the Clipper chip, Clinton's 1996 Antiterrorism and Effective Death Penalty Act expanded the federal government's wiretap authority, permitting "roving" wiretaps on a person and not a specific place as in the past.[27]

Thus the most profound change in the relationship between national security and the right to privacy during the 1990s was presented not by drug lords and terrorists but by technology. The opening of the internet to the public, the ubiquitous use of cellphones, the development of direct messaging systems, the ever-increasing sophistication of operating systems, and other elements of the information revolution also drove a revolution in intelligence gathering. The ability of spies, terrorists, and transnational criminals to commit espionage, communicate, recruit, raise and distribute funds, share information, and plot attacks grew swiftly and dramatically. Furthermore, the amount of information that was now being exchanged electronically was vast, presenting America's enemies with a treasure trove of classified material and sensitive data to plunder either openly or surreptitiously. But this same quantum leap in the amount of information available and the use made by spies, criminals, and terrorists of technology presented the US intelligence community with the opportunity to massively expand its surveillance of US citizens and with a justification for doing so.

Terrorism, Counterterrorism, and Homeland Security

George W. Bush faced unprecedented circumstances with the attack on US soil on September 11, 2001. President Bush amended Executive Order 12333 with three different updates: Executive Order 13284 (January 3, 2003), Executive Order 13355 (August 27, 2004), and Executive Order 13470 (July 30, 2008). In conjunction with the updates to counterterrorism intelligence gathering, Congress passed the Intelligence Reform and Terrorism Prevention Act (IRTPA) in 2004.[28] This bipartisan legislation had two major objectives: to ensure that the Intelligence Community agencies coordinated more closely than they had prior to 9/11, and to avoid mistakes made with misinformation regarding weapons of mass destruction in Iraq prior to the invasion in 2003. To better realize this reform effort, the IRTPA created a new position — the director of national intelligence (DNI). The DNI was created to centralize intelligence efforts and encourage more effective collaboration among the Intelligence Community, as first articulated by EO 12333.

Students can be invited to read a short report produced by the Congressional Research Service, which outlines the history and role of the DNI.[29] Students will note that under the DNI's "Responsibilities" as enumerated in the document, EO 12333 (as amended) continues to be the basis for the restructuring of the intelligence agencies. As the document also indicates, the DNI acts as principal intelligence adviser to the president, the National Security Council, and the Homeland Security Council for issues relating to national security. The DNI holds an increasingly influential position in government and, most recently under the Trump administration (see below), has been subject to partisan appointments.

In addition to the "beefing up" of intelligence gathering and operations represented by the revisions to EO 12333, the Bush administration also urged Congress to pass the USA Patriot Act, overhauled the federal government with the creation of the Department of Homeland Security, and signed a series of laws that gave the NSA, CIA, and FBI the ability to conduct surveillance without adhering to FISA guidelines or seeking court-approved warrants.[30] For example, Bush launched a

separate intelligence gathering apparatus, known as the President's Surveillance Program, in which warrantless intelligence was collected under
the code name Stellar Wind.[31]

The results of the Bush administration's concerns about domestic
terrorism led to racial and religious profiling of Muslims, South Asians,
and Black Americans by the NSA and the FBI, as countless court cases
taken up by individuals as well as by organizations such as the Anti-
Defamation League, the American Civil Liberties Union, and the Southern Poverty Law Center indicate.[32] In October 2011, the Civil Rights
Division of the Justice Department published a report, "Confronting
Discrimination in the Post-9/11 Era: Challenges and Opportunities Ten
Years Later," which explored and documented "the civil rights issues
that Muslims, Arabs, Sikhs and South Asians in America have faced
since the 9/11 terrorist attacks."[33] The twenty-two-page report—or at
least excerpts of it—would be another excellent source for students to
consider as evidence that the government itself recognized the problem
of balancing national security with respect for civil liberties. The Bush
administration's counterterrorist intelligence operations on American
soil set the stage for future justification of unwarranted data collection
and electronic surveillance in the name of homeland security by his presidential successor, Barack Obama.

Obama Lengthens the Leash

The Obama administration was also subject to the pressures to secure the nation in a global war on terrorism. For two years,
the administration continued the practices begun by President Bush's
warrantless surveillance program.[34] A *New York Times* exposé that includes a time line is an excellent source for students to compare similarities between the G. W. Bush and Obama administrations' electronic
surveillance programs.[35] Students will note the ways in which national
security took precedence over civil liberty protections during the Obama
administration with Section 215 of the Patriot Act; the NSA's expansion
of surveillance to telephone and internet communications among for-
eigners and Americans, which had begun under operation Stellar Wind;
and intelligence gathered through internet sites such as Google, Yahoo,
and, later, Facebook and Twitter. Intelligence officers who were familiar with the program viewed it as a direct violation of American civil
liberties.[36] One of those analysts was Edward Snowden.

In 2013, former NSA and CIA analyst Edward Snowden leaked confidential CIA and NSA documents to reporter Glenn Greenwald of the *Guardian* and several American journalists. Both the *Guardian* and the *Washington Post* published articles revealing details of the NSA PRISM program, which collected stored internet data from companies such as Google Inc. and Yahoo! for analysis. The revelations that the US government had been gathering mass surveillance data on all Americans provoked major controversy, similar in many respects to the Church Committee findings of the mid-1970s. In addition, some of the leaked documents revealed that racial profiling after 9/11 extended to government agencies—both the NSA and the FBI had been racially profiling Muslims in the United States, including tracking prominent Islam American leaders.[37]

In addition to leaking documents to journalists, Snowden uploaded hundreds of documents for public access to a site called WikiLeaks that had been created by a purported journalist, Julian Assange. A very quick exercise to demonstrate the historical legacy of Snowden's actions, and of the power of the internet to expand them, is to invite students to go to https://wikileaks.org/ and to encourage students to consider the site as an "archive" of primary sources. At WikiLeaks, which posted for public access the vast majority of the documents that Snowden leaked, students can search on any term of interest, of course, but to begin they can be directed to search on the word "Snowden." Among other documents, students will find a statement by Snowden from July 1, 2013, in which Snowden criticizes the Obama administration for obstructing Snowden's request for asylum to another country.[38] In the statement, Snowden asserts, "In the end the Obama administration is not afraid of whistleblowers like me. . . . No, the Obama administration is afraid of you. It is afraid of an informed, angry public demanding the constitutional government it was promised—and it should be."[39] Students can be asked to compare this brief statement with the Department of Justice press release that they reviewed at the start of the lesson. Do they see any common themes?

At the time of this writing, Snowden is still living in Moscow and is unlikely to return to the United States, as he will be convicted of espionage. Snowden's reputation as hero or villain is an excellent example of the tensions that exist between national security and democracy. Students can be asked how they might characterize Snowden's actions. Did he betray the trust of the US government? Did he betray the trust of the

American people? What motivated his activities? For some contemporary observers, with hindsight and given the current climate of American politics, Snowden's actions may have "weakened national security, but strengthened American democracy."[40] And the extent to which WikiLeaks has weakened national security is still a matter of debate.[41]

The Obama administration prosecuted Edward Snowden under the Espionage Act of 1917.[42] The act, which was originally intended to thwart potential spies (as the name suggests) during World War I, criminalizes the release of "national defense" information by anyone "with intent or reason to believe that it is to be used to the injury of the United States or to the advantage of a foreign nation." President Obama used the law against intelligence leaks in the government and in the press against a total of ten people—more than any of the previous administrations combined.[43] Many observers claim that the Espionage Act is sorely in need of updating, as both Presidents Obama and Trump (see below) have used the law to prosecute whistleblowers, rather than domestic spies. The ACLU has issued a public statement, which students can view on YouTube, as to the dangers to democracy posed by the recent applications of the Espionage Act against whistleblowers.[44]

The Trump Administration

The Trump administration returned, in many respects, to a Reagan-era approach to National Security primacy. EO 12333 remains the "north star" of intelligence coordination and gathering among the seventeen institutions in the Intelligence Community working today. The important distinction between previous administrations and the Trump administration, however, is the overt conflict that existed between the White House and the Intelligence Community.

In 2018, the NSA collected data from 534 million records of phone calls and text messages from American telecommunications providers such as AT&T and Verizon, according to a report published by the Office of the Director of National Intelligence. According to the NSA report, these numbers include data that is allowed via FISA, but they do not include the volume of Americans' communications or metadata gathered by the NSA's work abroad, where its activities are regulated by Executive Order 12333.[45]

In February 2018, Director of National Intelligence Daniel Coats issued Intelligence Community Directive 107 calling for "protecting civil liberties and privacy and promoting greater transparency, consistent with United States values and founding principles consistent with a democratic society."[46] This emphasis was reiterated in the National Intelligence Strategy of the United States, published in 2019 under the auspices of DNI Coats. Students would benefit from close reading of the following excerpt:

> The IC must be accountable to the American people in carrying out its national security mission in a way that upholds the country's values. The core principles of protecting privacy and civil liberties in our work and of providing appropriate transparency about our work, both internally and to the public, must be integrated into the IC's programs and activities. Doing so is necessary to earn and retain *public trust* [my emphasis] in the IC, which directly impacts IC authorities, capabilities, and resources. Mission success depends on the IC's commitment to these core principles.[47]

In late July 2019, President Trump tweeted that DNI Coats would be stepping down and that the president would be nominating a new DNI to replace him. Trump appointed Joseph Maguire and then Richard Grenell to serve as acting director of national intelligence until his nominee, John Ratcliffe, could be approved.[48] In the meantime, the White House instructed a thorough reorganization of the ODNI, including cutting staff, without mandated congressional approval.[49] According to the Intelligence Reform and Terrorism Prevention Act (IRTPA) of 2004, which created the ODNI, the president does not have the power to randomly appoint an acting DNI, but Trump defied the authority of the law by appointing these politicians to the role. Ratcliffe, a former US representative from Texas and a staunch supporter of the Trump administration, was sworn into the role in May 2020. He had minimal national security experience, but more troubling still to many intelligence experts and other observers was the explicit partisanship reflected in the appointment.[50]

The tension between protecting national security secrets and guarding against potential abuses of authority—and the public's right to know about them—is nothing new. Students might be surprised to learn that the Continental Congress passed the first whistleblower legislation in 1777, just months after signing the Declaration of Independence. The law declared it "the duty of all persons in the service of the United

States, as well as all other inhabitants thereof, to give the earliest information to Congress or any other proper authority of any misconduct, frauds or misdemeanors committed by any officers or persons in the service of these states, which may come to their knowledge."[51] But the legal right and responsibility exercised by whistleblowers to report "misconduct, frauds or misdemeanors" committed by government during the Trump administration was called into question.

In the fall of 2019, President Trump and Republican members of Congress were infuriated when a whistleblower released evidence that the Trump administration had reached out to the president of Ukraine, Volodymyr Zelensky, to aid in obstructing the nomination of Joe Biden as the Democratic candidate for the 2020 presidential election. The Trump administration went to war with this particular whistleblower as well as with the concept itself.[52] In September 2019, at a United Nations event for US diplomats in New York, Trump was recorded as saying that any government official who provided information to the whistleblower who first raised concerns about the president's call was "almost a spy."[53] And he added: "You know what we used to do in the old days when we were smart? Right?" Trump provocatively asked the diplomats in the room. "The spies and treason, we used to handle it a little differently than we do now."[54]

In October, Trump faced impeachment proceedings, largely as a consequence of congressional concerns about Trump's phone call to President Zelensky. In the impeachment inquiry, Lt. Col. Alexander Vindman, the top Ukraine expert on the National Security Council, testified before Congress, verifying the whistleblower's original claims. In December, in yet another twist in the story, Trump retweeted the alleged name of the whistleblower, once again revealing not merely the president's distrust of but also his disdain for whistleblowers. During his four years in office, Trump employed the Espionage Act of 1917 to arrest and prosecute eight whistleblowers in the intelligence agencies. The Trump administration used the act to punish officials who exposed the policies of the federal government.

A final case for the students to analyze is that of Terry J. Albury. The son of an Ethiopian refugee, Albury was a seventeen-year veteran of the FBI and the only Black agent in the Minneapolis field office.[55] Albury was found guilty of leaking documents to *The Intercept*, which later published an in-depth story exposing the ways in which the FBI continues to target immigrant and religious communities, in spite of antiprofiling policies. The report, titled "The FBI's Secret Rules," explains, "After the famous Church Committee hearings in the 1970s exposed the FBI's wild overreach, reforms were enacted to protect civil liberties. But in recent years, the bureau has substantially revised those rules with very little public scrutiny."[56] The exposé relies on Albury's and others' leaked documents, including three FBI training manuals, to show that the FBI under the Trump administration's guidance was "using race and religion when deciding who to target."[57]

In 2018, Albury was sentenced to four years in prison for having leaked the documents. After his sentencing, FBI director Christopher Wray stated: "Every FBI agent has a solemn obligation to protect classified information from unauthorized disclosure to safeguard our national security. Terry Albury betrayed that responsibility, and he betrayed the *trust* [my emphasis] bestowed on him by the American people."[58] Albury publicly apologized to his fellow FBI agents for his actions but defended them by explaining that he had been motivated to act in the name of "justice," and that he viewed his disclosures as "an act of conscience" in the face of racism at the FBI.[59]

In response to Albury's sentencing, the organization Defending Rights and Dissent, which was founded in 1960 as the National Committee to Abolish the House Un-American Activities Committee, published an open letter protesting the Trump administration's use of the Espionage Act of 1917 to silence legitimate complaints about wrongdoing at the federal level and especially at the national security level.[60] Students would benefit from learning more about Albury's case by reading the press release issued by the Department of Justice and the open letter from Defending Rights and Dissent. They could then be asked to respond to the same questions posed at the start of this lesson.

- What was Albury's crime?
- Are there any benefits from sharing secret information with the public?
- Are trust and loyalty necessary for national security?
- Are trust and loyalty necessary for democracy?

Many observers—including intelligence officers—perceive the purging of whistleblowers by the Trump administration as a direct threat to the constitutional balance of powers and to democracy itself.[61] As the lawyers on behalf of the CIA whistleblower in the call with Ukraine asserted in a *New York Times* op-ed, "We hope our former client's moral courage and personal integrity will inspire others to follow the law and speak up when they see something they reasonably believe to be wrong." The lawyers went on to remind readers, "Lawful whistle-blowers should always—always—be protected from reprisal. That is the foundation of our democracy."[62] And as Allison Stanger, the author of *Whistleblowers: Honesty in American from Washington to Trump*, asserted in a different *New York Times* Opinion piece: "Like the president, intelligence community employees swear an oath to preserve, protect and defend the Constitution of the United States. In insisting on speaking truth to power at great personal sacrifice, whistle-blowers serve their country and challenge all of us to think for ourselves. What could be more American than that?"[63]

Conclusion

Contemporary historical evidence reveals that the government's perceived vulnerability to national security risks in the United States posed by potential "terrorists" or "spies" has led in turn to government efforts to disrupt or obstruct their activities by spying on *them*—and, as it turns out, on the American population at large—or by seeking retaliation against them.

At the end of this lesson, big questions remain for students to contemplate: To what extent and under what circumstances does domestic intelligence gathering (even if legal) constitute a violation of individual rights? To what extent and under what circumstances is the prosecution of or retaliation against federal employees justified in the name of securing the nation? To what extent do these activities affect the social contract and the mutual *trust* between government and its citizens in a healthy democracy? What might have been done differently to resolve the tension between national security and civil liberties? What alternative actions might have been taken? What can we learn about how people made decisions to do the things they did?

Clearly, these questions have no easy answers, and they require a higher level of historical thinking. But students would benefit nonetheless from grappling with the challenge of thinking through the issues, and from a close reading and analysis of the documents, as they weigh the various factors that have affected the balance between national security and civil liberties since 1980. These decisions continue to affect all Americans and are sure to remain a constant tension in the history of US democracy.

NOTES

1. American Historical Association, "Historical Issues: Analysis and Decision-Making," https://www.historians.org/teaching-and-learning/teaching -resources-for-historians/teaching-and-learning-in-the-digital-age/the-histo ry-of-the-americas/the-conquest-of-mexico/for-teachers/setting-up-the-project/ historical-thinking-skills#5.

2. Strikingly few contemporary studies have been conducted with regard to the democratic implementation of foreign policy and national security policies, with important exceptions. See Russell A. Miller, *U.S. National Security, Intelligence, and Democracy: The Church Committee to the War on Terror* (London: Routledge, 2009); Andrea Friedman, *Citizenship in Cold War America: The National Security State and the Possibilities of Dissent* (Amherst: University of Massachusetts Press, 2014); and Lloyd Gardner, *The War on Leakers: National Security and American Democracy from Eugene Debs to Edward Snowden* (New York: New Press, 2016).

3. David R. Segal, "National Security and Democracy in the United States," *Armed Forces and Society* 20, no. 3 (Spring 1994): 375–93.

4. For a statistical analysis of the ways in which Americans viewed this delicate balance after 9/11, see Carroll Doherty, "Balancing Act: National Security and Civil Liberties in Post-9/11 Era," Pew Research Center, June 7, 2013, https://www.pewresearch.org/fact-tank/2013/06/07/balancing-act-national-se curity-and-civil-liberties-in-post-911-era/.

5. Office of Public Affairs, Department of Justice, "West Virginia Woman Admits to Willful Retention of Top Secret National Defense Information and International Parental Kidnapping," press release, July 6, 2020, https://www .justice.gov/opa/pr/west-virginia-woman-admits-willful-retention-top-secret -national-defense-information-and.

6. Ibid.; John Raby, "Woman Pleads Guilty in Scheme to Offer Information to Russia," *Washington Post*, July 6, 2020, https://www.washingtonpost.com/ national/woman-pleads-guilty-in-scheme-to-offer-information-to-russia/2020/ 07/06/d4caf450-bfd8-11ea-8908-68a2b9eae9e0_story.html.

7. Raby, "Woman Pleads Guilty."

8. For a list of identified cases since 1975, see Defense Personnel Security Center, "Espionage and Other Compromises of National Security: Case Summaries from 1975 to 2008," US Department of Defense, Personnel Security Research Center, November 2, 2009, https://fas.org/irp/eprint/esp-summ.pdf.

9. The relationship between trust and national security has been a topic of discussion in some circles. See, for example, Robert D. Shadley and Camilla Vance Shadley, "The Biggest Threat to U.S. National Security Is a Lack of Trust in Senior Military Leadership," *Military Times*, April 7, 2020, https://www.military times.com/opinion/2020/04/07/opinion-the-biggest-threat-to-us-national-secu rity-is-a-lack-of-trust-in-senior-military-leadership/; Mieke Eoyang, Ben Freeman,

Ryan Pougiales, and Benjamin Wittes, "Confidence in Government on National Security Matters: December 2018," Lawfare, January 17, 2019, https://www.law fareblog.com/confidence-government-national-security-matters-december-2018; Conor Friedersdorf, "Why Does Anyone Trust the National-Security State?," Atlantic, November 13, 2013, https://www.theatlantic.com/politics/archive/2013/ 11/why-does-anyone-trust-the-national-security-state/281429/.

10. Ayten Tartici, "The People Who Pledge Allegiance to the U.S. Constitution," Atlantic, September 23, 2017, https://www.theatlantic.com/politics/archive/ 2017/09/the-people-who-pledge-allegiance-to-the-us-constitution/540828/.

11. "Social Contract," Wikipedia, last edited June 7, 2021, https://en.wikipe dia.org/wiki/Social_contract.

12. The Truman Library provides excellent sources and lesson plans for teaching about the loyalty program. Harry S. Truman Library and Museum, "Truman's Loyalty Program," National Archives, https://www.trumanlibrary .gov/education/presidential-inquiries/trumans-loyalty-program (accessed August 10, 2021).

13. Beginning in the 1960s, the government conducted a sister campaign to Project Shamrock called Project Minaret, which targeted individuals suspected of being sympathetic to Fidel Castro's communist regime in Cuba.

14. Seymour Hersh, "Huge C.I.A. Operation Reported in U.S. against Anti-War Forces, Other Dissidents in Nixon Years," New York Times, December 22, 1974, 1, 26.

15. Ibid., 26.

16. "Intelligence Related Commissions, Other Select or Special Committees and Special Reports," US Senate Select Committee on Intelligence, https://www .intelligence.senate.gov/resources/intelligence-related-commissions.

17. US Senate Select Committee to Study Governmental Operations with Respect to Intelligence Activities, Intelligence Activities and the Rights of Americans, book 2, April 26, 1976 (Washington, DC: US Government Printing Office, 1976), https://www.intelligence.senate.gov/sites/default/files/94755_II.pdf.

18. Ibid., 1.

19. "Executive Order No. 12036," Section 2–202, January 24, 1978, https:// fas.org/irp/offdocs/eo/eo-12036.htm.

20. United States Foreign Intelligence Surveillance Court (FISC), "Public Filings," https://www.fisc.uscourts.gov/ (accessed August 14, 2021).

21. There are many explanations for this reputation, including the Westminster Speech and the establishment of the National Endowment for Democracy. See David Lowe, "History: Idea to Reality: NED at 30," National Endowment for Democracy, approximately 2013, https://www.ned.org/about/history/ (accessed August 14, 2021). For a primary source analysis of Reagan's speech to Parliament at Westminster, see "Ronald Reagan Address Parliament, 8 June 1982,"

Voices & Visions, University of Wisconsin Digital Resources, http://vandvreader
.org/ronald-reagan-address-parliament-6-june-1986/.

22. Federal Register, "Executive Order 12333: United States Intelligence
Activities," December 4, 1981, National Archives, https://www.archives.gov/
federal-register/codification/executive-order/12333.html.

23. Ibid.

24. Brad Heath, "U.S. Secretly Tracked Billions of Calls for Decades," *USA
Today,* updated April 8, 2015, https://www.usatoday.com/story/news/2015/04/
07/dea-bulk-telephone-surveillance-operation/70808616/.

25. Steven Levy, "Battle of the Clipper Chip," *New York Times Magazine,* June
12, 1994, https://www.nytimes.com/1994/06/12/magazine/battle-of-the-clipper
-chip.html.

26. Ibid.

27. David Cole and James X. Dempsey, *Terrorism and the Constitution: Sacri-
ficing Civil Liberties in the Name of National Security* (New York: New Press, 2006),
chapter 9.

28. "Intelligence Reform and Terrorism Prevention Act of 2004," Public Law
108–458, December 17, 2004, 108th Congress, https://www.govinfo.gov/content/
pkg/PLAW-108publ458/pdf/PLAW-108publ458.pdf.

29. Congressional Research Service, "The Director of National Intelligence
(DNI)," updated May 10, 2019, https://fas.org/sgp/crs/intel/IF10470.pdf.

30. James Risen and Eric Lichtblau, "Bush Secretly Lifted Some Limits on
Spying in the U.S. after 9/11, Officials Say," *New York Times,* December 15, 2005,
https://www.nytimes.com/2005/12/15/politics/bush-secretly-lifted-some-lim
its-on-spying-in-us-after-911.html.

31. James Risen and Eric Lichtblau, "Bush Lets U.S. Spy on Callers without
Courts," *New York Times,* December 16, 2005, https://www.nytimes.com/2005/12/
16/politics/bush-lets-us-spy-on-callers-without-courts.html.

32. See, for example, "Sanctioned Bias: Racial Profiling since 9/11," American Civil Liberties Union, February 2004, https://www.aclu.org/report/racial
-profiling-911-report.

33. "Confronting Discrimination in the Post-9/11 Era: Challenges and Opportunities Ten Years Later," Department of Justice Civil Rights Division, October
19, 2011, https://www.justice.gov/sites/default/files/crt/legacy/2012/04/16/post
911summit_report_2012-04.pdf.

34. Glenn Greenwald and Spencer Ackerman, "NSA Collected U.S. Email
Records in Bulk for More than Two Years under Obama," *Guardian* (Manchester),
June 27, 2013, https://www.theguardian.com/world/2013/jun/27/nsa-data-min
ing-authorised-obama.

35. "Electronic Surveillance under Bush and Obama," *New York Times,* June
7, 2013, https://archive.nytimes.com/www.nytimes.com/interactive/2013/06/07/
us/07nsa-timeline.html#/#time254_7504.

36. Shortly before leaving office, President Obama expanded the role of the NSA by allowing the agency to share the raw streams of communications it intercepts directly with agencies, including the FBI, the DEA, and the Department of Homeland Security. Charlie Savage, "N.S.A. Gets More Latitude to Share Intercepted Communications," *New York Times*, January 12, 2017, https://www.nytimes.com/2017/01/12/us/politics/nsa-gets-more-latitude-to-share-intercepted-communications.html. Some observers have questioned Obama's motivations for this end-of-presidency act, including that he intended to prevent President Trump from extending surveillance even further. See Kaveh Waddell, "Why Is Obama Expanding Surveillance Powers Right before He Leaves Office," *Atlantic*, January 13, 2017, https://www.theatlantic.com/technology/archive/2017/01/obama-expanding-nsa-powers/513041/.

37. Glenn Greenwald and Murtaza Hussain, "Meet the Muslim-American Leaders the FBI and NSA Have Been Spying on," *The Intercept*, July 8, 2014, https://theintercept.com/2014/07/09/under-surveillance/; Tom Risen, "Racial Profiling Reported in NSA, FBI Surveillance: Prominent Muslim-Americans Targeted by Government Surveillance, Reports Say," *U.S. News and World Report*, July 9, 2014, https://www.usnews.com/news/articles/2014/07/09/racial-profiling-reported-in-nsa-fbi-surveillance.

38. "Statement from Edward Snowden in Moscow," July 2, 2013, https://wikileaks.org/Statement-from-Edward-Snowden-in.html.

39. Ibid.

40. Thomas Rid, "Reassessing Edward Snowden," *Washington Post*, May 13, 2020, https://www.washingtonpost.com/outlook/reassessing-edward-snowden/2020/05/13/fc7a9054-8a23-11ea-9dfd-990f9dcc71fc_story.html. See also Barton Gellman, *Dark Mirror: Edward Snowden and the American Surveillance State* (New York: Penguin Books, 2020); and Barton Gellman, "Since I Met Edward Snowden, I've Never Stopped Watching My Back," *The Atlantic*, June 2020, https://www.theatlantic.com/magazine/archive/2020/06/edward-snowden-operation-first-fruits/610573/?utm_source=share&utm_campaign=share. Snowden has warned against giving the federal government extended surveillance powers due to the Coronavirus. See Isobel Asher Hamilton, "Edward Snowden Says COVID-19 Could Give Governments Invasive New Data-Collection Powers That Could Last Long after the Pandemic," *Business Insider*, March 27, 2020, https://www.businessinsider.com/edward-snowden-coronavirus-surveillance-new-powers-2020-3.

41. Greg Myer, "How Much Did WikiLeaks Damage U.S. National Security?," National Public Radio, April 12, 2019, https://www.npr.org/2019/04/12/712659290/how-much-did-wikileaks-damage-u-s-national-security.

42. In 2019, the Trump administration indicted Julian Assange on seventeen counts of violating the Espionage Act. These expanded charges provoked

observers to ask if First Amendment rights were at risk, given that Assange was a journalist. Charlie Savage, "Assange Indicted under Espionage Act, Raising First Amendment Issues," *New York Times*, May 23, 2019, https://www.nytimes.com/2019/05/23/us/politics/assange-indictment.html.

43. For a full list of the whistleblowers who had been prosecuted by the Obama administration, see Elizabeth Shell and Vanessa Dennis, "The 11 'Leakers' Charged with Espionage," Public Broadcasting System, updated August 21, 2013, https://www.pbs.org/newshour/spc/multimedia/espionage/.

44. "Why Are Whistleblowers Being Prosecuted as Spies?," American Civil Liberties Union, https://www.aclu.org/video/why-are-whistleblowers-being-prosecuted-spies (accessed August 14, 2021).

45. Charlie Savage, "N.S.A. Triples Collection of Data from U.S. Phone Companies," *New York Times*, May 4, 2018, https://www.nytimes.com/2018/05/04/us/politics/nsa-surveillance-2017-annual-report.html.

46. Office of the Director of National Intelligence, "Intelligence Community Directive 107: Civil Liberties, Privacy, and Transparency," February 28, 2018, https://www.dni.gov/files/documents/ICD/ICD-107.pdf; "DNI Affirms Commitment to Transparency: Revised Intelligence Community Directive Focuses on Greater IC Transparency," Office of the Director of National Intelligence, approximately February 2018, https://www.intelligence.gov/publics-daily-brief/public-s-daily-brief-articles/798-dni-affirms-commitment-to-transparency.

47. "National Intelligence Strategy of the United States of America, 2019," https://www.dni.gov/files/ODNI/documents/National_Intelligence_Strategy_2019.pdf.

48. "Opinion: Trump Puts an Unqualified Loyalist in Charge of National Intelligence," *Washington Post*, February 20, 2020, https://www.washingtonpost.com/opinions/global-opinions/trump-puts-an-unqualified-loyalist-in-charge-of-national-intelligence/2020/02/20/d1d8506a-540a-11ea-b119-4faabac6674f_story.html.

49. Adam Mazmanian, "ODNI Shakes Up Cyber Structure," *Federal Computer Week*, May 8, 2020, https://fcw.com/articles/2020/05/08/odni-reorg-cyber-grenell.aspx.

50. "Opinion: The Job Is Essential to U.S. Security: Trump's Nominee Is Not Qualified," *Washington Post*, March 2, 2020, https://www.washingtonpost.com/opinions/global-opinions/the-job-is-essential-to-us-security-trumps-nominee-is-not-qualified/2020/03/02/a19c43d4-5ca7-11ea-9055-5fa12981bbbf_story.html; Robert Draper, "Unwanted Truths: Inside Trump's Battles with U.S. Intelligence Agencies," *New York Times Magazine*, August 8, 2020, https://www.nytimes.com/2020/08/08/magazine/us-russia-intelligence.html.

51. Steven M. Kohn, "The Whistle-Blowers of 1777," *New York Times*, June 12, 2011, https://www.nytimes.com/2011/06/13/opinion/13kohn.html. See also

Christopher Klein, "U.S. Whistleblowers First Got Government Protection in 1777," September 26, 2019, https://www.history.com/news/whistleblowers-law -founding-fathers.

52. Yet another whistleblower—Dr. Rick Bright, a federal scientist— explained that he had suffered retaliation by the Trump administration for hav- ing protested the president's mishandling of the Coronavirus pandemic and thus resigned from the National Institutes of Health. Will Stone, "Government Scientist Adds to Whistleblower Complaint and Quits NIH," National Public Radio, October 6, 2020, https://www.npr.org/sections/coronavirus-live-updates/ 2020/10/06/920985099/government-scientist-tops-up-whistle-blower-complaint -and-quits-nih. See also Bright's op-ed: "I Couldn't Sit Idly and Watch People Die from Trump's Chaotic, Politicized Pandemic Response, So I Resigned," *Washington Post*, October 7, 2020, https://www.washingtonpost.com/opinions/ rick-bright-trump-coronavirus-response-nih/2020/10/07/3ed36cb4-08c3-11eb -859b-f9c27abe638d_story.html.

53. "Listen: Audio of Trump Discussing Whistleblower at Private Event: 'That's Close to a Spy,'" *Los Angeles Times*, September 26, 2019, https://www .latimes.com/politics/story/2019-09-26/trump-at-private-breakfast-who-gave- the-whistle-blower-the-information-because-thats-almost-a-spy.

54. Ibid.

55. Maggie Astor, "Former F.B.I. Agent Admits He Shared Classified Doc- uments," *New York Times*, April 17, 2018, https://www.nytimes.com/2018/04/17/ us/politics/fbi-leaker-terry-albury.html.

56. "The FBI's Secret Rules," *The Intercept*, https://theintercept.com/series/ the-fbis-secret-rules/about/.

57. Cora Currier, "Despite Anti-Profiling Rules, the FBI Uses Race and Reli- gion When Deciding Who to Target," *The Intercept*, January 31, 2017, https:// theintercept.com/2017/01/31/despite-anti-profiling-rules-the-fbi-uses-race -and-religion-when-deciding-who-to-target/.

58. U.S. Department of Justice, "Former FBI Agent Sentenced for Leaking Classified Information," press release, October 18, 2018, https://www.justice.gov/ opa/pr/former-fbi-agent-sentenced-leaking-classified-information.

59. Astor, "Former F.B.I. Agent Admits."

60. "End Espionage Act Prosecutions of Whistleblowers," Defending Rights and Dissent, April 9, 2018, https://rightsanddissent.org/wp-content/uploads/ 2018/04/End-Espionage-Act-Prosecutions-of-Whistleblowers.pdf.

61. Recent calls have been made to request the pardoning of whistleblower Reality Winner, who was sentenced to prison for five years and three months for leaking documents with respect to foreign meddling in the 2016 presidential election. The very same evidence was made publicly available under subsequent investigations by Robert Mueller.

62. Andrew P. Bakaj and Mark S. Zaid, "We Represented the Whistle-Blower. The Law Needs Urgent Help," *New York Times*, March 1, 2020, https://nyti.ms/2PCSziK.

63. Allison Stanger, "Why America Needs Whistle-Blowers," *New York Times*, October 6, 2019, https://nyti.ms/2oWSLiu. See also Allison Stanger, *Whistleblowers: Honesty in America from Washington to Trump* (New Haven, CT: Yale University Press, 2019).

Explaining Waco

How Historians Come to Different
Conclusions about What Really
Happened

Andrew R. Polk

Why Teach This Lesson?

Few secondary students will know much about the tragic events of February 1993. Yet the Waco standoff is a valuable object of historical study for two important reasons. First, the government's stand-off with members of the Branch Davidians in Waco, Texas, became national and international news just as twenty-four-hour news networks were gaining traction among the American public and at the very onset of the internet. Americans could access an unprecedented amount of information about the incident. That volume resulted in an increasing amount of speculation among both the media and the public, with an increasing number of Americans convinced that there was more to the story than officials were willing to share. The resultant distrust in both the government and media helped contribute to the increasing popu-larity of conspiracy theories and the proliferation of militia groups ded-icated to putting their distrust into often violent action. In 1995, on the second anniversary of the final raid on the compound, Timothy McVeigh bombed the Alfred P. Murrah Federal Building in Oklahoma City, Oklahoma, killing 168 people for what he declared was revenge for the government's murder of the Davidians in Waco. Consequently, to study Waco is to study Americans' distrust in their own institutions, a development that has had profound implications on the late twentieth and early twenty-first centuries.

Second, to study Waco is also to study how and why Americans come to understand their past and present. In December 1975, US Secretary of Defense James R. Schlesinger, quoting financier Bernard Baruch, said that "everybody is entitled to his own views; everybody is not entitled to his own facts."[1] Sometimes the work of historians is to investigate and correct the factual errors in popular historical narratives, especially since most people tell stories of the past to give meaning to the present. When people use history to make points about how the world does or should work today, it is important that the story they are telling is factually accurate. Consequently, this lesson will help students think through the differences between facts, opinions, and conjecture.

However, there are also times when two well-meaning and well-informed people tell decidedly different stories of the same event, even though both are basing their narratives on evidence and fact. These contradictory narratives, though both factually accurate, still tell different parts of a story, often for very different reasons. In other words, since they want to make two different points about the present, they highlight or ignore various aspects of the past, either consciously or unconsciously. Subsequently, this fifty-minute lesson is not designed to primarily argue about the "truth" of the federal government's standoff with the Branch Davidians but rather is intended to allow students to see the ways that historical narratives and our understanding of past events are determined in large part by what aspects of a narrative are emphasized. In many ways, this lesson is a culmination of the historical thinking skills students have practiced throughout the year. They will source documents, ascertain biases, and corroborate evidence. However, they will also examine why and how two accounts can examine the same incident and come to completely contrary interpretations of what *really* happened.

Introduction

Federal law enforcement's infamous standoff outside of Waco, Texas, began on the morning of February 28, 1993. For months, agents of the federal Bureau of Alcohol, Tobacco, and Firearms (ATF) had been investigating an obscure religious group, an offshoot of the Davidian Seventh-day Adventist Church known as the Branch Davidians, who lived in a residential complex on Mount Carmel outside of Waco. The group was expecting an imminent end to the world, but reports from numerous sources and an undercover agent led the ATF to believe the group was trying to hasten that end by stockpiling a trove of illegal drugs, firearms, and explosives and was actively converting AR-15 type rifles into fully automatic machine guns. On Saturday, the previous day, the Waco *Herald Tribune* began publishing a dramatic series called "The Sinful Messiah" about the Branch Davidians and their leader, Vernon Howell, who had taken the name David Koresh. The article accused Koresh and the Davidians of polygamous sexual relationships, child abuse, and paramilitary exercises. Fearing violent repercussions from Koresh, the ATF finally decided to serve the "search and arrest" warrant it had been holding in reserve. At 7:30 am, an eighty-vehicle convoy, including two cattle trailers loaded with over seventy heavily armed ATF agents, convened at a staging area a few miles from the Branch Davidians' compound. Local newspaper and television journalists, already alerted to the raid, had previously gathered and were filming the scene by the time the agents advanced on the compound at 9:00 am, accompanied by two National Guard helicopters.

By the time the first agents arrived at the front door, gunshots had been fired, though exactly who shot first was debated. Koresh claimed that when the agents approached the front door, he shouted, "We have women and children in here; let's talk," but this was met with a hail of bullets from the agents. His attorney would later claim that the Davidians were, in fact, the first to fire, but they did so in what they assumed was self-defense after the accidental discharge of an ATF firearm. ATF officers swore they shouted that they were federal agents issuing a warrant but were met with intense gunfire as soon as they set foot on the front porch. Regardless of who fired the first shots, an intense gunfight ensued for several hours. A few minutes into the raid, Davidians called 911 from the compound and asked that the agents stop shooting, yet other Davidians continued to fire upon the agents. By noon a ceasefire had been established, with agents pulling back from the compound. Four federal agents had been killed and more than a dozen injured in the shootout. At least six Davidians had also been killed with another dozen injured in the battle.

The specialized Hostage Rescue Team of the Federal Bureau of Investigation (FBI) was called in. By the end of the day, national news organizations, including all of the major broadcast news networks and the ascendant cable news channels, had sent reporters to Waco to cover the standoff that lasted a total of fifty-one days. Federal agents allowed

Koresh's lawyer to visit the compound, delivered letters from the Davidians' families and friends, and even recorded videos introducing the Hostage Rescue Team to the group, in hopes of humanizing and connecting with the members. Dozens of Davidians willingly left the compound over the next few weeks, but Koresh consistently failed to act on his promises of surrender. Agents eventually cut power to the complex and—at night—shone bright lights and blasted loud music at the compound to put pressure on the remaining Davidians. Eventually, newly appointed attorney general Janet Reno gave permission to assault the compound with a slowly increasing amount of tear gas (CS gas) to compel the Davidians outside. The assault began just after 6:00 am on Monday, April 19. Specially equipped M60 tanks punched holes in the compound and pumped in CS gas. Over the next few hours, four Bradley tanks were added to the assault, and agents shot 40 mm canisters of CS gas through the compound's windows. Although the FBI and ATF swore for years that no incendiary devices were used in the assault, an investigation later revealed they had been lying, as some of the canisters used an incendiary charge to deploy the gas.

The wind was high that day, and much of the gas seemed to blow away as soon as it was inserted. Most to the remaining women and children had been moved to the "bunker," a concrete-block room near the middle of the compound, but the men continued to shoot at the agents. Around noon, smoke could be seen rising from three different points within the compound, with flames soon pouring out of second-floor windows. Gunshots could also be heard within the buildings. Fueled by the high winds, the fire engulfed the whole compound. Within an hour, the entire structure had burned to the ground. Nine people managed to escape the flames, but investigators ultimately found over seventy bodies, including around two dozen children. Autopsies found that most died of smoke inhalation, but several died of gunshot wounds, including Koresh.

Covered nearly nonstop by local and national news organizations, especially the burgeoning twenty-four-hour cable news networks, CNN and CNBC, the government's handling of the standoff drew harsh criticism from many. Attorney General Reno later expressed regret for the raid and its consequences but maintained that the government was not responsible for the fires or, ultimately, the deaths of the Davidians. An extensive congressional investigation determined that although the ATF and FBI committed numerous breaches in protocol and exercised questionable judgment, only Koresh was truly responsible for the many deaths that occurred. However, some viewed the federal standoff with the Branch Davidians as a gross abuse of governmental authority, and scholars see it as a significant factor in the subsequent popularization of both conspiracy theories as well as American militias and paramilitary groups.[2] By the late 1990s, Americans all knew what really happened at Waco in 1993, but most disagreed with each other over what that was.

Scholarly Debate

The ATF's and FBI's standoff with the Branch Davidians was controversial as soon as it began, and the fact that it intersects with issues of religion, politics, and law means that scholars have examined numerous aspects of the event. Much of the scholarly debate over the standoff centers on the government's understanding of the Davidians as a "cult" and on the religious and sociopolitical ramifications of that designation. Although scholars had been interested in new religious movements for several decades, work on the intentional designation of religious movements as cults had begun again in earnest after social psychologist Jeffrey Pfeifer's work the year before the Waco standoff.[3] Consequently, soon after the incident sociologists and religious scholars generally concluded that the ATF and FBI both shallowly accepted and strategically endorsed the designation of the Davidians as a dangerous cult.[4] However, other scholars argued that too much emphasis had been placed on the cult designation and that other, more influential factors contributed to the deadly encounter. For instance, sociologist and legal scholar Stuart A. Wright has argued that although the cult designation was highly problematic, the FBI's increasingly militaristic posturing, both in negotiations and preparations, was a greater factor in the botched final raid.[5] Others have contended that the Davidians' own apocalyptic worldview, when combined with the ATF's aggressive tactics, doomed negotiations before they started.[6]

Beyond the actions of government agents during the standoff, scholars have also been interested in the public displays and understanding of the event in the years since 1993. Much of that interest has centered on the criminal and civil trials relating to the event and the governmental reports on it.[7] Scholars have also examined the role of the media in the standoff, both in its coverage and in the ensuing trials, principally concluding that most journalists too easily accepted the government's position without further challenge or investigation.[8] Dick Reavis has also argued that the religious beliefs of the Davidians had little impact on the federal government's response, and he places significantly more blame on the government's actions than do many scholars.[9] Recent work has also examined the role of Waco in the popularization of both conspiracy theories and militias in America.[10]

Lesson Plan

Student Learning Objectives

Students will be able to do the following:

- Use primary sources to analyze two narratives of the federal standoff with the Branch Davidians,
- Source documents to determine potential bias,
- Corroborate evidence to ascertain historical validity,
- Use evidence-based analysis to assess or defend a position,
- Construct a narrative based on evidence (*optional*).

Procedure

1. The teacher can begin the lesson by briefly introducing students to the event (using the introductory narrative in this chapter as a resource), though this can also be done by simply asking students to recall for the class what, if anything, they know about the event. The teacher should emphasize that the standoff has been controversial, both in the 1990s and up to the present day. It has garnered numerous conspiracy theories and has been cited by many Americans as fueling their distrust of the government, despite the fact that numerous investigations were conducted. Impress upon the students that the disparate accounts of the event have as much to do with what someone emphasizes and who one trusts as sources. Students will have a chance to investigate two different understandings of the event and will use primary sources to analyze and critique the perspectives.

2. After introducing students to the subject and objectives, split students into groups of four to eight, depending on the size of the class and the needs of your classroom. Groups of six tend to allow

the requisite cooperation and discussion, while maintaining the appropriate classroom management. Once students are placed in their groups, give all students Documents A and B. Document A is from religious scholar Catherine Wessinger, who has been highly critical of the federal government's actions during the crisis, most especially the ATF's and FBI's depiction and understanding of the Davidians as a dangerous "cult." Document B is an excerpt of the introduction to the Department of the Treasury's initial, publicly released report on the incident, which was supportive—and many argued defensive—of the ATF's and FBI's actions before, during, and after the standoff. Have the students read both documents and answer questions (individually, as a group, or in two equal subgroups) that highlight the differences between the two accounts, both in details of the incident, word choices and their effects, and the overall tone and "story" that each account tells. A sample questionnaire with such questions has been provided (Resource 1), but teachers can alter, substitute, or add any questions they wish. The principal differences between the accounts are the descriptions of the initial and final raids, the source of the fires, descriptions of the Davidians, and which casualties are emphasized.

3. Once students have noted the differences in the accounts, split each student group into two equal subgroups and assign each subgroup one of the accounts (Document A or Document B). Explain that each subgroup will be examining a set of primary sources (Documents C–H) and will be required to use those sources to support their assigned account. However, both groups receive the same set of primary sources, so some sources will be primarily supportive of one narrative, while others may contain information that could support either narrative. Students should also keep an eye out for any information that directly contradicts their assigned narrative. Teachers can have students organize this information in several ways. Some teachers find it helpful to have students highlight the information in different colors, with supportive information in one color and contradictory information in another. Students could also simply underline any pertinent information and note which narrative it supports. Teachers can also have students sort the information using a scaffolding organizer, such as the samples supplied (Resource 2 or Resource 3). Teachers can also combine these organizing techniques, such as having students

underline or highlight information in the sources individually and then convene in their subgroups to discuss and organize their findings. Time will likely be the determinate factor, and the length of the lesson will depend on how talkative students are and what concluding activity the teacher chooses (group discussion, whole-class discussion, analysis of History Channel video, etc.).

4. Once students have organized the supportive and contradictory information from the sources, have students defend their assigned account with evidence from the sources. This can be done within the original groups (each subgroup reporting to the other) or as a whole class, with the teacher inviting, or calling on, students supportive of each narrative to defend their position with evidence from the documents. Insist that students directly reference the documents when supporting their account. Stress at the beginning of this exercise that the point is not to determine which position is "right"; both positions are based on evidence. Rather, students should see how each account can understand the event in such different ways.

5. The lesson's concluding activity should have students discuss both the differences in how each account constructs and supports its argument and why the authors might perceive the event the way they do. Students should also note any claims or statements that seem factually inaccurate or that cannot be supported by the available evidence. This can be achieved with a whole-class discussion about what students have learned, with the central focus on why the accounts might differ. Alternatively, or if time allows in addition, the teacher can play the five-minute video from the History Channel (Document H) about the "Waco Siege." Have students compare the video to the two previous accounts and ask them which account they think it best supports. Is it a "neutral" or "balanced" account since it comes from the History Channel? If not, why do students think the video might highlight one version of events over others? Teachers can also ask students to describe what they think happened at the event and/or construct their own narrative of the events.

6. The teacher should end the lesson by emphasizing the perspectival, and ultimately biased, nature of all historical narratives. Whenever someone tells a story of the past, they are merely telling *a* story and never *the* story. As historians, we must be aware of the perspectival

nature of the past and train ourselves to understand and analyze not just history but also historical narratives themselves.

Document A

Catherine Wessinger. "The Deaths of 76 Branch Davidians in April 1993 Could Have Been Avoided—So Why Didn't Anyone Care?," *The Conversation*, April 12, 2018. https://theconversation.com/the-deaths-of-76 -branch-davidians-in-april-1993-could-have-been-avoided-so-why-didnt -anyone-care-90816.

Catherine Wessinger is a religious scholar who specializes in new religious movements. She has written extensively on the Branch Davidians, including an oral history project with former members that culminated in three autobiographical works that she edited. She has been critical of the government's actions during the standoff, especially its portrayal of the Davidians as a dangerous "cult" and the implications of that portrayal during and after the standoff. The following is an excerpt from an article she wrote on the standoff.

Twenty-five years ago, on February 28, 1993, Bureau of Alcohol, Tobacco and Firearms [ATF] agents attempted to execute a "dynamic entry" into the home of a religious community at Mount Carmel, a property 10 miles east of Waco, Texas.

David Koresh and his Bible students—who became known as the Branch Davidians—were living at Mount Carmel. The ATF had obtained a search warrant and an arrest warrant for Koresh, whom they suspected was in possession of illegal weapons. The raid prompted a shootout that resulted in the deaths of four ATF agents and six Branch Davidians.

On March 1, 1993, FBI agents took control of the property, and ended up presiding over what became a 51-day siege. On April 19, the siege ended in a second tragedy when FBI agents carried out a tank and tear gas assault, which culminated in a massive fire. Seventy-six Branch Davidians, including 20 children and two miscarried babies, died. Nine Branch Davidians escaped the fire.

Throughout the ordeal, media coverage of the ATF raid and FBI siege depicted the Branch Davidians as a cult with David Koresh exercising total control over mesmerized followers. It was a narrative that federal law enforcement agencies were happy to encourage, and it resonated with the public's understanding of so-called "cults."

Document B

Report of the Department of the Treasury on the Bureau of Alcohol, Tobacco, and Firearms Investigation of Vernon Wayne Howell also known as David Koresh, p. 1. Washington, DC, Department of the Treasury, September, 1993. http://www.policefoundation.org/wp-content/uploads/2018/02/DOT-Report-ATF-Investigation-of-David-Koresh_Sept-1993.pdf.

In September 1993, shortly after the failed standoff between federal agents and the Branch Davidians at Waco, the Department of the Treasury issued a report on the ATF's investigation and actions during the standoff. The report exonerated the ATF and FBI of any culpability in the deaths during either the initial or final raids, though the report did critique some decisions made by commanding officers. This excerpt is from the introduction to the report, where the Treasury first describes the standoff.

On February 28, 1993, near Waco, Texas, four agents from the Treasury Department's Bureau of Alcohol, Tobacco, and Firearms (ATF) were killed, and more than 20 other agents were wounded when David Koresh and members of his religious cult, the Branch Davidians, ambushed a force of 76 ATF agents. The ATF agents were attempting to execute lawful search and arrest warrants at Mount Carmel, the Branch Davidian Compound. Tipped off that the agents were coming, Koresh and more than 100 of his followers waited inside the Compound and opened fire using assault weapons before the agents even reached the door. This gunfire continued until the Branch Davidians agreed to a cease-fire. The ensuing standoff lasted 51 days, ending on April 19, when the Compound erupted in fire set by cult members after the Federal Bureau of Investigation (FBI) used tear gas to force its occupants to leave. The fire destroyed the Compound, and more than 70 residents died, many from gunshot wounds apparently inflicted by fellow cult members.

Document C

Report to the Deputy Attorney General of the Events at Waco, Texas: The Aftermath of the April 19 Fire. Section D, "The Arson Investigation." US Department of Justice, October 8, 1993. https://www.justice.gov/archives/publications/waco/report-deputy-attorney-general-events-waco-texas-aftermath-april-19-fire.

The arson report identifies three points of origin for the fire. The investigators were able to determine these points [of] origin based on the videotapes of the fire, including the infrared aerial tape, provided by the FBI. The items found at the scene, including the presence of fuel containers in certain locations and the presence of chemical accelerants, confirmed the finding of three separate points of origin. . . .

The arson team also discussed the efforts of the arson detection dog. The dog alerted to the presence of chemical accelerants at numerous points throughout the compound, including at the three points of origin. The dog was also exposed to various items of clothing taken from the survivors of the fire, and the dog alerted to the presence of chemical accelerants on several pieces of that clothing.

Document D

Jim McGee, interview in *Waco: Madman or Messiah?* A&E. Two episodes. Written and directed by Christopher Spencer. RAW TV Limited. 90 minutes. Premier dates January 28 and 29, 2018. Quoted in Stuart A. Wright, "Waco after Twenty-Five Years: Media Reconstructions of the Federal Siege of the Branch Davidians," *Nova Religio* 22, no. 3 (February 2019), https://muse.jhu.edu/article/737595.

James "Jim" McGee was a principal negotiator with the FBI's Hostage Rescue Unit, who negotiated with Koresh during the standoff.

I wanted to do an assault. I wanted [Koresh] to pay for killing those four ATF agents.

Document E

"Statement of Attorney General Janet Reno before Committee on the Judiciary, US House of Representatives, Concerning the Events Surrounding the Branch Davidian Cult Standoff in Waco, Texas, presented on April 28, 1993 [modified]." https://www.justice.gov/archive/ag/speeches/1993/04-28-1993b.pdf.

During the week of April 5, the FBI advised me that they were developing a plan for the possible use of teargas in an effort to increase the pressure on those in the compound to surrender. . . . The threshold question I asked was whether the gas could cause permanent injury to the children. . . . Then, the primary question I asked again and again during the ensuing discussion was "Why now?," "Why not wait?" . . . At this time, a number of things were readily apparent to me. Most important, I was convinced that, short of allowing David Koresh to go free, he was not coming out voluntarily. Given that unacceptable result, allowing the status quo to remain was not going to lead to an ultimate peaceful resolution and eliminate any risk to the safety of the innocent children in the compound, the public at large, or the government agents at the scene. On the contrary, the passage of time only increased the likelihood of incidents and possible attendant injuries and harm.

Document F

Investigation into the Activities of Federal Law Enforcement Agencies toward the Branch Davidians. Thirteenth Report by the Committee on Government Reform and Oversight, House Report 104–749, 104th Congress, 2nd session, House of Representatives, US Government Printing Office. https://www.congress.gov/104/crpt/hrpt749/CRPT-104hrpt749.pdf.

But for the criminal conduct and aberrational behavior of David Koresh and other Branch Davidians, the tragedies that occurred in Waco would not have occurred. The ultimate responsibility for the deaths of the Davidians and the four Federal law enforcement agents lies with Koresh. . . .

David Koresh could have been arrested outside the Davidian compound. The ATF chose not to arrest Koresh outside the Davidian residence and instead were determined to use a dynamic entry approach. In making this decision ATF agents exercised extremely poor judgment, made erroneous assumptions, and ignored the foreseeable perils of their course of action. . . .

The ATF's raid plan for February 28 was significantly flawed. The plan was poorly conceived, utilized a high risk tactical approach when other tactics could have been successfully used, was drafted and commanded by ATF agents who were less qualified than other available agents, and used agents who were not sufficiently trained for the operation. Additionally, ATF commanders did not take precautions to ensure that the plan would not be discovered.

Document G

Bonnie Haldeman. *Memories of the Branch Davidians: The Autobiography of David Koresh's Mother*, edited by Catherine Wessinger, p. 103. Waco, TX: Baylor University Press, 2007.

> I don't know why that happened the way it did in 1993. I just really admire my son for having the guts to stand up to the United States government for his beliefs. He might not have done everything the way the world thinks he should have, but the Bible tells us not to judge lest you will be judged.

Document H

Jeremy Schwartz. "Lessons for Media Still Echo from Waco Tragedy." *Statesman*, April 19, 2018. https://www.statesman.com/NEWS/20180419/ Lessons-for-media-still-echo-from-Waco-tragedy.

> Several journalists, including [Tommy] Witherspoon and the news crew at KWTX in Waco, received tips about the Sunday morning raid and were at Mt. Carmel even before the bullets started flying.
>
> But KWTX cameraman Jim Peeler found himself lost on the desolate roads near the compound and asked a passing mailman for directions. During their brief conversation, Peeler apparently revealed that a law enforcement operation was underway.
>
> Unbeknownst to Peeler, the mail carrier, David Jones, was a member of the Branch Davidians, and he promptly raced to the compound to tell Koresh the news.

Document I (optional)

What Happened at the Waco Siege? History Channel, March 19, 2018, video, 4:58. https://www.youtube.com/watch?v=vhKmRtBfxjo.

Resource 1

After reading both Document A and Document B, answer the following questions.

1. Complete the chart, noting how each document describes the following people or events. Quote directly from the documents whenever possible.

People or Group	How Described in Document A	How Described in Document B
Koresh and Branch Davidians		
Initial Raid		
Final Raid		
Casualties		
Fires in Compound		

2. Are there any additional differences that you notice between the two accounts? If so, list them below.

a. _____

b. _____

c. _____

3. After looking at the differences between each account, who does each account determine, or imply, is at fault for the tragic events in Waco?

a. Document A _____

b. Document B _____

Resource 2

After reading Documents C–G, fill out the chart with the information that supports your account, noting the document the information is in. Quote directly from the source whenever possible.

Information That Supports Your Assigned Account	Document

Resource 3

Use this space to organize the most persuasive evidence that supports your assigned account and, after hearing the presentation from the other group members, the most persuasive evidence in support of the opposing account.

Document A: Catherine Wessinger Account: List the three pieces of evidence that best support this account.

Information That Supports Your Assigned Account	Document

Document B: Department of Treasury Account: List the three pieces of evidence that best support this account

Information That Supports Your Assigned Account	Document

Follow-up: After reading both accounts and sorting through the evidence, list any factually inaccurate statements or accusations made in either Document A or Document B:

NOTES

1. William K. Wyant Jr., "Colby Says CIA Has Made Contribution to Peace," *St. Louis Post-Dispatch*, December 4, 1975, 7A.

2. For the most complete example of this argument and its antecedents, see Kathryn S. Olmsted, *Real Enemies: Conspiracy Theories and American Democracy, World War I to 9/11* (New York: Oxford University Press, 2009), 195–99.

3. Jeffrey Pfeifer, "The Psychological Framing of Cults: Schematic Representations and Cult Evaluations," *Journal of Applied Social Psychology* 22, no. 7 (April 1992): 531–44, https://doi.org/10.1111/j.1559-1816.1992.tb00988.x.

4. For example, see James D. Tabor and Eugene V. Gallagher, *Why Waco? Cults and the Battle for Religious Freedom in America* (Berkeley: University of California Press, 1995); Stuart A. Wright, ed., *Armageddon in Waco: Critical Perspectives on the Branch Davidian Conflict* (Chicago: University of Chicago Press, 1995); and Catherine Wessinger, "The FBI's 'Cult War' against the Branch Davidians," in *The FBI and Religion: Faith and National Security before and after 9/11*, ed. Sylvester A. Johnson and Steven Weitzman (Oakland: University of California Press, 2017), 203–43.

5. Stuart A. Wright, "Anatomy of a Government Massacre: Abuses of Hostage-Barricade Protocols during the Waco Standoff," *Terrorism and Political Violence* 11, no. 2 (1999): 39–68; Stuart A. Wright, "Why Negotiations at Mount Carmel Really Failed: Disinformation, Dissension and Psychological Warfare," in *Waco: Ten Years after*, ed. David Tabb Stewart, 2003 Fleming Lectures in Religion (Georgetown, TX: Southwestern University, 2003), 42–56, available at https://www.scribd.com/document/303188239/Waco-Ten-Years-After-by-Stewart-and-others; Stuart A. Wright, "Explaining Militarization at Waco: Construction and Convergence of a Warfare Narrative," in *Controversial New Religions*, ed. James R. Lewis (New York: Oxford University Press, 2005), 75–97.

6. Eugene V. Gallagher, "'Theology Is Life and Death': David Koresh on Violence, Persecution, and the Millennium," in *Millennialism, Persecution, and Violence*, ed. Catherine Wessinger (Syracuse, NY: Syracuse University Press, 2000), 82–100; Jayne Seminare Docherty, *Learning Lessons from Waco: When Parties Bring Their Gods to the Negotiation Table* (Syracuse, NY: Syracuse University Press, 2001); Kenneth G. C. Newport, "A Baptism by Fire: The Branch Davidians and Apocalyptic Self-Destruction," *Nova Religio* 13, no. 2 (November 2009): 61–94.

7. Jean E. Rosenfeld, "The Use of the Military at Waco: The Danforth Report in Context," *Nova Religio* 5, no. 1 (October 2001): 171–85; Jayne Seminare Docherty, "Why Waco Has Not Gone Away: Critical Incidents and Cultural Trauma," *Nova Religio* 5, no. 1 (October 2001): 186–202; Stuart A. Wright, "A Critical Analysis of Evidentiary and Procedural Rulings in the Branch Davidian Civil Trial," in *New Religious Movements and Religious Liberty in America*, ed. Derek Davis (Waco: Baylor University Press, 2002), 101–13; Matthew D. Wittmer, "Traces of

the Mount Carmel Community: Documentation and Access," *Nova Religio* 13, no. 2 (November 2009): 95–112.

8. For example, see James T. Richardson, "'Showtime' in Texas: Social Production of the Branch Davidian Trials," *Nova Religio* 5, no. 1 (October 2001): 152–70; and Stuart A. Wright, "Waco after Twenty-Five Years: Media Reconstructions of the Federal Siege of the Branch Davidians," *Nova Religio* 22, no. 3 (February 2019): 108–20.

9. Dick J. Reavis, *From the Ashes of Waco: An Investigation* (Syracuse, NY: Syracuse University Press, 1998).

10. Kenneth S. Stern, *A Force upon the Plain: The American Militia Movement and the Politics of Hate* (New York: Simon & Schuster, 1996); Michael Barkun, *A Culture of Conspiracy: Apocalyptic Visions in Contemporary America* (Berkeley: University of California Press, 2003); Olmsted, *Real Enemies*.

FOR FURTHER READING

Doyle, Clive. *A Journey to Waco: Autobiography of a Branch Davidian*. Edited by Catherine Wessinger and Matthew D. Whittmer. New York: Rowman and Littlefield, 2002.

Haberman, Clyde. "Memories of Waco Siege Continue to Fuel Far-Right Groups." *New York Times*, July 12, 2015. https://www.nytimes.com/2015/07/13/us/memories-of-waco-siege-continue-to-fuel-far-right-groups.html.

Noesner, Gary. *Stalling for Time: My Life as an FBI Hostage Negotiator*. New York: Random House, 2010.

Thibodeau, David, Leon Whiteson, and Aviva Layton. *Waco: A Survivor's Story*. New York: Hatchett Books, 2018.

A Nation at Risk?

Education Debates and Policies
from Reagan to Trump

CARL P. WATTS

Why Teach This Lesson?

For many instructors a constant tension exists between the number of topics that they need to teach and the limited time in which they have to teach them. This is particularly the case when teaching survey courses, in which hard choices have to be made about the focus of study. When thinking about the significance of education policy in the United States, it is useful to recognize how the history of education relates to other aspects of contemporary American politics and society. This chapter seeks to correct the perception that education is an isolated area of domestic policy in US history by showing the ways in which education policy is inextricably linked to defining American national identity and its projection of power on the global stage. This lesson provides students with an opportunity to trace the historical evolution of education as it relates to larger national conversations about the future of the United States and its role in the world.

Introduction

This chapter suggests three possible connections that exist between US education policy and larger issues in American life: the fear of national decline, the increasing role of the federal government, and the culture wars. First, debates about US education performance can be seen as part of a recurrent angst about national decline and the rise of competitors on the international stage. This relationship is reflected in the title of this chapter, which refers to the 1983 report *A Nation at Risk* published by President Ronald Reagan's National Commission on Excellence in Education. Second, the increasing federal role within the field of education policy since the 1960s—which has accelerated considerably during the period covered by this book—reveals a great deal about the nature of federal-state relations. This lesson provides opportunities for students to develop their analytical skills by evaluating primary sources excerpted from the US Constitution, legislation, executive orders, and Supreme Court decisions. Third, it is abundantly clear that education is one of the most controversial aspects of public policy in the United States. Any course on contemporary US history cannot avoid grappling with the culture wars, which have grown in intensity since the 1990s and reached a crescendo during the Trump administration. Controversial topics offer tremendous opportunities for student engagement through presentations and debates. Students may, for example, engage the controversies surrounding prayer in public schools and arguments about how US history should be taught. The latter has attracted an enormous level of scrutiny as a result of the conservative reaction against the *New York Times'* Pulitzer Prize–winning 1619 Project. A lesson plan is appended to this chapter to illustrate how students can engage the 1619 Project through a formal debate. However, engaging students through controversial material also demands that instructors should give some careful thought to their approach. This chapter therefore affords some space to consider a few philosophical and practical issues before turning to the three substantive themes identified above.

Articulating an Approach to Teaching US Education Policy

As is already apparent, multiple themes surface in the debates about education policy in the United States; education is a particularly controversial topic when viewed through the analytical lens of the culture wars. For this reason, teachers should think carefully about how their approach to teaching education policy might be influenced by their own political bias and educational philosophy. With the decline of academic tenure, and the attenuation of academic freedom that is associated with that privilege, many educators who are not tenured or on the tenure track may feel understandably reluctant to foreground the controversies that are associated with the study of history. This reluctance may be compounded if instructors have not received much formal training in education methods. Fortunately, instructors may avail themselves of many useful articles that provide advice and guidance to help them formulate an approach to teaching controversial topics.[1] Research on the teaching of history and social studies has shown that educators may take a range of approaches, including avoiding controversial topics; denying that topics are controversial (simply asserting truth); privileging a particular perspective; and adopting a balance between competing perspectives. The general academic consensus is that students benefit from evaluating rather than avoiding controversial issues. Students are able to develop critical thinking skills by weighing evidence associated with the issue under debate and build tolerance for different points of view.[2] Instructors should therefore emphasize the purpose of engaging with controversial topics in the classroom and explain whether they are going to privilege a particular viewpoint or adopt a balanced approach. Instructors might wish to encourage students to read some of the literature on the teaching of controversial topics in order to establish transparency about their approach. There is also considerable value in asking students to reflect on how they have been taught controversial topics in the past, and how they have formed their political views, since this may help build self-awareness and receptiveness to information and interpretations that contradict their own beliefs.

Moving beyond broad philosophical concerns, instructors will need to give some thought to the principles of instructional design in order to establish a coherent lesson or unit of study on the history of US education policy. The process known as understanding by design, or "backward design," has become very influential during the last two decades.[3] Instructors usually adopt a "forward design" process, which means that they first consider how to teach the content—the teaching and learning activities they will implement, and the assessments they will use—then they attempt to draw connections to the student learning outcomes (SLOs). In contrast, "backward design" suggests that instructors should first consider the learning outcomes, which encompass the knowledge, skills, and affective traits that students are expected to have attained by the end of the lesson or unit of study. Next, instructors should consider the enabling objectives (EOs) that define more specific requirements and are necessary to give effect to the learning outcomes. Learning outcomes and enabling objectives should be framed using Bloom's Taxonomy, which establishes a hierarchy for the cognitive and affective domains.[4] The advantages of this "backward design" process are that it helps avoid disconnecting the learning outcomes from the teaching and learning activities and ensures that assessment methods are correctly aligned. Based on the content of this chapter, suitable learning outcomes and enabling objectives might be framed in the following terms:

- SLO 1: Students will be able to recall and categorize the main developments in the history of US education policy since 1950.
  - EO 1a: Students will be able to list the major milestones in a time line from 1950 to the present.
  - EO 1b: Students will be able to identify the political, economic, and cultural aspects of US education policy since 1950.
- SLO 2: Students will be able to analyze debates about US education policy in relation to concerns about the decline of the United States.
  - EO 2a: Students will be able to assess the relationship between education and international economic competitiveness.
  - EO 2b: Students will be able to assess the relationship between education and the capacity of the public to scrutinize the conduct of US foreign relations.
- SLO 3: Students will be able to evaluate the nature and effects of federalism in US education policy.
  - EO 3a: Students will be able to explain the constitutional basis of federalism for education policy.
  - EO 3b: Students will be able to evaluate the effects of federalism in relation to education outcomes.
- SLO 4: Students will be able to evaluate the effects of the culture wars on US education policy.
  - EO 4a: Students will be able to analyze the controversy over history and national identity.
  - EO 4b: Students will be able to analyze the controversy over secularization in schools.

Useful Sources for US Education Policy

Before turning to the substantive themes in this chapter, instructors will obviously wish to know what materials are available to teach the history of US education policy. As with any other topic, students can gain an understanding of chronological developments and a sense of the salient issues in education policy by examining the relevant parts of general US history texts, such as those written by Joshua Freedman, James Patterson, and David Reynolds.[5] This broader historical context will enable them to construct a time line for the period since 1950, which is necessary to give full context for the period from Reagan to Trump. Once students have identified the major developments and themes, they can then engage the specialized sources on the history of US education. In addition to the textbooks, a handful of bibliographic guides might prove helpful. Instructors might find it efficacious to divide their students into groups so that they can explore the utility of various types of materials including primary sources, journals, textbooks, monographs, professional association resources, and so forth.[6] For example, instructors will find the collection of documents edited by James Fraser, *The School in the United States: A Documentary History*, to be particularly useful. This includes primary sources and commentaries on education in the United States since colonial times, with the last five chapters covering developments since 1950, and the final two devoted to the period since 1980.[7] These bibliographic guides and documents will also allow students to quickly familiarize themselves with the contours of the historiography, which in the last few decades has focused in particular on the social history of ethnic minorities, urban schooling, and social reform movements. To further scaffold the lesson, instructors might also make use of some award-winning (but controversial) documentaries that have been produced during the last decade, examining various issues in education including teaching standards, standardized curriculum, testing and student achievement, and the comparative performance of different types of educational institutions.[8]

Education and the Debate about National Decline

Concerns about the relationship between education and national power stretch back to the second decade of the Cold War. The furor over the Soviet launch of the satellite *Sputnik* in October 1957—which revealed that the United States was behind in the space race and the development of ballistic missile technology—undermined conservative opposition to greater federal spending on education. The National Defense Education Act (NDEA) of 1958 declared the existence of "an educational emergency" that required action by the federal government.

It opened the way for dramatic growth in higher education that went far beyond the expansion brought about by the GI Bill after the Second World War. In 1946, 2 million students were enrolled in higher education programs, which increased to 3.5 million in 1960, and 8 million by 1970. By 1961 the federal budget for research and development more than doubled to $9 billion. Although targeted toward science and engineering, this money could be absorbed into general overhead costs so it also benefited nonscientific university departments.[9] The rapid expansion of higher education meant that premier research universities sought to differentiate themselves from the burgeoning number of lower-tier institutions. This hierarchical differentiation resulted in the widespread adoption of the Scholastic Aptitude Test (SAT) and the American College Test (ACT) as a means by which to sort and select applicants.[10] This change was significant because standardized testing became a marker of performance that has profoundly shaped approaches to educational reform since the 1980s.

The NDEA was predicated on the belief that schools, as well as universities, were now a battleground in the Cold War. A commission led by Admiral Hyman Rickover prescribed more rigorous standards, particularly for the teaching of mathematics and science.[11] One historian of the United States during the Cold War has commented wryly, "Grade-schoolers who scoffed at classroom air raid drills became truly rattled as they heard rumors that the nation would demand additional homework."[12] Historians have emphasized the significance of the NDEA because it constituted a historic break with the earlier practice of assigning educational spending primarily to state and local authorities. However, they also tend to observe that it was conceived in terms of national security and not as an endorsement of the broader principle of federal aid for public education.[13] This is a reasonable interpretation, but it is also true that key officials were quite prepared to use the *Sputnik* crisis so that they could push through legislation primarily in order to improve the quality of instruction in schools.[14]

In 1965, Congress enacted the Elementary and Secondary Education Act (ESEA). Title I of the ESEA allocated federal funds to schools with a high concentration of economically and socially disadvantaged students.[15] Spending per pupil increased, student-teacher ratios improved, and educators seized the moment to implement curriculum reform.[16] Nevertheless, by the late 1970s, there was a widespread belief that schools were failing. There was of course a great deal of controversy over the failure to racially integrate schools (which is also noted in the next section of this chapter). The business community, however, drew attention to academic failures. On the one hand, SAT scores had been dropping since the mid-1960s and reached a nadir in 1980; on the other hand, grade inflation at both the secondary and university levels was evident. Business leaders contended that unless there was an improvement in educational standards, the United States would be at a disadvantage in a technologically complex and competitive global economy.[17]

The publication in 1983 of *A Nation at Risk* by President Ronald Reagan's National Commission on Excellence in Education was a major landmark in education policymaking. The report contributed heavily to the perception that American schools were failing:

> Our nation is at risk. Our once unchallenged preeminence in commerce, industry, science, and technological innovation is being overtaken by competitors throughout the world. . . . Our society and its educational institutions seem to have lost sight of the basic purposes of schooling, and of the high expectations and disciplined effort needed to attain them.[18]

The report brought enormous national attention to education policymaking and led to a flurry of further reports from the federal government, state governments, private foundations, and corporations. The range of prescriptions for the American educational malady included greater emphasis on science, mathematics, and communication skills; better civics education; more time in the classroom; greater discipline; and improvements in the education, status, and remuneration of teachers.[19] *A Nation at Risk* and other reports set the stage for local, state, and federal education reforms predicated on free market principles that profoundly shaped the US education system.[20]

Despite national attention to education as an engine of national competitiveness and vehicle for individual economic improvement, only around one-half of people born in 1980 earn more today than their parents did at a similar age. Education is one of the factors that explains this decline in intergenerational economic gain. The productivity of the education sector in the United States is declining rapidly, as costs soar but learning has stagnated. According to the Organisation for Economic Co-operation and Development (OECD), the numeracy and literacy skills of people born in the United States since 1980 are no greater than for those born between 1968 and 1977. The United States spends more per student on education than most OECD countries, but ranks last out twenty-six countries tested on math gains and second to last on literacy gains.[21] Although education costs have increased dramatically, public schools have actually suffered funding cuts. Most states cut public education funding in response to the economic crisis of 2008, and tax cuts in some of those states compounded the effect of the funding crisis. By 2015, twenty-nine states were still providing less funding per student than before the onset of the Great Recession.[22] The various statistical analyses provide opportunities for students to enhance their awareness of education inequalities within the United States. Students can also develop their understanding of economic and geopolitical concerns in education policy by comparing the education performance of the United States relative to its competitors, particularly India and China.[23]

Yet another dimension is apparent in the debate about US decline and its relationship to education. Writing in the late 1980s, Gerald Dorfman and Paul Hanna observed:

> Education has drawn so much attention in recent years because it is a central part of a wider discontent about the condition of our nation. We are dissatisfied with our educational system because we believe that it is not producing skilled, informed, and effective citizens for the future.[24]

Two decades on, Dorfman and Hanna would have been no happier about the capacity of the US education system to produce informed and effective citizens. In 2006, a national survey on geographic literacy revealed that young Americans were hugely deficient in even the most basic geographic knowledge. For example, 60 percent of Americans between the ages of eighteen and twenty-four were unable to find Iraq on a map of the Middle East, and 90 percent were unable to locate Afghanistan on a map of Asia.[25] This was despite the fact that the United States had been conducting military operations in Afghanistan for five years and in Iraq for three years. Students of US education policy might wish to consider the implications of this dire lack of knowledge. The economic costs of the wars in Iraq and Afghanistan are highly significant. In 2008 it was estimated that the United States would face a total bill of $3 trillion. However, the cost of these wars has escalated over time, and a more recent analysis has put the cost at around $6.4 trillion.

This includes long-term costs such as veterans' benefits and disability care, which will obviously continue for decades to come.[26] Students should be encouraged to consider the opportunity costs in connection with these staggeringly large sums of money. The United States faces multiple domestic economic problems, including the health-care costs associated with a growing and aging population, the need to repair and replace infrastructure that is decades old, and the management of the novel coronavirus pandemic. Students might well conclude that many young Americans have not acquired the knowledge and skills that are necessary to become effective citizens if they know little about the effects of US foreign policy in the domestic sphere.

Education and Federalism

The education system in the United States is based on a division between federal, state, and local authorities. The federal government has expanded its involvement in educational policy since the 1960s, and its role has accelerated dramatically in the period covered by this book, but public education remains the primary responsibility of state and local governments. Article I, Section 8, of the Constitution specifies the "enumerated powers" that Congress exercises, and the Tenth Amendment grants state autonomy in a wide range of matters, including education. A key consequence of this division of power within the federal system is that it preserved state control over its internal affairs, including the segregation of schools in southern states well into the twentieth century. The Supreme Court decision in *Brown v. Board of Education* (1954) was of course a landmark because it declared legalized school segregation unconstitutional. However, the implementation of this historic decision struggled to gain traction, partly due to determined southern resistance and partly due to the reluctance of the Eisenhower administration to enforce integration. A decade later, fewer than 2 percent of Black public school children in the South attended racially integrated schools. The North hardly served as a model of integration: in 1989, estimates suggested that more than 30 percent of Black schoolchildren attended public schools that were at least 90 percent nonwhite.[27] Notwithstanding the failure of racial integration in schools, it is clear that from the 1960s the federal government was becoming more keenly attuned to the needs of disadvantaged students, which produced a flurry of rights legislation during the 1970s.[28]

154

Ronald Reagan was inclined toward a smaller role for the federal government and had pledged to abolish the Department of Education, which had been established by his predecessor, Jimmy Carter. However, Reagan was disappointed to find that he was constrained in his instincts by the enormous level of attention that followed the publication of *A Nation at Risk*. Reagan's successor, George H. W. Bush, promised during his election campaign that he would be "the education president." Although he served for only one term, and he passed no education bills during his time in office, his administration is recognized as having far-reaching consequences in education policy.[29] In the fall of 1989, Bush called the state governors together for an education summit, and in April 1991 he asked Congress to approve his education plan, dubbed America 2000.[30] Bush's plan revealed a shift away from federal funding and called for greater entrepreneurialism and accountability in education. Liberals in Congress initially rejected this vision, but over the course of the next two decades administrations of all political stripes came to embrace it. Under the Clinton administration a consensus began to build around the need for the federal government to foster a greater focus on student achievement, and in March 1994 Bill Clinton signed the Goals 2000: Educate America Act, which was predicated upon outcomes-based education.[31] The new direction in education policy became entrenched with the No Child Left Behind Act (NCLB), signed by President George W. Bush in January 2002.[32] This greatly emphasized increased accountability at the state level through student testing, teacher evaluation, and school rankings. The NCLB regime required annual testing of students at the elementary grades in core subject areas, mandated the hiring of highly qualified teachers, and granted state and local agencies substantial authority in taking corrective actions to turn around failing schools.[33] Students could practice historical thinking skills by corroborating these primary source documents. They could be invited to read and analyze excerpts of all three pieces of legislation in order to identify change over time and patterns of continuity and change with regard to the history of federal education policy.

Initially it seemed that President Obama would continue the emphasis of his predecessor through the Race to the Top initiative in elementary and secondary education.[34] States were asked to compete for relatively small federal education resources. In exchange for these funds, states were required to adopt measures that would not have looked out of place during the Bush era: raise the caps on charter schools; implement prescribed strategies to improve the performance of low-achieving schools; and develop promotion standards for teachers based on student achievement. In 2015, however, Congress replaced NCLB with the Every Student Succeeds Act (ESSA).[35] This returned the initiative in education policy to the state and local levels. ESSA restricts requirements for intervention in low-performing schools and no longer requires states to adopt common core standards in exchange for federal funds. It also specifies that the federal government cannot use fiscal and regulatory incentives to encourage certain accountability practices, such as teacher evaluation systems based on metrics like student test outcomes. On the other hand, the Obama era is noted for much tighter regulation of higher education.[36]

Beginning in early 2017, during the Trump administration, Education Secretary Betsy DeVos adopted a clear effort toward decentralization of education policies. In February 2017, for example, DeVos rescinded the guidance that protected transgender students and advised that the administration would take a much narrower view of Title IX laws prohibiting sex discrimination in education. DeVos requested less money for her department from Congress, which was consistent with her position of reducing federal education spending (a move that Congress rebuffed). One area for which DeVos was prepared to seek more funding was to expand choice via charter schools and private school vouchers. Education Freedom Scholarships would have provided up to $5 billion a year for children to attend the school of their choice, including nonpublic and religious schools. However, although this idea had previously attracted bipartisan support in Congress, it now languished partly because so many Democratic legislators regarded the Education Secretary as a polarizing figure whose policies they could not support. That polarization extended beyond the halls of Congress, as shown by the vilification of the Education Secretary during the teachers' strikes in early 2018. When educators in West Virginia walked off the job to protest low pay and the underfunding of public schools, it generated a wave of similar labor action in other states.[37]

Under the strain of the novel coronavirus pandemic, the Trump administration adopted a more coercive approach to federal-state relations in education. Enormous controversy ensued when Trump and DeVos insisted that schools should reopen for face-to-face teaching during the pandemic. They threatened to cut off federal funding for districts that did not comply, but this was meaningless because federal funds for schools are appropriated by Congress and not by the executive branch. Critics observed that the attempt at coercion ran contrary to DeVos's ideological emphasis that education is a matter for local authorities. Defenders of her position pointed to the fact that remote learning did not best serve the needs of vulnerable children, particularly students of color, in deprived areas without access to the necessary resources. However, this argument was contradicted by the main thrust of DeVos's education policy, which had all along suggested that education authorities should be free to offer instruction through virtual schools. With the 2020 presidential election bearing down, there was a strong perception that the Trump administration was pushing for schools to reopen as part of its overall effort to create the impression that the pandemic was under control. The effect was to erode confidence in the intentions of the administration.[38]

Reflecting on the policies of successive administrations will allow students to see that federalism is an important theme in education. Students may be able to draw on what they have learned in the political science curriculum to classify cooperative, competitive, and coercive approaches to federal-state relations.[39] Students will certainly need to come to a conclusion about the effects of free-market approaches to education reform. They might engage the documentaries by Bob Bowden and Davis Guggenheim (referenced above), which been controversial because they have endorsed conservative views about the causes of, and solutions to, problems in public education. In particular, they have suggested that teachers' unions and tenure systems are an obstacle to improving education standards, and that fostering greater parental choice in public education—through the use of school vouchers and increasing numbers of charter schools—can address the failure of urban schools. Instructors could ask students to evaluate the claims made in these documentaries either through presentations or in a formal debate. To do so they can draw on the writings of critics such as Diane Ravitch, who has argued that despite these successive attempts at reform, there has been little appreciable improvement in educational outcomes, and state legislatures continue to spend billions of tax dollars to fund separate, unfair, and unequal systems of public education.[40] Kimberly Jenkins Robinson has argued that to achieve better outcomes, federalism in education policy must be restructured to reflect the policymaking strengths of each level of government while ensuring that all levels of government aim to achieve equitable access to an excellent education.[41]

Education and the Culture Wars

It should be evident from the previous two sections that concerns about the role of education in national decline and the dynamics of the federal-state relationship in education have a history that predates the Reagan government by several decades. By contrast, the cultural conflict over education in the United States has antecedents that stretch back well into the nineteenth century, which saw struggles over the moral dimensions of public education and antipathy between Protestants and Catholics.[42] This battle in the culture wars did not subside during the period between the Reagan and Trump administrations. The reason for this is easy to discern, as James Davison Hunter has commented:

> The education of the public at every level—from elementary school through college—is not a neutral process of imparting practical knowledge and technical skills. Above and beyond that, schools are the primary institutional means of *reproducing community and national identity* for succeeding generations of Americans. This is where we first learn and where we are continually reminded with others of our generation— through courses in history, geography, civics, literature, and the like— what it means to be an American. Thus, when the meaning of our identity as Americans is contested, as it is in the contemporary culture war, the conflict will inevitably reach the institutions that impart these collective understandings to children and young adults.[43]

Students are very well placed to engage with the controversies over education and national identity because they can draw on their own experiences to reflect on how they have been taught and how this intersects with other influences on their views including family, peer groups, churches and community groups, political institutions, and the media. However, instructors will need to emphasize that this does not obviate the need for careful research on controversial topics such as the secularization of education and the teaching of history in a multicultural society.

James Fraser has noted that that multiculturalism became a central focus of the discourse on education during the late twentieth century, addressing questions such as

- How can schools attract and reflect increasing diversity in their student bodies?
- How can schools celebrate the contributions to American culture that many different ethnic groups have made?
- How can schools counter discrimination by race, class, or gender that has so long been a part of the American story? [44]

This multicultural approach has provoked fierce debates, with some conservatives pushing back against the desirability of multicultural education. Fraser suggests that in order to explore differing perspectives readers should read works by Sonia Nieto and Arthur M. Schlesinger Jr.[45] Samuel Huntington's book on US national identity is another controversial source that can be read alongside Schlesinger.[46]

Students will likely become quite animated if they are asked to evaluate President Trump's statements about US history and national identity. Trump issued his "Executive Order on Combating Race and Sex Stereotyping" on September 22, 2020.[47] The order pushes back against "the pernicious and false belief that America is an irredeemably racist and sexist country; that some people, simply on account of their race or sex, are oppressors; and that racial and sexual identities are more important than our common status as human beings and Americans." The order also prohibited federal entities from suggesting through diversity training that the United States is "fundamentally racist or sexist." Some confusion followed as to whether this order applied to educational institutions in receipt of federal funds. The order was part of the Trump administration's broader assault on critical race theory, exemplified by the White House Conference on American History.

Referring to the *New York Times'* Pulitzer Prize–winning 1619 Project, Trump warned that "students in our universities are inundated with critical race theory. This is a Marxist doctrine holding that America is a wicked and racist nation, that even young children are complicit in oppression, and that our entire society must be radically transformed. Critical race theory is being forced into our children's schools, it is being imposed into workplace trainings, and it's being deployed to rip apart friends, neighbors and families."[48] Such statements were clearly hyperbolic and a product of the heated political environment in which they were being tossed around, but they offer a superb opportunity for students to see how US history is often misused.[49]

159

Another dimension to the culture wars in US education is the secularization of schools. A possible starting point for exploring this would be the landmark 1962 Supreme Court decision in the case of *Engel v. Vitale*. A decade earlier, the New York State Board of Regents wrote a nondenominational prayer to be used in some school districts at the start of each school day. The justices ruled (with only one dissenting vote) that this violated the First Amendment prohibition of government-established religion. The following year the Supreme Court extended its ruling in *Abington School District v. Schempp*, stating that reciting the Lord's Prayer or reading Bible verses in classrooms was also unconstitutional.[50] Bill Bright, the founder of Campus Crusade for Christ, declared the 1963 ruling "the darkest hour in the history of the nation."[51] The liberalism of the Supreme Court alarmed many evangelical Christians, who were spurred into challenging the teaching of evolution and sex education, and other aspects of "secular humanism."[52] Students can be invited to explore the role of religion in the culture wars as they pertain to education through the many battles that have been fought over curricula, the content of school textbooks, and the status of religious schools. These issues can be evaluated through the framework of core democratic values, which enables students to see that balancing rights in a pluralist society is no easy task.

Conclusions

This chapter has posited three key points for educators and their students about the study of US education policy. First, it is clear that external and domestic considerations drive reform attempts. This was true throughout the Cold War and more recently as the United States has become increasingly concerned about the rise of China. Second, the US Constitution limits the ability of the federal government to reform education, which has been evidenced by the federal government's inability during the last four decades to narrow gaps in educational attainment and skill levels between more advantaged and less advantaged students. Finally, it is abundantly clear that education debates demonstrate the political and social fractures in the United States, which makes democracy in the United States more fragile. The consequence is that the United States can still be considered a "nation at risk."

Lesson Plan

This lesson invites students to debate the merits of a recent legislative proposal to restrict federal funding to states that seek to incorporate the 1619 Project into their curriculum. Instructors should recognize that the Saving American History Act of 2021, which was initially introduced into the US Senate in July 2020 and reintroduced in June 2021, is controversial and will be sensitive for many students. The intention of this lesson is that students should evaluate *both sides* of the debate and reflect on their own thinking.

Outcome and Objective

- SLO 4: Students will be able to evaluate the effects of the culture wars on US education policy.
  - EO 4a: Students will be able to analyze the controversy over history and national identity.

Establishing the Terms of the Debate

The Motion is the subject of the debate. In this case the language is taken directly from the Saving American History Act of 2021: "Proposed: A Bill to prohibit Federal funds from being made available to teach the 1619 Project curriculum in elementary schools and secondary schools, and for other purposes."

Preparation

To ensure the success of a debate, preparation is essential for *all students*, not just those who are assigned to the debate teams. Instructors may use an online discussion forum in the weeks prior to the debate, which will allow students to engage the academic materials listed below and rehearse their arguments and counterarguments. Instructors should press students to clarify their thinking and avoid logical fallacies that are often characteristic of uninformed opinions. Instructors should chair the debate. They should take care to establish the rules ahead of time and emphasize the need for civility.

The Teams

It is the job of the Proposition to speak in favor of the Motion. The Opposition will speak against it. It is usual to have two or three speakers on each side. The first Proposition speaker (1st Prop.) will open the debate. It is their job to

1. Define the Motion;
2. Outline the Proposition case (a good team will have planned out the argument in advance and divided the material appropriately);
3. Begin to develop the case.

The first Opposition speaker (1st Opp.) then responds to the 1st Prop. It is their job to

1. Rebut (attack) any weak points in the 1st. Prop. case;
2. Outline the Opposition case (a good team will have anticipated the Proposition arguments in advance and divided the rebuttal material appropriately);
3. Begin to develop the case.

The second Proposition speaker (2nd Prop.) then responds to the 1st Opp. It is their job to

1. Rebut any weak points in the 1st. Opp. case;
2. Restate the Prop. case;
3. Continue to develop the case.

The second Opposition speaker (2nd Opp.) then responds to the 2nd Prop. It is their job to

1. Rebut (attack) any weak points in the 2nd Opp. case;
2. Restate the Opp. case;
3. Continue to develop the case.

Floor Debate

A Floor Debate may follow. Speakers from the Floor (all students who are not assigned to the Proposition or Opposition) have the opportunity to contribute to the debate by putting a difficult question to the speakers, or they may give their opinions when invited to do so by the Chair.

Summary Speeches

It is usual for the Opposition team to summarize first. The speaker should

1. Respond to some (but not too many) issues raised by the Floor;
2. Outline the main areas of disagreement between the two sides;
3. Give reasons why the Opposition has won the debate.

The Proposition will conclude the debate. The speaker should

1. Respond to some (but not too many) issues raised by the Floor;
2. Outline the main areas of disagreement between the two sides;
3. Give reasons why the Proposition has won the debate.

Concluding the Debate

The debate should conclude with a vote in order to determine which side has prevailed. This could be achieved through a simple show of hands, but in order to preserve anonymity and to make the experience more authentic, instructors may wish to set up an electronic poll that students can access via a smart device.

Consolidation

After the debate students could write an essay about the controversy over history and national identity or about how the 1619 Project demonstrates the nature of historical interpretation. Alternatively, students could write a critical reflection on what they have learned as a result of the debate. This type of exercise is particularly valuable because it allows students to reflect on what they already knew (or thought they knew) about US history, how their knowledge has changed, and why history is important to their identity. Instructors should provide a scaffold for critical reflection in order to guide students through the process of metacognition.

NOTES

1. See, for example, Pillarisetti Sudhir, ed., "Controversy in the Classroom: A Matter for Debate," *Perspectives on History* 48, no. 5 (May 2010), https://www.historians.org/publications-and-directories/perspectives-on-history/may-2010/controversy-in-the-classroom-a-matter-for-debate.

2. Sarah Philpott et al., "Controversial Issues: To Teach, or Not to Teach? That Is the Question!" *Georgia Social Studies Journal* 1, no. 1 (Spring 2011): 32–44.

3. Grant P. Wiggins and Jay McTighe, *Understanding by Design*, 2nd ed. (Alexandria, VA: Association for Supervision and Curriculum Development, 2005).

4. Benjamin S. Bloom, *Taxonomy of Educational Objectives: The Classification of Educational Goals* (New York: David McKay, 1965); Lorin W. Anderson and David R. Krathwohl, eds., *A Taxonomy for Learning, Teaching, and Assessing: A Revision of Bloom's Taxonomy of Educational Objectives* (New York: Addison Wesley Longman, 2001). Sam Wineburg has challenged the utility of Bloom's Taxonomy in the history classroom. Teachers will be familiar with the pyramid that is used to represent Bloom's Taxonomy, in which knowledge provides the base for students to ascend through comprehension, application, analysis, synthesis, and evaluation. Wineburg contends that in historical thinking this pyramid should be inverted, because historians have to evaluate what they do not know in order to constantly piece together a more accurate story about the past. He observes that the sourcing heuristic used by professional historians when they approach evidence analytically leads to the creation of new knowledge. See Sam Wineburg, *Why Learn History (When It's Already on Your Phone)* (Chicago: University of Chicago Press, 2018), ch. 4. There is some merit in Wineburg's observations, but it might also be suggested that in order to more accurately capture the dynamic nature of historical inquiry Bloom's Taxonomy should not be conceptualized as a pyramid but as a *cycle*.

5. Joshua B. Freedman, *American Empire: The Rise of a Global Power, the Democratic Revolution at Home* (New York: Viking, 2012); James T. Patterson, *Grand Expectations: The United States, 1945–1974* (New York: Oxford University Press, 1996); James T. Patterson, *Restless Giant: The United States from Watergate to "Bush v. Gore"* (New York: Oxford University Press, 2005); David Reynolds, *America, Empire of Liberty: A New History of the United States* (New York: Basic Books, 2009).

6. David J. Roof, "Mapping Knowledge: A Survey of U.S. Educational Historiography," *Critical Questions in Education* 6, no. 2 (2015): 55–74, https://files.eric.ed.gov/fulltext/EJ1065824.pdf; Christopher M. Span, "History of Education in the United States," 2013, *Oxford Bibliographies*, https://www.oxfordbibliographies.com/view/document/obo-9780199756810/obo-9780199756810-0013.xml.

7. James W. Fraser, *The School in the United States: A Documentary History*, 3rd ed. (New York: Routledge, 2014).

8. Bob Bowdon, *The Cartel* (Bowdon Media/Moving Picture Institute, 2009); Davis Guggenheim, *Waiting for "Superman"* (Walden Media, 2010).

9. Freedman, *American Empire*, 165–66, 188; Fraser, *School in the United States*, 242–48; Derek Leebaert, *The Fifty-Year Wound: The True Price of America's Cold War Victory* (Boston: Little, Brown, 2002), 219; Reynolds, *America, Empire of Liberty*, 331–32.

10. Freedman, *American Empire*, 188–89.

11. Fraser, *School in the United States*, 252–55.

12. Leebaert, *Fifty-Year Wound*, 219.

13. Freedman, *American Empire*, 166; Patterson, *Grand Expectations*, 421; Reynolds, *America, Empire of Liberty*, 331.

14. Patricia Albjerg Graham, *Schooling America: How the Public Schools Meet the Nation's Changing Needs* (New York: Oxford University Press, 2005), 108.

15. Fraser, *School in the United States*, 302, 308–11; Patterson, *Restless Giant*, 34–35.

16. Fraser, *School in the United States*, 302, 308–11; Patterson, *Restless Giant*, 34; Diane Ravitch, *The Troubled Crusade: American Education, 1945–1980* (New York: Basic Books, 1983), ch. 7.

17. Patterson, *Restless Giant*, 33–34.

18. Fraser, *School in the United States*, 333. For the full text of the report, see https://edreform.com/wp-content/uploads/2013/02/A_Nation_At_Risk_1983.pdf.

19. Gerald A. Dorfman and Paul R. Hanna, "Can Education Be Reformed?," in *Thinking about America: The United States in the 1990s*, ed. Annelise Anderson and Denis L. Bark (Stanford, CA: Hoover Institution Press, 1988), 383–90.

20. Maris A. Vinovskis, *From "A Nation at Risk" to "No Child Left Behind": National Education Goals and the Creation of Federal Education Policy* (New York: Teachers College Press, 2009).

21. Jonathan Rothwell, "The Declining Productivity of Education," Brookings Institute, December 23, 2016, https://www.brookings.edu/blog/social-mobility-memos/2016/12/23/the-declining-productivity-of-education/.

22. Michael Leachman, Kathleen Masterson, and Eric Figueroa, "A Punishing Decade for School Funding," Center on Budget and Policy Priorities, November 29, 2017, https://www.cbpp.org/research/state-budget-and-tax/a-punishing-decade-for-school-funding.

23. Donna Cooper, Adam Hersh, and Ann O'Leary, *The Competition That Really Matters: Comparing U.S., Chinese, and Indian Investments in the Next-Generation Workforce* (Washington, DC: Center for American Progress and the Center for the Next Generation, 2012), https://www.americanprogress.org/wp-content/uploads/2012/08/USChinaIndiaEduCompetitiveness.pdf.

24. Dorfman and Hanna, "Can Education Be Reformed?," 383.

25. *National Geographic–Roper Public Affairs 2006 Geographic Literacy Survey*, https://media.nationalgeographic.org/assets/file/Roper-Poll-2006-Highlights.pdf.

26. Linda J. Bilmes and Joseph Stiglitz, *The Three Trillion Dollar War: The True Cost of the Iraq Conflict* (New York: W. W. Norton, 2008); "Costs of War: Economic Costs," Watson Institute for International and Public Affairs, page updated September 2021, http://watson.brown.edu/costsofwar/costs/economic.

27. Fraser, *School in the United States*, 270–71, 277–80; Freedman, *American Empire*, 148–52; Patterson, *Grand Expectations*, 388–99, 411–16; Ravitch, *Troubled Crusade*, ch. 4; Reynolds, *America: Empire of Liberty*, 336–40.

28. Patterson, *Restless Giant*, 35–36; Fraser, *School in the United States*, ch. 11.

29. Patterson, *Restless Giant*, 238–40; Valerie Strauss and Jack Schneider, "How President George H. W. Bush Helped Pave the Way for Education Secretary Betsy DeVos," *Washington Post*, December 4, 2018, https://www.washington post.com/education/2018/12/04/how-president-george-hw-bush-helped-pave -way-education-secretary-betsy-devos/.

30. See "America 2000: An Education Strategy, Report No. ED/oS91–13," Department of Education, May 1991, https://eric.ed.gov/?id=ED327985.

31. See James B. Stedman, "Goals 2000: Overview and Analysis," Congressional Research Service Report CRS 94–490-EPW, June 3, 1994, https://files.eric .ed.gov/fulltext/ED359637.pdf.

32. "No Child Left Behind: A Desktop Reference," Department of Education, 2002, https://eric.ed.gov/?id=ED471334.

33. Patterson, *Restless Giant*, 240; Fraser, *School in the United States*, ch. 13; Vinovskis, *From "A Nation at Risk."*

34. "Race to the Top: Executive Summary," US Department of Education, November 2009, https://eric.ed.gov/?id=ED557422.

35. See "Every Student Succeeds Act (ESSA)," US Department of Education, https://www.ed.gov/essa?src=rn.

36. Frederick M. Hess, "The Real Obama Education Legacy," *National Affairs*, September 2015, https://www.nationalaffairs.com/publications/detail/the-real -obama-education-legacy; Doug Lederman and Paul Fain, "The Higher Education President," *Inside Higher Ed*, January 19, 2017, https://www.insidehighered .com/news/2017/01/19/assessing-president-obamas-far-reaching-impact-high er-education.

37. Cory Turner, "How Education Secretary Betsy DeVos Will Be Remembered," National Public Radio, November 19, 2020, https://www.npr.org/2020/ 11/19/936225974/the-legacy-of-education-secretary-betsy-devos.

38. Laurie Garrett, "America's Schools Are a Moral and Medical Catastrophe," *Foreign Policy*, July 24, 2020, https://foreignpolicy.com/2020/07/24/ameri cas-schools-are-a-moral-and-medical-catastrophe/; Erica L. Green, "DeVos Abandons a Lifetime of Local Advocacy to Demand Schools Reopen," *New York Times*, July 13, 2020, https://www.nytimes.com/2020/07/13/us/politics/betsy-de vos-schools-coronavirus.html; Laura Meckler, Michael Sherer, and Josh Dawsey, "Trump Trains His Eyes on Education as He Hunts Path to Victory," *Washington*

Post, July 23, 2020, https://www.washingtonpost.com/local/education/trump
-trains-his-eyes-on-education-as-he-hunts-path-to-victory/2020/07/22/4bc3c9f6
-c835-11ea-8ffe-372be8d82298_story.html.

39. Joseph R. Marbach, Ellis Katz, and Troy E. Smith, eds., *Federalism: An Encyclopedia*, 2 vols. (Westport, CT: Greenwood Press, 2005), https://encyclope dia.federalism.org/index.php?title=Federalism_in_America:_An_Encyclopedia &oldid=1702.

40. Diane Ravitch, *The Death and Life of the Great American School System: How Testing and Choice Are Undermining Education*, 3rd ed. (New York: Basic Books, 2016); Diane Ravitch, *Reign of Error: The Hoax of the Privatization Movement and the Danger to America's Public Schools* (New York: Knopf, 2013); Diane Ravitch, *Slaying Goliath: The Passionate Resistance to Privatization and the Fight to Save America's Schools* (New York: Knopf, 2020).

41. Kimberly Jenkins Robinson, "The High Cost of the Nation's Current Framework for Education Federalism," *Wake Forest Law Review* 48 (2013): 287– 331; Kimberly Jenkins Robinson, "Education Federalism: Why It Matters and How the United States Should Restructure It," in *The Oxford Handbook of U.S. Education Law*, ed. Kristin L. Bowman (Oxford: Oxford University Press, 2020), https://www.oxfordhandbooks.com/view/10.1093/oxfordhb/9780190697402 .001.0001/oxfordhb-9780190697402-e-8.

42. James Davison Hunter, *Culture Wars: The Struggle to Define America* (New York: Basic Books, 1991), 198–201.

43. Ibid., 198.

44. Fraser, *School in the United States*, 332.

45. Sonia Nieto, *Affirming Diversity: The Sociopolitical Context of Multicultural Education*, 6th ed. (New York: Pearson, 2019); Arthur M. Schlesinger Jr., *The Disuniting of America: Reflections on a Multicultural Society*, rev. ed. (New York: W. W. Norton, 1998); Fraser, *School in the United States*, 344–54.

46. Samuel P. Huntington, *Who Are We? The Challenges to America's National Identity* (New York: Simon and Schuster, 2004).

47. "Executive Order on Combating Race and Sex Stereotyping," White House, September 22, 2020, https://trumpwhitehouse.archives.gov/presidential -actions/executive-order-combating-race-sex-stereotyping/.

48. Colleen Flaherty, "Diversity Work, Interrupted," *Inside Higher Ed*, October 7, 2020, https://www.insidehighered.com/news/2020/10/07/colleges-cancel -diversity-programs-response-trump-order; Olivia B. Waxman, "Echoing Decades of Fighting over U.S. History Classrooms, President Trump Announces a Push for 'Patriotic Education,'" *Time*, September 17, 2020, https://time.com/588 9907/trump-patriotic-education/.

49. Students should be encouraged to read James W. Loewen, *Lies My Teacher Told Me: Everything Your American History Textbook Got Wrong* (New York: New

Press, 2018); and Loewen, *Teaching What Really Happened: How to Avoid the Tyranny of Textbooks and Get Students Excited about Doing History*, 2nd ed. (New York: Teachers College Press, 2018).

50. Fraser, *School in the United States*, 302, 305–7; Freeman, *American Empire*, 198.

51. Hunter, *Culture Wars*, 203.

52. Hunter, *Culture Wars*, 203–5; Patterson, *Restless Giant*, 136–37.

FOR FURTHER READING

DEBATES

Bailey, J., and G. Molyneaux. *The Oxford Union Guide to Schools' Debating*. Oxford: Oxford Union Society, 2005. https://outspokenela.files.wordpress.com/2017/02/the-oxford-union-guide-to-schools-debating-copy.pdf.

English-Speaking Union. "Debate Formats." https://www.esu.org/debate-formats/.

National Speech and Debate Association. https://www.speechanddebate.org/.

THE 1619 PROJECT

116th Congress. "Saving American History Act of 2020." https://www.blackburn.senate.gov/services/files/254B1925-6B7C-4B06-8BC6-A1F59CCB0B6C.

"The 1619 Project." *New York Times Magazine*, August 14, 2019. https://www.nytimes.com/interactive/2019/08/14/magazine/1619-america-slavery.html.

Ellison, S. "How the 1619 Project Took Over 2020." *Washington Post*, October 13, 2020, https://www.washingtonpost.com/lifestyle/style/1619-project-took-over-2020-inside-story/2020/10/13/af537092-00df-11eb-897d-3a6201d6643f_story.html.

Fleming-Hunter, S. "Project 1619 Revisited: Black Children, Racism, and Reparations." *Phylon*, 57, no. 1 (Summer 2020): 76–93.

Forman, S. "The 1619 Project: Believe Your Lying Eyes." *Academic Questions* 33, no. 2 (June 2020): 299–306.

Gasman, M. "What History Professors Really Think about 'The 1619 Project.'" *Forbes*, June 3, 2021. https://www.forbes.com/sites/marybethgasman/2021/06/03/what-history-professors-really-think-about-the-1619-project/?sh=343656b37a15.

Harris, L. M. "I Helped Fact-Check the 1619 Project: *The Times* Ignored Me." *Politico*, March 6, 2020. https://www.politico.com/news/magazine/2020/03/06/1619-project-new-york-times-mistake-122248.

Morel, L. E. "A Review of the 1619 Project Curriculum: The Heritage Foundation Backgrounder #3570." December 15, 2020. https://files.eric.ed.gov/fulltext/ED612928.pdf.

RealClear Public Affairs. "Engaging the 1619 Project." https://www.realclear publicaffairs.com/public_affairs/american_civics/1619_project/.

Riley, N. S. "'The 1619 Project' Enters America's Classrooms." *Education Next* 20, no. 4 (Fall 2020). https://www.educationnext.org/1619-project-enters-amer ican-classrooms-adding-new-sizzle-slavery-significant-cost/.

Sandefur, T. "The 1619 Project: An Autopsy." October 27, 2020. Cato Institute. https://www.cato.org/commentary/1619-project-autopsy.

Serwer, A. "The Fight over the 1619 Project Is Not about the Facts." *Atlantic,* December 23, 2019. https://www.theatlantic.com/ideas/archive/2019/12/his torians-clash-1619-project/604093/.

Singer, A. J. "Defending the 1619 Project in the Context of History Education Today." December 12, 2020. History News Network. https://historynewsnet work.org/article/178586.

PART TWO

Beyond the Borders of the United States

Undermining the Sandbags

How Neoliberalism Encouraged Undocumented Migration from the 1980s to the Early 2020s

BENJAMIN C. MONTOYA

> The forces of globalization often seem to roar through the atmosphere like the jet stream. They are powerful but abstract and hard to see well from the ground.
> DAVID FITZGERALD, *A NATION OF MIGRANTS: HOW MEXICO MANAGES ITS MIGRATION*

Why Teach This Lesson?

As a student of history you have been asked to consider how the United States has developed and changed over time. Immigration is a central historical force that has defined the nation civically and racially; as such, it is a topic that will likely interest you. Even as citizens disagree about the perceived political benefits and costs of immigration, the nation's economic development is indelibly tied to the movement of people into the United States. This lesson will help you understand the complicated relationship between immigration and economics in the recent history of the United States. Economic globalization, which seeks to eliminate trade barriers in order to lower consumer prices and to expand foreign investment opportunities, paved the way for increased immigration, much of it undocumented (often derisively called "illegal"). United States immigration law and border enforcement hardened during this period to confront what was increasingly

173

considered the national security threat of undocumented Mexican migration. Additionally, this lesson will help you develop the analytical skill of historical empathy by asking you to examine primary sources created by Mexican migrants and their families. Such analysis will illuminate the hardships that Mexicans face when they and their loved ones choose to migrate to the United States.

Introduction

Following World War II, the United States led the effort to lower barriers to trade in order to create an international system (called "liberal internationalism") that would benefit the United States, help create a set of capitalist economies that would successfully compete against the Communist/socialist economies of the Cold War, and presumably help those countries emerging from colonization and other underdeveloped countries to attain the level of development modeled by the United States and Western Europe. However, economic difficulties in the 1970s led the United States to try to greatly reduce—if not eliminate—Mexican migration across the border that had helped both nations' economies in the previous decades. In other words, US policymakers sought to diminish the migration of labor while enhancing the free movement of goods, as exemplified by the North American Free Trade Agreement (NAFTA). Historians and economists have termed this policy "neoliberalism," and it has had profound effects on both the Mexican and American economies and peoples that continue to reverberate to this day.

Xenophobia and New Laws Make Mexican Migrants "Illegal" in the 1980s

The economic challenges of the 1970s—double-digit inflation, rising gas prices, and plummeting US economic competitiveness—led American policymakers to double down on neoliberal reforms and globalization at the same time that they codified new immigration laws between the 1980s and 1990s that effectively marginalized undocumented Mexican migrants. For example, President Ronald Reagan (1981–89) signed into law the Immigration Reform and Control Act (IRCA) in November 1986. It sought to penalize and fine employers who knowingly hired undocumented workers and stated that aliens who had resided in the United States since 1982 could apply for legal status ("amnesty").[1]

The IRCA did not solve the problem of undocumented migration for several reasons. First, paradoxically, employers were shielded from legal consequences of hiring undocumented workers as long as they filled out and kept on file the routine I-9 employee verification form. The burden of proving the veracity of the information on the I-9 form did not fall upon the employer but was rather placed on the migrant workers themselves, who faced greater risks such as workplace raids by the Immigration and Naturalization Service (INS).[2] Related to this, the law stimulated the production of false identification documents for those who sought to meet the growing need within the US economy for migrant workers.[3] Ancillary to these design flaws was the lack of enthusiasm for enforcement by federal officials who found that the IRCA had transformed their primary job from immigration regulation to immigration reduction.[4] The new law seemed to work in the short term, as the rate of undocumented migration to the United States slowed during the late 1980s. By the early 1990s, however, these rates were back to levels witnessed *before* passage of the IRCA.[5]

The IRCA's ignominious legacy was to exacerbate the undocumented Mexican migration issue by ending the flexibility of circular migration that had served the interests of the US and Mexican governments and economies for decades. Historically, Mexican migrants (documented and undocumented) had worked seasonally in the United States and returned to Mexico. Consequently, the permanent Mexican immigrant population in the United States was relatively low compared to other immigrant groups. Much of this had to do with ease of return to Mexico for migrants. But the IRCA's criminalization of undocumented migration ended this mutually beneficial system of circular migration. Not coincidentally, the permanent population of Mexican *immigrants* (no longer migrants) in the United States grew after passage of the IRCA. Before 1986 roughly 45 percent of Mexicans returned to Mexico; by the early 2000s that return rate was down to 25 percent. As a result, from 1980 to 1995, the population of Mexicans in the United States tripled. It increased by another 30 percent in just five years between 1997 and 2002, from 7 million to 10 million.[6]

Border enforcement measures became more stringent during the late 1980s and early 1990s as the permanent population of Mexican immigrants in the United States grew and as the rate of undocumented

Mexican migration to the United States persisted.[7] Notable examples of such efforts were the grand sweeps of "illegals" by US Border Patrol agents in areas along border regions. "Operation Hold the Line" of September 1993 saw 450 Border Patrol agents sweep a twenty-mile area of the border around El Paso, Texas. Similar sweep operations took place in the San Diego area in 1994 ("Operation Gatekeeper") and along the Arizona-Mexico borderland in 1996 ("Operation Safeguard"). These actions were successful in reducing unauthorized border crossings, but only in the short term. The limits of this "Maginot-Line strategy" soon became clear: suppressing the flow of illegal border crossings in one area simply directed it elsewhere, often to more remote and dangerous parts of border regions.[8] The proportion of migrants passing through nontraditional areas doubled during the 1990s in response to enhanced border sweep operations by the Border Patrol. Customarily, migrants would enter the United States through high-volume passageways such as those that connected Tijuana and San Diego or Ciudad Juárez and El Paso. Starting in the late 1980s, however, migrants increasingly traveled through sparsely populated, arid regions of the border in the wake of the IRCA and especially in response to border sweep operations. Consequently, a growing number of migrants died while attempting to enter the United States. The number of migrant fatalities was negligible before 1986; by contrast, nearly five hundred migrants were dying annually in the early 2000s.[9] Migrant fatalities are usually attributable to exposure.[10] The "illegalization" of Mexican migrants in US society and the lethality of border crossing between the mid-1980s and the mid-1990s have been the ultimate effect of immigration laws and enforcement practices that criminalize undocumented migrants and marginalize their traditional migration pathways.

NAFTA and Border Sweeps during the Clinton Administration

The North American Free Trade Agreement (NAFTA) of 1994 was a culmination of neoliberal efforts to expand trade and investment. For US leaders, heady with the success of the liberal-democratic model that the end of the Cold War seemed to highlight, NAFTA represented an attempt to achieve financial hegemony throughout the Western Hemisphere. While the principle of globalization relies on the free movement of capital, information, and people, architects of NAFTA believed they could construct a trade agreement that would curb, not abet, Mexican migration to the United States. American leaders hoped they could keep out Mexican laborers as they relaxed barriers to trade.[11]

There has been a great deal of scholarly and public debate about NAFTA's successes and failures. NAFTA has been unquestionably successful in expanding North American trade: a 400 percent increase in intraregional trade, from $290 billion in 1993 to $1.1 trillion in 2012. Roughly $1 *billion* worth of goods and services cross the US-Mexico border *daily*. Mexico is the second largest export market of the United States. Production chains between Canada, Mexico, and the United States have become intertwined, basically meaning that assembly and production costs are shared and profits enjoyed in all three countries. Cross-border investment has grown rapidly, which has led to job growth in all three countries. NAFTA has even been credited with a boom in tourism, which for Mexico has resulted in billions of tourist dollars. On the face of it, NAFTA has succeeded in making Mexico a more modern nation.[12]

Underneath the superficial layer, beyond the broad, macroeconomic measures, however, NAFTA has placed Mexico and especially poor Mexicans in a perilous state. Per capita income growth has just barely doubled over the past twenty years, rising in 2014 dollar terms from $4,500 (1994) to $9,700 (2012), or an average yearly rate of just 1.2 percent. That is below per capita rates of other major Latin American countries. And while intraregional trade has risen, that has not resulted in job growth within Mexico. Production at the border maquilas (manufacturing plants where workers *assemble* durable goods such as automobiles with premade parts in border towns) is stagnant, resulting in the creation of relatively few *new* jobs. Maquilas were created to tamp down on Mexican migration to the United States. If more jobs were created in Mexico, it was believed, then Mexicans would have less need to go to the United States for work. It did not work out that way. In fact, maquilas destabilized the Mexican economy and made Mexico even more economically dependent on the United States than it already was. Mexico became a "direct appendage" of US manufacturing.[13] Between 1994 and 2014 the maquila industry created just 700,000 jobs, as 20 *million* Mexicans entered the job market during those same twenty years.[14] Because maquilas are not *production* sites where parts and technology are created and innovated, it helps explain why Mexican wages are stagnant, especially when compared to US wages, which are much higher.[15] Whereas the dramatic increase in trade because of NAFTA created 23 million US jobs between 1994 and 2008, Mexican jobs have fallen victim to the forces of globalization—to the very economic phenomenon that created them in the first place. One estimate shows that 30 percent of maquila jobs have been lost since the 1990s, as US assembly subsidiaries have moved to nations in Asia where wages are even lower.[16] In this sense, Mexico is going through a simultaneous process of *underdevelopment* and *deindustrialization*: the establishment of subsidiary, US-owned, export-oriented assembly plants in Mexico has undermined the growth of entrepreneurial enterprises among native industries, while the stagnation and decline in manufacturing employment is showing the limits of maquila-led industrialization. Instead of working to modernize the Mexican economy, globalizing industrialization has only continued Mexico's dependence upon larger, developed economies such as the United States.[17]

NAFTA and neoliberalism have made Mexico and Mexicans more vulnerable to the disruptive influences of globalization, which is especially evident in Mexico's agricultural sector. As Mexico entered the free-trade agreements, Mexican farmers were fully exposed to the harsh realities of globalizing free-trade competition. They were no match for the productivity and automation of commercialized agriculture in the United States. Such free-trade competition displaced many Mexican farmers, as their products could not compete on the global market or even in many domestic markets. This inability to survive in a globalizing, transnational marketplace made it increasingly difficult for Mexicans to stay on their farms and led many to migrate northward to scratch out livings as a "nomadic mass of migrant workers."[18]

This further explains why the number of Mexican nationals entering the United States has jumped during the twenty years since the creation of NAFTA, from 6.2 million in 1994 to 12 million in 2013. Over 2 million Mexican workers lost their jobs just between 1994 and 1996. In short, not only has NAFTA failed in its goal of ending Mexican migration to the United States by creating more jobs in Mexico, but it has actually exacerbated the migration issue by ruining Mexico's agricultural economy and displacing its citizens.[19]

New Laws in the Mid-1990s Further Marginalize Mexican Migrants

Fifteen million Latino and Asian immigrants entered the United States between 1980 and 1995. About one-third of legal immigrants and about one-half of undocumented migrants went to California, where, during these same years, economic recession led to federal and state cuts to welfare, education, and social services. This combination of economic insecurity and racial anxiety culminated in Californians' passage of Proposition 187 (Prop 187) in November 1994.[20] It was designed to prevent undocumented immigrants living in the state from accessing a variety of publicly funded social services, including health care and education.[21] The measure helped to redefine the illegality of Mexican immigrants by claiming that the people of California were "suffering" economic hardship and higher rates of crime because of the presence of illegal aliens.[22] By describing illegal aliens as threats to California, Prop 187 was both the result of and the cause of nativist rhetoric that had increasingly criminalized the act of undocumented migration in the years following passage of the IRCA in 1986. A foreign national in the United States was not simply illegal, they were a threat—both to society and individual citizens. The development of such "alien terminology" helped to rationalize the harsh treatment of Mexican immigrants.[23]

Prop 187 was ultimately struck down by a US District Court in California in late 1995, just a year after California voters passed it. Yet its social and legal legacy was immediately apparent as a Republican-controlled US Congress in turn passed a slew of legislation in 1996 that reflected the same fear and xenophobia of Prop 187. Within this batch of laws was, first, the Personal Responsibility and Work Opportunity Reconciliation Act (nicknamed the "welfare reform bill"), passed on August 22, 1996, which dramatically scaled back legal immigrants' access to publicly funded social services, such as Medicaid and food stamps, and devolved authority over select welfare services to states by ending the Aid to Families with Dependent Children, which was a program founded in 1935 that offered cash assistance to low-income families.[24] Second, and most important, was the Illegal Immigration Reform and Immigrant Responsibility Act (IIRIRA), passed on September 30, 1996, which made it harder for undocumented immigrants to adjust their status to that of a legal immigrant while simultaneously making it much easier for these undocumented immigrants—including minors and children—to be apprehended and deported. Now local and state police could be trained to enforce federal immigration law, more offenses were deemed deportable, it was easier to deport criminals, and deportation decisions were made by immigration courts with straitened judicial review procedures.[25]

A notable difference between the IIRIRA of 1996 and the IRCA of 1986 was that the new act, which significantly increased criminal penalties on undocumented immigrants, did nothing to penalize US employers of undocumented workers. Also, the 1996 law dramatically strengthened the US government's ability to apprehend and deport undocumented migrants at the border and from the nation's interior. In this sense, the IIRIRA deterritorialized the US-Mexican border: not just as they tried to enter the United States but even after they did so, undocumented immigrants were always illegal in the eyes of the law and were subsequently liable to be deported.[26] Not coincidentally, since passage of the IIRIRA, the number of mass worksite raids—think of them as interior versions of border sweeps—expanded markedly as did the number of nonviolent, noncriminal immigrants arrested (and families separated) for immigration violations. The persistent legacy of the IIRIRA has been "a series of ever-expanding efforts to deter illegal immigration through higher penalties and fewer options."[27]

Post-9/11 Focus on Securing and Deterritorializing Borders

Public fear and anxiety about Mexican immigration receded a bit during the late 1990s, as the United States enjoyed robust economic growth with low unemployment rates and significant job growth. Suddenly immigrant labor was in high demand.[28] There was even a moment, during the first year of the administration of George W. Bush (2001–9), when the US and Mexican governments attempted comprehensive immigration reform that included a temporary worker program as well as an initiative to legalize undocumented Mexican workers. A booming US economy, which not coincidentally caused an upsurge in undocumented Mexican immigration to the United States, was behind this moment of détente. Whatever progress was made in these negotiations was undermined by the terrorist attacks of September 11, 2001. The subsequent focus for the Bush administration was national security and anti-terrorism laws.[29] The events of 9/11 only heightened nativist fears of Mexican immigrants; therefore, after September 2001, efforts were accelerated to militarize the US-Mexico border as well as to heighten restrictions on immigration.[30] The first step toward this end was the consolidation and centralization of border enforcement agencies into the Department of Homeland Security in November 2002.

The US government broadened its immigration restriction authority beyond the confines of the physical boundaries after 9/11. New regulations between 2002 and 2006 allowed immigration officials to expeditiously return undocumented migrants found within one hundred miles of the border up to fourteen days after their actual crossing.[31] Such processes of "expedited removal" blurred the line between the perimeter and interior of the United States.[32] Increased surveillance was another element of post-9/11 border crossings. The Border Security Act of May 2002 required foreign nationals to have machine-readable passports to enter the United States,[33] and the Real ID Act of May 2005 required state motor vehicle agencies and other institutions responsible for issuing identification documents to verify that license holders were legally authorized to be in the United States.[34] These new methods of mass surveillance were combined with tried-and-true internal enforcement efforts of immigration regulation as the newly created Immigration and Customs Enforcement Agency (ICE), founded in March 2003, conducted sweeping raids looking to deport undocumented immigrants.[35]

The stated purpose of this legislation was to enforce the border security of the United States from terrorist threats. Yet the principal effect of such acts and legislation has been to "terrorize" immigrant workers.[36] Indeed, in the post-9/11 United States, border security was fused with anti-terrorist measures despite the fact that none of the 9/11 terrorists had crossed the US-Mexico border. Nonetheless, since the early 2000s the "illegal alien" has been likened to the foreign terrorist.[37]

Laying the Foundations for a Border Wall, Bush to Trump

Even as the post-9/11 era saw a novel move toward deterritorialized surveillance, concrete, territorially bound measures toward border security were also implemented. The Bush administration signed into law the Secure Fence Act in October 2006, which authorized the construction of 670 miles of reinforced wall along the US-Mexico border. Such an effort to literally block undocumented Mexican migrants from entering the United States was not without precedent. A ten-foot high wall (eventually expanded to fourteen feet) of thin corrugated steel was constructed along seven miles of the border from the ocean inland, between San Diego and Tijuana in 1991. The wall's purpose, like the border sweeps of the early 1990s, was to keep out undocumented migrants and to channel their migration routes through more isolated and dangerous areas. Mexican leaders viewed the wall as an insult and criticized the administration of George H. W. Bush (1989–93) for constructing it while simultaneously trying to economically integrate the United States and Mexico—efforts that were eventually finalized in NAFTA. Additionally, critics of this border wall highlighted the irony between the collapse of the Berlin Wall in November 1989, which effectively represented the end of the Cold War, and the United States building a wall along the border of one its closest—proximately, culturally, economically, historically—neighbors.[38]

While the IIRIRA of 1996 had empowered the US government to construct barriers along other parts of the border, legal hurdles as well as opposition from various domestic groups prevented further border wall construction outside of San Diego up to the early 2000s. However, the Secure Fence Act of 2006, amid a larger US effort to shore up borders in the face of foreign threats, provided a new impetus for border wall construction. By 2009, the first year of the administration of Barack Obama (2009–17), there were over one hundred miles of wall built along the Texas-Mexico border and seventy miles along the Arizona-Mexico border despite opposition from environmental groups, human rights groups, academics, landowners on the border, and Mexican leaders.[39]

The border wall issue was weaponized politically when Donald Trump announced his intention to campaign for the US presidency in 2016. He shocked and awed Americans in July 2015 by likening all Mexican immigrants to drug-dealing criminals: "When Mexico sends its people, they're not sending the best. . . . They're not sending you, they're sending people that have lots of problems and they're bringing those problems. They're bringing drugs, they're bringing crime. They're rapists and some, I assume, are good people, but I speak to border guards and they're telling us what we're getting."[40] Trump boldly declared that if elected president, he would build a "big" and "beautiful" border wall that would keep Mexican immigrants out of the United States. He even stated that he would get Mexico to pay for construction of the wall. The border wall issue was a primary plank of the Trump campaign by the fall of 2016.

Trump won the presidency and pursued his effort to build a wall, facing opposition from human rights groups, landowners along the border, US lawmakers, and Mexican leaders. The Trump administration attempted to appropriate funding through Congress when it became clear by 2018 that he could not follow through on his promise to "get Mexico to pay for it." The border wall issue grew so contentious that negotiations over the federal budget broke down, leading to a government shutdown between December 22, 2018, and January 25, 2019. After that time, the Trump administration tried to cobble together border wall construction money by redirecting defense appropriations. Such actions raised questions about executive overreach and legal impropriety. Some funding was also raised by private donors.[41] By the end of 2020, the Trump administration crowed about fulfilling its promise to build a wall by lauding completion of 450 miles of border construction.[42] Less than 10 percent (40 of 450 miles) of this wall represented new construction, while the great majority of the construction replaced older, extant fencing.[43] The irony of a global business tycoon sponsoring a garish symbol of illiberalism would be rich indeed if the reality of apprehension, deportation, and family separation of Mexican and Central American immigrants since 2017 were not so egregious.

Globalization was promoted to encourage economic integration between the United States and Mexico. Instead, it exacerbated the conditions that led to increased migration across the border by undocumented Mexican migrants. US immigration law and border enforcement policies became stricter and more sophisticated as Mexican migration to the United States reached new highs between the 1980s and early 2000s. The increasingly restrictive nature of US border security measures and immigration laws have worked not only to marginalize the Mexican immigrant's place within US society but also to reduce the basic human rights of Mexican nationals who attempt to enter the United States as undocumented migrants. The tensions between economic globalization and "illegal" immigration go a long way in explaining the heavy-handed and misguided attempts at border security that are witnessed today.

Lesson Plans on Retablos: Pictorial Representations of the Migration Experience

The chapter's introduction helped you to understand the larger economic, social, and political forces that have driven Mexican immigration to the United States in recent decades. It explained how prolonged economic stagnation in Mexico led to increased Mexican immigration to the United States between the 1970s and 1980s. At nearly the same time, neoliberal reforms in both the United States and Mexico culminated in the early 1990s to reduce barriers to trade between the two countries. The most notable example of these reforms was the

North American Free Trade Agreement (NAFTA), which dramatically increased the rate of US-Mexican trade. Ironically, that same reform— by reducing trade protections of certain sectors of Mexico's economy, most notably agriculture—increased the pressures that had already been spurring along Mexican immigration to the United States for years. The chapter introduction also showed that the issue of immigration is not just a matter of economics, but rather an issue that touches deeply upon the sociopolitical soul of a nation. This is evidenced by the discussion in the chapter introduction of a resurgent nativism during the last decades of the twentieth century in reaction to Mexican immigration. US government policies seemed to reflect the noticeable public mood of antipathy toward Mexican immigrants as it passed laws to restrict immigrant access to social services, enhanced border enforcement, broadened its abilities to apprehend and detain immigrants, and even took steps to construct a physical wall along the US-Mexican border. Considering all that has been detailed—economic downturns, political economic reforms, government action, and social reaction—this lesson plan illustrates—literally—how Mexican immigrants and their families reacted to those larger economic, social, and political forces.

Textual references rarely exist to account for undocumented Mexican migrants, and migrants are little inclined to leave a documentary trail of their migration, especially as their movement across borders has been criminalized in recent decades. Within this void of historical records, *retablos*, or small paintings commissioned to document migration experiences, offer students a distinct perspective on how Mexican immigrants conceive and react to the challenges of immigration and living in the United States. Retablos "get at the heart of the matter" in a way that academic reports and analyses by specialists on migration never can.[44] An analysis of retablos allows students to see the issue of immigration from the perspective of immigrants themselves.

What Are Retablos?

The word "retablo" comes from the Latin *retro-tabula*, or "behind the altar." Retablos are typically small paintings on tin that are left at religious shrines to offer public thanks to a divine image for a miracle or a favor received.[45] According to Jorge Durand and Douglas Massey, two historians who have studied retablos, these icons provide a *"spiritual and cultural anchor* for Mexicans in the northern diaspora, giving them a familiar cultural lens through which they can interpret and assimilate the fragmented and often disorienting experiences of life in an alien land."[46]

Retablo paintings, which are generally commissioned works of untrained popular artists who specialize in such paintings, embrace a flexible artistic style that is not wedded to a particular time or place. The typical technical and stylistic features of a retablo are as follows. Each pictorial space is separated into sections that correspond to different points in time—before, during, and after the miraculous happening. Another common device is to display all members of a supplicant's family within the painting: sometimes five, ten, fifteen, or twenty people are shown lined up and giving thanks to the holy image. Finally, figures are frequently shown appealing to multiple images, which are arrayed across the top of the painting.[47]

Three basic elements comprise every retablo painting: a holy image, a graphic rendering of a threatening occurrence or miraculous event, and a text explaining what happened. The holy image is conveyed in such a way that it is recognizable by the audience; expressions of gratitude draw upon a standard vocabulary of faith and devotion. The miraculous event is the central, most important feature of any retablo painting. Bold bright colors are used to augment the emotional effect of the scene. Pictorial space is deliberately and self-consciously manipulated to underscore the drama of the unfolding events. "Actions occurring before, during, and after the miracle are shuffled and recombined for maximum psychological effect."[48] Actions that occurred sequentially are broken down to represent simultaneous occurrence. The ultimate goal of the retablo painting, Durand and Massey argue, is less "adherence to appearances" and more to "the dramatization of the ghastly event or the miraculous encounter" between the supplicant and the holy figure.[49]

Most important for our purposes, retablo paintings are not meant to aesthetically please the eye of the beholder. Instead, they are supposed to convey, or *document*, to viewers the testing times overcome through the intercession of holy figures on behalf of thankful subjects, who are oftentimes illiterate migrants. In short, retablos are both personal prayers of thanksgiving and historical documents recounting the treacherous nature of migrating. The viewer is meant to share "the intensity of the fear and sorrow . . . the relief of delivery and the unmitigated joy that follow an unbelievable stroke of good luck."[50] Finally, retablos give immigrants a sense of order by integrating symbols of the celestial world to bring order to the problematic nature of the temporal world. As anthropologist David Sandell writes, "[Religious objects such as retablos] orient people to a way of being that infuses the supernatural into space and time, giving a sense of order that is felt to be as much a part of the exterior world as it is an emanation from an interior one."[51]

Analyzing Retablos as Historical Documents on Mexican Immigration

Migrants face unique difficulties: pain of separation from loved ones, hazards of moving north, risks of crossing the border, fear of falling sick in a strange land, threat of arrest and deportation, issue of documentation, getting lost, difficulty of finding a job, accidents at work, and falling victim to crime and exploitation. As such, retablos are the perfect medium for capturing the travails of immigration for Mexicans. Often entering the United States surreptitiously, undocumented migrants are exposed to all kinds of dangers pertaining to crossing the border, avoiding both Mexican and American border authorities, exploitation on the job, harsh working conditions, loneliness, isolation, racism. Retablos provide solace that enables migrants to construct an "inner Mexico" within the larger alien culture of the United States.[52]

Two forms of expression are at work and are interwoven in the retablos you will analyze. First, in religious terms these paintings provide a way for expressing devotion to a favored icon. Historically, most Mexican migrants to the United States derive from the western Mexican states of Guanajuato, Jalisco, San Luis Potosí, and Zacatecas. Perhaps not coincidentally, those states have been at the center of production of retablo art in Mexico. By far the most important icon of the western states of Mexico is La Virgen de San Juan de los Lago. No other image approaches this in attracting the devotion of migrants to the United States. The town of San Juan is located in Jalisco, in a region known as los Altos (the highlands). The town is situated in a shallow valley carved out of the surrounding hills by the San Juan River. The rolling hills and craggy ridges contain a number of small ponds and lakes that give the community its name: San Juan de los Lagos.[53]

Second, in cultural terms, these retablo paintings represent one of the few ways common people can give public expression to their anxieties, needs, fears, and sufferings. Retablos are a catharsis, they are personal testimonies, they are confessions, and they are expressions of gratitude or remorse that are difficult to articulate publicly. "Retablos give voice to the joys, celebrations, sufferings, illnesses, disgraces, enmities, losses, and tragedies of the human condition." As the famous Mexican muralist Diego Rivera once said, retablos are the "one true and present pictorial expression of the Mexican people."[54]

In recent decades retablos have come to reflect an increasing concern over the legal problem of documentation. In 1976, for the first time ever, the United States placed an annual immigration quota of 20,000 on Mexico. Two years later, in 1978, Mexico was placed under a worldwide annual ceiling of 290,000 immigrants, which was subsequently reduced to 270,000 in 1980. These changes have reduced the number of immigrant visas available to Mexican nationals, causing a great deal of panic among potential immigrants about obtaining proper documentation to immigrate. The subjective shift toward legal problems in retablo paintings may stem from the Immigration Reform and Control Act (IRCA) passed by the US Congress and signed into law by President Ronald Reagan in November 1986. This legislation put a premium on documentation by requiring migrants to prove that they had worked in the US agriculture sector during 1985 or 1986. Not coincidentally, many retablos of the late 1980s reflect gratitude for holy icons for managing to qualify for legal status.[55]

As you analyze each retablo, you should not only recognize what the painted prayer depicts but also reflect on the broader context of economics and shifting US immigration law. How do the paintings depict the difficulties of migration?

In conclusion, retablos show how migration to the United States has become a "core part of the collective experience" of the Mexican people. Retablos also show us how immigration is a true transnational experience; retablos speak to the indomitability of the human spirit to face multiple odds.[56]

Learning Objectives

- To gather a sense of the challenges Mexican migrants face when they choose to migrate to the United States.
- To form an appreciation of how primary documents are constructed and interpreted. To understand the utility of primary documents to the subjects that produce them.

- To understand the agency, as well as vulnerability, of migrants in the process of immigration

Resources Needed for the Lessons

At least one copy of *Miracles on the Border* by Jorge Durand and Douglas Massey and access to the Mexican Migration Project (https://mmp.opr .princeton.edu/home-en.aspx).[57] Full color versions of the images are available at the companion website (http://GoldbergSeries.org/UT ContemporaryUSHistory).

Selected Retablos to Analyze
from Miracles on the Border

Retablo #6. The harshness of crossing the border, 1986. (Retablo photos courtesy of the Mexican Migration Project)

Retablo #7. Escaping migration authorities, undated. (Retablo photos courtesy of the Mexican Migration Project)

Retablo #12. Problem of arranging papers, 1990. (Retablo photos courtesy of the Mexican Migration Project)

Retablo #13. Thanks for leaving prison, 1988. (Retablo photos courtesy of the Mexican Migration Project)

Retablo #38. Thanks for the healing of one son, hope for return of three other sons from US, 1977. (Retablo photos courtesy of the Mexican Migration Project)

Retablo #39. Thanks that a son has returned from the north and thanks for arranging papers, undated. (Retablo photos courtesy of the Mexican Migration Project)

Retablo #40. Thanks for return of husband from US, undated. (Retablo photos courtesy of the Mexican Migration Project)

Lesson Plan Number 1: In Class

The instructor gives a brief overview of retablo painting based on lesson plan introduction; the instructor could use one of the seven selected retablos as an example of analysis that will follow the criteria below (5–7 minutes).

In groups of 3 or 4, students look at a pair of the retablos and answer the Discussion Prompts below (8–10 minutes).

The same groups repeat that process two more times for the remaining four or five retablos (8–10 minutes × 2 = 16–20 minutes).

In a class response session, groups are invited to share their responses to each of the seven retablos (10–12 minutes).[58]

In the last few minutes of class (8–10 minutes), the instructor asks big concept questions: How do the paintings depict the difficulties of migration? How do these paintings inform, even change, your view of immigration and Mexican migrants? How do these paintings line up with and display larger themes or problems associated with immigration?

Discussion prompts:

- What do you see?
- What miraculous event is depicted?
- For what is the commissioner of the retablo thankful?
- What kind of psychological effect is sought upon the viewer by the use of objects, use of space, and choice of colors?
- What is the retablo *not* telling us? What is it taking for granted?
- If a year is given, what was the historical context that surrounded this painting?

Lesson Plan Number 2: Outside Class

Each student develops a retablo that represents the oral story that they have read from the Oral Histories section of the Mexican Migration Project website. This would practice skills in construction of primary documents as well as interpretation of primary documents.

In anticipation of this activity, the instructor could cull oral stories to share with the class. Those selected stories could be assigned to individual students or small groups of students. Students would construct their retablo interpretations of the migration experience based on the oral story they read. They would bring their completed retablos to class, present them to their classmates (explaining how the scene they created describes the oral interviewee's migration experience), and compare their interpretations with the interpretations of their classmates.

For simplicity, all students could construct their retablos around the most commonly depicted saint in actual retablos, La Virgen de San Juan de los Lago.

Notable Oral Histories to draw on include the following: "The North is like the Sea," "The North is like a battle," and "Working and wearing oneself down." The Oral Histories can be accessed by following this virtual crumb trail: Mexican Migration Project homepage (https://mmp .opr.princeton.edu/home-en.aspx)—Oral Histories—Stories.

Additional Primary Source Suggestions

- Bracero Oral History Project. Audio clips and transcripts of interviews of Mexican migrants (in Spanish). https://scholarworks.utep.edu/ bracero/.
- Dick Reavis Papers. Reavis was a journalist who frequently worked on border issues. http://legacy.lib.utexas.edu/taro/utlac/00113/lac-00113 .html.
- Los del Valle Oral History Project. http://legacy.lib.utexas.edu/taro/ utlac/00459/lac-00459.html.
- Political Asylum Project of Austin (PAPA) Records. http://legacy.lib .utexas.edu/taro/utlac/00104/lac-00104.html.
- Storycorps Historias. 2,500 interviews done in the National Public Radio "StoryCorps" style comprising the Latino subset of StoryCorps. Search on the page for the term "immigration" to find hundreds of mentions. http://legacy.lib.utexas.edu/taro/utlac/00354/lac-00354.html.

NOTES

1. Timothy J. Dunn, *The Militarization of the U.S.-Mexico Border, 1978–1992: Low-Intensity Conflict Doctrine Comes Home* (Austin: University of Texas, 1995), 37, 42; A. Zolberg, "Reforming the Back Door: The Immigration Reform and Control Act of 1986 in Historical Perspective," in *Immigration Reconsidered*, ed. Virginia Yans-McLaughlin (Oxford Scholarship Online, October 2011), 323, 334–35, https://www.doi.org/10.1093/acprof:oso/9780195055108.001.0001; Leo Chavez, *The Latino Threat: Constructing Immigrants, Citizens, and the Nation* (Stanford, CA: Stanford University Press, 2008), 8.

2. Marc R. Rosenblum and Leo B. Gorman, "The Public Policy Implications of State-Level Worksite Migration Enforcement: The Experiences of Arizona, Mississippi, and Illinois," in *Taking Local Control: Immigration Policy Activism in U.S. Cities and States,* ed. Monica Varsanyi (Stanford, CA: Stanford University Press, 2008), 115; Nicholas Degenova, "Migrant Illegality and Deportability in Everyday Life," *Annual Review of Anthropology* 31, no. 1 (October 2002): 437.

3. Mary Giovagnoli, "Overhauling Immigration Law: A Brief History of Basic Principles of Reform," *Immigration Policy Center* (2013), 7; Daniel James, *Illegal Immigration: An Unfolding Crisis* (Lanham, MD: University Press of America, 1991), 7.

4. Rosenblum and Gorman, "Public Policy Implications," 115; Dunn, *Militarization of the U.S.-Mexico Border,* 42; Patricia Fernández-Kelly and Douglas S. Massey, "Borders for Whom? The Role of NAFTA in Mexico-U.S. Migration," *Annals of the American Academy of Political and Social Science* 110, no. 1 (2007): 107.

5. Dorothee Schneider, *Crossing Borders: Migration and Citizenship in the Twentieth Century United States* (Cambridge, MA: Harvard University Press, 2011), 246–47.

6. Fernández-Kelly and Massey, "Borders for Whom?," 110–13.

7. One study shows that around 2 to 3 million unauthorized persons were present in the United States in the late 1980s and that the net flow of illegal aliens ranged from 200,000 to 300,000 persons per year. George Borjas, "The Economics of Immigration," *Journal of Economic Literature* 32, no. 4 (December 1994): 1669.

8. Peter Andreas, "U.S.: Mexico: Open Markets, Closed Border," *Foreign Policy* 103 (Summer 1996): 65.

9. Fernández-Kelly and Massey, "Borders for Whom?," 110–11.

10. See Luis Alberto Urrea's, *The Devil's Highway: A True Story* (New York: Back Bay Books, 2004) for grisly accounts of the danger of border crossing in remote areas. "Death by sunlight, hyperthermia, was the main culprit. But illegals drowned, froze, committed suicide, were murdered, were hit by trains and trucks, were bitten by rattlesnakes, had heart attacks" (19).

11. Fernández-Kelly and Massey, "Borders for Whom?," 99–104.

12. Carla Hills, "NAFTA's Economic Upsides: The View from the United States," *Foreign Affairs* 93, no 1 (January/February 2014): 122–27; Jorge Castañeda, "NAFTA's Mixed Record," *Foreign Affairs* 93, no. 1 (January/February 2014): 134–37.

13. Andreas, "Open Markets, Closed Border," 59–60.

14. Castañeda, "NAFTA's Mixed Record," 137–38.

15. Castañeda, "NAFTA's Mixed Record," 138; M. Angeles Villarreal and Ian F. Fergusson, "NAFTA at 20: Overview and Trade Effects," *Congressional Research Service,* April 28, 2014, http://nationalaglawcenter.org/wp-content/up loads/assets/crs/R42965.pdf, p. 19.

16. Stephen W. Hartman, "NAFTA: The Controversy," *International Trade Journal* 25, no. 1 (2010): 16–17.

17. Gilbert Gonzalez and Raul Fernandez, "Empire and the Origins of Twentieth-Century Migration from Mexico to the United States," *Pacific Historical Review* 71, no. 1 (February 2002): 54; Hartman, "NAFTA," 21.

18. Hartman, "NAFTA," 19; Gonzalez and Fernandez, "Empires and the Origins," 54–57, quote on 57; Villarreal and Fergusson, "NAFTA at 20," 17–18; Andreas, "Open Markets, Closed Border," 61.

19. Lisa Marie Cacho, "'The People of California Are Suffering': The Ideology of White Injury in Discourses of Immigration," *Cultural Values* 4, no. 4 (2000): 392; Castañeda, "NAFTA's Mixed Record," 139.

20. Cacho, "People of California Are Suffering," 389.

21. Monica W. Varsanyi, "Immigration Policy Activism in U.S. States and Cities: Interdisciplinary Perspectives," in *Taking Local Control*, ed. Varsanyi, 1–2.

22. Cacho, "People of California Are Suffering," 393, emphasis mine.

23. Kevin Johnson, "'Aliens' and the U.S. Immigration Laws: The Social and Legal Construction of Nonpersons," *University of Miami Interamerican Law Review* 28, no. 2 (Winter 1996): 268–69.

24. Cacho, "People of California Are Suffering," 408; James T. Patterson, *Restless Giant: The United States from Watergate to "Bush v. Gore"* (Oxford: Oxford University Press, 2005), 374.

25. Varsanyi, "Immigration Policy Activism," 1–2.

26. Andreas, "Open Markets, Closed Border," 62; Varsanyi, "Immigration Policy Activism," 1–2; Giovagnoli, "Overhauling Immigration Law," 2; Chavez, *Latino Threat*, 8–9; Schneider, *Crossing Borders*, 246–47; Johnson, "'Aliens' and the U.S. Immigration Laws," 281; Cacho, "People of California Are Suffering," 389; Ayelet Schachar, "Territory without Boundaries: Immigration beyond Territory: The Shifting Border of Immigration Regulation," *Michigan Journal of International Law* 30 (Spring 2009): 815–17.

27. Giovagnoli, "Overhauling Immigration Law," 3.

28. Chavez, *Latino Threat*, 36–37.

29. Giovagnoli, "Overhauling Immigration Law," 2; David Fitzgerald, *A Nation of Emigrants: How Mexico Manages Its Migration* (Berkeley: University of California Press, 2009), 60–62; Chavez, *Latino Threat*, 37; Rosenblum and Gorman, "Public Policy Implications," 115.

30. Chavez, *Latino Threat*, 23, 38–39. See Alan D. Bersin, "Lines and Flows: The Beginning and End of Borders," *Brooklyn Journal of International Law* 37, no. 2 (March 2012): 394–96, for a countervailing view that holds that 9/11 was a shock that changed how immigration was viewed.

31. Bersin, "Lines and Flows," 395–96.

32. Schachar, "Territory without Boundaries," 811, 817–18.

33. Ibid., 824, 827, 835.

34. Rosenblum and Gorman, "Public Policy Implications," 119.

35. Fernández-Kelly and Massey, "Borders for Whom?," 108.

36. Ibid., 108.

37. Chavez, *Latino Threat*, 38–39. It is worth noting that the 9/11 terrorists were all in the United States legally on student, tourist, or business visas.

38. Dunn, *Militarization of the U.S.-Mexico Border*, 66–67; Andreas, "Open Markets, Closed Border," 63–64. A sign soon appeared on the San Diego–Tijuana wall with the words "Welcome to the New Berlin Wall."

39. Denise Gilman, "Seeking Breaches in the Wall: An International Human Rights Law Challenge to the Texas-Mexico Wall," *Texas International Law Journal* 46 (Spring 2011): 258–60.

40. "Trump Stands by Statements on Mexican Illegal Immigrants, Surprised by Backlash," Fox News Network, last updated December 20, 2015, https://www.foxnews.com/politics/trump-stands-by-statements-on-mexican-illegal-immigrants-surprised-by-backlash.

41. Nick Miroff and Adrian Blanco, "Trump Ramps Up Border-Wall Construction ahead of 2020 Vote," *Washington Post*, February 6, 2020, https://www.washingtonpost.com/graphics/2020/national/immigration/border-wall-progress/.

42. There was even a website dedicated to tracking the construction progress of "Trump's Wall": https://www.trumpwall.construction/ (accessed January 5, 2021).

43. Anna Giaritelli, "Trump Hits 450-Mile Goal for 2020 Border Wall Construction," *Washington Examiner*, January 5, 2021, https://www.washingtonexaminer.com/news/trump-hits-450-mile-goal-for-2020-border-wall-construction.

44. Jorge Durand and Douglas Massey, *Miracles on the Border: Retablos of Mexican Migrants to the United States* (Tucson: University of Arizona Press, 1995), 67, 121.

45. Ibid., 3, 6.

46. Ibid., 4, emphasis mine.

47. Ibid., 9, 18–19, 29.

48. Ibid., quote on 26.

49. Ibid., quote on 26.

50. Ibid., 23–26, quote on 27.

51. David P. Sandell, "Mexican Retablos," *Journal of Folklore Research* 51, no. 1 (January–April 2014): 13–47, quote on 33. It does not take a student of art to know that a figure's proportion in an illustration often denotes its overall significance in the image at large. The importance given religious imagery for retablo subjects is paramount and is demonstrated by most retablos, notably in Retablo #13, dated February 1988, in which a full third of the illustration's face is dedicated to a holy image.

52. Durand and Massey, *Miracles on the Border*, 63, 70, 72–75. See Retablo #6, dated June 5, 1985, in which a migrant gives thanks for helping him and his companions to remigrate into the United States despite the extreme heat, thirst, and scarce water. See also Retablo #7, undated, in which migrants give thanks to the Virgin of San Juan for "delivering us" (*librarnos*; "sustaining" or "freeing" are also possible translations) from the Mexican border patrol so they could "migrate to Los Angeles."

53. Durand and Massey, *Miracles on the Border*, 15, 59, 62, 68.

54. Ibid., 62. Retablos #38 and #40 demonstrate how several of these themes—joy, celebration, suffering—can be expressed simultaneously. In #38, dated early July 1977, Maria Marcos Rebolloso gives thanks for the return of her son, Leonardo Arsola, while also praying for her three other sons who are still in the United States. Retablo #40, undated, is an intensely emotional and personal historical document, in which Carmen Ortiz gives thanks to the Virgin of San Juan for the return of her husband, Mateo Hernandez, from the United States. The personal nature of the illustration is driven home by the artist including the initials "C. O." and "M. H." next to the two figures depicting wife and husband. One even gets a sense of the transnational spatiality central to the familial relations between migrants and the loved ones they leave behind; the artist has painted an American flag and Mexican flag in the bottom left and bottom right corners, respectively.

55. Ibid., 78, 82. See Retablo #12, dated November 20, 1990, in which Juan Sanchez R. gives thanks for "solving the problem of arranging [*arreglar*] important papers" to enter the United States. See also Retablo #39, undated, in which a mother gives thanks to God that her son was able to arrange his papers (*ha[b] iendo arreglado sus papeles*) and return from the United States (*regrasara del Norte*).

56. Ibid., 120.

57. The Mexican Migration Project (https://mmp.opr.princeton.edu/home-en.aspx), a website created to accompany *Miracles on the Border* by authors Jorge Durand and Douglas Massey, offers myriad opportunities for instructors to illustrate the immigration experience to students. This website has great information on retablos and even has a gallery of images (*Expressions—Retablo Gallery*) that arranges retablos chronologically. This same group of links has a section called *Artists* in which retablo artists are interviewed. Most important, there is a section on oral histories (*Expressions—Oral Histories—Stories*) both in English and Spanish. The chronology of the experiences recounted predominantly ranges from the 1940s to the 1980s; the interviews were largely conducted in the early 1990s.

58. This activity could take place after 30 minutes of student analysis or could be intermingled after each group looks at a pair of retablos. The problem with intermingling discussion is that students' observations of the retablos could be influenced by the observations they will have heard from their classmates.

Racializing Legality in Post-1965 Immigration Debates

NATALIE MENDOZA

Why Teach This Lesson?

The 1965 Immigration and Naturalization Act created the concept of an "illegal alien," and in the years following its passage, Mexican immigrants came to be viewed as synonymous with an "illegal alien" problem in the United States. This lesson will help students understand how government officials, politicians, the media, and anti-immigrant proponents from the late 1960s into the 1990s contributed to this process of racializing legality. Additionally, students will see how public and political discussions about "illegal aliens" overemphasized the role of immigrants as the sole determinant of unauthorized migration into the United States, obscuring the role of federal and state policy (see, for instance, Benjamin Montoya's chapter on NAFTA). This lesson aims to reframe how students understand current immigration debates by focusing on the historical origins and process of linking Mexican immigrants to legality in the late twentieth century.

"Save Our State"

On May 13, 1994, California governor Pete Wilson ran a television ad for his reelection campaign on a highly contentious issue in the state, undocumented immigration—or "illegal immigration," as it was commonly referred to at the time. The thirty-second-long ad began with black-and-white footage of people running across several lanes on Interstate 5 at the US-Mexico border into San Diego County. A narrator immediately began speaking over the grainy footage. "They keep coming," he intoned. "Two million illegal immigrants in California. The federal government won't stop them at the border, yet requires us to pay billions to take care of them." In the first half of the ad, the narrator had quickly set up an us-versus-them narrative in which Californians were forced to contend with undocumented immigrants who, according to the narrator, imposed a serious financial burden on the state's economy. And the federal government was not without blame—it was cast as contributing to the problem by not fulfilling its responsibility of enforcing immigration policy at the border. The rest of the ad continued this narrative by turning to Governor Wilson and the work he had done and intended to do on behalf of Californians: sending the National Guard to support the US Border Patrol, his current effort to sue the federal government "to force [it] to control the border," and a promise to "[work] to deny state services to illegal immigrants."[1] Wilson's last promise reflected his support for Proposition 187 (also known as the "Save Our State" referendum), a voter-led ballot initiative that sought to deny public benefits and services to undocumented immigrants. The measure also called for public employees to report to federal authorities any individuals they suspected of entering the United States without authorization.[2]

Wilson's television ad and Proposition 187 both reflect long-standing themes in immigration history. They are one example, for instance, of how xenophobia and nativism have both consistently driven the scapegoating of immigrants during periods of economic instability in the United States.[3] They both also demonstrate the tension between federal, state, and local governments over the enforcement of immigration policy, as well as the role of the public in shaping immigration legislation.[4] Lastly, the debates surrounding Proposition 187 reflect one episode in a longer history of anti-Mexican sentiment in the United States, in which Mexican immigrants have been regarded as a social burden and threat to American society.[5]

California's Proposition 187 also embodies the racialization of legality in immigration policy debates that had begun after Congress passed the Immigration and Naturalization Act of 1965 (also known as the Hart-Celler Act). Several scholars have contributed to a rich literature on racialization that broadly defines it as the process of attaching racial meanings to a group, social practice, behavior, particular issue, or relationship. Over time, race comes to be accepted and normalized as the key factor for understanding said group, practice, behavior, issue, or relationship—even if unfounded.[6] With the 1965 act, legality had been placed front and center in immigration policy debates, and in the decades to follow government officials, politicians, the media, and the public would come to link legality to race—that is, racialize legality—in specific reference to immigrants and immigration from Mexico. This chapter focuses on how legality was racialized in post-1965 immigration debates, with special attention to how this manifested in California politics with the Proposition 187 campaign.

Immigration and Naturalization Act of 1965

The issue of undocumented immigration—or legality—as a focal point in policy debates began after the passage of the Immigration and Naturalization Act of 1965. The act had been hailed as progressive legislation at the time because it had eliminated the national origins criterion that had been set by 1920s legislation that many had come to see as racist and discriminatory (indeed, lawmakers were greatly influenced by the emerging American eugenics movement, in which proponents racialized nationality). The 1921 Emergency Quota Act had created an immigration hierarchy that ranked immigrants based on nationality, using a quota system that favored immigration from northern Europe and that placed an annual ceiling on immigration from eastern and southern European countries. Importantly, the Western Hemisphere was excluded from quotas because agribusiness in the southwestern United States had lobbied hard to protect the pool of Mexican migrant workers it heavily relied upon. A subsequent act, the 1924 Immigration Act (also known as the Johnson-Reed Act), further restricted immigration by reducing the annual ceiling. The 1965 act had eliminated the racialized national origins criterion but retained the quota system, relying instead upon two other criteria (family reunification and occupational skills) for determining who could immigrate to the United States. It also raised the annual ceiling on immigration for the Eastern Hemisphere and imposed—for the first time—quotas on the Western Hemisphere. The new quotas placed on the Western Hemisphere were highly restrictive. When the law went into effect in 1968, it failed to accommodate the reality of Mexican migration in previous years, which had steadily been on the rise and would continue to do so into the 1970s. This was certainly a moment, then, in which the number of Mexican migrants entering the

United States was indeed increasing. But as historian Mae Ngai has astutely pointed out, the 1965 Immigration and Naturalization Act recast what had previously been legal migration from Mexico as "illegal." Legality, in other words, was not fixed. And in the case of Mexican immigration, the law could be at odds with actual migration patterns that had been historically shaped by labor policies and economic ties between the United States and Mexico.[7]

Following the passage of the 1965 immigration act, policy debates would come to center on the question of legality. This did not mean, however, that notions of race were left out of discussions.[8] In fact, several scholars have shown that in the post-1965 period the language of and ideas about legality and immigration became racialized as distinctly Mexican in origin. In particular, government officials and the media began to increasingly use the term "illegal" as a way to describe the unauthorized immigration from Mexico, and especially as a dangerous threat to the nation's social and economic infrastructures. William Saxbe, the US attorney general under President Gerald Ford, described unauthorized immigration as "a severe national crisis" that contributed to unemployment, crime, and welfare costs. The solution, according to Saxbe, was to deport one million "illegal immigrants," most of whom he identified as Mexican. In 1978, William E. Colby, the former director of the Central Intelligence Agency, expressed concern about a "Spanish-Speaking Quebec in the US Southwest," claiming that undocumented immigration from Mexico posed far more danger to the United States than the Soviet Union.[9]

The media painted a picture of an "illegal alien invasion" from Mexico in the immediate post-1965 period by increasing its coverage of issues related to undocumented immigration. The *New York Times*, for instance, went from publishing an average of 8.5 articles per year between 1970 and 1972 to publishing an average of more than 57 articles each year between 1973 and 1980. This increase in publication by more than 650 percent coincided with a period of economic decline and greater focus among politicians and government officials on undocumented immigration as a national problem. In the same set of years, the average number of *New York Times* articles that related unauthorized immigration specifically to Mexico increased from 1.3 percent to 20.6 percent. Imagery was also effective in creating an impending sense of danger. In December 1974, the *American Legion Magazine* chose to highlight one of its articles, "Our Illegal Alien Problem," on its cover through cartoon: in the image, Mexican caricatures wearing sombreros were depicted as forcing their way into the United States to take jobs away from Americans, and as placing a burden on the country's education system and social and medical services.[10] The cover sent a clear message that the "illegal alien problem" was largely a Mexican one.[11] Into the 1980s, the media would continue to portray undocumented immigration through an "immigrant invasion" metaphor and to describe the situation at the US-Mexico border as "out of control."[12]

Modern Anti-Immigration Movement

No one did more to reinforce the narrative of "illegal immigrants" as a threat to the nation than perhaps John Tanton. Considered the father of the modern anti-immigration movement that emerged in the 1980s, Tanton had founded the Federation for American Immigration Reform (FAIR) in 1979 in response to what he saw as an immigrant overpopulation problem that threatened white Americans. Policymakers had just eliminated the national origins criterion—what many had decried as racist—which meant Tanton would need to marshal a campaign for restrictionist legislation that avoided using overtly racist language to frame immigration debates, especially those centered on unauthorized migration. Tanton had created what historian Carly Goodman has described as an "anti-immigration ecosystem" of organizations that shaped the way the media and lawmakers talked about immigration—as a clear-cut issue of legal versus illegal migration—that oversimplified what was, in reality, a complicated situation. This ecosystem included FAIR as well as other organizations Tanton had founded or funded: the Center for Immigration Studies (CIS), NumbersUSA, and the Immigration Reform Law Institute. Tanton had created CIS to conduct research as a think tank independent of FAIR (though it was not) and to provide a "greater appearance of objectivity" to the movement.[13]

By the mid-1980s, it became increasingly clear that Tanton's work was driven by nativist and xenophobic ideas that mirrored those of the eugenics movement that had shaped the restrictionist legislation of the 1920s. A memo, for instance, that Tanton had written in 1986 for a brainstorming retreat with colleagues focused on immigration from Latin America, most notably the supposed hyperfertility of Latinas and what this would mean for the future of white America.[14] In a letter to a significant donor, Tanton had expressed his concern "about the decline of folks who look like you and me," and he told a friend in another instance that "for European-American society and culture to persist requires a European-American majority, and a clear one at that."[15] Tanton had also helped cultivate and circulate nativist and xenophobic ideas. Beginning in 1985, his organization hosted writers' workshops for nativists, such as Peter Brimelow, author of *Alien Nation*, and Ann Coulter. In 1990, Tanton established The Social Contract Press, which published a regular journal and books, including an English-language edition of *The Camp of Saints*, a French novel that depicted a dystopian future in which France and white Europe are invaded by dark-skinned refugees. Tanton's work in the 1980s created a modern-day anti-immigration movement, complete with an ecosystem for circulating ideas and language that would allow proponents to debate immigration without specific reference to race.[16]

California's Proposition 187

California's Proposition 187 campaign in the early 1990s offers the clearest snapshot of both the racialized legality that had developed in recent decades and the considerable influence the anti-immigration movement had on public thinking. Proposition 187 was a 1994 voter-led initiative that proposed denying public benefits—medical services and education—to undocumented immigrants. It called for stricter penalties for falsifying documentation and cooperation between local law enforcement and the Immigration and Naturalization Service (INS), the precursor to the Immigration and Customs Enforcement (ICE). The initiative also required all public state employees to report undocumented immigrants, turning private citizens into agents in the enforcement of federal immigration policy.[17] For proponents of Proposition 187, the initiative would achieve what the federal government had failed to do—enforce immigration law at the US-Mexico border—and end the "economic hardship" that the "People of California" suffered "by the presence of illegal aliens" in the state.[18]

The authors of Proposition 187 were a somewhat mixed group of individuals that had mobilized around the issue of undocumented immigration. While some had previous relationships with each other, they had not collectively worked together prior to writing Proposition 187. Barbara Coe was an analyst for the Anaheim Police Department when she began self-publishing an anti-immigration newsletter from her Huntington Beach home. In early 1992, Coe created Citizens for Action Now (CAN) with Bill King, a former US Border Patrol chief. CAN recruited members through ads it placed in conservative magazines, such as the *National Review*, the language of which criminalized immigrants and immigration. By May 1992, CAN had merged with other immigration restrictionist groups to create the California Coalition for Immigration Reform (CCIR), instantly creating a collective membership of four thousand. In October 1993, a small group of individuals from within this network met in Orange County to draft what became Proposition 187. Both Coe and King attended the meeting, among others including Harold Ezell, who had once been the western regional commissioner for the INS (and under whom King had worked). Alan Nelson, who had been Ezell's boss at the INS, also attended the October meeting. At the time, Nelson was working as a lobbyist for FAIR—the group Tanton had created in 1979—in Sacramento.[19] (Tanton would help fund CCIR in 1994 in the midst of the Proposition 187 campaign).[20]

Governor Pete Wilson had chosen to support Proposition 187 in the last months of a reelection campaign that was not doing well. The state was also going through an especially tense period in its history. Wilson had been elected governor in 1990, during which time the state had been experiencing a declining economy—the worst since the Great Depression—alongside a drastic demographic shift. California's overall population had increased by 25 percent in the 1980s, causing the white proportion to drop from 71 to 59 percent as a result of higher rates of migration from Asia and Latin America. The newest migration transformed the racial and ethnic makeup of neighborhoods, schools, and workplaces, contributing to interracial tensions between groups. Moreover, the police brutality that the African American population had long experienced became devastatingly apparent to the public when a video of Los Angeles police officers beating motorist Rodney King surfaced in 1991. The city erupted into riots a year later after the police officers were acquitted of charges in the beating. It was within this context that Wilson had chosen to embrace a "war on illegal immigration" platform that blamed undocumented migrants for the state's economic decline and that cast white Californians as victims. Wilson also blamed the federal government. In August 1993, Wilson wrote an open letter to President Bill Clinton, published in the *New York Times*, *USA Today*, and the *Washington Times*, in which he charged the federal government with incentivizing undocumented immigration and failing to enforce the law at the border. Wilson would file three lawsuits against the federal government for expenses he claimed undocumented immigrants generated in the state.[21]

The criticisms opponents leveled against Proposition 187 were numerous and varied. On the ballot pamphlet sent to voters, the California legislative analyst explained that while the state could potentially save $200 million annually by denying services to undocumented immigrants, the costs involved in verifying status could amount to at least $100 million. Denying medical services could also lead to future costs since this could potentially increase the risk of spreading contagious diseases in the general population. The US-born children of undocumented immigrants could develop health issues if their mothers were denied prenatal care. The analyst also pointed out that Proposition 187 would not actually result in savings to public education since the initiative violated the Supreme Court case *Plyler v. Doe* (1982), which held that a state could not deny a public education to students based on immigration status.[22]

While a range of organizations—civil rights and immigrant rights groups, taxpayer organizations, and labor unions—opposed Proposition 187, many were slow to mobilize out of a concern that publicizing the initiative would have the unintended consequence of promoting its message and thus helping secure its passage. It was only after June 1994—after Proposition 187 qualified for the November ballot—that leaders in these organizations and the Democratic Party organized a group, called No on S.O.S., to defeat the initiative. Groups and individuals who opposed the measure, including law enforcement officials, teachers, and health professionals, oftentimes legitimized the message that unauthorized migrants were a threat to the state and reinforced the link between undocumented immigrants and criminality described in the proposition. The challenge these opponents posed was that Proposition 187 was "not a real solution" to these issues. An immigrant rights group, Californians United Against 187, emphasized the discriminatory implications of the initiative, stating that its passage would lead to racial profiling. Citizens and migrants with proper documentation would be "burdened with proving their immigration status." Moreover, elected officials and public leaders failed to address the xenophobic and nativist underpinnings of the debate, preventing—even if implicitly—

any meaningful discussion that examined the causes of undocumented immigration. In doing so, they did not dispute Proposition 187 as a viable policy solution and instead sent a message that it was worth debating (despite the statements they made to the contrary).[23]

The media helped set the tone for how undocumented immigration from Mexico was discussed by using metaphors of danger that harkened back to the news reporting of the late 1960s. Sociolinguist Otto Santa Ana examined over one hundred articles the *Los Angeles Times* published on Proposition 187 and found that most dehumanized and racialized Mexican migrants by using metaphor to report on the immigration debate. Phrases such as "awash under a brown tide," "the flood of legal and illegal immigrants streaming," "Third World takeover," and "state of siege in California" were some of the ways Mexican immigrants and migration were described in these articles, and Santa Ana categorized these phrases as falling under "dangerous moving water" and "war" metaphors. Moreover, Santa Ana argued that these metaphors demonstrate that Proposition 187 was less about economic concerns— the alleged cost undocumented immigrants posed to taxpayers—as proponents claimed since the metaphors rarely, if at all, referred to fiscal arguments but to cultural threats instead.[24]

The debates surrounding Proposition 187, then, were limited to a legality dichotomy that created a false dilemma rooted in racialized notions of criminality. Political scientist Robin Dale Jacobson describes this understanding of legality in immigration—"illegal" and "legal" immigrants—as part of a "metaschema of color-blind conservatism" based in ideas about fairness and equal treatment. When charged with racism, color-blind conservatives could claim their motives were based in lawfulness and nothing else. Despite a claim to race neutrality, most anyone listening in on the Proposition 187 debate would have understood that legality was not about any and all immigrants, but that it was coded language used to talk about a *specific* immigrant group (Mexicans) that had long been racialized and criminalized. This dichotomy also falsely framed the debate as an either/or discussion premised on an understanding of legality as a universal (timeless and therefore fixed) ideal. Such a binary ignored the complicated history of immigration policymaking, its enforcement, and how the meaning of legality has changed over time.[25] It also obscured the dialectical relationship between the public, politicians, and the media in policy discussions. Not paying attention to this relationship meant overlooking how policy could end up realigning and reinforcing racial categories.[26]

Californians would approve Proposition 187 in the November 1994 election, with 59 percent of the electorate casting a vote in its favor. Immediately following the election civil rights groups brought a legal challenge before the California Superior Court and the US District Court and were successful—the US District Court declared Proposition 187 unconstitutional since immigration regulation was not the responsibility of the state, but of the federal government. The newly elected Democratic governor, Gray Davis, dropped the state's appeal.[27]

Despite failing to become policy in California, Proposition 187 reverberated nationally in at least two ways. The first was to amplify the modern anti-immigration movement and legitimize its new brand of nativism that employed a color-blind conservatism to great effect. Conservative thinkers and commentators, such as Peter Brimelow, former presidential candidate Patrick Buchanan, and Harvard political scientist Samuel Huntington, had been helping to mainstream the anti-immigration ideas that drove the Proposition 187 campaign. The second impact was in shaping federal policy. Many of the proposition's core pieces were included in federal welfare and immigration policies that responded to the perception of an "immigration crisis." This "crisis" was defined by ideas that drove the Proposition 187 campaign: the criminalization of undocumented immigrants, the view that immigrants were undeserving and should not have access to public benefits and services, and the belief that the only solution to the problem was to militarize the US-Mexico border. Every presidential administration since Bill Clinton's has developed policy that contributed to an expanded immigration enforcement apparatus that located, arrested, detained, and deported the growing number of immigrants who entered the United States.[28]

In 2016, Donald Trump did not need to use color-blind conservatism to win the American presidency. His explicit use of xenophobic, nativist, and racist language when describing immigrants did not turn off but rather resonated with many voters. And for those who were less comfortable with Trump's overtly racist rhetoric, his "Make America Great Again" slogan was perhaps the coded message they needed to satisfy their color-blind conservatism.[29] But racializing legality did not begin with Trump, nor will it end with him. Rather, its origins are found in the aftermath of the 1965 Immigration and Naturalization Act, when the idea of an "illegal alien" was not only created but also racialized. Racializing legality has had the effect of placing an overemphasis on immigrants, rather than policy, as the sole determinant of unauthorized migration into the United States. That is, focusing on migrants meant shifting attention away from how federal policy contributed to the problem of unauthorized entry (see, for instance, Benjamin Montoya's chapter on NAFTA), but also from the historical role United States foreign policy and economic ties with Mexico had played in shaping Mexican migration patterns. Understanding the contours of immigration policy debates, especially those taking place in the present day, necessarily rests upon examining how the discussion around legality has emerged and, more importantly, how it has been racialized historically. In doing so we learn how ideas about race have intersected with beliefs about migration and citizenship, and the central role this has played in creating immigration policy.

Primary Source Lesson: Learning Goals, Lesson Plan, and Implementation

Students will critically read and write about a set of three primary sources on public discussions about Proposition 187, which are included at the end of this chapter. The lesson includes three parts that can be implemented in whatever way best meets your course curriculum design and student needs: getting context, reading and writing about the primary source set, and sharing a "Why It Matters" paragraph.

The first part of the lesson entails providing students with the context they need—drawn largely from this chapter—in order to answer a set of questions in the second part that are meant to guide them through the discipline-specific ways historians read, analyze, and write about primary sources. This includes sourcing, summarizing, contextualizing, and identifying evidence for argument. Students will then choose a single primary source they identify as especially useful for understanding the Proposition 187 debates and write a short "Why It Matters" paragraph in which they explain its significance to the topic. In the last part of the lesson, students will use the paragraph to share their ideas about the primary source they chose with their classmates in a variation of the well-known "Think-Pair-Share" activity.[30]

Part 1: Getting Context

Students will need a basic understanding of how immigration policy has been racialized. You may have already taught, for instance, the 1882 Chinese Exclusion Act, the 1917 Immigration Act, the 1921 Emergency Quota Act, and the 1924 Immigration Act (some of which were briefly discussed in this chapter), which are important for establishing how restrictionist immigration policy developed over time at the federal level. The passage of the 1965 Immigration and Naturalization Act was a turning point in this narrative because, as noted in the chapter, the question of legality was added to the focus on race from the earlier immigration debates. From here the story continues to show how legality and race became linked in the media in the 1970s, for instance, and especially with the emergence of the modern anti-immigration movement in the 1980s. This will give students a solid grasp of how notions of racialized legality were well established in immigration debates by the 1990s.

The central goal in sharing this context with students is to provide them with sufficient historical background to help them answer questions about the primary sources. What counts as "sufficient" will understandably vary from course to course. One thing to keep in mind is that the primary source set activity is meant to build upon students' *preliminary* understanding of the topic by giving them a chance to critically read primary sources on their own. Rather than try to "cover" everything with students, aim instead to give them a contextual foundation on which they can build from their reading and writing about the primary sources and ultimately develop a more advanced and nuanced understanding of how legality was racialized and discussed in immigration debates.

Part 2: Reading and Writing about the Primary Source Set

After students have sufficient context (as determined by the instructor), ask them to read and think about the primary source set on their own as described below.

Read *each* primary source and consider the following:

- *Sourcing:* What type of primary source is it? Who created it? For what audience? When? Where?

- *Summarize:* What is the primary source about? What is the main message(s) or idea(s) of the primary source? Try to limit your thinking in this step to describing the source rather than analyzing it (that is the next step).
- *Analysis:* What do we learn from the primary source? What new understanding, insight, or meaning do you gain of this topic or period of time?
- *Evidence:* What specific parts of the primary source support your analysis? Paraphrase your evidence or identify a direct quote that supports your analysis. Jot it down for easy reference.

Choose *one* primary source. Which primary source was most interesting to you? Provide an example (evidence) from the primary source that illustrates why this is interesting (or important, revealing, surprising, noteworthy) to you.

Identify what *additional information* you need to further analyze the primary source. What additional information would help you make better sense of this particular primary source? What will help you contextualize your chosen primary source? Do you need:

- *Historical Information:* This is basic information about what was happening in this historical moment and which is not something you were able to know from reading the primary source alone. This can be something as simple as factual information (a date, for instance) or something more substantive (biographical information or a sequence of events) that helps you situate the primary sources in the historical moment under study.
- *Clarifying Information:* This is information that helps clarify something that was referenced in the primary source and which you knew little or nothing about prior to reading about it in the primary source.
- *Missing Information:* This is information that is absent from the primary source. Just like clarifying information, it is information you suspect will be useful for gaining a better or more complete understanding of the primary source and the historical moment.

How does this new information affect your initial analysis of the primary source? Does it reinforce or challenge your original analysis?

Write "Why It Matters" paragraph.

- In a short paragraph, explain the significance of this particular primary source for studying how the public debated immigration in 1990s California. Use the following question to guide you in writing your paragraph: *What makes the primary source especially useful—compared to the others in the set—for understanding the Proposition 187 debates? What makes it stand out, in other words, from the other primary sources?*

- A strong paragraph will have a clear and well-articulated response to the question, as well as at least one example (evidence) from the primary source that supports your reasoning. Comparing your chosen primary source to the others in the set may also help strengthen your argument about its significance for understanding the Proposition 187 debates. Additionally, you might consider if your analysis of the primary source (the one you chose or all of them) holds any significance to present-day debates on immigration.

Part 3: Sharing the "Why It Matters" Paragraph

Writing the "Why It Matters" paragraph is meant to prepare students for a discussion with their classmates about the primary source set.[31] The general structure for doing this is the familiar "Think-Pair-Share" activity. In this method, the instructor first poses a question to students and provides them with time to think about and develop an answer to the question. Students are then paired up with a classmate (or put into small groups, if that works better) in which they discuss their answers with each other, responding with feedback, comments, or questions. And lastly, the whole class reconvenes to share the smaller discussions that had taken place.

The "Why It Matters" paragraph can be easily graded as a low-stakes assignment using a three-point scale. The assignment could fall, for instance, under the participation portion of the final course grade. When grading the paragraphs, consider the following three criteria: Does the student provide an answer about the significance of the primary source? How effectively does the student use evidence to support their claim? And did the student articulate their answer in a clear and well-written manner? A strong paragraph would earn two points, an acceptable paragraph would earn one point, while a paragraph that did not meet any of the criteria would earn zero points (what counts as "strong" versus "acceptable" is best left to the discretion of the instructor).

"Think-Pair-Share" is a useful teaching and assessment tool for three reasons.[32] First, it is a good way to ensure that most, if not all, students are engaging the material and sharing their thoughts about it with someone—even if it is not the instructor. Second, the whole class discussion is a great way to quickly reinforce or clarify ideas, concepts, and use of skills among students. If a student has misunderstood a piece of legislation in their analysis, for instance, the instructor can step in and clarify for everyone at once. Or perhaps a student made particularly good use of evidence in their analysis, thus providing the instructor the chance to offer praise and encourage students to follow that example. Third, when the "Think" portion includes a written component that is turned in—such as the "Why It Matters" paragraph—the instructor now has a relatively easy and informal way to gauge student learning as it is happening during the semester (as opposed to at the end of the semester when the final assignment is submitted). Using the three-point grading scale and criteria provides the instructor with a snapshot of what students know, both in terms of content and skill. Do most students seem to be learning what you intended? Or are a significant number of students having trouble with something that needs addressing before moving on to the next lesson? Gauging student learning in this way is critical since it means that instructors can assess in real time whether they can move forward with teaching as planned, or if they need to readjust their lessons and teaching to meet the immediate needs of their students.

THE PRIMARY SOURCE SET

Buchanan, Patrick J. "What Will America Be in 2050?" *Los Angeles Times*, October 28, 1994, p. B7. (Word version of edited document available on companion website [http://GoldbergSeries.org/UTContemporaryUSHistory].)

Muñoz, Daniel. "Governor Wilson/Prop 187 Is Not about Immigration but Racial War in California!" *La Prensa San Diego*, October 28, 1994, University of California San Diego, Special Collections and Archives, Herman Baca Papers, MSS 0649, https://library.ucsd.edu/dc/object/bb8124229j.

"Pete Wilson 1994 Campaign Ad on Illegal Immigration." www.youtube.com/watch?v=lLIzzs2HHgY.

Scheer, Robert. "Prop 187 Is a Search for Scapegoats." *Los Angeles Times*, October 27, 1994, p. VYB17. (Word version of edited document available on companion website [http://GoldbergSeries.org/UTContemporaryUSHistory].)

NOTES

1. "Pete Wilson 1994 Campaign Ad on Illegal Immigration," www.youtube.com/watch?v=lLIzzs2HHgY (accessed June 16, 2020); Daniel M. Weintraub, "Wilson Ad Sparks Charges of Immigrant-Bashing," *Los Angeles Times*, May 14, 1994, p. A22.

2. Erika Lee, *America for Americans: A History of Xenophobia in the United States* (New York: Basic Books, 2019), 254.

3. Lee, *America for Americans*, specifically, the introduction.

4. Hidetaka Hirota, *Expelling the Poor: Atlantic Seaboard States and the Nineteenth-Century Origins of American Immigration Policy* (New York: Oxford University Press, 2017); Adam Goodman, *The Deportation Machine: America's Long History of Expelling* (Princeton, NJ: Princeton University Press, 2020); Erika Lee, *At America's Gates: Chinese Immigration during the Exclusion Era, 1882–1943* (Chapel Hill: University of North Carolina Press, 2003); Kelly Lytle Hernández, *Migra! A History of the US Border Patrol* (Berkeley: University of California Press, 2010); S. Deborah Kang, *The INS on the Line: Making Immigration Law on the US-Mexico Border, 1917–1954* (New York: Oxford University Press, 2017); Mae Ngai, *Impossible Subjects: Illegal Aliens and the Making of Modern America* (Princeton, NJ: Princeton University Press, 2004).

5. For a sampling of works on how the population has been characterized as a "problem," see Natalia Molina, *Fit to Be Citizens? Public Health and Race in Los Angeles, 1879–1939* (Berkeley: University of California Press, 2006); Cybelle Fox, *Three Worlds of Relief: Race, Immigration, and the American Welfare State from the Progressive Era to the New Deal* (Princeton, NJ: Princeton University Press, 2012); Mark Hendrickson, *American Labor and Economic Citizenship: New Capitalism from World War I to the Great Depression* (New York: Cambridge University Press, 2013); Carey McWilliams, *North from Mexico: The Spanish-Speaking People of the United States*, new edition updated by Matt S. Meier (New York: Praeger, 1948, 1990).

6. Scholars continue to examine racialization in all of its manifestations. The foundational text remains Michael Omi and Howard Winant, *Racial Formation in the United States*, 3rd ed. (New York: Routledge, 2015). For an overview, see also Karim Murji and John Solomos, eds., *Racialization: Studies in Theory and Practice* (Oxford: Oxford University Press, 2005). For a sampling that focuses on Latinos, see Hana E. Brown, Jennifer A. Jones, and Andrea Becker, "The Racialization of Latino Immigrants in New Destinations: Criminality, Ascription, and Countermobilization," *Russell Sage Foundation Journal of the Social Sciences* 4, no. 5 (August 2018): 118–40, https://doi.org/10.7758/rsf.2018.4.5.06; Natalia Molina, *How Race Is Made in America: Immigration, Citizenship, and the Historical Power of Racial Scripts* (Berkeley: University of California Press, 2014).

7. Ngai, *Impossible Subjects*, 6, 261; Jonathan Peter Spiro, *Defending the Master Race: Conservation, Eugenics, and the Legacy of Madison Grant* (Burlington: University of Vermont Press, 2009), 138–40, 157–58. For historical migration patterns between the US and Mexico, see Mark Overmyer-Velazquez, ed., *Beyond La Frontera: The History of Mexico-US Migration* (New York: Oxford University Press, 2011).

8. The emergence of this type of racially coded language when talking about immigration policy is similar to what happened in many white communities in the American South following the passage of the Civil Rights Act of 1964 and the Voting Rights Act of 1965. See Dan T. Carter, *The Politics of Rage: George Wallace, the Origins of the New Conservatism, and the Transformation of American Politics* (Baton Rouge: Louisiana State University Press, 2000); Kevin Kruse, *White Flight: Atlanta and the Making of Modern Conservatism* (Princeton, NJ: Princeton University Press, 2007); Matthew Lassiter, *The Silent Majority: Suburban Politics in the Sunbelt South* (Princeton, NJ: Princeton University Press, 2007).

9. Joseph Nevins, *Operation Gatekeeper and Beyond: The War on "Illegals" and the Remaking of the US-Mexico Boundary*, 2nd ed. (New York: Taylor & Francis, 2010), 79; Nicholas De Genova, *Working the Boundaries: Race, Space, and 'Illegality' in Mexican Chicago* (Durham, NC: Duke University Press, 2005), 237–38.

10. *American Legion Magazine* 97, no. 6 (December 1974), https://archive .legion.org/handle/20.500.12203/4191?show=full.

11. Nevins, *Operation Gatekeeper and Beyond*, 141–42.

12. Lee, *America for Americans*, 253, 256–58.

13. Carly Goodman, "John Tanton Has Died: He Made America Less Open to Immigrants—and More Open to Trump," *Washington Post*, July 18, 2019, https://www.washingtonpost.com/outlook/2019/07/18/john-tanton-has-died-how -he-made-america-less-open-immigrants-more-open-trump/.

14. "'WITAN Memo' III," *Intelligence Report*, Southern Poverty Law Center, October 10, 1986, https://www.splcenter.org/fighting-hate/intelligence-report/ 2015/witan-memo-iii.

15. As quoted in Jason DeParle, "The Anti-Immigration Crusader," *New York Times*, April 17, 2011, https://www.nytimes.com/2011/04/17/us/17immig.html.

16. Carly Goodman, "The Shadowy Network Shaping Trump's Anti-Immigration Policies," *Washington Post*, September 27, 2018, https://www.wash ingtonpost.com/outlook/2018/09/27/shadowy-network-shaping-trumps-anti -immigration-policies/.

17. Lee, *America for Americans*, 264.

18. *California Ballot Pamphlet, General Election, November 8, 1994* (Sacramento: California Secretary of State, 1994), 91, https://repository.uchastings.edu/ca_ ballot_pamphlets/ (accessed June 25, 2020).

19. Daniel Martinez HoSang, *Racial Propositions: Ballot Initiatives and the Making of Postwar California* (Berkeley: University of California Press, 2010), 162–67.

20. Goodman, "Shadowy Network."

21. HoSang, *Racial Propositions*, 161; Lee, *America for Americans*, 265–68. Democrats also responded to undocumented immigrants in ways that aligned with Wilson's sentiments. California's two US senators, Democrats Dianne Feinstein and Barbara Boxer, supported his lawsuits against the federal government.

22. Lee, *America for Americans*, 264. *Plyler* also extended the protections of the Fourteenth Amendment to the US-born children of undocumented immigrants. Elizabeth F. Cohen, *Illegal: How America's Lawless Immigration Regime Threatens Us All* (New York: Basic Books, 2020), 144.

23. As quoted in Lee, *America for Americans*, 270–72; "not a real solution" quote originally in all uppercase letters.

24. Otto Santa Ana, *Brown Tide Rising: Metaphors of Latinos in Contemporary American Public Discourse* (Austin: University of Texas Press, 2002), 68–78, 82–87, 95. See also Leo R. Chavez, *Covering Immigration: Popular Images and the Politics of the Nation* (Berkeley: University of California Press, 2001). Sociologist Kitty Calavita has argued that, for its supporters, Proposition 187 was a symbolic expression of politics, rather than a policy statement, based in an ideology of "balanced-budget conservatism" and new nativism. Kitty Calavita, "The New Politics of Immigration: 'Balanced-Budget Conservatism' and the Symbolism of Proposition 187," *Social Problems* 43 no. 3 (August 1996): 285, 295–98.

25. Leo Chavez, "Immigration Reform and Nativism: The Nationalist Response to the Transnationalist Challenge," in *Immigrants Out! The New Nativism and the Anti-Immigrant Impulse in the United States*, ed. Juan F. Perea (New York: New York University Press, 1997), 73; Robin Dale Jacobson, *New Nativism: Proposition 187 and the Debate over Immigration* (Minneapolis: University of Minnesota Press, 2008), 49, 51–53, 56–58, 64; Gerald L. Neuman, "Aliens as Outlaws: Government Services, Proposition 187, and the Structure of Equal Protection Doctrine," *UCLA Law Review* 42, no. 6 (1995): 1429, 1451–52.

26. Nevins, *Operation Gatekeeper and Beyond*, 98; Ngai, *Impossible Subjects*, 7.

27. Lee, *America for Americans*, 272.

28. Ibid., 272–84.

29. Ibid., 284–88.

30. In developing the lesson described here, I drew upon the following scholarly research in history education: Lendol Calder, "Uncoverage: Toward a Signature Pedagogy for the History Survey," *Journal of American History* 92, no. 4 (March 2006): 1358–70, https://doi.org/10.2307/4485896; Arlene Díaz, Joan Middendorf, David Pace, and Leah Shopkow, "The History Learning Project: A Department 'Decodes' Its Students," *Journal of American History* 94, no. 4 (March 2008): 1211–24; Laura Westhoff, "Historiographic Mapping: Toward a Signature Pedagogy for the Methods Course," *Journal of American History* 98, no. 4 (March 2012): 1114–26; and Sam Wineburg, "On the Reading of Historical Texts: Notes

on the Breach between School and Academy," *American Educational Research Journal* 28, no. 3 (Fall 1991): 495–519.

31. The "Why It Matters" paragraph and the grading criteria are an adaptation of the "Point Paragraph" developed by historian Lendol Calder. Lendol Calder, "Points of Interest," *Perspectives on History*, January 12, 2018, https://www.historians.org/publications-and-directories/perspectives-on-history/january-2018/points-of-interest-encouraging-class-participation-with-the-preparatory-point-paragraph.

32. For an overview on assessment, see Michael R. Fisher Jr. and Joe Bandy, "Assessing Student Learning," Vanderbilt University Center for Teaching, 2019, https://cft.vanderbilt.edu/assessing-student-learning/.

Something Old, Something New, Something Purple?

US Military Adaptation from the Renewed Cold War to Resurrected Confrontation

HAL M. FRIEDMAN

Why Teach This Lesson?

Since 1980, the United States military has gone through enormous changes in tumultuous times. Following a largely conventional Cold War in the last decades of the twentieth century, the American military had to adjust again to unconventional warfare with the Global War on Terrorism in Afghanistan and Iraq in the first decades of the twenty-first century. These global conflicts took place in a context of rapidly changing technologies—especially stealth and cyber technologies—as well as monumental changes in the internal structure and culture of the military. Especially significant was a mandated shift away from interservice rivalry toward "jointness," which is symbolized by the color purple—the color that emerges if one combines the colors of all traditional US military uniforms.

Every teacher will likely want to cover different aspects of this broad history, which ranges from traditional military operations such as the invasions of Kuwait and Iraq to social histories of women moving into combat roles and new policies on the integration of LGBTQ+ personnel into the military. Therefore, the opening essay is meant to provide the instructor with an overview of these changes, and then the accompanying lesson focuses on questions of determining historical significance using customizable time lines (which are Word documents on the companion website [http://GoldbergSeries.org/UTContemporary USHistory]).

Introduction

The US military is the primary way in which the country defends itself from external foes and projects its power abroad; as such, it is existentially important to the nation. Both the executive and legislative branches of the federal government are constantly engaged in thinking about the military as a tool for pursuing US objectives abroad and about its role as a social institution and a huge consumer of the national budget at home. Additionally, the military—and each of its branches—is also constantly involved in planning and training for new missions based on its knowledge of the past, new technologies, and an understanding that new threats are always appearing. All commanders in chief therefore inherit a military built by their predecessors that they try to mold and develop to meet the challenges of tomorrow. This introductory essay will help instructors understand the main innovations and challenges (military, social, and economic) that all of the commanders in chief have faced since 1980, with the underlying theme that every president faced new challenges that he could not have imagined heading into the Oval Office.

Reagan: Facing Détente and the Cold War

Ronald Reagan ran for office based on repudiating President Jimmy Carter's SALT (Strategic Arms Limitation Treaty) II negotiations with the Soviet Union, kicking the "Vietnam Syndrome" by taking up a more interventionist foreign policy, calling for higher defense spending to do this at the expense of domestic programs, and ultimately realizing but not publicly admitting that the Carter administration had already taken steps in this direction. His first administration held pretty closely to this blueprint, but his second administration required significant adaptation and innovation. While he signed on to the new Strategic Defense Initiative (SDI, pejoratively called "Star Wars" at the time) to provide a missile defense system to prevent a nuclear missile attack on the United States, he also adapted to the seismic shifts happening in the Soviet Union under the leadership of Mikhail Gorbachev and negotiated the INF (Intermediate-Range Nuclear Forces) Treaty with the USSR, which called for eliminating an entire class of nuclear weapons.[1]

Reagan's rhetoric is as important to understanding the history of the military buildup as were his actions. Reagan and other conservatives made great hay in both the 1976 and 1980 presidential elections that the SALT I and II treaties constituted a sellout of American defense, since the treaties gave the Soviet Union higher numbers of weapons. The reality—which was clear to Reagan and others who were privy to classified information—was that Soviet weaponry was so deficient compared to that of the United States that the Soviets were given higher numbers as a way of giving them some measure of a second-strike capability in a mutual assured destruction (MAD) context.[2] Additionally, Reagan's massive spending on the defense buildup was actually begun by the Carter administration and did not seriously impact American force structure until at least 1983. Yet the Soviets were very visibly demonstrating outward signs of weakness before the mid-1980s, were significantly crippled by the late 1980s, and ceased to exist by 1991, a fact that the Central Intelligence Agency (CIA) noted repeatedly.[3]

Soon after his election in 1980, Reagan conducted increased forward deployments of naval forces as well as increased ground and air unit deployments to forward bases in Western Europe, East Asia, the Middle East, and Latin America—demonstrating that he would not be deterred by fears of "another Vietnam." The US invasion of the island of Grenada in 1983 is a good example for students to analyze.[4] Operation Urgent Fury was purportedly launched to stop Grenada from becoming a Soviet-Cuban satellite in the Caribbean and to prevent American medical students on the island from being taken as hostages. This operation at first appeared to be a sledgehammer crushing an egg, but there were major fiascos in the operation, highlighted by the story of an 82nd Airborne trooper who was forced to use a phone card to call the army at the Pentagon to receive navy air support offshore because of incompatible radios.[5] This incident in Grenada led Congress and the White House to address the bitter interservice rivalries in the US military. The resulting bipartisan Goldwater-Nichols Act of 1986 sought to eliminate these rivalries by having the chair of the Joint Chiefs of Staff serve as the sole military adviser for the president and by giving the assigned combatant commanders of each geographic region operational command to coordinate the actions of all the branches in that area.[6]

The Reagan administration was decidedly less successful in managing the domestic politics of some of its more adventuresome policies. When in August 1982 the president deployed US troops as part of a multinational force to Lebanon to facilitate the withdrawal of both Palestinian and Israeli forces from that country, those troops became targets. On October 23, 1983, terrorists drove a truck bomb into the US Marine barracks in Beirut, killing 241 and prompting the February 7, 1984, announcement that American troops would be withdrawn. Even more controversial was the Iran-Contra scandal that emerged toward the end of Reagan's second term. Reagan's political and military commitments to the Contras (fighting against the Sandanista regime in Nicaragua) and his attempts to get American hostages out of Lebanon resulted in a convoluted plot in which arms were illegally sold to the Contras and the profits sent to Iran (also illegal) in order to presumably exercise influence over the hostage takers in Lebanon. Ironically, National Security Council staffer Marine Corps Lieutenant Colonel Oliver North came out of the "Iran-gate" scandal with an extraordinarily popular following instead of being court-martialed for assisting in these illegal operations.[7] Garnering less attention but having longer-term and more positive consequences for the US military as an institution were the increasing standards of living across the military during the 1980s that undergirded the All-Volunteer Force by increasing pay and benefits, requiring higher levels of education, and supporting military families. All of this resulted in more reenlistments, more married troops, and more highly trained troops to carry out the AirLand Battle doctrine's calls for rapid maneuver and precision strikes from artillery and the air in an imagined future European battle against the Soviet Union.[8]

Ultimately, the Reagan administration is probably best known for influencing the significant internal changes in the Soviet Union that brought about the end of the Cold War and ultimately the dissolution of the USSR. Reagan-era military spending has often been credited for speeding these internal processes, though it was actually the Carter administration that initiated the increased spending and increasingly confrontational posture against the USSR. The Strategic Defense Initiative (SDI) was an especially splashy incidence of this. In a nationwide television address on March 23, 1983, President Reagan proposed to spend millions developing a land-, sea-, and space-based defense system to protect the United States from a Soviet intercontinental ballistic missile (ICBM) attack. Critics quickly pointed out that it violated several international treaties (including the Outer Space Treaty of 1967) and mocked it with the nickname "Star Wars" for its seeming improbability. Nonetheless, the SDI Organization was officially established within the Department of Defense just four days after Reagan's address, and it served as a stumbling block to a nuclear agreement when Reagan and Soviet premier Mikhail Gorbachev met at Reykjavik, Iceland, in the fall of 1986. Nonetheless, the two leaders persisted and signed the INF Treaty in December 1987, gradually eliminating intermediate-range nuclear forces.[9]

Kicking the Vietnam Syndrome:
The First Persian Gulf War

When Vice President George Bush succeeded Reagan in the 1988 election, it was clear that he would continue the work of the previous commander in chief in overseeing improved relations with the Soviet Union, although the 1991 dissolution of that nation was unanticipated. In many ways signifying the end of the Cold War for the US military was that its operations shifted from preparations against the Soviet Union to preparations for what eventually became the Bush-era invasions of both Panama and Kuwait, supposedly distancing the country from its "Vietnam Syndrome" and improving on the practice of "jointness." On the home front, however, the "Tailhook" scandal revealed a permissive military culture that allowed and even encouraged sexual harassment and assault of women within the ranks.[10]

Operation Just Cause—the invasion of Panama to take its dictator, Manuel Noriega, into custody, which started in late 1989—seemed to show the effectiveness of the reforms and jointness mandated after the invasion of Grenada six years earlier. A joint force of more than 20,000 US troops deployed from the United States and Panama, striking 27 different locations simultaneously to overwhelm the Panamanian Defense Forces within 30 hours while simultaneously protecting the Panama Canal Zone and 30,000 US nationals in the country. These military forces departed as the elected government of President Guillermo Endara assumed power.[11]

An additional degree of difficulty was added with the subsequent invasion of Iraqi-occupied Kuwait, as US troops were part of a large multinational force. The Bush administration's efforts to secure as many allies as possible, especially Middle East countries, was a direct response to the American public—and even elements of Congress—being skittish about post-Vietnam military deployments. Reluctance to support military deployments could also be seen in Bush's strong statements that the Persian Gulf War would not be "another Vietnam."[12] The president was similarly quick to change his public rhetoric when he was accused of fighting a war for oil resources. Bush quickly reversed Secretary of State James Baker's assertion that the war was about oil resources, the economy, and jobs to argue that the intervention in the Persian Gulf was instead about confronting international lawlessness.[13]

Militarily, the first Persian Gulf War was a swiftly successful, limited war, but there were a number of contradictions built into the conflict. Although Iraqi forces constituted one of the largest armies in the world, it was a significantly weakened institution after a decade-long conflict with Iran, and it was facing a large US military as a result of previous administrations' budgets. Despite being a joint operation, a culture of jointness was largely absent among the US forces; each branch tried to outshine the other, knowing that Bush's fiscal conservancy, the dissolution of the Soviet Union, and the size of the US national debt would prompt postwar budget cuts. Although Iraq's ground forces collapsed in less than one hundred hours of combat in February 1991 with just four hundred US service members killed in action, nearly half of these deaths came from accidents and friendly fire. Nonetheless, President Bush claimed that the Vietnam Syndrome had been "kicked," and the nation celebrated with a ticker-tape parade down Fifth Avenue in New York City. Despite the exuberant celebration, some observers and analysts called for caution about assessing the war and its results.[14]

The victory in Iraq also did not shield the US military from scandal. Shortly after the war's end, events at the September 1991 annual meeting of the Tailhook Association (a private lobbying organization primarily consisting of active and retired naval aviators) prompted a female American naval officer in June 1992 to publicly accuse her fellow officers of sexually assaulting her and then actively seeking to cover up the crime. Just two days later, President and Mrs. Bush invited Lieutenant Paula Coughlin to meet with them. The commander in chief offered her an apology and promised her a full investigation, which led to the firing of the secretary of the navy in the short term and sweeping changes in all branches of the military and Department of Defense over the long term. Specifically, in 1993, Secretary of Defense Les Aspin announced that women could serve in almost any aviation capacity, and Congress passed legislation allowing women to serve on combat ships, effectively reversing the Pentagon's Combat Exclusion Policy.[15]

"Don't Ask, Don't Tell"

When it came to the United States military, President William (Bill) J. Clinton—the first baby boomer and nonveteran to serve in the nation's highest office since World War II—took a different approach. Clinton was open to the idea of expanding rights for gays and lesbians in American society in general and was also clearly supportive of military policy being first step in that regard. While Clinton's policy eventually became a weak compromise of "Don't Ask, Don't Tell" that satisfied neither the military—which was opposed to any changes— nor advocates of gay rights, Clinton's compromise was a product not only of the natural give and take of the political system but also the commander in chief's weak credentials (having avoided military service during the Vietnam War). Clinton was visibly uncomfortable at first with being commander in chief, and instances of service members' indiscipline and disrespect toward him marred his early administration.[16]

However, for a president who was very unfamiliar with military affairs, Clinton eventually came to employ the military with a high operational tempo, perhaps too high given that the military had shrunk from 2.1 million service members during the Reagan administration to 1.4 million by the time the Bush/Clinton-era drawdown ended.[17] Having inherited Bush's peacekeeping mission to Somalia, Clinton learned quickly how military operations could go badly and how politically poisonous US casualties—especially the bodies of dead soldiers appearing on television news—could be. Clinton also deployed the US military against a dictatorship in Haiti and then again to Bosnia, despite significant opposition from Congress, elements of the media and public, and even outgoing Joint Chiefs chair General Colin Powell. By most accounts, Clinton's rationale for US participation in the NATO peacekeeping operations in Bosnia and then Kosovo to end ethnic cleansing in the Balkans was fear that instability in the Balkans could spread to the rest of Europe. Nonetheless, the Clinton administration chose not to intervene in the subsequent deadly genocide in the African nation of Rwanda.[18] The Clinton administration also oversaw the expansion of NATO, with that organization absorbing the former Soviet-bloc nations of Poland, Hungary, and the Czech Republic in 1999; Bulgaria, Estonia, Latvia, Lithuania, Romania, Slovakia, and Slovenia in 2004; and Albania and Croatia in 2009. For the military itself, carrying out more missions with fewer personnel was worrisome, but the Clinton administration's version of doing more with less paled in comparison to that of the George W. Bush administration.[19]

George W. Bush and the Global War on Terrorism

Counterterrorism became the primary mission during George W. Bush's administration after al-Qaeda's attack on the United States on September 11, 2001. Although the United States—especially the military—had been subjected to terrorist attacks in 1996, 1998, and again in 2000, the 9/11 strike was the most surprising attack on the country since the Japanese strike on Pearl Harbor and caused even more deaths, this time primarily among civilians. *The 9/11 Commission Report* pointed out that the US federal government had been unprepared for these types of attacks, significantly due to interdepartmental rivalries in the national security establishment.[20]

These attacks prompted a hunt for those responsible for the terrorist attacks, the opening of a special prison at the US military base in Guantanamo (Cuba) to detain those arrested without granting them the constitutional protections that would be due to them on US soil, and an invasion of the nation of Afghanistan, which had provided a safe haven to Osama bin Laden and al-Qaeda to plan and launch terrorist attacks on US targets. The invasion of Afghanistan aimed not only to destroy al-Qaeda's base in Afghanistan but also to assist and train the Afghan Northern Alliance in an attempt to reform that nation so that it ceased to be a base for terrorists. Instead, the United States found itself bogged down in a lengthy nation-building and counter-insurgency campaign against al-Qaeda, which it could disrupt but not destroy.[21]

Despite its inability to stabilize the situation in Afghanistan and remove US troops, George W. Bush's administration prepared to launch another invasion. Using innuendo and manufactured intelligence, the president (supported by several close advisors) convinced the American people that Iraqi leader Saddam Hussein was linked to al-Qaeda and was still developing weapons of mass destruction (WMD), specifically nuclear weapons. Although the US intelligence community and the United Nations' inspection teams had illustrated that UN sanctions against Iraq in the wake of its invasion of Kuwait had shut down Hussein's WMD programs, the specter of a "nuclear 9/11" swayed American public opinion and Congress into supporting a conventional ground invasion of Iraq. Worse still, once the administration became determined to pursue an invasion of Iraq, State and Defense Department specialists were largely locked out of the planning for both the invasion and the postwar occupation.[22]

Although the administration strove to put the gloss of victory over the 2003 invasion, it was almost immediately clear that the more difficult mission would be to secure the peace. Secretary of Defense Donald Rumsfeld's attempt to illustrate that fewer American troops could carry out the operation and occupation in what was termed a "just in time" war resulted in too few troops for the invasion, the near defeat of US troops on several occasions, and such sparse occupation forces that the United States could not prevent post-operation looting nor weapons acquisitions by Baathist Party members who had been fired by Provisional Administrator Paul Bremer.[23] Additionally, scandals—such as the abuse of Iraqi prisoners at the Abu Ghraib prison that became public in April 2004 and the killing of twenty Iraqis by private defense contractors for the Blackwater firm on September 16, 2007—angered many Iraqis, who increasingly turned against the US occupation. Collectively, these wartime and postwar missteps by the United States led to a vicious counterinsurgency campaign that lasted for years in Iraq, consumed much of the US military—including large portions of the Reserve and National Guard—and resulted in repeated tours of duty by a smaller force that totaled less than 1 percent of the American population.[24]

The irony was that the Bush administration had invaded Iraq not just to topple Hussein but also to deny Iraqi oil to a rising China. Yet once the situation exploded in Iraq, the United States had little to no military force to face off against more serious threats such as China or the recovering power of Russia. President George W. Bush's Global War on Terrorism and his focus on the "axis of evil" of Iraq, Iran, and North Korea left much to be desired and left the military more stretched than ever.[25] In effect, the Bush administration had planted the United States squarely into another Vietnam-like quagmire resulting in significant US casualties, serious civil liberty abuses, and the nation being gripped in a national security culture that in some ways rivaled the Cold War paranoia of the 1950s.

The Obama Administration

The new president, Barack Obama, sought to help the United States recover from the Great Recession of 2008 and disengage from the costly wars of the previous administration. He consistently drew down troops in both Afghanistan and Iraq, even as new threats arose in the Middle East, most notably the Islamic State of Iraq and Syria (ISIS). Instead, the president invested in new technologies—including drones and the modernization of US nuclear forces—to project American power abroad while reducing military personnel and budgets.[26] On the home front, Obama administration initiatives dovetailed with the military's need to effectively recruit a broader cross section of young Americans.[27]

Even though the Middle East had not stabilized from an American perspective and had in fact become even more chaotic, it was clear that neither the American public nor the nation's military leadership wanted much more to do with nation-building missions in the Middle East. The Obama administration drew down US troop levels in Iraq to a few hundred and in Afghanistan to a few thousand just as civil war between the US-backed regime and ISIS began. Instability and warfare spread to Syria as well, but the Obama administration deployed military aid to allies and drone technology almost exclusively in the new conflict against ISIS.[28] Relatively inexpensive both monetarily and in terms of risking the lives of American aircrew, drone missile strikes seemed to be the perfect way to utilize US military technology to pursue the Global War on Terrorism, minimize American casualties, and allegedly minimize civilian casualties or what the Pentagon called "collateral damage." That the technology did not always work as advertised when it came to collateral damage is not surprising from a military historical perspective. Nor is it a shock that al-Qaeda, ISIS, and the Taliban characterized such strikes as particularly cowardly ways of fighting and therefore used them in recruitment. The situation on the ground also became increasingly complicated, as Russian troops reinforced the regime of Bashar al-Assad in Syria, Kurdish troops clashed with Turkish troops, and everyone presumably fought against the Islamic State, whose power started to wane toward the end of the Obama administration. The entry of Russia on the scene further signaled that country's resurgence following its 2014 annexation of Crimea from Ukraine. Obama's foreign policy was more and more confrontational with Vladimir Putin's Russia, including continuing and intensifying George W. Bush's rotational deployments of American forces to Eastern European members of NATO such as Poland and Romania.[29]

Domestically, military personnel who had been deployed in Iraq and Afghanistan often struggled to reenter American society. At the same time that the military was often the only institution that the public would claim as trustworthy in polls and many of their fellow citizens thanked veterans for their service, this group suffered from physical wounds and disabilities as well as disproportionately from post-traumatic stress disorder (PTSD), homelessness, joblessness, and suicide. The Veterans Affairs (VA) health system struggled and failed to keep up with the needs of these new veterans, with delays in medical service becoming a veritable national scandal by mid-2014.[30]

In the midst of such stories and a significant economic recovery, the US military struggled to recruit sufficient new volunteers in terms of both quantity and quality. The December 2010 discarding of the costly "Don't Ask, Don't Tell" policy of the Clinton administration allowed the military to better compete with civilian employers as unemployment rates fell.[31] This was all the more important as a Joint Chiefs of Staff study in the fall of 2009 found that 25 percent of the country's military age-eligible population—eighteen- to twenty-six-year-olds—was ineligible for military service because of obesity. This statistic lent a national-security dimension to the Obama administration's efforts to improve the nutritional content of school lunches and to provide health care to a broader cross section of American citizens with the Affordable Care Act.[32]

President Trump's Ambivalent Relationship with the Military

The election of Donald Trump as president demonstrated the military's place in the new cultural order. On the one hand, Trump frequently lauded those who had served and went even further than previous presidents in appointing retired generals to key positions such as national security advisor, secretary of defense, and secretary of home-land security, at least early in his term of office.[33] On the other hand, the rivalry between Trump and the Vietnam War hero and Republican sen-ator John McCain over—among other things—Trump's lack of military service and Trump's insult of McCain's time as a prisoner of war in North Vietnam revealed the administration's conflict not only with the military establishment itself but with the culture of the US military.[34]

Trump promised during his campaign and his administration to allocate greater financial support for the military, including continuing very expensive programs such as the F-35 Joint Strike Fighter, more ships for the navy, and a more aggressive stance by American naval forces against Chinese military forces and artificial bases in the South China Sea. His actions, however, were really more a continuation of the Obama administration's policies when it came to these military matters. The last coincided with Trump's tougher stance against the PRC (People's Republic of China) on trade issues, but Trump failed to focus on China and Russia as the most serious national security threats to the United States. He also first zeroed in on but then minimized North Korea's nuclear capabilities. His administration also oversaw continued mili-tary withdrawal from the Middle East, even as he withdrew the coun-try from its treaty commitments over Iran's nuclear stance. Moreover, Trump failed to confront Russian interference in Eastern Europe and the Middle East, not surprising given that his pre-election activities cre-ated at least the impression of questionable if not treasonable actions vis-à-vis Putin and the Russian Republic. It also continued to be unclear at the end of his administration what future the United States military would have given the extraordinarily poor fiscal health of the country and the literally poor physical health of a large portion of America's youth who might be recruited.[35]

Perhaps more centrally, the Trump administration and future pres-idential administrations as well as the Congress, the media, and the public have to deal with what has been called the state of "never-ending" war in which the United States has been engaged since 9/11. The cyber war that has been going on between the United States, Rus-sia, and China for the past several years is a perfect example of this, since no one—not even the US military—can provide a good definition of cyber war or can describe how one knows if one's country has been attacked or has attacked, how one of these conflicts is declared or started, or when one ends, if a cyber war even has an end to it.[36]

Conclusion

The history of the US military from the Reagan through the Trump administrations allows teachers to have their students explore not just the US military and its overseas activities but also major aspects of post–Vietnam War American society. First, students can learn about the military as an institution, both its unique aspects and the ways in which it reflects its larger society in terms of its politics, social composition, and change over time. In addition, this history allows students to explore how each president has interacted with and used the military in terms of rhetoric and reality as seen through primary sources.

Lesson Plan for Thinking about Historical
Significance in US Military Affairs since 1980

In this lesson plan, we invite students into the work of historians—especially historians of recent American history—by answering questions such as how do historians make sense of long lists of events and how do historians decide what is historically significant? These are some of the historical thinking skills that this lesson will highlight.

Having read through a summary of military affairs in the Reagan through Trump presidencies preceding this lesson, teachers should be prepared to guide students to further develop their historical thinking skills. On the companion website (http://GoldbergSeries.org/UTContemporaryUSHistory), you will find chronological time lines for each of the presidencies since 1980 as Word documents. Events related to the military, national security, current and former military personnel, and weapons systems are listed in chronological order for each administration, with links to visual and textual primary sources where available. You can edit these chronologies to best fit your focus, your students' abilities, and your classroom needs. For example, depending on the time you have available, you could cover military affairs from 1980 to the present in a single lesson—perhaps shortening the chronologies, dividing them among small groups, and having each group report to the rest of the class. Or you could revisit these materials and use the full chronologies at several points toward the end of the semester as you get to these administrations.

You will design and tailor the lesson to best fit your needs, but here are some suggestions.

Preparation and Patterns

Have students read through a chronology and relevant primary source(s) as homework or in class individually or in groups (if an in-class assignment, you will likely want to shorten the chronologies). Have students identify any patterns they see emerging within each administration. Ask students to report on the patterns they have identified in writing or orally. If students do not notice, the teacher should point out that these patterns often cross presidential administrations. For example, fighting the Islamic State was the work of the G. W. Bush, Obama, and Trump administrations. And students should notice, and the teacher might want to emphasize, that there are persistent issues across the past four decades, including US involvement in the Middle East and efforts to curb nuclear proliferation and reduce existing nuclear stockpiles. I suggest starting by identifying patterns, because historical significance often is defined by an event's position within a larger pattern or movement. Is it the cause of, the result of, or a powerful example of this pattern or movement?

Defining Historical Significance

If you have not already discussed historical significance over the course of the semester, I would suggest an opening discussion or exercise in which students develop their own working definition of historical significance based on their previous studies over the course of the semester or year. For example, the instructor might write several terms on the board (e.g., *Brown v. Board of Education*, the bombing of Pearl Harbor, and the Nineteenth Amendment) and ask students (1) if these are historically significant events and (2) what makes them historically significant. Through discussion, develop by consensus a classroom working definition of "historical significance." This step is key to a fruitful discussion of the historically significant events in the chronologies.[37]

Class Activity

If you have already discussed historical significance previously in this semester or school year, or once you have developed your classroom definition (using the previous step), you can use the provided chronologies (one at a time or several at a time) and ask students (individually or in small groups) to identify the most historically significant event on their time line and to defend their interpretation. Other students or small groups may have different interpretations and defenses, which allows for a robust discussion in which students can explore why and how some events are more historically significant than others. And like the best historical questions for classroom discussion, there is not a single, clear answer.

Discussion

I believe that this lesson is particularly well suited for wrestling with the challenges all historians and students face when trying to determine what is historically significant while it is happening. You might point to some items in the chronology that struck people at the time as historically significant (such as the terrorist attacks on 9/11), but then point to some items in the chronology that only seemed historically significant later or in light of later events (such as the bombing of the US embassies in Tanzania and Kenya or the attack on the USS *Cole* as precursors to the 9/11 attacks). You can also address students' potentially unidentified assumptions about the flow of history. For example, because many of the stories that Americans tell about themselves and that students are taught in K–12 show progress and have "happy endings," students might be surprised that all of the work, time, lives, and billions of dollars in US aid spent toward developing sustainable governments in Afghanistan and Iraq utterly failed to produce states that could survive the withdrawal of US troops.

Another rich element of this lesson is that while it works with time lines, it very much calls into question conventional chronologies. For example, students' textbooks likely identify the civil rights movement as starting in 1953 with the *Brown v. Board of Education* US Supreme Court decision and ending with passage of the 1965 Voting Rights Act, but this overlooks that President Harry Truman ordered desegregation of the US military in 1948. This example also raises the question of whether the military has led the country in promoting social change or reflects the social changes of the home front. We also see within these chronologies the "end" of the Cold War with the dissolution of the Soviet Union in 1991, but there are significant continuities to the present in US conflicts with the communist or autocratic governments of Russia and the People's Republic of China that have led contemporary observers to call current events a "new" Cold War.

Closing Activity

At this point, students may have already noticed that it seems to be "harder" or that there is more discussion and dispute about what is historically significant the closer that we get to the present. You can reinforce or surface this with a final exercise that asks students to apply all that they have learned about historical significance to the chronology of the Biden administration, which at this writing is the shortest of all of the chronologies (although we hope to continue updating this on the website). Start by asking students if there is anything missing from the chronology and have them add events as appropriate. Then, as students have already done previously in the lesson, have them identify the most historically significant event of the Biden administration. Call on students or small groups for their answers and justification. See if there is consensus (there might be, because there may be fewer events on the chronology) or if there is difficulty in identifying significance—since we do not know how the story will end.

Conclusion

I would suggest that you wind up this discussion—which will come toward the end of the school year or semester—by discussing how history is equipped to give us the tools to better understand what is going on around us in life. Students can start seeing patterns of change and continuity, they can critically analyze sources ranging from news stories to people's opinions on social media, they can identify the context that shapes events or people, they can exercise historical empathy to better understand other people's actions, and they can be better citizens in this democracy as a result.

Assessment

Depending on your student learning outcomes, you can assess students' historical thinking skills (social studies practice objectives in some state standards) through their homework, class discussion, group work, and a concluding assignment that, for example, might ask students to identify and justify the historical significance of an event. Additionally, you might want to have students do further research on the event that they identify as significant or have them provide evidence from the primary source associated with the event or pattern.

NOTES

1. For the pattern of the Carter administration's origins of the defense buildup, see Brian Auten, *Carter's Conversion: The Hardening of American Defense Policy* (Columbia: University of Missouri Press, 2008).

2. "Strategic Arms Limitations Talks (SALT I) Texts," Federation of American Scientists, https://fas.org/nuke/control/salt1/text/index.html; "Strategic Arms Limitation Talks (SALT II) Texts," Federation of American Scientists, https://fas .org/nuke/control/salt2/text/index.html. For Reagan's views on SALT and nuclear matters, see Rowland Evans and Robert Novak, "Reagan's SALT Measure," *Washington Post*, July 16, 1986, p. A15; Ronald Reagan, "Message to the Congress Transmitting a Report on Soviet Noncompliance with Arms Control Agreements," March 10, 1987, Reagan Library, https://www.reaganlibrary.gov/re search/speeches/031087c; and Ronald Reagan, "The President's News Conference," January 29, 1981, American Presidency Project, University of California, Santa Barbara, https://www.presidency.ucsb.edu/documents/the-presidents -news-conference-992.

3. For an example of the CIA estimates, see Douglas J. MacEachin, "CIA Assessments of the Soviet Union," January 1997, https://www.cia.gov/static/bc 2e3557eaea99d155f41b6065efc3bd/cia-assessments-soviet-union.pdf.

4. Ronald Cole, *Operation Urgent Fury: The Planning and Execution of Joint Operations in Grenada, 12 October–2 November 1983* (Washington, DC: Joint History Office, 1997), https://www.jcs.mil/Portals/36/Documents/History/Monographs/ Urgent_Fury.pdf.

5. During the invasion, US Army units, pinned down by enemy fire, tried to call for fire support from navy warships offshore, but they discovered that army and navy radio systems were incompatible. One of the 82nd Airborne troopers supposedly used a phone card to call the Pentagon, so the army could contact its navy counterparts in Washington, DC, who in turn would contact their ships offshore. See William Schmidt, "2 Soldiers, Back from Grenada, Tell of Landing under Heavy Fire," *New York Times*, October 28, 1983, https://www .nytimes.com/1983/10/28/world/2-soldiers-back-from-grenada-tell-of-landing -under-heavy-fire.html.

6. Gordon Lederman, *Reorganizing the Joint Chiefs of Staff: The Goldwater- Nichols Act of 1986* (Westport, CT: Greenwood Press, 1999).

7. Malcolm Byrne, *Iran-Contra: Reagan's Scandal and the Unchecked Abuse of Presidential Power* (Lawrence: University Press of Kansas, 2014); James David Barber, "How Irangate Differs from Watergate," *New York Times*, August 9, 1987,

https://www.nytimes.com/1987/08/09/opinion/how-irangate-differs-from-water
gate.html.

8. James Kitfield, *Prodigal Soldiers: How the Generation of Officers Born of Vietnam Revolutionized the American Style of War* (New York: Simon & Schuster, 1995);
Douglas W. Skinner, "AirLand Battle Doctrine," Professional Paper 463, Center
for Naval Analyses, September 1988, https://apps.dtic.mil/sti/pdfs/ADA202888
.pdf.

9. US State Department, "Intermediate-Range Nuclear Forces Treaty (INF
Treaty), 1987," https://2001-2009.state.gov/r/pa/ho/time/rd/104266.htm.

10. For some of the primary sources, see "Tailhook: Scandal Time," *Newsweek*, July 5, 1992, https://www.newsweek.com/tailhook-scandal-time-200362;
and "Tailhook '91," *Frontline*, https://www.pbs.org/wgbh/pages/frontline/shows/
navy/tailhook/91.html. For a secondary source analyzing the event and the navy
from an ethical perspective and also including selected primary sources, see
Joselyn Ogden, "Tailhook '91 and the U.S. Navy," Case Studies in Ethics, Kenan
Institute for Ethics, Duke University, https://kenan.ethics.duke.edu/wp-content/
uploads/2018/01/TailhookUSNavy_Case2015.pdf.

11. Lt. Col. James H. Embrey, "Operation Just Cause: Concepts for Shaping
Future Rapid Decisive Operations," in *Transformation Concepts for National Security in the 21st Century*, ed. Williamson Murray (Carlisle, PA: Strategic Studies
Institute, Army War College, September 2002), 198–99, https://www.globalsecur
ity.org/military/library/report/2002/ssi_murray.pdf.

12. "Oral History: Colin Powell," *Frontline*, https://www.pbs.org/wgbh/
pages/frontline/gulf/oral/powell/1.html; Helen Thomas, "Bush Says a Gulf War
Would Not Be Another Vietnam," UPI, December 18, 1990, https://www.upi
.com/Archives/1990/12/18/Bush-says-a-gulf-war-would-not-be-another-Viet
nam/7507661496400/.

13. Rick Atkinson, *Crusade: The Untold Story of the Persian Gulf War* (New
York: Houghton Mifflin, 1993); Michael Gordon and General Bernard Trainor,
The Generals' War: The Inside Story of the Conflict in the Gulf (New York: Little,
Brown, 1995). For the controversy over war aims, see "Oral History: James
Baker," *Frontline*, https://www.pbs.org/wgbh/pages/frontline/gulf/oral/baker/1
.html; and William Safire, "Neither Oil nor Jobs," *Baltimore Evening Sun*, Novem-
ber 20, 1990, https://www.baltimoresun.com/news/bs-xpm-1990-11-20-1990324
139-story.html.

14. Jeffrey Engel, *When the World Seemed New: George H. W. Bush and the End
of the Cold War* (New York: Houghton Mifflin, 2017); Steven Beardsley, "'Mother
of All Battles' Lasted Only 100 Hours," *Stars and Stripes*, February 25, 2016,
https://www.stripes.com/mother-of-all-battles-lasted-only-100-hours-1.395996;
Atkinson, *Crusade*, 469–500; Gordon and Trainor, *Generals' War*, 433–77; "National
Victory Celebration Parade," C-SPAN, June 8, 1991, https://www.c-span.org/
video/?18328-1/national-victory-celebration-parade; Christopher Layne, "Why

the Gulf War Was Not in the National Interest," *Atlantic Monthly*, July 1991, https://www.theatlantic.com/past/docs/unbound/flashbks/saudiara/layne .htm; "General Norman Schwarzkopf Speech to West Point Corps of Cadets," May 1, 1991, https://www.youtube.com/watch?v=uGfrMzqNZqc.

15. See note 10 above.

16. For primary source analyses of the "Don't Ask, Don't Tell" policy, see Title V: Military Personnel Policy, Subtitle G: Other Matters, House Resolution 2401, National Defense Authorization Act for Fiscal Year 1994, 103rd Congress (1993–1994), https://www.congress.gov/bill/103rd-congress/house-bill/2401; Lieutenant Colonel Kevin Connors, "Clinton's Policy Relating to Gays in the Military: A Lesson in Politics at the National Level," National War College Seminar Paper, 1999, https://apps.dtic.mil/dtic/tr/fulltext/u2/a442396.pdf.

17. Melissa Healy, "Clinton Defense Budget Cuts into Troops, Ships," *Los Angeles Times*, March 27, 1993, https://www.latimes.com/archives/la-xpm-1993 -03-27-mn-15800-story.html.

18. Andrew Bacevich, *American Empire: The Realities and Consequences of U.S. Diplomacy* (Cambridge, MA: Harvard University Press), 79–197. For primary sources, see Helen Thomas, "Clinton Orders U.S. Military Attack against Iraq," UPI, June 26, 1993, https://www.upi.com/Archives/1993/06/26/Clinton-orders -US-military-attack-against-Iraq/7662741067200/; Office of the Historian, State Department, "Intervention in Haiti, 1994–1995," *Milestones: 1993–2000*, https:// history.state.gov/milestones/1993-2000/haiti; John Broder, "Clinton: A Vocal Dove Turned Hesitant Hawk," *New York Times*, March 28, 1999, https://archive. nytimes.com/www.nytimes.com/library/world/europe/032899kosovo-com mand.html; and Kathleen Pate et al., "What Should the United States Do about the Kosovo Crisis?," in *Advise the President: William J. Clinton*, William J. Clinton Presidential Library and Museum, 1999, https://www.archives.gov/files/presi dential-libraries/advisethepresident/clinton-kosovo.pdf.

19. Bacevich, *American Empire*, 79–197; Healy, "Clinton Defense Budget."

20. National Commission on Terrorist Attacks, *The 9/11 Commission Report* (New York: W. W. Norton, 2004); Alfred Goldberg, Sarandis Papadopoulos, Diane Putney, Nancy Berlage, and Rebecca Welch, *Pentagon 9/11* (Washington, DC: Office of Secretary of Defense Historical Office, 2007).

21. For the invasion and attempted occupation of Afghanistan early in the Global War on Terrorism, see Sean Naylor, *Not a Good Day to Die: The Untold Story of Operation Anaconda* (New York: Berkley Books, 2005).

22. For a comprehensive account of the US invasion of Iraq, see Michael Gordon and General Bernard Trainor, *Cobra II: The Inside Story of the Invasion and Occupation of Iraq* (New York: Vintage Books, 2007). See also the PBS *Frontline* episode "Rumsfeld's War," https://www.pbs.org/wgbh/pages/frontline/shows/ pentagon/view/ (posted October 26, 2004).

23. The concept of a "just in time" war emerged within the context of the revolution in military affairs (RMA), supposedly a situation in which the United States had such overwhelming military technology that future foes would be easily defeated or even cowed into submission without much of a fight.

24. See sources in note 22.

25. President George W. Bush, "State of the Union Address," CNN, January 29, 2002, http://edition.cnn.com/2002/ALLPOLITICS/01/29/bush.speech.txt/.

26. For Obama's defense budget, see Louis Jacobson and Amy Sherman, "PolitiFact Sheet: Military Spending under Obama and Congress," December 14, 2015, https://www.politifact.com/truth-o-meter/article/2015/dec/14/politifact -sheet-our-guide-to-military-spending-/. For an analysis of the Triad modern-ization, see Jon Wolfsthal, Jeffery Lewis, and Marc Quint, *The Trillion Dollar Nuclear Triad: US Strategic Nuclear Modernization over the Next Thirty Years* (Mon-terey, CA: James Martin Center for Nonproliferation Studies, 2014).

27. See Thomas Spoehr and Bridget Handy, *The Looming National Security Crisis: Young Americans Unable to Serve in the Military*, Center for National Defense, Heritage Foundation, February 13, 2018, https://www.heritage.org/defense/report/the-looming-national-security-crisis-young-americans-unable-serve-the -military.

28. For the argument that Obama's national security policy was more about continuity with George W. Bush's rather than change, see Andrew Bacevich, *Washington Rules: America's Path to Permanent War* (New York: Metropolitan Books, 2010), 245–50. For the primary sources from 2011 and 2017, see White House, "President Obama Has Ended the War in Iraq," October 21, 2011, https://obamawhitehouse.archives.gov/blog/2011/10/21/president-obama-has -ended-war-iraq; Mark Thompson, "Obama Slows Down U.S. Troop Pullout from Afghanistan," *Time*, July 6, 2016, https://time.com/4394955/afghanistan -barack-obama-troops-pullout/; "Obama Leaves Complicated Legacy in Iraq, Afghanistan, and Iraq," *PBS Newshour*, January 13, 2017, https://www.pbs.org/newshour/show/obama-leaves-complicated-legacy-iraq-afghanistan-syria.

29. For the origins of the renewed confrontation with Russia, see Stephen Cohen, *Failed Crusade: America and the Tragedy of Post-Communist Russia* (New York: W. W. Norton, 2000). For related primary sources, see David Frum, "Obama Just Made the Ultimate Commitment to Eastern Europe," *Atlantic*, September 3, 2014, https://www.theatlantic.com/international/archive/2014/09/obama-commit ment-eastern-europe-russia-nato/379581/; and Abel Romero, "Thanks, Obama: Tracking the President's Missile Defense Embrace," *RealClear Defense*, January 26, 2017, https://www.realcleardefense.com/articles/2017/01/27/the_presidents_ missile_defense_embrace_110702.html.

30. For some of the costs of the Global War on Terrorism, see Rear Admiral Michael Baker, "Casualties of the Global War on Terror and Their Future Impact on Health Care and Society: A Looming Public Health Crisis," *Military Medicine*

179, no. 4 (April 2014): 348–55, https://academic.oup.com/milmed/article/179/4/348/4160773; and Oriana Pawlyk, "Lawmakers: End Afghanistan War, Give Every GWOT Vet a $2,500 Bonus," March 5, 2019, https://www.military.com/daily-news/2019/03/05/lawmakers-end-afghanistan-war-give-every-gwot-vet-2500-bonus.html.

31. For the repeal of Don't Ask, Don't Tell, see Public Law 111–321, December 22, 2010, 111th Congress, https://www.congress.gov/111/plaws/publ321/PLAW-111publ321.pdf. For Obama's statement on the repeal, see Office of the White House Press Secretary, "Statement by the President on Certification of Repeal of Don't Ask, Don't Tell," July 22, 2011, https://obamawhitehouse.archives.gov/the-press-office/2011/07/22/statement-president-certification-repeal-dont-ask-dont-tell. For the financial costs of Don't Ask, Don't Tell, see Crosby Burns, "What DADT Cost Us: Misguided Policy Wasted Taxpayer Dollars, Military Talent," Center for American Progress, September 20, 2011, https://www.americanprogress.org/issues/security/news/2011/09/20/10399/what-dadt-cost-us/.

32. Spoehr and Handy, *Looming National Security Crisis*.

33. For Trump's initial love affair with the generals, see Glenn Fleishman, "Trump Once Called Them 'My Generals': After Mattis Resigns, They'll All Be Gone," *Fortune*, December 20, 2018, https://fortune.com/2018/12/20/trump-mattis-resignation-letter-my-generals-flynn-kelly-mcmaster/; and Jonathan Marcus, "Why Did Trump's Love Affair with US Generals Turn Sour?," BBC News, January 6, 2019, https://www.bbc.com/news/world-us-canada-46766271.

34. For Trump's insults toward McCain, see Bess Levin, "It Sure Sounds Like Trump Just Implied John McCain Is Rotting in Hell," *Vanity Fair*, June 26, 2019, https://www.vanityfair.com/news/2019/06/donald-trump-john-mccain-greener-pastures; and Davie Boyer, "Trump Says He's 'Making Up' for Lack of Military Service with Defense Buildup," *Washington Times*, June 5, 2019, https://www.washingtontimes.com/news/2019/jun/5/donald-trump-says-hes-making-lack-military-service/.

35. See Bryan Bender, "Russia Beating U.S. in Race for Global Influence, Pentagon Study Says," *Politico*, June 30, 2019, https://www.politico.com/story/2019/06/30/pentagon-russia-influence-putin-trump-1535243; Frederick Kempe, "Trump's Escalating Trade War Gives Heat to Putin and Xi's Growing Bromance," *CNBC Newsletters*, June 1, 2019, https://www.cnbc.com/2019/05/31/trumps-escalating-trade-war-gives-heat-to-putin-and-xis-growing-bromance.html; and James Miller and Michael O'Hanlon, "Quality over Quantity: U.S. Military Strategy and Spending in the Trump Years, Policy Brief," Brookings Institution, January 2019, https://www.brookings.edu/wp-content/uploads/2019/01/FP_20190103_military_strategy_spending.pdf.

36. For the concept of the "forever war," see Bacevich, *Washington Rules*, 6–34, 222–50. See also Michael Harriot, "Report: Intelligence Officials Won't Brief

Trump on Cyberattacks against Russia for Fear He Might Get Mad and Tell Putin," *Root,* June 16, 2019, https://www.theroot.com/report-intelligence-officials -wont-brief-trump-on-cybe-1835560314; and Office of the President, *National Cyber Strategy of the United States of America,* September 2018, https://trump whitehouse.archives.gov/wp-content/uploads/2018/09/National-Cyber-Strat egy.pdf. For an assessment of Trump's military legacy, see Tom Bowman, "Trump and the Military: What an Erratic Commander in Chief Leaves Behind," National Public Radio, January 4, 2021, https://www.npr.org/2021/01/04/951203 109/trump-and-the-military-what-an-erratic-commander-in-chief-leaves-behind.

37. Bruce A. Lesh, *"Why Won't You Just Tell Us the Answer?": Teaching Historical Thinking in Grades 7–12* (Portsmouth, NH: Stenhouse Publishers, 2011), 137–52; Bob Bain, "Into the Breach: Using Research and Theory to Shape History Instruction," in *Knowing, Teaching, and Learning History,* ed. Peter Stearns, Peter Sexias, and Sam Wineburg (New York: New York University Press, 2000); Martin Hunt, "Teaching Historical Significance," in *Issues in History Teaching,* ed. James Arthur and Robert Phillips (London: Routledge, 2000).

Arctic Nation

Climate Change Changes Policy

JEREMY M. MCKENZIE AND

LAURA KRENICKI

Why Teach This Lesson?

The Arctic has been important to the United States since the purchase of Alaska from Russia in 1867. Its strategic significance grew during World War II (when Lend-Lease supplies from the United States traversed the area) and the Cold War (when nuclear weapons were imagined to fly over it).[1] American policy in the Arctic has always been a balance between environmental protection and development. Yet, global warming has made the polar region dramatically more important in the past decade to policymakers, because the Arctic is warming twice as fast as the lower latitudes. As a result, recent US presidents have increasingly sought to balance environmental preservation with the opportunities that a melting ice pack could bring (including new sea routes, resources, and economic development for Arctic communities, which some have termed a potential "cold rush"[2]). Tracing both the continuities and changes in Arctic policy since 1980 provides students with an exceptional case study of how climate change is impacting US policy from the economy to national security.

Introduction

The Arctic—one of earth's most unique and transnational regions, consisting of the Arctic Ocean, adjacent seas, and parts of Alaska

(United States), Canada, Finland, Greenland (Denmark), Iceland, Norway, Russia, and Sweden—is experiencing an astonishing transformation due to climate change.[3] The consequences of global warming—including rising temperatures, loss of sea ice, and melting of the Greenland ice sheet—have been accompanied by a renewed strategic interest in the area's extraordinary resources that were previously largely inaccessible as well as its increasingly accessible waterways.[4] For example, on August 2, 2007, the Russians planted a flag on the seabed at the North Pole. In response, a number of articles declared that a new "great race" was beginning for the Arctic's resources.[5] In January 2009, just days before his final day in office, President George W. Bush signed National Security Presidential Directive (NSPD) 66, which built on President Nixon's Arctic policy and which set policy and strategy precedents that continued into the administrations of both Presidents Obama and Trump. In the lesson below, students will examine the changes in US Arctic policy in the seven key areas that these presidents

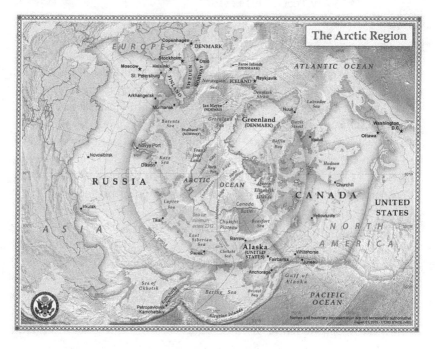

State Department geographers created this map of the Arctic as part of the US chairmanship of the Arctic Council. (https://2009-2017.state.gov/e/oes/ocns/opa/arc/uschair/258202.htm)

identified: environmental protection, sustainable development, international cooperation, security, preservation of the freedom of navigation, the establishment of an Interagency Arctic Policy Group, and scientific exploration.[6]

Understanding the importance of the Arctic requires looking at the earth from a different perspective. As students reorient their geographic perspective, they recognize that the United States is an Arctic nation. They also recognize that the United States and Russia are neighbors but also rivals for access to the region. Additionally, students can discover transit across the Arctic could dramatically reduce shipping distances (by as much as one-third) versus traditional routes using the Panama and Suez canals.[7] For all of these reasons, the US government has its eye on the Arctic and began developing policy and strategy toward the region beginning in the 1970s, which it prioritized in the 1980s.

The Arctic "Warrants Priority Attention"

Ronald Reagan's Arctic policy—National Security Decision Directive 90: United States Arctic Policy—largely reaffirmed Richard Nixon's earlier 1971 policy. The Reagan directive begins with the proclamation "It is clear that the United States has unique and critical interests in the Arctic region," and reiterates interests stated earlier. Reagan's directive notes, however, "In light of the region's growing importance, it warrants priority attention by the United States."[8] This attention resulted in the creation of the Interagency Arctic Research Policy Committee (IARPC) in 1984 and the Arctic Research Commission in 1985.[9] Having strengthened the US stance toward the Arctic, Reagan was ready to promote international cooperation, as witnessed by the inclusion of the Arctic on the agenda of his December 1987 summit with Soviet general secretary Mikhail Gorbachev. The resulting joint statement emphasized "expanded contacts and cooperation on" Arctic issues, including "bilateral and regional cooperation," "coordination of scientific research," and "protection of the region's environment."[10]

President George Bush's administration continued his predecessor's focus on developing international cooperation around the Arctic as well as preserving key US strategic interests. From 1989 to 1991, the United States worked with the other seven Arctic countries (Finland, Sweden, Iceland, Norway, Denmark, Canada, and Russia) to establish the Arctic Environmental Protection Strategy (AEPS, the precursor to today's

This iceberg is surrounded by sea ice and polar bear tracks in Storfjorden in the Svalbard archipelago. A scene like this is probably what most people imagine when they think about the Arctic. (photo by Jeremy M. McKenzie)

Arctic Tromsø, Norway, is a direct contrast to what most people think of as the Arctic. The Arctic is inhabited by about four million people. (photo by Jeremy M. McKenzie)

Arctic Council) with a mandate for environmental protection. On June 1, 1990, Bush and Gorbachev signed a maritime boundary agreement resolving the maritime boundary in the Bering Sea and placing 70 percent of that sea under US control. Following the Soviet Union's collapse, the Russian government failed to ratify the agreement, yet it has been provisionally enforced by both sides.[11]

Acknowledging that the end of the Cold War provided a "significant shift of emphasis in US Arctic policy," the Clinton administration's 1994 Arctic policy prioritized cooperation and environmental sustainability and added the policy goal of "involving the Arctic's Indigenous peoples in decisions that affect them."[12] To these ends, the United States signed the Ottawa Declaration in 1996, which created the Arctic Council—a high-level, intergovernmental forum that sought active Indigenous participation for discussion of common regional issues, especially sustainable development and environmental protection.[13] The Clinton White House did not, however, solely focus on international cooperation and environmental issues in the Arctic. It set a new precedent in October 1998 by including the region in its US national security document *A National Security Strategy for a New Century*. In keeping with both the Clinton administration's priorities and the geopolitical situation of the world, the strategy especially focused on working "to mitigate nuclear and non-nuclear pollution in the Arctic."[14]

New Century, New Security Threats, and a New Focus on the Arctic

The twenty-first century brought to the fore new priorities with regard to US policy toward the Arctic region. President George W. Bush entered office wanting to lessen US reliance on energy from the Middle East and Russia, and the 9/11 terrorist attacks meant that new national security imperatives largely defined his administration. Popular concern about the dangers of climate change also grew more demanding during his presidency. The planting of a Russian flag at the North Pole in 2007 helped focus the administration on the Arctic.[15] The result was a new and more intensive attention on the Arctic, including two key statements of US policy toward the polar region under the George W. Bush administration. First, in May 2008, the Bush administration adopted the Ilulissat Declaration, whereby Canada, Denmark, Norway, Russia, and the United States agreed that the United Nations

Convention on the Law of the Sea "provides a solid foundation for responsible management" of the Arctic Ocean and that there was therefore no need for a separate treaty regime, such as that for Antarctica.[16] The Illulissat Declaration can be seen as a preemptive move by the five Arctic coastal states to ensure that a new treaty regime would not be imposed that could limit their rights in the region. Second, at the end of his second term, President Bush published a significant new Arctic strategy that is still guiding US policy today. It starts by asserting, "The United States is an Arctic nation, with varied and compelling interests in that region." Then it points to the reasons for issuing a new policy, including "altered national policies on homeland security and defense, the effects of climate change and increasing human activity in the Arctic region, the establishment and ongoing work of the Arctic council, and a growing awareness that the Arctic region is both fragile and rich in resources." This was the first US Arctic strategy document to mention climate change as a driving force in US policy development. Other notable changes from previous Arctic policies include anti-terrorism efforts and a call for the Senate to ratify the UN Convention on the Law of the Sea, both as a means to govern the Arctic as well as furthering US national security objectives outside the region.[17]

Bush's policy highlighted key goals—some of them new—that demonstrated a commitment to a multilateral approach to protecting the fragile Arctic environment while at the same time ensuring US national security. Alongside the commitment to meeting national security and homeland security needs relevant to the Arctic region was the commitment to conserving its biological resources and ensuring that its natural resource management and economic development were environmentally sustainable. To meet these goals, the policy also called for strengthening cooperation among the eight Arctic nations, involving the Arctic's Indigenous communities in decision-making, and enhancing scientific monitoring and research into local, regional, and global environmental issues. President George W. Bush's initiative put a spotlight on the Arctic, laying the groundwork for at least twenty-five high-level, executive branch statements of US policy in the region during the Obama and Trump administrations.

The Obama administration followed in the footsteps of its predecessor, focusing on national security and climate change in the Arctic. The importance of the region in strategic formulations becomes evident in how we see Arctic considerations diffusing throughout the federal national security bureaucracy. The US Navy published its "Arctic road-map" in October 2009, which made it clear that climate change was driving US government interest in the region.[18] The Department of Defense (DoD) released its *Quadrennial Defense Review* (*QDR*) in February 2010. The report mentions the Arctic on eight occasions—while Russia gets four mentions and China eleven.[19] Shortly thereafter, President Obama's first *National Security Strategy*, published in May 2010, also included Arctic considerations. It unambiguously asserts:

> The United States is an Arctic Nation with broad and fundamental interests in the Arctic region, where we seek to meet our national security needs, protect the environment, responsibly manage resources, account for Indigenous communities, support scientific research, and strengthen international cooperation on a wide range of issues.[20]

In pursuing these goals, President Barack Obama also sought to improve coordination of Arctic issues across the federal government and to strengthen international cooperation among the Arctic states. In 2010, the president created the Interagency Arctic Research Policy Committee (under the leadership of the director of the Office of Science and Technology Policy).[21] Additionally, in May 2011, Secretary of State Hillary Rodham Clinton signed another Arctic Council multinational agreement (the Agreement on Cooperation on Aeronautical and Maritime Search and Rescue in the Arctic).[22] Nonetheless, the most significant initiatives in the Obama administration's work on the Arctic—and on climate change—came in his second term.[23]

May 2013 was an extraordinary month for Arctic policy under the Obama administration, as it began to ramp up efforts to take over the chairmanship of the Arctic Council in 2015. The administration released the first U.S. *National Strategy for the Arctic Region*, conceived "to meet the reality of a changing Arctic environment, while we simultaneously pursue our global objective of combating the climatic changes that are driving these environmental conditions." The strategy laid out three main goals: advancing US security interests, pursuing responsible stewardship in the region, and strengthening international cooperation. It also reiterated the goal of consulting and coordinating with Alaska Natives.[24] That same month, the administration signed another Arctic Council agreement (on cooperation on marine oil pollution preparedness and response in the Arctic), and the United States Coast Guard released its first *Arctic Strategy*. The Coast Guard strategy document identifies three strategic objectives for the service in the Arctic: "improving maritime domain awareness, modernizing governance to oversee maritime activities while safeguarding national interests, and broadening partnerships across the public and private sectors."[25] Later in 2013, the Department of Defense released its first *Arctic Strategy* with a clear statement that the Arctic must remain "a secure and stable region where US national interests are safeguarded, the US homeland is protected, and nations work cooperatively to address challenges."[26]

Between February 2014 and January 2020, the Obama administration authored seven more documents that further clarified US strategy in the Arctic. The documents ranged across the federal bureaucracy from the US Navy and DoD to the National Oceanic and Atmospheric Administration (NOAA).[27] This flurry of documents demonstrated the significance of the Arctic within the administration's efforts to "confront climate change," which was reinforced by the president's appointment of the former commandant of the US Coast Guard, Admiral Robert J. Papp, to serve as the US special representative for the Arctic. All of this activity also pointed to the need for additional policy coordination, which we see in Obama's executive order to create the Arctic Executive Steering Committee that was chaired by the Mark Brzezinski, the former US ambassador to Sweden.[28] Finally, the Obama administration also joined Canada, Denmark, Norway, and Russia in a "Declaration Concerning the Prevention of Unregulated High Seas Fishing in the Central Arctic Ocean."[29]

The Obama administration's commitment to the Arctic reached beyond writing strategies and reports, however. Obama became the first US president to travel to Arctic Alaska in 2015, with the stated goal to "shine a spotlight on what Alaskans in particular have come to know: Climate change is one of the biggest threats we face, it is being driven by human activity, and it is disrupting Americans' lives right now."[30] As the *New York Times* highlighted in the title of an article about his visit, "Obama's Alaska Visit Puts Climate, Not Energy, in Forefront." President Obama's visit to Alaska further demonstrated the administration's efforts to prioritize the Arctic as part of its strategy in confronting climate change.[31] However, as the Obama administration wound down, critics noted that despite significant climate change triumphs—highlighted by his 2016 signature on the Paris Agreement on Climate Change—much of his legacy could be reversed by incoming President Donald Trump.[32]

Trump Changes Course on
Climate Change and the Arctic

The Trump administration's Arctic policy can be summarized as a policy that focused on security, national defense, and resource extraction above all else; it effectively removed the mitigation of climate change as a goal. Indigenous relations and environmental protection were also relegated to lower priorities. Trump's Arctic policy was based on confronting potential great power competition from China and Russia, extracting natural resources, and achieving "better outcomes" in international forums—it could be said that all of this was about seizing the potential opportunities for exploitation of the region, due to climate change.[33]

The Trump administration's "America First" platform had a direct impact on its policy toward the Arctic. When the Arctic Council met in May 2017, Secretary of State Rex Tillerson signed the Agreement on Enhancing International Arctic Scientific Cooperation, but the administration asked for six last-minute changes to the meeting declaration, all of which had the intention of watering down any language on climate change. And for the same reason that Obama had highlighted the Arctic in his national security strategy, the Trump administration's 2017 *National Security Strategy* downplayed the Arctic—mentioning it only once, under a section titled "Achieve Better Outcomes in Multilateral Forums."[34]

The US Navy made three key moves in 2018 and 2019 that signaled a change in its posture toward the Arctic as well. First, in 2018 the navy reestablished the US Second Fleet to counter Russia in the North Atlantic and the Arctic. Then, later in 2018, the USS *Harry S. Truman* participated in an exercise north of the Arctic Circle, marking the first time that a carrier strike group had operated in the Arctic since the fall of the Soviet Union.[35] The navy's new *Strategic Outlook for the Arctic* was published January 2019 and immediately became the subject of criticism for its brevity and generalities, with one observer joking, "It looks like some commander was told to type this up on a Sunday night."[36] The Department of Defense's unclassified *Summary of the 2018 National Defense Strategy*, released in January 2019, does not mention the Arctic or climate change; it was notable for carefully describing the impacts of climate change using the words "changing physical environment."[37] Cumulatively, these documents prompted Congress to order an update to the DoD's Arctic strategy in the John S. McCain National Defense Act for Fiscal Year 2019.[38] Experts such as Heather Conley of the Center for Strategic and International Studies have noted that the "DoD wouldn't have done this on its own if it hadn't been a requirement."[39]

In contrast, the Coast Guard's April 2019 *Arctic Strategic Outlook* is noteworthy for being a professionally polished document that still clearly shows a shifting US Arctic policy. The document lays out three completely new lines of strategy:

1. Enhance capability to operate effectively in a dynamic Arctic domain,
2. Strengthen the rules-based order, and
3. Innovate and adapt to promote resilience and prosperity.

The second paragraph of the Executive Summary describes the "resurgence of nation-state competition."[40] Although there were critics of the new direction, the administration supported the shift, most visibly by its vocal support of the new Polar Security Cutter program.[41] When President Trump gave the commencement speech at the United States Coast Guard Academy in New London, Connecticut, in May 2017, he gave his full-throated support to the Coast Guard's icebreaker acquisition plans, proclaiming:

> Out of the five branches of our Armed Services, it's only the Coast Guard that has the power to break through 21 feet of rock-solid Arctic ice, right? You're the only ones. And I'm proud to say that under my administration, as you just heard, we will be building the first new heavy icebreakers the United States has seen in over 40 years. We're going to build many of them. (Applause.) We need them. We need them.[42]

Similarly, a June 2020 presidential memorandum proclaimed that "the United States requires a ready, capable, and available fleet of polar security icebreakers that is operationally tested and fully deployable by Fiscal Year 2029." The Coast Guard's icebreaker acquisition program was also a key element of Arctic policy under the Trump administration, emphasizing security and remaining silent on climate change.

The Trump administration's increased focus on security was accompanied by a decrease in multilateralism. The May 2019 meeting of the Arctic Council marked "the first time since its formation in 1996 that the council had been unable to issue a joint declaration spelling out its priorities."[43] US objections to language about climate change and the Paris Agreement meant that the statement by the chair (Timo Soini, the minister of foreign affairs of Finland) could only conclude, "A majority of us regarded climate change as a fundamental challenge facing the Arctic."[44]

Despite the change of focus on the Arctic, there was still broad agreement about the importance of the region to US national security. The Department of the Air Force followed up DoD's *Arctic Strategy* with a strategy of its own in July of 2020. The Air Force notes, "The Arctic's capacity as a strategic buffer is eroding, making it an avenue of threat to the homeland, due to advancements by great power competitors." The Air Force *Arctic Strategy* remains focused on four lines of effort including vigilance, power projection, cooperation, and preparedness. This document was significant as the first published Arctic strategy from this service, showing the Arctic's continuing importance to US policy-makers.[45] The Senate Appropriations Defense Subpanel has called on the army to join the other branches in recognizing the importance of the Arctic by acquiring "equipment and vehicles necessary for Arctic and cold weather operations" and creating "overland mobility capabilities in the Arctic."[46] In addition, the State Department appointed a coordinator for the Arctic region, James P. DeHart, with primary responsibility for coordinating the State Department's "policy-making and diplomatic engagement" related to the Arctic. The appointment of a high-level coordinator for managing US diplomacy in the region demonstrates the Arctic's continuing importance under the Trump administration.[47]

Greenland played a unique role in the Trump administration's Arctic policy. In August 2019, media reported that the Trump administration was thinking about buying Greenland from Denmark. When asked by reporters about the idea, President Trump asserted, "It's just something we've talked about."[48] That talk ultimately resulted in a diplomatic row with Danish prime minister Mette Frederiksen, who called the idea "absurd."[49] President Trump responded by canceling his scheduled visit to Denmark via Twitter and then calling the prime minister's comments "nasty" before asserting, "All she had to do was say 'No, we wouldn't be interested.' She's not talking to me, she's talking to the United States of America."[50] However, the spat provides a window on the strategic importance of Greenland and the genuine security concerns raised by Greenland's drive for independence from Denmark.[51]

Ultimately, the Trump administration settled on a "softer" approach to the strategic implications in Greenland. First, the administration provided $12 million of economic development aid in April 2020, which prompted both "praise and suspicion in Denmark." Then, in June 2020, the State Department announced the reopening of its consulate in Greenland—a move likely meant to counter growing Chinese influence in the region.[52] A coincidental exercise of "soft power" in Greenland came in November 2020 when a junior member from the US Coast Guard Cutter *Campbell* bought dinner for a man sitting by himself in a diner—the man turned out to be Greenlandic prime minister Kim Kielsen. To reciprocate the kindness, Kielsen visited the *Campbell*, met the crew, and gave the commanding officer a driving tour of the capital, Nuuk. Captain Thomas Crane asserted that the interaction "directly strengthened our nation's position in an increasingly competitive Arctic domain."[53]

Conclusion

US Arctic policy over the past forty years has been generally consistent, but as this chapter asserts, the policy has evolved due to climate change, including a dramatic shift from 2008 forward.[54] The Arctic is changing rapidly due to anthropogenically induced climate change—warming twice as fast as the lower latitudes. An area that was once inaccessible is increasingly easy to access—as a result of climate change and technological advances. This change can be seen in the relative importance placed on the Arctic since 1970, but most recently since 2008. The US government has issued almost three times more Arctic policy statements in the last ten years than it did in the preceding four decades, largely due to climate change and its impact on the region.

This chapter is meant to provide a primer for teachers on this evolving policy landscape so that they can, in turn, invite students to grapple with an evolving policy area and explore how the US government has responded to climate change over time. In the lesson plan below, students can study US policy across nine presidential administrations with an eye toward how climate change shifted and drove US Arctic policymakers from 2009 onward. Students also have the opportunity to consider the ways in which different stakeholders in the region have different perspectives on what government policy should be in the future.

The significant area of tension in this policy area is between national security, economic development, and environmental protection (all exacerbated by climate change). This tension helps make this policy such an interesting area for students to study. Do the environmental costs of climate change outweigh its potential security and economic benefits? From the perspective of the US government, the cost versus benefits analysis of the impact of global warming in the Arctic is far from decided. The debate on how the US should respond to anthropogenic warming is therefore likely to continue for the foreseeable future.

Lesson Plan

Compelling Question: How Has Climate Change Impacted US Policies toward the Arctic?

This lesson addresses the impact of climate change in the Arctic region since Reagan and how the impacts of climate change affect US strategies in the region. Among the issues that have influenced decisions in the Arctic are economic development (i.e., accessing energy reserves in the region), environmental protections, scientific exploration, freedom of navigation, protections for Indigenous or First Peoples (including residents of Alaska), international cooperation, domestic security, and international cooperation. Climate change has profoundly affected all of these issues.

This inquiry lesson asks students to do the following:

1. Examine the Arctic region's geography, consider how climate change may affect borders and sea access, and consider the consequences of climate change on cultural, economic, and political systems.
2. Choose (or the teacher may assign) a special-interest stakeholder who may be affected by climate change or who could take advantage of the changing climate. Using policies developed by previous administrations, students take the role of the stakeholder to research and develop an informed point of view.
3. Develop an outline of issues created by climate change that should be considered by the current administration or the Arctic Council.

4. Take informed action by getting involved in climate change initiatives.

This lesson provides three formative assessments with guiding questions, as well as a summative assessment, and a "taking informed action" task. All of the sources that are cited in this lesson are also available on the book's website (http://GoldbergSeries.org/UTContemporaryUS History).

Common Core Social Studies Standards

The Common Core is a set of high-quality academic standards in mathematics and English language arts/literacy (ELA) created by two state groups—the National Governors Association and Council of Chief State School Officers—in 2009 and 2010.[55] These learning goals outline what a student should know and be able to do at the end of each grade. What follows are selected Common Core State Standards for English Language Arts & Literacy in History/Social Studies for grades 11 and 12.

- CCSS.ELA-LITERACY.RH.11–12.3: Evaluate various explanations for actions or events and determine which explanation best accords with textual evidence, acknowledging where the text leaves matters uncertain.
- CCSS.ELA-LITERACY.RH.11–12.6: Evaluate authors' differing points of view on the same historical event or issue by assessing the authors' claims, reasoning, and evidence.
- CCSS.ELA-LITERACY.RH.11–12.7: Integrate and evaluate multiple sources of information presented in diverse formats and media (e.g., visually, quantitatively, as well as in words) in order to address a question or solve a problem.
- CCSS.ELA-LITERACY.RH.11–12.9: Integrate information from diverse sources, both primary and secondary, into a coherent understanding of an idea or event, noting discrepancies among sources.

Staging the Compelling Question

Compelling question: How has climate change impacted US policies toward the Arctic?

Scenario: A newly elected presidential administration is determining the next ten-year policy on the Arctic based on historical precedent, input from stakeholders, and the administration's own strategic priorities.

Who: The Arctic region is a special focus because of a number of factors: different national groups are claiming areas, First Peoples and Indigenous peoples have land rights and cultural connections to the region, and scientists, environmentalists, and explorers are working in the region. In addition to these groups, there are competing claims for shipping routes, navigation and trade, national security concerns, energy initiatives, and environmental protections.

Why: Climate change is rapidly changing the Arctic, and there is a race to exploit the resources and possibilities of innovation, industry, cooperation, and jockeying for control of the region that has dwindling ice. The potential for sustainable economic development must be weighed against national interests. In addition, there are many different nations vying for a stake of the Arctic, making the already impacted region vulnerable to bad actors and subject to international diplomacy.

For the inquiry: In this lesson, small groups of students will represent stakeholders. In order to provide sufficient perspective, having at least five stakeholder groups represented will help students recognize differing points of view. The stakeholders may be governmental groups or nongovernmental organizations. The following list is broadly worded so that students may start with a key interest and find an organization, a company, or special-interest group to research. These may include but are not limited to the following:

- economic development groups (i.e., groups seeking natural resources, energy production, etc.)
- environmental protection agencies
- international affairs (i.e., governments, diplomatic groups, or national agencies)
- domestic or international security systems
- those seeking freedom of navigation or trade (such as fishermen, shipping companies, etc.)
- Interagency Arctic Policy Group
- Indigenous or First Peoples groups (including residents of Alaska)
- scientists
- other nongovernmental groups with interests in the region.

Performance Task Number 1

Guiding/Supporting Questions: What do the maps of the Arctic tell you about the region? Who has interests in the region? How might climate change affect decisions made in the region?

Compare the geographic elements among the five maps noted below. Note which political powers are in the area, what details each map reveals, and how climate change might affect the region. Give special consideration to the people who live and work in the region and how their lives would be impacted by the decisions and policies made by governmental leaders.

- Arctic Region: "Arctic Ocean," *The World Factbook*, Central Intelligence Agency, https://www.cia.gov/the-world-factbook/oceans/arctic -ocean/
- Arctic Council Member and Observer States: Arctic Portal, https://arcticportal.org/images/maps/8.1.3_rgb%20s_ap-05.jpg
- Arctic Continental Shelf beyond 200 nautical miles from shore, with sea ice extent data: IBRU Centre for Borders Research, Durham University, https://www.dur.ac.uk/resources/ibru/resources/ibru_ arctic_map_27-02-15.pdf
- Indigenous population in the Arctic: Nordregio, https://nordregio.org/ wp-content/uploads/2019/03/02286b_Arctic_indi_2018.jpg
- Arctic Resources: European Environment Agency, https://www.eea .europa.eu/data-and-maps/figures/arctic-resources

Performance Task Number 2

Guiding/Supporting Questions: How are policies decided or negotiated by stakeholders? In what way have these decisions influenced presidential policies?

Students will compare and contrast two presidential policies using the documents below to show how their attitudes toward the Arctic were driven by stakeholders or national interests. Students should also use at least one additional supporting document (located after the administration documents) to support their answers. Annotate the texts to demonstrate how their stakeholder position would be affected by the policies.

Arctic Policy Documents by Administration

- President Reagan
  - April 1983 — "National Security Decision Directive Number 90," Ronald Reagan Presidential Library, https://www.reaganlibrary .gov/public/archives/reference/scanned-nsdds/nsdd90.pdf
  - January 1985 — "Executive Order 12501 on Arctic Research," Ronald Reagan Presidential Library, https://www.reaganlibrary.gov/ research/speeches/12885d
- President Clinton
  - June 1994 — "Presidential Decision Directive/NSC-26," White House, https://fas.org/irp/offdocs/pdd/pdd-26.pdf
- President George W. Bush
  - January 2009 — "National Security Presidential Directive-66, Homeland Security Directive-25," Homeland Security Digital Library, https://www.hsdl.org/?abstract&did=232474
- President Obama
  - May 2013 — *National Strategy for the Arctic Region*, https://obamawhite house.archives.gov/sites/default/files/docs/nat_arctic_strategy.pdf
  - May 2013 — *United States Coast Guard Arctic Strategy*, https://www .uscg.mil/Portals/0/Strategy/cg_arctic_strategy.pdf
  - January 2014 — *Implementation Plan for the National Strategy for the Arctic Region*, https://obamawhitehouse.archives.gov/sites/default/ files/docs/implementation_plan_for_the_national_strategy_for_the_ arctic_region_-_fi....pdf
  - January 2015 — "Executive Order 13689: Enhancing Coordination of National Efforts in the Arctic," https://obamawhitehouse.archives .gov/the-press-office/2015/01/21/executive-order-enhancing -coordination-national-efforts-arctic
  - September 2015 — "President Obama's Trip to Alaska," https:// obamawhitehouse.archives.gov/2015-alaska-trip#:~:text=President %20Obama%20traveled%20to%20Alaska,disrupting%20 Americans'%20lives%20right%20now
- President Trump
  - May 2017 — Remarks by President Trump at United States Coast Guard Academy Commencement Ceremony, https:// trumpwhitehouse.archives.gov/briefings-statements/remarks -president-trump-united-states-coast-guard-academy -commencement-ceremony

- April 2019—United States Coast Guard, *Arctic Strategic Outlook*, https://www.uscg.mil/Portals/0/Images/arctic/Arctic_Strategic_ Outlook_APR_2019.pdf
- June 2020—"Memorandum on Safeguarding U.S. National Interests in the Arctic and Antarctic Regions," https://trumpwhitehouse .archives.gov/presidential-actions/memorandum-safeguarding-u-s -national-interests-arctic-antarctic-regions/

Additional Supporting Documents

Students should consider how the policies made by these administrations will affect their stakeholder group. Then, students must choose one of the following and consider how the rapidly changing climate will continue to affect their stakeholder group.

- 1973 Agreement on the Conservation of Polar Bears, https:// polarbearagreement.org/about-us/1973-agreement
- Arctic Research and Policy Act of 1984 (amended 1990), National Science Foundation, https://www.nsf.gov/geo/opp/arctic/iarpc/arc_ res_pol_act.jsp
- 1996 Declaration on the Establishment of the Arctic Council, Arctic Council, https://oaarchive.arctic-council.org/bitstream/ handle/11374/85/EDOCS-1752-v2-ACMMCA00_Ottawa_1996_ Founding_Declaration.PDF?sequence=5&isAllowed=y
- 2008 Ilulissat Declaration, Centre for International Law, https://cil.nus .edu.sg/wp-content/uploads/formidable/18/2008-Ilulissat-Declaration .pdf
- 2019 Statement by the Chair, Timo Soini, Arctic Council, https:// oaarchive.arctic-council.org/bitstream/handle/11374/2343/Rovaniemi -Statement-from-the-chair_FINAL_840AM-7MAY.pdf?sequence=1& isAllowed=y

Performance Task Number 3

Guiding or supporting question: What is the impact of climate change? Should nongovernmental stakeholders influence policy- and decision-makers on climate issues?

Using the information and resources students brought from Performance tasks 1 and 2, determine an outline of issues and talking points from the point of view of their stakeholder group. Additional research will be required to accurately reflect the current position of the political administration, and reputable current sources should be found that reflect the stakeholder group interests. Students should be able to answer the following questions:

- How has climate change impacted your group?
- How would you inform the public about the impact?
- Why should we care?
- How would you get others to support your stakeholder position?

Using their notes and annotated documents, students should develop an outline of issues to present to the current administration or the Arctic Council. They should also consider the positions already established by the Arctic Council as part of their research; two relevant sources are as follows:

- A Brief History of the Arctic Council, https://www.thearcticinstitute .org/wp-content/uploads/2020/05/TAI_Infographic-History-Arctic -Council.pdf
- Declaration on the Establishment of the Arctic Council, https:// oaarchive.arctic-council.org/bitstream/handle/11374/85/EDOCS-1752 -v2-ACMMCA00_Ottawa_1996_Founding_Declaration.PDF?sequence =5&isAllowed=y

Summative Assessment

Compelling question: How has climate change impacted US policies toward the Arctic?

Argument prompt for students: As a stakeholder in the Arctic, you are presenting your proposed policy to the current administration and to the Arctic Council. Ensure you are addressing the compelling question in your argument. Using your research from the three performance tasks, you may present your argument as a paper, a letter, a TED Talk, a podcast, a news story, or website, but it must include the historical precedent of policies of previous administrations. If you agree or disagree with current policy, you may say so, but be sure to be clear in your argument to explain why, as a stakeholder, you hold that opinion and provide evidence to support your claim. (If students are working in groups, each student should contribute to the argument so that all voices are heard.)

Extension/Enrichment

Have your class create a climate action group or civics webpage to post their digital work.

Taking Informed Action

Encourage students to take their work to social media and share their research with TED Talks, Global Citizen, Instagram, Twitter, TikTok, and other places where social action can make a difference.

Encourage students to share their work with local, state, and national leaders, as well as nongovernmental groups they may have researched. They could use the support of young people who are passionate about making a difference.

NOTES

1. Stephen Haycox, "Arctic Policy of the United States: An Historical Overview," in *The Palgrave Handbook of Arctic Policy and Politics*, ed. Ken S. Coates and Carin Holroyd (New York: Springer Nature, 2019), 233–50; Robert W. Murray and Anita Dey Nuttall, *International Relations and the Arctic: Understanding Policy and Governance* (Amherst, NY: Cambria Press, 2014).

2. Martin Breum, *Cold Rush: The Astonishing True Story of the New Quest for the Polar North* (Montreal: McGill-Queen's University Press, 2018).

3. We use the terms "global warming" and "climate change" interchangeably in this chapter, but it is important to note that global warming is one aspect of long-term climate change.

4. The Arctic is home to an estimated $1 trillion in rare earth minerals, 30 percent of the world's undiscovered gas, and 10 percent of the world's undiscovered oil reserves. See United States Coast Guard, *Arctic Strategy*, May 2013, https://www.uscg.mil/Portals/0/Strategy/cg_arctic_strategy.pdf; Shannon Hall, "These Researchers Spent a Winter Trapped in Arctic Ice to Capture Key Climate Data," *Nature*, May 22, 2020, https://www.nature.com/immersive/d41586 -020-01446-x/index.html; and Henry Fountain, "Arctic's 'Last Ice Area' May Be Less Resistant to Global Warming," *New York Times*, last updated August 5, 2021, https://www.nytimes.com/2021/07/01/climate/arctic-sea-ice-climate-change .html.

5. Scott G. Borgerson, "Arctic Meltdown: The Economic and Security Implications of Global Warming," *Foreign Affairs* 87, no. 2 (March–April 2008): 15; Zoë Schlanger, "An International Race for the Arctic? Try a Slow, Science-Driven Crawl," *Newsweek*, September 3, 2015, https://www.newsweek.com/internation al-race-arctic-try-slow-science-driven-crawl-368557.

6. "National Security Decision Memorandum 144: United States Arctic Policy and Arctic Policy Group," December 22, 1971, https://fas.org/irp/offdocs/ nsdm-nixon/nsdm-144.pdf.

7. Jeremy McKenzie, "America Is an Arctic Nation: It's Time We Acted Like It," *Pacific Council on International Policy Magazine*, January 30, 2019, https:// www.pacificcouncil.org/newsroom/america-arctic-nation%E2%80%94it%E2% 80%99s-time-we-acted-it; David Fairhall, *Cold Front: Conflict Ahead in Arctic Waters* (Berkeley, CA: Counterpoint, 2010).

8. "National Security Decision Directive Number 90: United States Arctic Policy," April 14, 1983, Ronald Reagan Presidential Library, https://www.rea ganlibrary.gov/public/archives/reference/scanned-nsdds/nsdd90.pdf. See also Samuel Frye, "Feature: The Arctic and US Foreign Policy, 1970–90," *Department of State Dispatch* 2, no. 14 (1991): 242–46.

9. "Arctic Research and Policy Act of 1984," July 31, 1984, National Science Foundation, https://www.nsf.gov/geo/opp/arctic/iarpc/arc_res_pol_act.jsp; "Executive Order 12501: Arctic Research," January 28, 1985, Reagan Presidential Library, https://www.reaganlibrary.gov/research/speeches/12885d.

10. "Joint Statement by Reagan, Gorbachev," *Washington Post*, December 11, 1987, https://www.washingtonpost.com/archive/politics/1987/12/11/joint -statement-by-reagan-gorbachev/cd990a8d-87a1-4d74-88f8-704f93c80cd3/.

11. Paul Goble, "Moscow May Soon End 'Provisional Enforcement' of 1990 Bering Strait Accord with US," *Eurasia Daily Monitor* 17, no. 12 (January 30, 2020), https://jamestown.org/program/moscow-may-soon-end-provisional-enforce ment-of-1990-bering-strait-accord-with-us/; Jennifer Cook, "A Brief History of the Arctic Council," 2019, https://www.thearcticinstitute.org/wp-content/up loads/2020/05/TAI_Infographic-History-Arctic-Council.pdf; Frye, "Feature: The Arctic and US Foreign Policy."

12. William J. Clinton, "Presidential Decision Directive/NSC-26: United States Policy on the Arctic and Antarctic Regions," Federation of American Scientists, June 9, 1994, https://fas.org/irp/offdocs/pdd/pdd-26.pdf.

13. "Ottawa Declaration," Arctic Council Archive, September 19, 1996, https://oaarchive.arctic-council.org/handle/11374/85; Cook, "A Brief History of the Arctic Council."

14. White House, *A National Security Strategy for a New Century*, October 1998, http://nssarchive.us/wp-content/uploads/2020/04/1998.pdf.

15. Philip Steinberg, "Maintaining Hegemony at a Distance: Ambivalence in US Arctic Policy," in *Polar Geopolitics? Knowledges, Resources and Legal Regimes,*

ed. Richard C. Powell and Klaus Dodds (Northampton, MA: Edward Elgar, 2014), 113–30; Rob Huebert, "United States Arctic Policy: The Reluctant Arctic Power," University of Calgary, *School of Public Policy Briefing Papers* 2, no. 2 (May 1, 2009), https://www.researchgate.net/publication/292257748_United_ States_Arctic_Policy_The_Reluctant_Arctic_Power.

16. "2008 Ilulissat Declaration," Centre for International Law, National University of Singapore, May 28, 2008, https://cil.nus.edu.sg/wp-content/uploads/ formidable/18/2008-Ilulissat-Declaration.pdf.

17. White House, "National Security Presidential Directive/NSPD-66, Homeland Security Presidential Directive/HSPD-25," National Archives and Records Administration, January 9, 2009, https://catalog.archives.gov/id/26082871.

18. Task Force Climate Change and the Oceanographer of the Navy, *U.S. Navy Arctic Roadmap*, October 2009, https://www.wired.com/images_blogs/dan gerroom/2009/11/us-navy-arctic-roadmap-nov-2009.pdf.

19. Department of Defense, *Quadrennial Defense Review: Report*, February 2010, https://www.hsdl.org/?view&did=29786.

20. White House, *National Security Strategy*, May 2010, https://obamawhite house.archives.gov/sites/default/files/rss_viewer/national_security_strategy.pdf.

21. White House, "Presidential Memorandum: Arctic Research and Policy Act," July 22, 2010, https://obamawhitehouse.archives.gov/the-press-office/pres idential-memorandum-arctic-research-and-policy-act.

22. Arctic Council, "Agreement on Cooperation on Aeronautical and Maritime Search and Rescue in the Arctic," 2011, https://oaarchive.arctic-council .org/handle/11374/531.

23. Marianne Lavelle, "2016: Obama's Climate Legacy Marked by Triumphs and Lost Opportunities," *Inside Climate News*, December 26, 2016, https://inside climatenews.org/news/26122016/obama-climate-change-legacy-trump-policies/.

24. White House, *National Strategy for the Arctic Region*, May 10, 2013, https:// web.archive.org/web/20210215024218/https://obamawhitehouse.archives.gov/ sites/default/files/docs/nat_arctic_strategy.pdf.

25. Arctic Council, "Agreement on Cooperation on Marine Oil Pollution Preparedness and Response in the Arctic," 2013, https://oaarchive.arctic-coun cil.org/handle/11374/529; United States Coast Guard, *Arctic Strategy*, May 2013, https://www.uscg.mil/Portals/0/Strategy/cg_arctic_strategy.pdf.

26. Department of Defense, *Arctic Strategy*, November 2013, https://dod.de fense.gov/Portals/1/Documents/pubs/2013_Arctic_Strategy.pdf. See also White House, *Implementation Plan for the National Strategy for the Arctic Region*, January 2014, https://obamawhitehouse.archives.gov/sites/default/files/docs/implemen tation_plan_for_the_national_strategy_for_the_arctic_region_-_fi....pdf.

27. Navy Task Force on Climate Change, *U.S. Navy Arctic Roadmap, 2014– 2030*, February 2014, https://www.hsdl.org/?abstract&did=756030; Department of Defense, *Quadrennial Defense Review*, 2014, https://history.defense.gov/Por

tals/70/Documents/quadrennial/QDR2014.pdf?ver=tXH94SVvSQLVw-ENZ -a2pQ%3d%3d; NOAA Arctic Program, *NOAA's Arctic Action Plan*, National Oceanic and Atmospheric Administration, April 2014, https://arctic.noaa.gov/ Arctic-News/ArtMID/5556/ArticleID/308/NOAAs-Arctic-Action-Plan; President Barack Obama, "Executive Order 13689: Enhancing Coordination of National Efforts in the Arctic," January 21, 2015, https://obamawhitehouse.archives.gov/ the-press-office/2015/01/21/executive-order-enhancing-coordination-national -efforts-arctic; White House, *National Security Strategy*, February 2015, http:// nssarchive.us/wp-content/uploads/2020/04/2015.pdf; Arctic Executive Steering Committee, *2015 Year in Review: Progress Report on the Implementation of the National Strategy for the Arctic Region*, March 2016, https://obamawhitehouse .archives.gov/sites/whitehouse.gov/files/documents/Progress%20Report%20 on%20the%20Implementation%20of%20the%20National%20Strategy%20 for%20the%20Arctic%20Region.pdf; Department of Defense, "Report to Congress on Strategy to Protect United States National Security Interests in the Arctic Region" (OUSD [Policy], December 2016), https://www.sullivan.senate.gov/ imo/media/doc/2016_ArcticStrategy-Unclass.pdf.

28. White House, *National Security Strategy*, February 2015. See also Barack Obama, "Executive Order 13689: Enhancing Coordination of National Efforts in the Arctic," https://www.govinfo.gov/content/pkg/DCPD-201500039/pdf/ DCPD-201500039.pdf; John Kerry, "Retired Admiral Robert Papp to Serve as U.S. Special Representative for the Arctic," US Department of State, July 16, 2014, https://2009-2017.state.gov/secretary/remarks/2014/07/229317.htm; White House, "Ambassador Mark Brzezinski Appointed Executive Director of the Arctic Executive Steering Committee," August 13, 2015, https://obamawhitehouse .archives.gov/blog/2015/08/13/ambassador-mark-brzezinski-appointed-execu tive-officer-arctic-executive-steering.

29. "Declaration Concerning the Prevention of Unregulated High Seas Fishing in the Central Arctic Ocean," Ocean Conservancy, July 15, 2015, https:// oceanconservancy.org/wp-content/uploads/2017/04/declaration-on-arctic-fish eries-16-july-2015-1.pdf.

30. White House, "President Obama's Trip to Alaska," 2015, https://obama whitehouse.archives.gov/2015-alaska-trip.

31. Julie Hirschfeld Davis, "Obama's Alaska Visit Puts Climate, Not Energy, in Forefront," *New York Times*, August 30, 2015, https://www.nytimes.com/2015/ 08/31/us/politics/obama-to-urge-aggressive-climate-action-in-visit-to-arctic-ala ska.html.

32. Lavelle, "2016: Obama's Climate Legacy"; White House, "President Obama: The United States Formally Enters the Paris Agreement," September 3, 2016, https://obamawhitehouse.archives.gov/blog/2016/09/03/president-obama -united-states-formally-enters-paris-agreement.

33. White House, *National Security Strategy of the United States of America*, December 2017, https://trumpwhitehouse.archives.gov/wp-content/uploads/20 17/12/NSS-Final-12-18-2017-0905-2.pdf, p. 40.

34. Sabrina Shankman, "Leaked Draft Shows How U.S. Weakened Climate Change Wording in the Arctic Declaration," *Inside Climate News*, May 19, 2017, https://insideclimatenews.org/news/18052017/arctic-council-climate-change-rex -tillerson-donald-trump; White House, *National Security Strategy*, December 2017.

35. Sam LaGrone, "Navy Reestablishes U.S. 2nd Fleet to Face Russian Threat: Plan Calls for 250 Person Command in Norfolk," *USNI News*, May 4, 2018, https://news.usni.org/2018/05/04/navy-reestablishes-2nd-fleet-plan-calls-for -250-person-command-in-norfolk; David Larter, "US Navy Declares New Fleet Created to Confront Russia Fully Operational," *Defense News*, December 31, 2019, https://www.defensenews.com/naval/2019/12/31/us-navy-declares-new-fleet -stood-up-to-confront-russia-fully-operational/; Meghan Eckstein, "Truman Carrier Strike Group Operating North of Arctic Circle: First Time for US Navy since 1991," *USNI News*, October 19, 2018, https://news.usni.org/2018/10/19/ truman-carrier-strike-group-operating-north-arctic-circle-first-time-us-navy -since-1991.

36. Melody Schreiber, "The US Navy's New Arctic Strategy Is Limited in Scope and Details, Say Critics," *ArcticToday* (blog), April 29, 2019, https://www .arctictoday.com/the-us-navys-new-arctic-strategy-is-limited-in-scope-details -say-critics/. See also Chief of Naval Operations, *Strategic Outlook for the Arctic*, United States Navy, January 2019, https://www.navy.mil/strategic/Navy_Stra tegic_Outlook_Arctic_Jan2019.pdf.

37. Department of Defense, "Summary of the 2018 National Defense Strategy of the United States of America: Sharpening the American Military's Competitive Edge," January 2019, https://dod.defense.gov/Portals/1/Documents/ pubs/2018-National-Defense-Strategy-Summary.pdf.

38. Melody Schreiber, "Congress Calls for a New US Arctic Defense Strategy," *ArcticToday* (blog), August 9, 2018, https://www.arctictoday.com/congress -calls-new-us-arctic-defense-strategy/.

39. As quoted in Melody Schreiber, "U.S. Arctic Defense Strategy Ramps up Rhetoric without Committing Resources, Experts Say," *ArcticToday* (blog), June 11, 2019, https://www.arctictoday.com/u-s-arctic-defense-strategy-ramps-up -rhetoric-without-committing-resources-experts-say/.

40. United States Coast Guard, *Arctic Strategic Outlook*, April 2019, https:// www.uscg.mil/Portals/0/Images/arctic/Arctic_Strategy_Book_APR_2019.pdf, pp. 6, 4. See also Ben Werner and Sam LaGrone, "Coast Guard Renames New Icebreaker Program 'Polar Security Cutter,'" *USNI News*, September 27, 2018, https://news.usni.org/2018/09/27/36846.

41. Andreas Østhagen, "What the New US Coast Guard Strategy Tells Us about the Arctic Anno 2019," *The Arctic Institute* (blog), April 25, 2019, https:// www.thearcticinstitute.org/new-us-coast-guard-strategy-arctic-anno-2019/.

42. White House, "Remarks by President Trump at United States Coast Guard Academy Commencement Ceremony," May 17, 2017, https://trump whitehouse.archives.gov/briefings-statements/remarks-president-trump-unit ed-states-coast-guard-academy-commencement-ceremony/.

43. Somini Sengupta, "U.S. Pressure Blocks Declaration on Climate Change at Arctic Talks," *New York Times*, May 7, 2019, https://www.nytimes.com/2019/ 05/07/climate/us-arctic-climate-change.html.

44. Timo Soini, "Statement by the Chair," Arctic Council, May 6–7, 2019, https://oaarchive.arctic-council.org/bitstream/handle/11374/2343/Rovaniemi -Statement-from-the-chair_FINAL_840AM-7MAY.pdf?sequence=1&isAl lowed=y.

45. Department of the Air Force, *Arctic Strategy*, July 21, 2020, https://www .af.mil/Portals/1/documents/2020SAF/July/ArcticStrategy.pdf, p. 4.

46. Jen Judson, "Lawmakers Want US Army to Quicken Purchase of Arctic-Capable Vehicles," *Defense News*, November 15, 2020, https://www.defensenews .com/land/2020/11/13/lawmakers-want-army-to-speed-up-arctic-capable-vehi cles-buy/.

47. Office of the Spokesperson, "Appointment of U.S. Coordinator for the Arctic Region," US Department of State, July 29, 2020, https://2017-2021.state .gov/appointment-of-u-s-coordinator-for-the-arctic-region/index.html.

48. As quoted in Scott Neuman, "No Joke: Trump Really Does Want to Buy Greenland," National Public Radio, August 19, 2019, https://www.npr.org/2019/ 08/19/752274659/no-joke-trump-really-does-want-to-buy-greenland.

49. "Danish PM Says Trump's Idea of Selling Greenland to U.S. Is Absurd," Reuters, August 18, 2019, https://www.reuters.com/article/us-usa-trump-green land-idUSKCN1V80Mo.

50. Scott Neuman and Sasha Ingber, "Trump Skips Visit to Denmark, Calls Danish Leader 'Nasty' for Greenland Sale Rebuff," National Public Radio, August 21, 2019, https://www.npr.org/2019/08/21/752989771/trump-to-skip-visit ing-denmark-after-prime-minister-says-greenland-not-for-sale.

51. Jeremy McKenzie, "Instead of Buying Greenland, Enhance Security & Cooperation," Pacific Council on International Policy, November 26, 2019, https://www.pacificcouncil.org/newsroom/instead-buying-greenland-enhance -security-cooperation.

52. Martin Selsoe Sorensen, "U.S. Aid for Greenland Prompts Praise and Suspicion in Denmark," *New York Times*, April 23, 2020, https://www.nytimes .com/2020/04/23/world/europe/us-greenland-denmark.html. See also Conor Finnegan, "After Trump Tried to Buy Greenland, US Gives Island $12M for Economic Development," ABC News, April 23, 2020, https://abcnews.go.com/ Politics/trump-buy-greenland-us-island-12m-economic-development/story?id =70305163; US Embassy and Consulate in the Kingdom of Denmark, "Reopen-ing of US Consulate Nuuk," June 12, 2020, http://dk.usembassy.gov/reopening -of-u-s-consulate-nuuk/.

53. Chad Garland, "A Coast Guardsman Bought Dinner for a Stranger in Greenland: He Turned out to Be the Prime Minister," *Stars and Stripes*, November 30, 2020, https://www.stripes.com/a-coast-guardsman-bought-dinner-for-a-stranger-in-greenland-he-turned-out-to-be-the-prime-minister-1.653712.

54. At the time, a handful of observers identified 2008 as a turning point of Arctic policy due to climate change. See most notably Scott G. Borgerson, "Arctic Meltdown: The Economic and Security Implications of Global Warming," *Foreign Affairs* 87, no. 2 (March–April 2008): 63–77; and Kenneth S. Yalowitz, James F. Collines, and Ross A. Virginia, *The Arctic Climate Change and Security Policy Conference: Final Report and Findings*, December 2008, Carnegie Endowment for International Peace, https://carnegieendowment.org/files/arctic_climate_change.pdf.

55. National Governors Association Center for Best Practices, "English Language Arts Standards » History/Social Studies » Grade 11–12," in *Common Core State Standards*, ed. Council of Chief State School Officers, National Governors Association Center for Best Practices, 2010, www.corestandards.org/ELA-Literacy/RH/11-12/ (accessed April 4, 2022).

Pushing Back

*Nuclear Disarmament and Peace Activism
during the Cold War and Beyond*

LORI CLUNE

Why Teach This Lesson?

In 1945, the United States became the first country to develop the atomic bomb and the only country to drop it on an enemy nation during wartime. Eight other countries have since joined the nuclear club, but the United States has maintained its lead by conducting more nuclear tests than any other country.[1] Antinuclear crusades in the United States and around the world date back to a handful of scientists in the 1930s who pushed back against the prospect of an atomic bomb. After the United States ordered these bombs dropped on Japan in August 1945, antinuclear activism spread beyond the scientific community and grew into a global protest movement.

This chapter addresses how we can teach about nuclear disarmament and peace activism in the tumultuous years since 1980. It includes themes likely addressed throughout the semester, including issues of war and peace, engagement in the political process, cultural production, citizen activism, and citizen rights. The story is rich and complex—and has important lessons for today. AP Historical Thinking Skills used in this lesson include C2 (compare different historical processes), C3 (situate historical developments within a broader context), D1 (explain long- and short-term effects of a historical development), D2 (evaluate the relative significance of different causes and effects on historical events), D3 (identify patterns of continuity and change over time), D4 (explain how patterns of continuity and change over time relate to larger historical themes), and D6 (evaluate whether a particular event could be considered a turning point between different historical periods).

Introduction

In the mid-1980s, during my last semesters of college, I wore a black armband. Each morning I pulled the grosgrain band up my left arm, as did a dozen of my fellow activists. If someone asked who had died, as one of my professors did, I replied, "We all could." If anyone asked why I was wearing it, and many did, I said I pledged to wear it until there was a mutually verifiable nuclear arms freeze. When my mother begged me to take it off "just for Thanksgiving dinner," I refused, claiming that bombs don't care about national holidays. After two years, only two of us still wore the armband. As we each headed off to graduate school, we decided it was time to take it off, even though there was no freeze. Nearly four decades later, there still isn't. I tossed the armband in the trash but remained fascinated by the movement that pushed back against this existential global threat.

Scholars have been exploring the development and use of nuclear weapons since 1945. Broad works, such as McGeorge Bundy's 1988 exploration of the political impact of the bomb, *Danger and Survival*, often disparage antinuclear activism.[2] Devoting just one page to the nuclear freeze movement in a six-hundred-page book, Bundy belittles the nuclear freeze movement, believing that a bilateral and verifiable freeze remains a hard sell because "opposition to *American* weaponry" was "never dominant in more than a minority of American minds."[3]

In contrast, Allan M. Winkler, in *Life under a Cloud*, emphasizes the power engaged American citizens have to impact nuclear policy.[4] The US government seized complete control over nuclear technology from the scientists and, under Cold War constraints, kept nuclear technology secret under wraps and avoided international control. Winkler argues that American nuclear disarmament activists—such as those with the National Committee for a Sane Nuclear Policy (SANE)—emphasized nuclear dangers and incrementally helped shift policy.

Numerous scholars have highlighted nuclear tragedies, and these works have served as inspiration for antinuclear activists. Here is a sample, from which I pull a short selection for students to read and reflect on. Jonathan Schell motivated many in the disarmament movement with his 1982 bestseller, *The Fate of the Earth*.[5] Schell describes in painful detail the impact of full-scale nuclear war on people and the planet, and how humans can mitigate the threat. Philip L. Fradkin, in *Fallout: An American Nuclear Tragedy*, examines the devastating impact of radiation on the people and livestock living downwind from Nevada nuclear test sites.[6] Several scholars—such as Kate Brown in her 2013 work *Plutopia*—have addressed the disturbing history of nuclear accidents and experiments.[7]

No historian has chronicled the antinuclear protest movement more thoroughly than historian Lawrence S. Wittner. He highlights the role the massive global nuclear disarmament movement has played in saving the planet from nuclear war, arguing that "omitting this nuclear disarmament campaign from explanation of nuclear restraint makes about as much sense as omitting the US civil rights movement from explanations for the collapse of racial segregation."[8] Wittner's trilogy on the disarmament movement remains a classic in the field.

Instructors may want to explore with students the connections between civil rights and disarmament, which Martin Luther King Jr. observed in 1968.[9] In *African Americans against the Bomb*, Vincent J. Intondi tells this history, explaining that "since its inception, the Congressional Black Caucus has included some of the most outspoken critics of nuclear weapons" and concluding that "the right to live without fear of nuclear war is not only a black issue but a human issue."[10] Students may also sample works in *Peace and Change*—the official journal of the Peace History Society, in print since 1972.[11]

This is a vibrant, growing field of research, and scholars have begun to internationalize this global story.[12] Researchers can access the records of the Institute for Defense and Disarmament Studies (1974–2007) held at Cornell University's Division of Rare and Manuscript Collections.[13] Randall Forsberg founded the institute, and the collection contains documentation from the United States and around the world. The London School of Economics was due to hold a conference on "Global Histories of Anti-Nuclear and Peace Activism in the Late Cold War" in May 2020, postponed due to COVID-19. They hoped to push the scholarship beyond the largest NATO countries and to bring together sociologists, political scientists, and cultural studies scholars, along with historians, from all over the world, "to broaden the scope beyond the North Atlantic by inviting papers on protest that opposes various aspects of nuclear technologies in any country."[14]

It is also worthwhile to remind students that the right to peacefully protest is in the US Constitution. Having students read the First

Amendment with their mind to political activism can solidify this point. I like to have them read it out loud, together.

> Congress shall make no law respecting an establishment of religion, or prohibiting the free exercise thereof; or abridging the freedom of speech, or of the press; or the right of the people peaceably to assemble, and to petition the Government for a redress of grievances.

Instructors can also direct students to the American Civil Liberties Union (ACLU), which supports each citizen's right to protest, and remind them: "The right to join with fellow citizens in protest or peaceful assembly is critical to a functioning democracy and at the core of the First Amendment."[15] While protesters of all groups have experienced challenges over the past forty years—law enforcement's use of arrest, force, curfews, intimidation, and new surveillance technologies—the ACLU and other groups monitor the US government's actions concerning the right to protest. It may go without saying, but I believe it is important for instructors to introduce students to the long and rich history of protest movements in US history.

I have broken down the antinuclear/disarmament/peace protest movement into three periods of study. I include a wide range of primary sources from which instructors may choose, and I explain how I teach with these sources. Instructors may prefer to tackle peace activism as a stand-alone lesson, covering one to two class meetings. Alternately, one could address each period as it comes up chronologically in the course, comparing and contrasting previous protests. Either way, one will address the following learning outcomes. Students will be able to

- detail instances where Americans engaged with nuclear disarmament/ peace activism, and how those methods changed between the 1980s and 2020;
- explain how cultural products (art, film, music, games) reflect the unique periods in which they are produced, and how those products have changed over time.

Reagan, the 1980s, and the Cold War

There were growing Cold War tensions in the final year of the Carter administration, especially after the president postponed action on the SALT II nuclear weapons treaty, recalled the US ambassador to Moscow, and considered the use of nuclear weapons if the Soviets followed their invasion of Afghanistan with further ventures into the Persian Gulf.[16] Peace activists shifted focus from Vietnam and, with growing environmental concerns about nuclear energy, embraced nuclear disarmament.[17] During the 1980 presidential campaign, hardline cold warrior and Republican Party nominee Ronald Reagan opposed every nuclear arms control agreement while embracing expanding American nuclear capabilities.[18] His running mate, George H. W. Bush, claimed that nuclear wars were winnable.[19]

Reagan's inauguration in January 1981 was a shot of adrenaline into the antinuclear movement. Americans who had never been politically active before read about the dangers of the nuclear arms race, joined organizations, and took to the streets. On June 12, 1982, an estimated one million protesters demonstrated in New York City's Central Park at the Nuclear Disarmament Rally.[20] Jonathan Schell declared it "not only the largest antinuclear demonstration but the largest political demonstration of any description in American history."[21]

By the early 1980s, dozens of antinuclear organizations operated in the United States and around the world, including SANE, the Campaign for Nuclear Disarmament, and the Plowshares—composed of antinuclear and Christian pacifists. The groups pushed for a nuclear freeze, resulting in freeze resolutions sponsored in Congress by more than a dozen senators and one hundred members of the House in March 1982. The legislation stalled, and critics labeled the propositions impractical, but others credited the debate that the freeze proposition prompted as "useful in educating the public."[22]

Events in 1983—including International Day of Nuclear Disarmament, commemorated in fifty American cities; the takedown of a Korean airliner, KAL 007, which the Soviets mistook for a threat; and the misunderstanding and near–nuclear confrontation surrounding the Able Archer test—all motivated the disarmament movement. I also address a different source that emerged at around the same time, Dr. Seuss's *The Butter Battle Book*.

In 1984, at the age of seventy-nine, Dr. Seuss (aka Theodor Geisel) wrote an anti–nuclear war parable that the *New York Times* labeled a Notable Book of the Year. *The Butter Battle Book* is a pointed critique of the nuclear arms race and mutually assured destruction. It was animated for television a few years later. Unlike the book, the TV special ends with a final screen shot: "The End (maybe)."[23] This is terrific to show in class; students discuss its impact, especially on children.

Political cartoons of the era are another way to explore opposition to the nuclear arms race. There are hundreds of cartoons available online for students to study.[24] I then ask students to create their own cartoon, stressing that drawing ability is not important. They draw as well as they can and include a paragraph that explains what their cartoon means.

Students can explore the issues around the Strategic Defense Initiative (SDI) by reading letters Reagan wrote to Soviet general secretary Mikhail Gorbachev in March 1985. Reagan expressed his hope that the Nuclear and Space Talks (NST) planned for Geneva later that year would "provide us with a genuine chance to make progress toward our common ultimate goal of eliminating nuclear weapons," and Gorbachev agreed.[25] However, negotiations broke down over the future of SDI. Critics labeled the program "Star Wars," mimicking the name of the film series.[26] Antinuclear activists were frustrated by the failed negotiations, and in March 1986, hundreds of activists walked from Los Angeles to Washington, DC, in the Great Peace March for Global Nuclear Disarmament.

Later that month, the Chernobyl Nuclear Power Plant became the site of the worst nuclear disaster in history, killing thirty-one and leaking an enormous amount of radiation, resulting in exposure deaths in the decade that followed. It reminded Americans of the accident at Three Mile Island Nuclear Generating Station in Pennsylvania in 1979 and reaffirmed to protesters the dangers of nuclear power.[27]

There are numerous cultural products for students to explore to help understand this period. I organize students into groups of three to six and ask each group to research an item from the list. They present to the class a brief summary of the piece and the impact of the item.

Video Games

- *Balance of Power* (1985)—a strategy game designed by Chris Crawford for the Macintosh where one plays as either the president of the United States or the general secretary of the Soviet Union. Players have eight turns, representing eight years, to improve their country's standing in the world while navigating brinksmanship situations and avoiding nuclear war. Should a player cause a nuclear war, the game ends with the following message: "You have ignited a(n accidental) nuclear war.

And no, there is no animated display of a mushroom cloud with parts of bodies flying through the air. We do not reward failure."[28]

Films

- *If You Love This Planet* (1982)—a short recording of a lecture by physician and antinuclear activist Helen Caldicott on the dangers of nuclear weapons.[29]
- *WarGames* (1983)—a Hollywood film about a teenager (Matthew Broderick) who hacks into a government computer and accidently triggers global thermonuclear war.[30]
- *Silkwood* (1983)—a biographical film starring Meryl Streep as Karen Silkwood, a labor activist and nuclear whistleblower who died in a car accident while investigating misconduct at a plutonium plant.[31]
- *Testament* (1983)—a film that depicts the impact of nuclear war on a small suburban town near San Francisco.[32]
- *The Day After* (1983)—a made-for-television movie that first aired to an audience of more than 100 million viewers on November 20, 1983. It shows a full-out nuclear war and its impact on several towns in Kansas and Missouri.[33]
- *Threads* (1984)—a British apocalyptic television film about the impact of nuclear war on a city in Northern England.[34]

Songs

- "Breathing" (1980)—from Kate Bush, English singer/songwriter, from the perspective of a fetus anxious about nuclear fallout.[35]
- "Enola Gay" (1980)—from British Orchestral Manoeuvers in the Dark (OMD), including the line "Enola Gay you should have stayed at home yesterday."[36]
- "99 Luftballons" (1984)—from German band Nena, with the line "99 years of war."[37]
- "Two Minutes to Midnight" (1984)—from British heavy metal band Iron Maiden, with the line "Two minutes to midnight to kill the unborn in the womb."[38]
- "Christmas at Ground Zero" (1986)—an original song from musical comedian "Weird Al" Yankovic. The video includes great footage, dark humor, and the line "What a crazy fluke, we're gonna get nuked on this jolly holiday."[39]

I also show students activism through print culture, especially bumper stickers and buttons: "Nuclear Waste is Not Healthy for Children and Other Living Things," "You Can't Hug a Child with Nuclear Arms," "Better Active Today than Radioactive Tomorrow." Then students create their own bumper sticker or button.

In the waning months of the existence of the Soviet Union, Mikhail Gorbachev declared a unilateral moratorium on nuclear testing. In 1992, the United States reciprocated. Four years later, the United States— along with more than 183 other nations—signed the Comprehensive Nuclear Test Ban Treaty, which banned all nuclear explosions and tests. More than a dozen countries, including the United States, have yet to ratify the 1996 treaty, but most nations have been following its provisions. Other countries—India, Pakistan, and North Korea—have not.

I end this period by exploring a near-cataclysmic event. On January 25, 1995, American and Norwegian scientists launched a research rocket off Norway's coast, triggering a high-level alert in Moscow.[40] Russian radar operators had not been informed and thought the rocket was a US missile attack. Officials brought President Boris Yeltsin the briefcase containing the nuclear codes, should he decide to authorize an attack.[41] Since we do not know what was said, I ask students to imagine what the conversations between Yeltsin and his advisers might have been like in those tense minutes. What prevailed in Moscow to allow Yeltsin

Button, 1984 (author's collection)

not to respond with a nuclear attack? This event shows that even with the end of the Cold War, nuclear weapons continue to make the world a very dangerous place.

Bush and Weapons of Mass Destruction

The attacks of September 11, 2001, prompted renewed concerns about weapons of mass destruction (WMD), especially nuclear weapons. The US government disclosed that its nuclear power plants were on the target list for the 9/11 terrorists and remained vulnerable to attack. President George W. Bush clarified that the United States was under threat by enemy nations and by individual terrorist groups, who possessed WMDs. The 2002 Bush Doctrine detailed the national security threat and the intended American response.[42] The US-led military action in Iraq represented an application of the Bush Doctrine against a nation the Americans presumed possessed WMDs and had a connection to the attacks of September 11. We know now that those claims were false, but there was significant pushback on the part of activists even in 2003.

As the Bush administration planned an American invasion of Iraq, antiwar organizers coordinated a day of protest, on February 15, 2003. Composed of more than 15 million protesters in eight hundred cities around the world, it is likely the largest antiwar protest in world history.[43]

The International Physicians for the Prevention of Nuclear War, which had won the Nobel Peace Prize back in 1985, launched the International Campaign to Abolish Nuclear Weapons (ICAN) in 2007. A coalition of more than five hundred nongovernmental organizations in more than one hundred countries, ICAN promotes "adherence to and implementation of the United Nations nuclear weapon ban treaty."[44] The organization is working to eliminate the existential threat that the more than fourteen thousand nuclear weapons in nine nuclear-armed states currently pose to the world. In 2017, ICAN was awarded the Nobel Peace Prize "for its work to draw attention to the catastrophic humanitarian consequences of any use of nuclear weapons and for its groundbreaking efforts to achieve a treaty-based prohibition of such weapons."[45]

Again, to help students grapple with the history of antiwar activism in this period, I invite them to work in groups to analyze a selection of the following cultural products.

Video Games

- *September 12th: A Toy World* (2010)—a simulation created by Games for Change that exposes the futility of the US-led War on Terror.[46]

Films

- *Why We Fight* (2005)—a documentary about the military-industrial complex as it questions post-9/11 US foreign policy.[47]
- *The Ground Truth* (2006)—a documentary about the American veterans of the Iraq War.[48]
- *We Are Many* (2014)—a documentary about the February 15, 2003, global day of protest against the Iraq War. Scholars consider this the largest protest in history.[49]

Songs

- "Boom" (2002)—from System of a Down, an Armenian American heavy metal band out of California. Michael Moore directed the music video as an anti-Iraq war piece in 2003.[50]
- "America First" (2003)—from Merle Haggard, the American country singer/songwriter, who urges Americans to "get out of Iraq" and "rebuild America first."[51]
- "Final Straw" (2004)—from indie rock band R.E.M., is an anti–Iraq War song.[52]
- "Radio Baghdad" (2004)—by Patti Smith, is a twelve-minute, improvised anti–Iraq War song about Americans bombing.[53]
- "Make Love Fuck War" (2005)—by Public Enemy and Moby, is an antiwar electronica hip-hop song.[54]
- "Christmas in Fallujah" (2007)—features Cass Dillon singing Billy Joel's song about war fatigue in Iraq and Afghanistan.[55]
- "Operation Iraqi Liberation (OIL)" (2007)—by David Rovics, indie singer/songwriter, is an antiwar song.[56]

Obama and Trump

In November 2008, the American people elected Barack Obama, whose antinuclear activism dated back to his days as an undergraduate at Columbia University.[57] In 2012, Obama explained his position:

I believe the United States has a unique responsibility to act; indeed, we have a moral obligation. I say this as a President of the only nation ever to use nuclear weapons. I say it as a Commander in Chief who knows that our nuclear codes are never far from my side. Most of all, I say it as a father, who wants my two daughters to grow up in a world where everything they know and love can't be instantly wiped out."[58]

The Obama administration supported ratification of the Comprehensive Nuclear Test Ban Treaty, but the Senate declined to act. The 2011 earthquake and tsunami, which resulted in the accident at the Fukushima Daiichi nuclear power station in Japan, pushed nuclear safety to the forefront, but activists had difficulty getting traction on the issue.

Nuclear disarmament and antiwar activism increased under the Trump administration. President Donald J. Trump surrounded himself with advisers who opposed international nuclear agreements.[59] The administration soon withdrew from the 1987 US/Soviet intermediate range missiles pact, withdrew from the Iran nuclear agreement, declared it would not seek ratification of the 1996 Comprehensive Nuclear Test Ban Treaty, and failed to halt the nuclear program in North Korea.[60] In 2020, administration officials discussed leaving the 2002 Treaty of Open Skies, which allows the thirty-four signature states to "conduct short-notice, unarmed, reconnaissance" over member nations to gather military information and promote transparency.[61]

In addition, on May 15, 2020, the Trump administration discussed the possibility of resuming nuclear testing.[62] Dissenting opinions have emerged, calling the resumption unnecessary and dangerous, with a director at the Federation of American Scientists declaring it "completely nuts."[63] Issues include the use of Nevada's underground nuclear test site, the impact of leaking tests on "downwinders" in Utah, and the possibility that other countries might resume testing.[64]

Students can grapple with cultural products of the Obama and Trump years to piece together the state of the protest movement. Here is a list, but instructors should add items as they become available.

1. By watching the 2010 documentary *Countdown to Zero*, students explore the dangers nuclear weapons pose in the post–Cold War world.[65] In addressing terrorism, nonstate nuclear actors, accidents—and the horrific fact that not all the estimated twenty-three thousand nuclear weapons in the world can be located—the film argues that it is more dangerous now than ever

before, and that the only answer is worldwide nuclear disarmament.

2. Comedian and contemporary muckraker John Oliver addresses nuclear weapons in an episode of *Last Week Tonight with John Oliver* in July 2014. Oliver exposes the dangers of storing nearly five thousand outdated nuclear warheads in the United States.[66]

3. Eric Schlosser's 2016 documentary *Command and Control* explores a potentially devastating nuclear accident that occurred in Arkansas in September 1980. A dropped socket, a punctured fuel tank, and an intercontinental ballistic missile with a nuclear warhead combine to create a harrowing tale.[67]

4. Beginning in 1947, the *Bulletin of Atomic Scientists* has set its Doomsday Clock to reflect how dangerous the nuclear risk is to the future of humanity. Through the Cold War the clock has fluctuated between 2 minutes, in 1953, to 12 minutes to midnight during the 1960s and 1970s. During the Reagan administration, the clock moved to 3 minutes before midnight in 1984. The collapse of the Soviet Union was reflected in 1990 with a 17-minute setting. It has crept closer to midnight ever since, matching the 1953 record of 2 minutes in 2018 and setting a new record in 2020, with 100 seconds before midnight. Students can track the Doomsday Clock settings and reflect on the changes, the impact of policy, and the symbolic importance of the clock to protesters.[68]

5. *DEFCON: Everybody Dies* (2020)—a real-time strategy video game by British game developer Introversion Software visually represents global nuclear war on a "big board" screen leading to Armageddon.[69]

As students have observed change over time with protest movements since 1980, one can finish the lesson addressing the complications of protesting in the time of a pandemic.[70] As protesters attempt to socially distance, conduct drive-by protests, and turn to online activism, all while encouraging voting and fundraising, students can explore the creativity that nuclear disarmament protesters have displayed to exercise their First Amendment rights, impact policy, and be heard. Moving beyond buttons and bumper stickers, I ask students to create activist tweets.

Conclusion

In my experience, students become engaged in history that comes alive for them. Whether it is through oral histories, music, film, or games, there are many opportunities here to engage students. As often happens in the classroom, we are only limited by our own imaginations, and time. I hope that instructors will take these ideas, choose the ones that work for their students, and focus some attention on individual and group activism in the United States. These are excellent examples of ways that Americans can push back and have an impact on their government.

NOTES

1. Of the 2,053 detonations, the United States has the most with 1,032; the Russians have the second highest with 715. Isao Hashimoto, "A Time-Lapse Map of Every Nuclear Explosion since 1945," October 24, 2010, https://www.youtube.com/watch?reload=9&v=LLCF7vPanrY.

2. McGeorge Bundy, *Danger and Survival: Choices about the Bomb in the First Fifty Years* (New York: Random House, 1988).

3. Ibid., 582.

4. Allan M. Winkler, *Life under a Cloud: American Anxiety about the Atom* (New York: Oxford University Press, 1993). See also Ronald D. Cohen and Will Kaufman, *Singing for Peace: Antiwar Songs in American History* (New York: Routledge, 2015).

5. Jonathan Schell, *The Fate of the Earth* (New York: Knopf, 1982). This work prompted me to join the movement.

6. Philip L. Fradkin, *Fallout: An American Nuclear Tragedy* (Tucson: University of Arizona Press, 1989, 2004).

7. See Kate Brown, *Plutopia: Nuclear Families, Atomic Cities, and the Great Soviet and American Plutonium Disasters* (New York: Oxford University Press, 2013); Adam Higginbotham, *Midnight in Chernobyl: The Untold Story of the World's Greatest Nuclear Disaster* (New York: Simon & Schuster, 2019); Eric Schlosser, *Command and Control: Nuclear Weapons, the Damascus Accident, and the Illusion of Safety* (New York: Penguin, 2013); and Eileen Welsome, *The Plutonium Files: America's Secret Medical Experiments in the Cold War* (New York: Random House, 1999).

8. Lawrence S. Wittner, *Confronting the Bomb: A Short History of the World Nuclear Disarmament Movement* (Stanford, CA: Stanford University Press, 2009), xii. Here Wittner condenses a story he previously told in a trilogy, *The Struggle against the Bomb* (Stanford, CA: Stanford University Press, 1993, 1997, 2003). Volume 1, *One World or None*, covers the story from 1945 through 1953. Volume

2, *Resisting the Bomb,* addresses 1954 through 1970. The third volume, *Toward Nuclear Abolition,* brings the story to the early 2000s.

9. "It would be rather absurd to work to get schools and lunch counters integrated and not be concerned with the survival of a world in which to integrate." Martin Luther King Jr., "Vietnam Is upon Us," address, February 6, 1968, as quoted in Vincent Intondi, "Nuclear Weapons and the Legacy of Dr. King," *Outrider Post,* January 9, 2019, https://outrider.org/nuclear-weapons/articles/nuclear-weapons-and-legacy-dr-king/.

10. Vincent J. Intondi, *African Americans against the Bomb: Nuclear Weapons, Colonialism, and the Black Freedom Movement* (Stanford, CA: Stanford University Press, 2016), 111, 132.

11. *Peace & Change: A Journal of Peace Research,* Wiley Online Library, https://onlinelibrary.wiley.com/loi/14680130.

12. For example, see Nicholas Rostow, "The World Health Organization, the International Court of Justice, and Nuclear Weapons," *Yale Journal of International Law* 20, no. 1 (1995): 151–85, https://digitalcommons.law.yale.edu/yjil/vol20/iss1/5; David P. Fidler, "International Law and Weapons of Mass Destruction: End of the Arms Control Approach?," *Duke Journal of Comparative and International Law* 14 (2004): 39–88, https://www.researchgate.net/publication/241811978_International_Law_and_Weapons_of_Mass_Destruction_End_of_the_Arms_Control_Approach/link/56cefffa08ae059e37581f65/download.

13. The plan is to make part of the collection available digitally. See a history and description of the archive at Center for International Studies, "Reppy Institute for Peace and Conflict Studies," Cornell University, http://pacs.einaudi.cornell.edu/IDDS-Archive (accessed August 15, 2021); and Division of Rare Books and Manuscript Collections, "Institute for Defense and Disarmament Studies: Records, 1974–2007, Collection Number: 8588," Cornell University, https://rmc.library.cornell.edu/EAD/htmldocs/RMM08588.html#a1 (accessed August 15, 2021).

14. "Call for Papers: Global Histories of Anti-Nuclear and Peace Activism in the Late Cold War," Wilson Center, February 4, 2020, https://www.wilsoncenter.org/article/call-papers-global-histories-anti-nuclear-and-peace-activism-late-cold-war.

15. American Civil Liberties Union, "Rights of Protesters," https://www.aclu.org/issues/free-speech/rights-protesters (accessed August 15, 2021).

16. Richard Halloran, "Soviet Buildup near Iran Tested Carter," *New York Times,* August 27, 1986, https://www.nytimes.com/1986/08/27/world/soviet-buildup-near-iran-tested-carter.html.

17. Lawrence S. Wittner, "The Forgotten Years of the World Nuclear Disarmament Movement, 1975–78," *Journal of Peace Research* 40, no. 4 (July 2003): 435–56.

18. Such as the B-1 bomber, the neutron bomb, the Trident nuclear submarine, and the MX nuclear missile. See Wittner, *Confronting the Bomb,* chapter 6.

19. Wittner, *Confronting the Bomb*, 138.

20. Wittner, "Forgotten Years."

21. Jonathan Schell, "The Spirit of June 12," *Nation*, July 2, 2007, https://www.thenation.com/article/archive/spirit-june-12/.

22. "A Nuclear Freeze?," *Washington Post*, March 28, 1982, https://www.washingtonpost.com/archive/opinions/1982/03/28/a-nuclear-freeze/dobcec87-a654-4148-956e-ce58fc8424fe/.

23. Turner Network Television, *"Butter Battle Book,"* 1989, animated television special, https://www.youtube.com/watch?v=yeoggnNIg64.

24. Students can be invited to study political cartoons, such as those found online in the "Nuclear Weapons" lesson plan, History Teaching Institute of the Ohio State University, https://hti.osu.edu/opper/lesson-plans/nuclear-weapons (accessed July 21, 2022).

25. "President Ronald Reagan Letter to General Secretary Mikhail Gorbachev, March 11, 1985," National Security Archive, https://nsarchive2.gwu.edu/NSAEBB/NSAEBB172/Doc2.pdf.

26. Kathleen Hendrix, "'The Great Peace March' Forming Up in L.A.: Activists Are Gathering for 3,235-Mile Trek across United States Starting from Coliseum," *Los Angeles Times*, December 27, 1985, https://www.latimes.com/archives/la-xpm-1985-12-27-vw-25644-story.html.

27. See Kate Brown, "Uncovering the Realities of the Chernobyl Accident," Wilson Center, March 9, 2020, https://www.wilsoncenter.org/blog-post/kate-brown-uncovering-realities-chernobyl-accident.

28. "Balance of Power for the Apple II," https://www.youtube.com/watch?v=Jowy5yz6pnQ. Chris Crawford updated the game in 1990.

29. Terre Nash, dir., *If You Love This Planet* (Studio D, 1982), https://documentary.net/video/if-you-love-this-planet-1982-oscar-winning-film/.

30. John Badham, dir., *"WarGames* Official Trailer #1," 1983, https://www.youtube.com/watch?v=hbqMuvnx5MU.

31. Mike Nichols, dir., *"Silkwood* Official Trailer #1," 1983, October 5, 2012, https://www.youtube.com/watch?v=iNyrSR5JGh8.

32. Lynne Littman, dir., *"Testament* 1983 Trailer: Jane Alexander," June 8, 2017, https://www.youtube.com/watch?v=CyzHGSOJjeA.

33. Nicholas Meyer, dir., *"The Day After* 1983 Trailer," November 12, 2012, https://www.youtube.com/watch?reload=9&v=MOFsOA9VsBk.

34. Mick Jackson, dir., *"Threads* (1984) Original Trailer," April 10, 2018, https://www.youtube.com/watch?v=vgT4Y30DkaA.

35. Kate Bush, "Breathing: Official Music Video," April 14, 1980, https://www.youtube.com/watch?v=VzlofSthVwc.

36. Orchestral Manoeuvres in the Dark, "Enola Gay (Official Music Video)," September 20, 2010, https://www.youtube.com/watch?v=d5XJ2GiR6Bo.

37. NENA, "99 Luftballons," September 25, 2019, https://www.youtube.com/watch?v=7aLiT3wXk00.

38. Iron Maiden, "2 Minutes to Midnight (Official Video)," August 7, 2015, https://www.youtube.com/watch?v=9qbRHY1lovc.

39. "Weird Al" Yankovic, "Christmas at Ground Zero," 1986, https://www.youtube.com/watch?reload=9&v=t039p6xqutU.

40. David Hoffman, "Cold-War Doctrines Refuse to Die," *Washington Post*, March 15, 1998, https://www.washingtonpost.com/wp-srv/inatl/longterm/coldwar/shatter031598a.htm.

41. The American nuclear code briefcase is nicknamed the "football." See Michael Dobbs, "The Real Story of the 'Football' That Follows the President Everywhere," *Smithsonian Magazine*, October 2014, https://www.smithsonianmag.com/history/real-story-football-follows-president-everywhere-180952779/.

42. George W. Bush, "Address before a Joint Session of the Congress on the State of the Union," January 29, 2002, American Presidency Project, University of California, Santa Barbara, https://www.presidency.ucsb.edu/documents/address-before-joint-session-the-congress-the-state-the-union-22.

43. See Amir Amirani's film on the protests, *We Are Many*, trailer, https://www.youtube.com/watch?v=SgxlMJnxUl4

44. ICAN, https://www.icanw.org/ (accessed August 15, 2021). See also Lawrence S. Wittner, "A Rebirth of the Anti-Nuclear Weapons Movement?," *History News Network*, June 25, 2007, https://historynewsnetwork.org/article/40310.

45. "The Nobel Peace Prize 2017," Nobel Prize, https://www.nobelprize.org/prizes/peace/2017/summary/ (accessed August 15, 2021).

46. "*September 12th* sample," https://www.youtube.com/watch?v=N1OemWEk5ns.

47. Eugene Jarecki, dir., *Why We Fight*, trailer, https://www.imdb.com/video/vi1660748057?playlistId=tt0436971&ref_=tt_ov_vi.

48. Patricia Foulkrod, dir., *The Ground Truth*, trailer, https://www.youtube.com/watch?v=ReuzTgcboWo.

49. Amir Amirani, dir., *We Are Many*, trailer, https://www.youtube.com/watch?v=SgxlMJnxUl4.

50. System of a Down, "Boom! (Official Video)," https://www.youtube.com/watch?v=bE2r7r7VVic.

51. Merle Haggard, "America First," https://www.youtube.com/watch?v=UodJB1tRNVE.

52. R.E.M., "Final Straw," https://www.youtube.com/watch?v=XnVUosM3KUk.

53. Patti Smith, "Radio Baghdad," https://www.youtube.com/watch?v=Sj7dIhIvwb4.

54. Moby and Public Enemy, "Make Love Fuck War," https://www.youtube.com/watch?v=XN54kruANNk.

55. Cass Dillon, "Christmas in Fallujah," https://www.youtube.com/watch?v=R_qTuJ1UK2w.

56. David Rovics, "Operation Iraqi Liberation (OIL)," https://www.you tube.com/watch?v=AwKvR9mbYHo. See also David Rovics, "Who Would Jesus Bomb?," 2004, https://www.youtube.com/watch?v=VIFJltb8hcg.

57. In March 1983, Obama wrote in the campus newspaper that nuclear weapons were "linked to economics and politics and part of a much larger problem—militarism." As quoted in Intondi, *African Americans against the Bomb*, 109.

58. Barack Obama, "Remarks at Hankuk University of Foreign Studies in Seoul," March 26, 2012, American Presidency Project, University of California, Santa Barbara, https://www.presidency.ucsb.edu/documents/remarks-hankuk -university-foreign-studies-seoul.

59. Trump was born on the same day—June 12, 1946—that the United Nations held the first meeting of the Atomic Energy Commission (AEC). The AEC attempted to establish international control of nuclear technology, but the lack of an American-Soviet agreement resulted in the nuclear arms race. See Tomas Gaulkin, "Curious Coincidence: The Birth of Donald Trump and the Struggle to Abolish Nuclear Weapons," *Bulletin of the Atomic Scientists*, June 12, 2020, https://thebulletin.org/2020/06/curious-coincidence-the-birth-of-donald -trump-and-the-struggle-to-abolish-nuclear-weapons/?utm_source=Newslet ter&utm_medium=Email&utm_campaign=MondayNewsletter06152020&utm _content=NuclearRisk_Curious_06122020.

60. Experts agree that the collapsed US nuclear deal with North Korea, officially ended on June 12, 2020, has resulted in an expansion of North Korea's weapons program, particularly intercontinental ballistic missiles that could reach an American city. See Choe Sang-Hun, "North Korea Vows to Boost Nuclear Program, Saying U.S. Diplomacy Failed," *New York Times*, June 11, 2020, https://www.nytimes.com/2020/06/11/world/asia/north-korea-nuclear-trump.html.

61. See Arms Control Association, "The Open Skies Treaty at a Glance: Fact Sheets & Briefs," last reviewed June 2021, https://www.armscontrol.org/fact sheets/openskies.

62. John Hudson and Paul Sonne, "Trump Administration Discussed Conducting First U.S. Nuclear Test in Decades," *Washington Post*, May 22, 2020, https://www.washingtonpost.com/national-security/trump-administration-dis cussed-conducting-first-us-nuclear-test-in-decades/2020/05/22/a805c904-9c5b -11ea-b60c-3be060a4f8e1_story.html.

63. John Krzyzaniak, "Why a US Nuclear Test in Nevada Would Be Bad for the World—and Trump's Reelection," *Bulletin of the Atomic Scientists*, June 1, 2020, https://thebulletin.org/2020/06/why-a-us-nuclear-test-in-nevada-would-be -bad-for-the-world-and-trumps-reelection/.

64. Editorial, "Nevada Can Never Let Its Guard Down against Trump on Nuke Tests, Waste," *Las Vegas Sun*, May 31, 2020, https://lasvegassun.com/news/

2020/may/31/nevada-can-never-let-its-guard-down-against-trump/; Lee Davidson, "Utah Downwinders Denounce Trump's Talk of Restarting Nuclear Tests,"
Salt Lake Tribune, May 26, 2020, https://www.sltrib.com/news/politics/2020/05/
26/utah-downwinders-denounce/.

65. Lucy Walker, dir., *Countdown to Zero* (Magnolia Films, 2010), trailer,
https://www.youtube.com/watch?v=IXcH6xsq5zo; complete film, https://www
.youtube.com/watch?v=Js-CxhYO590.

66. "Nuclear Weapons," *Last Week Tonight with John Oliver*, July 28, 2014, on
HBO, https://www.youtube.com/watch?v=1Y1ya-yF35g.

67. Robert Kenner, dir., "Command and Control: The Long-Hidden Story
of the Day Our Luck Almost Ran Out," *American Experience*, April 25, 2017,
https://www.pbs.org/wgbh/americanexperience/films/command-and-control/.

68. "The Doomsday Clock: A Timeline of Conflict, Culture, and Change,"
Bulletin of the Atomic Scientists, https://thebulletin.org/doomsday-clock/past-state
ments/.

69. Introversion Software, "DEFCON Trailer, 2020," https://www.youtube
.com/watch?reload=9&v=tDVhWoNuR5I.

70. Emerson Sykes, "How to Protest in a Pandemic," American Civil Liberties Union, May 1, 2020, https://www.aclu.org/news/free-speech/how-to-protest
-in-a-pandemic/.

FOR FURTHER READING

Freeman, Stephanie. *Dreams for a Decade: Nuclear Abolitionism and the End of the
Cold War*. Philadelphia: University of Pennsylvania Press, forthcoming.

Goedde, Petra. *Politics of Peace: A Global Cold War History*. New York: Oxford
University Press, 2019.

Intondi, Vincent J. *African Americans against the Bomb: Nuclear Weapons, Colonialism, and the Black Freedom Movement*. Stanford, CA: Stanford University
Press, 2016.

Perry, William J., and Tom Z. Collina. *The Button: The New Nuclear Arms Race
and Presidential Power from Truman to Trump*. Dallas: Ben Bella Books, 2020.

Winkler, Allan M. *Life under a Cloud: American Anxiety about the Atom*. New York:
Oxford University Press, 1993.

Wittner, Lawrence S. *Confronting the Bomb: A Short History of the World Nuclear
Disarmament Movement*. Stanford, CA: Stanford University Press, 2009.

Framing America for the World

Understanding US Foreign Policy Rhetoric by Using Presidential Speeches before the UN General Assembly

AMY L. SAYWARD

Why Teach This Lesson?

The United Nations (UN) tends to bop in and out of Americans' consciousness depending on what is happening globally—such as pandemics, Security Council resolutions, and searches for weapons of mass destruction. Nonetheless, all US presidents—starting with Harry Truman—have addressed the global body, and Ronald Reagan initiated the practice of speaking annually to the General Assembly, the part of the United Nations with representatives from each of the member countries (157 when Reagan was inaugurated and 193 when Joe Biden was inaugurated).[1] As such, these speeches provide an opportunity for US presidents to frame their foreign policy for both an international and a domestic audience.

In the lesson attached to this chapter, students will have the opportunity to think about strategies that presidents use to frame their policies, which will help learners become better able to analyze rhetorical devices, as well see both change and continuity in the way that recent presidents have presented their foreign policy to a world audience. This lesson will fit well in your survey if you have focused on international issues and foreign policy, drawing links—for example—to the earlier

Cold War and the US war in Korea that took place under the auspices of the United Nations.

Although this lesson focuses on how US presidents have sought to frame American policies before the United Nations, Americans have frequently used both the League of Nations and the United Nations to challenge their own government's foreign and domestic policies. To provide just a handful of illustrative examples, early on the Cayuga people (Indigenous Americans) presented their grievances to the League of Nations in Geneva, Switzerland, in 1922. Then shortly after the founding of the United Nations in 1945, African Americans in the United States asked the UN Commission on Human Rights to stop what it defined as the ongoing genocide they were suffering as a result of racism. The NAACP (National Association for the Advanced of Colored People)— along with the Non-Aligned Movement—also pressed the UN to speed the process of decolonization that followed the Second World War. The League and United Nations have also worked on a wide variety of social issues that are crucial to many Americans, including human and drug trafficking, monitoring weapons of mass destruction and the spread of disease, the regulation of space and the oceans, ensuring the rights of women and children, and the protection of refugees and the global environment. Finally, a number of Americans forged reputations for their work within the United Nations, including Ralph Bunche, who became the first African American to earn the Nobel Peace Prize for his work in trying to mediate in the crisis between the Palestinians, Israel, and its Arab neighbors in the late 1940s. Further information and resources about these groups are available in the additional materials on the book's companion website for this chapter (http://GoldbergSeries .org/UTContemporaryUSHistory).

Introduction

Depending on the news cycle, many of your students may know little or nothing about the United Nations. For example, as I am writing this chapter, the COVID-19 global pandemic is ravaging the people of the globe, making more Americans aware of the World Health Organization (WHO)—both its guidance on how to deal with the disease and President Donald Trump's withdrawal from the organization for its "failure" to stop the planetary spread of this new virus.[2] In many ways, this is emblematic of how many Americans and also many scholars view the United Nations—which is made up of many parts.[3]

Historians, political scientists, commentators, diplomats, and politicians have written a lot about the United Nations since its founding in 1945 at the San Francisco Conference, but much of that writing has been primarily in terms of the "successes" and "failures" of the organization, which are usually defined by the highly idealized language of the UN Charter signed at San Francisco. In other words, has the United Nations— as stated in the Charter's Preamble—succeeded in saving people "from the scourge of war," promoting "the dignity and worth of the human person," securing "equal rights of men and women and of nations large and small," establishing "justice and respect" for international law, and promoting "social progress and better standards of life in larger freedom"?[4] Its handful of "successes" in these areas over the past seventy-seven years and, more often, its manifold "failures" have primarily been highlighted as lessons to be learned with the goal of "reforming" the United Nations to make it more "successful" at some point in the future.[5]

As I have written elsewhere, I think that historians would be better served to see the United Nations as an intersection or borderland, a location of diplomacy, or an international stage where many people, countries, and interests come together, collide, reconcile, advocate, negotiate, and bargain in an effort to forge a collective plan of action for the world while promoting their own interests. They do this primarily through language and secondarily—and far less often—through collective action, such as the peacekeeping efforts and economic sanctions that can result from UN Security Council resolutions.[6] Therefore language is especially important at the United Nations. US presidents have been very cognizant of the United Nations as a particularly important stage on which their words matter; those words help frame how the international community views each administration's initiatives both inside and outside of the United Nations, and those words help frame how the American people understand the wider world, US foreign policy goals within that world, and the role of the UN within that foreign policy.

Rhetorically, these are fascinating speeches, because they seek—at the same time—to frame American foreign policy in a way that aligns it with the goals and ideals of the United Nations *and* with the goals and ideals of the United States. As such, these speeches provide students with an opportunity to analyze presidential rhetoric in order to discern how these presidents frame their foreign policy, how they portray the United States—as well as its enemies, and how they want the United Nations to act in support of their policies. In other words, the speeches can be used simultaneously to see how respective presidents have sought to define their foreign policy, UN politics, and shifting definitions of the ideals of the United States.

Additionally, these speeches help students see that contemporary presidents have had very different views of the United Nations and its utility to their foreign policy, and sometimes a single president's views have shifted throughout his tenure. In the years leading up to his successful bid for the White House, Reagan largely defined the UN as an ineffective organization that could and should be ignored so long as it did not effectively address global communism, which he defined as the key threat to world peace. But the end of the Cold War brought about significant changes in his view of the New York–based international organization. This helped his successor, George H. W. Bush, who had previously served as the US ambassador to the United Nations, work through the organization to build an international consensus about the need to reverse the invasion of Kuwait by Saddam Hussein's Iraq. Bill Clinton initially thought that he could build on the post–Cold War consensus within the United Nations to build a more peaceful world, but botched efforts in Sudan and genocide in Rwanda put an effective end to such hopes.

The most recent US presidents have seemed to oscillate between nationalism and internationalism. The terrorist attacks of September 11, 2001, largely defined George W. Bush's presidency and prompted his subsequent decisions to invade both Afghanistan and Iraq mostly outside of the UN framework. Barack Obama embraced a more internationally focused foreign policy punctuated by the 2015 Joint Comprehensive Plan (exchanging limits on the Iranian nuclear effort for a lifting of the international sanctions regime against the Islamic republic) and the 2016 Paris Climate Change Agreement. However, his successor, Donald Trump, consistently sought to eliminate or minimize the international commitments of the United States—ranging from the Paris Agreement to NATO (the North Atlantic Treaty Organization)—and acted more unilaterally—for example, reinstating economic sanctions on Iran and renegotiating NAFTA (the North American Free Trade Agreement). But in the lesson below, students will be encouraged to identify similarities as well as differences between administrations.

Given that these speeches speak to a number of audiences simultaneously and have multiple contexts, this lesson seeks to give students specific tools to analyze the rhetoric of these addresses. With each student reading and analyzing a different speech as the preparatory homework for this lesson, the classroom lesson brings students together to "jigsaw" — teaching their peers what they have learned and in turn learning from their peers — so that they can see both changes and continuities between the ways that these presidents have defined US foreign policy for the world and for Americans.

In the lesson plan below, the Individual Homework worksheet that students will use (Worksheet 1) provides a framework for analyzing the rhetoric of these speeches, which I have borrowed from diplomatic historian Emily Rosenberg's cogent analysis of the rhetorical strategies employed in NSC-68 — that foundational 1950 document from the National Security Council (NSC) that created a framework for fighting the Cold War and mobilizing the home front for this unconventional, long-term conflict. That framework used the same types of binaries (good vs. evil, freedom vs. oppression) that President Harry S. Truman voiced when requesting aid for Greece and Turkey and enunciating his foreign policy doctrine. The second key element that Rosenberg identifies is the sense of emergency — or at least urgency — that encourages the listener or reader to take action immediately without seeking additional input or asking illuminating questions. And the third key ingredient to this type of foreign policy rhetoric is putting oneself on the right side of history, showing how the proposed actions are in line with the ideals of the United States and in this case the United Nations — even if they radically deviate from tradition (such as NSC-68's call for the creation and maintenance of a massive and permanent US military that could fight more than two wars around the world simultaneously). Teachers may want to read this short and accessible piece before teaching this lesson.[7] Training students to engage in this type of critical, rhetorical exercise can help improve their critical thinking skills as well as make them more thoughtful citizens, especially in their consumption of media.

Lesson Plan

This lesson has been designed for a single class session following completion of preparatory homework, but other and longer variations are listed below. I imagine that this would be a good lesson after surveying the Reagan administration and end of the Cold War. As such, this lesson—with its broad chronology—can help serve as a bridge to the next era and some of its key events. It also provides touchstones for future lessons and makes groups of students "experts" on each of the subsequent administrations.

Student Objectives

At the end of this lesson, students will be able to

- identify some of the key foreign policy goals of Presidents Reagan through Biden;
- use analytical skills to understand the rhetoric of presidential speeches before the UN General Assembly (lessons that can be applied to other contexts);
- identify changes and continuities between Presidents Reagan through Biden in terms of how they have described their foreign policy for an international audience.

Outline of Lesson

Preparatory homework: I have included an Individual Homework template (see Worksheet 1) at the end of the chapter and on the website [http://GoldbergSeries.org/UTContemporaryUSHistory]). In the class meeting ahead of this lesson, you will assign each student a speech to read and analyze (see the assignment chart, Assigning Presidential Speeches and Defining Small Groups). I recommend going over the

Assigning Presidential Speeches and Defining Small Groups

1	Reagan '82	Bush '89	Clinton '93	GWB '01	Obama '09	Trump '17
2	Reagan '83	Bush '90	Clinton '94	GWB '02	Obama '10	Trump '18
3	Reagan '84	Bush '91	Clinton '95	GWB '03	Obama '11	Trump '19
4	Reagan '85	Bush '92	Clinton '96	GWB '04	Obama '12	Trump '20
5	Reagan '86	Clinton '00	Clinton '97	GWB '05	Obama '13	Biden '21
6	Reagan '87	GWB '08	Clinton '98	GWB '06	Obama '14	Biden '22
7	Reagan '88	Obama '16	Clinton '99	GWB '07	Obama '15	Biden '23

front of the sheet with the students to answer their questions about the rhetorical analysis assignment. The worksheet is where students will show their analysis, which they will share with their small group in the subsequent class meeting.

Class Lesson

Preparation: As students come into the classroom, check their homework for completion (can be done quickly and does not penalize students for not "getting it") and have them sit with the other members of their group (laid out in the assignment chart).

Initial organization (approximately 3–5 minutes): Assign one member of the group to serve as the recorder (writing down the collective wisdom of the group), one member of the group to serve as the spokesperson (orally sharing the collective wisdom of the group), one member to serve as the leader of the group (ensuring that the group completes its work in the time allotted and that everyone in the group has an equal opportunity to contribute), and one member to serve as the timekeeper (assisting the leader with time management during the class period). If you do not have a current method of organizing roles in small-group activities, I like to assign roles based on birthdays—"Whose birthday is closest to today? Your present is you get to be your group's recorder today!" "Of the remaining people, whose birthday is closest to March 17, St. Patrick's Day? You get to be the group's spokesperson"— and so on. Make sure each person knows their role, and then hand out one copy of Group Work: Comparing and Contrasting Presidential Rhetoric (see Worksheet 2 at the end of the chapter and on the web page) to each group's recorder. Depending on your style, before you transition into the small-group discussion, you might want to start by asking for volunteers to share something that they thought was interesting or surprising in their speech and by modeling the type of analysis and discussion that you want to see in the small groups. Alternatively, you can have students simply start with their small-group discussion.

Small-group discussion, part 1 (approximately 18 minutes): Have students start by providing summaries of the key points that they picked up from their documents to the other members of their small group (approximately 3 minutes each), and have the recorder summarize these points on the front of their group worksheet (Worksheet 2). Circulate between the groups, asking questions and helping to deepen and move the discussion forward—also provide students with a two-minute warning to help them wind up their discussion in a timely manner.

Small-group discussion, part 2 (15–18 minutes): As students wind up their summary on the front of the sheet, invite them to start working on the back of the sheet (some groups may finish up earlier), which shifts the group's discussion to comparative analysis. Again, circulate among the groups, facilitating their discussion and asking them to provide (more) specific examples from their speeches to illustrate or support their answers (especially your groups that are moving quickly toward completion).

Whole-class discussion (approximately 10–12 minutes): Ask the spokesperson of one group to share the most significant similarity that they found among the speeches and ask clarifying questions. Write a summary on the board. Ask other groups if they also identified this as a similarity. Call on another group's spokesperson, asking for another significant similarity and following the same pattern of follow up until all groups have had an opportunity to contribute. If they seem to run out of similarities, you can ask the last group(s) to share a difference that they noted.

Assessment, connections, and closing (approximately 2–9 minutes): Wrap up by asking what the significance is that these similarities exist despite such significant differences in historical context (Cold War vs. post–Cold War vs. Global War on Terror) and individual presidents. If you prefer a more formal assessment, you could ask students to discuss and write this answer at the end of their group worksheets. Additionally or alternatively, you may want to have students compare these rhetorical strategies to other documents they might have read previously in the semester (such as the Truman Doctrine speech) or have students ask if they think that they could apply these rhetorical analysis skills to other speeches that presidents or presidential candidates might make. Have students turn in both their homework and their group work before leaving the classroom; this can be used as a formal, written assessment of student work and thinking. In the next class, the teacher can provide each small group with a packet that includes each of the group members' homework sheets, with the group worksheet as the cover sheet. This allows the instructor and students to refer back to this work later in the semester, introducing additional lessons or reinforcing ideas from this exercise.

Resources

Transcripts of each of the presidential addresses to the United Nations—with contextual and vocabulary footnotes to aid in student reading comprehension—are provided on this book's companion website (http://GoldbergSeries.org/UTContemporaryUSHistory). I have also included there links to audio and video versions of the addresses, which can be usefully assigned to English-language learners and struggling readers. Many of these are drawn from presidential libraries and the Miller Center of Public Affairs at the University of Virginia, which provide many other resources for studying US presidents and their foreign policies.[8]

Extended Lesson Activities and Ideas

The pandemic has me—and every other teacher (and parent)—thinking about how we might adapt lessons to "remote" learning. This lesson is well set up for a synchronous Zoom or Microsoft Teams class setting. After a short introduction to the lesson provided in the previous class meeting (or online), students work individually on their homework assignment (which is not easily answered via Google or similar search engine). Next they come together in small groups (Zoom break-out rooms) for their discussion and then reporting to the class as a whole. Both homework and group work can be submitted via email or some type of electronic drop box (easier since these assignments are provided in Word format on the book's companion webpage [http://GoldbergSeries.org/UTContemporaryUSHistory]).

If you are teaching this lesson in a class that is familiar with the United Nations, then you can shape the assignments a bit to add reflection on these US presidents' views of the international organization. If you want to do this, I would suggest adding or substituting this question on the homework assignment: "What does this speech identify as the primary strengths and weaknesses of the United Nations?" Many of the speeches are critical of the actual work of the UN while seemingly pointing to its "real" objectives and work (interesting rhetorical work). This, too, could be usefully unpacked as part of the small-group activity and whole-class discussion by either adding a chart where students fill in UN strengths versus weaknesses (in the president's opinion) or a chart on what the president wants the UN to do and not to do. This could also be substituted for one of the other questions (depending on time and preference). I believe that these speeches are fascinating in terms of framing the work of the United Nations, but that type of analysis would not be front-of-mind in a US history survey, for example.

If you are teaching in a slightly longer class period and have at least twelve students in class (so that there are at least two speeches read by each of the presidents), I would suggest that you have two different small-group activities. Ahead of the lesson plan laid out above, I would suggest having the students who read speeches by the same president gather together to specifically identify the changes and continuities they see in these speeches (see Worksheet 3, Group Work: Examining One President's Rhetoric at the end of this lesson and on the companion website [http://GoldbergSeries.org/UTContemporaryUSHistory]). They would spend approximately 8–15 minutes sharing information about the individual speech they read (depending on how big the class is and therefore how many people are in each of these groups) before pivoting to identifying similarities and differences (continuity and change) between the speeches for approximately 8–12 minutes. This activity will "warm up" students' thinking on themes of change versus continuity and will help them feel more confident in presenting their president's speech in their later small-group jigsaw, where others likely have not read a speech by their president. Also, it never hurts to practice historical thinking skills (such as identifying change versus continuity) multiple times.

One section of the homework sheet that is not currently part of the small-group work or whole-class discussion is the question of what might be a different way of looking at the issues the president raised and what might have been some of the criticisms. You may have additional time to pursue this line of questioning, which serves two different objectives: (1) to highlight the ways in which the rhetorical strategies employed often require the critic to dismantle the binaries and other rhetorical constructions before they can effectively address the core issues and (2) to emphasize that there are many perspectives on how to deal with the global issues raised in these speeches.

In connection with this rhetorical unpacking, the instructor might want to provide one or two specific historical examples that show how the rhetorical single point of view or binaries in one president's speech are often undermined or reversed by the very same president at a later date. For example, Reagan calls for significant international arms control in his first (1982) address to the UN General Assembly and is highly critical of the United Nations for its "failures" in this area. However, steps toward significant nuclear arms control do come toward the end of Reagan's second administration, in a very unexpected manner. Soviet leader Mikhail Gorbachev and Reagan met in 1986 in Reykjavik, Iceland, and agreed to the principles that led to the 1987 INF Treaty (eliminating intermediate-range nuclear forces), the 1991 START I Treaty (strategic offensive arms reductions), and further limitations on nuclear testing.[9] As such, this incident can be a useful example of how today's sense of urgency and binary—the Soviets are what is standing in the way of effective nuclear control—can become tomorrow's partnership. A similar example might be Trump's insultingly calling North Korean leader Kim Jong-un "rocket man" and a "mad man" who should have been dealt with long before (creating the sense of urgency) but later meeting North Korea's supreme leader in person in the demilitarized zone (DMZ) between North and South Korea.[10]

Further Reading

In addition to the sources identified in the notes for the chapter and the additional reading section on the companion webpage (http://GoldbergSeries.org/UTContemporaryUSHistory), Timothy J. Lynch, *In the Shadow of the Cold War: American Foreign Policy from George Bush Sr. to Donald Trump* (Cambridge University Press, 2020) offers one of the newest academic analyses of the foreign policy of most of the presidents in the time frame considered in this chapter. It provides a readable survey of the past thirty years, arguing for a fundamental continuity amid the changes wrought by the end of the Cold War; it also argues that US foreign policy has been fundamentally successful in this period, especially when presidents have applied the strategic lessons of the Cold War. This book also has a very strong but concise "Suggested Reading" section at the end—with an introduction and then a segment on each of the presidents—that offers analysis of the books, articles, and historians contributing to this emerging historiography, which Lynch characterizes as tending to deride or bemoan US foreign policy. Lise Morjé Howard's "Sources of Change in United States–United Nations Relations" also provides a good and clear summary of the changes in the Clinton and George W. Bush administrations in their stances toward the United Nations.[11]

Worksheet 1. Individual Homework: Analyzing Rhetoric in US Presidential Addresses to the United Nations

President: _____

Year of speech: _____

Important context (what had happened before this speech that is referred to in the speech—you might need to check the footnotes to your speech for this information):

Who is the "we" in the speech (usually Americans and some subset of the others in the world):	Who are the "they" in the speech (often communists, terrorists, or people currently in conflict with the United States):
What are the adjectives/phrases that the president uses to describe "us"? List them here and underline/highlight them in your copy of the speech to share with your classmates.	What are the adjectives/phrases that the president uses to describe "them"? List them here and underline/highlight them in copy of the speech to share with your classmates.

What course(s) of action is the president suggesting in this speech that the United Nations and the world should take?

_____

_____

_____

What reasons does he provide for this course of action?

_____

_____

What language does the president use to tell his audience that taking this course of action is important and urgent (needs to take place quickly)? For example, does he discuss the danger(s) that might result from delay or from not taking his suggested course of action? List key phrases/sentences below. You will also want to highlight/underline these in your copy of the speech.

_____

_____

_____

_____

How does the president's speech establish his point of view is in line with the ideals of

History (for example, appeals related to World War II and the Holocaust)	The United Nations (including the ideals in its Charter)	The United States (including its Constitution and Declaration of Independence)
Examples:	_Examples:_	_Examples:_

Can you imagine a different interpretation or angle of interpretation about what the president is saying? Who do you think might disagree with the president's suggested course of action? Why do you think they would be opposed?

_____

_____

_____

_____

Worksheet 2. Group Work: Comparing and Contrasting Presidential Rhetoric

In the boxes below, note the key points you identified from the speeches of each of these presidents:

Ronald Reagan	George Bush
Bill Clinton	George W. Bush
Barack Obama	Donald Trump
Joe Biden	

1. Did any of/most of/all of the speeches define a clear dichotomy (stark, mirror-image difference without nuance or complexity) between the goals of U.S. foreign policy and other international actors? Provide specific examples from your speeches below:

_____

_____

_____

2. List the action items that your speeches requested or called for below. Which were achieved? Which were not? What do you think explains the difference between achieving and not achieving these presidential goals?

_____

_____

_____

_____

_____

3. Did you find the appeals to history and authority (especially the foundational documents of the United States and the United Nations) effective in your speech? Why or why not?

_____

_____

_____

4. Did your speech foster a sense of urgency and/or danger? What was the danger? How did the president describe the danger?

_____

_____

_____

5. Despite significant differences between the times and personalities of the presidents, did you notice any significant similarities across these speeches? What were the similarities?

_____

_____

_____

6. What were the biggest differences you noted? What might explain those differences?

_____

_____

_____

Worksheet 3. Group Work: Examining One President's Rhetoric

You each read a speech by the same president before the United Nations General Assembly but each from a different year. Spend some time sharing the key points that you identified from each speech in the chart below:

President _____

Year:	Year:
Year:	Year:
Year:	Year:
Year:	Year:

1. What are the primary similarities/continuities that you see in this president's speeches? Are there similar ways that he portrays his goals and foreign policy? Does he use particular phrases and/or rhetorical strategies? Other similarities that you noticed?

_____

_____

2. What are the primary differences/changes that you see in this president's speeches?

_____

_____

NOTES

1. United Nations, "Growth in United Nations Membership, 1945–Present," https://www.unsecretariat.net/en/sections/member-states/growth-united-na tions-membership-1945-present/index.html (accessed June 23, 2020).

2. Morgan Ortagus, US Department of State spokesperson, "Update on U.S. Withdrawal from the World Health Organization," September 3, 2020, https://2017-2021.state.gov/update-on-u-s-withdrawal-from-the-world-health -organization/index.html.

3. See United Nations, "The United Nations System," https://www.un.org/ en/pdfs/un_system_chart.pdf. The chart shows the six principal organs of the United Nations and its fifteen specialized agencies, along with their myriad subsidiaries.

4. "Charter of the United Nations," https://www.un.org/en/charter-united -nations/. This webpage includes historical context for the signing of the charter in 1945 as well as a table of contents with clickable content. And at the bottom of the page is historical television footage of the signing of the charter.

5. John A. Krout, ed., *United Nations: Success or Failure?* (New York: Academy of Political Science, 1953); I. G. Edmonds, *The United Nations: Successes and Failures* (Boston: Bobbs-Merrill, 1974). Other works that do not have this success/failure dichotomy in the title but use it as their analytical focus include Paul Kennedy, *The Parliament of Man: The Past, Present, and Future of the United Nations* (New York: Vintage Books, 2006); James Barros, *The United Nations: Past, Present, and Future* (New York: Free Press, 1972); Tom J. Farer, "The United Nations and Human Rights: More Than a Whimper," *Human Rights Quarterly* 9 no. 4 (1987): 550–86; and Evan Luard, *A History of the United Nations*, vol. 1, *The Years of Western Domination, 1945–1955* (New York: St. Martin's, 1982).

6. Amy L. Sayward, *The United Nations in International History* (London: Bloomsbury, 2017).

7. Emily Rosenberg, "Rosenberg's Commentary," in *American Cold War Strategy: Interpreting NSC 68*, ed. Ernest R. May (Boston: Bedford/St. Martin's, 1993), 160–64.

8. Links to these presidential speeches (specific citation on the speech copies) and more information on these presidents and their foreign policies are available at University of Virginia, Miller Center for Public Affairs, https://millercen ter.org/, and the presidential libraries administered by the National Archives and Records Administration. There is also a now-outdated list and links of presidential addresses to the United Nations General Assembly at US State Department, "Presidential Remarks to the United Nations General Assembly," archived content, last updated January 20, 2017, https://2009-2017.state.gov/p/ io/potusunga/index.htm.

9. "Reagan and Gorbachev: The Reykjavik Summit," August 7, 2018, Atomic Heritage Foundation with the National Museum of Nuclear Science and History, https://www.atomicheritage.org/history/reagan-and-gorbachev-reykjavik-summit.

10. The "rocket man" and "mad man" quotations came from a Huntsville, Alabama, rally on September 23, 2017. Excerpts from the address are available from Guardian News, "Trump: I'll Handle 'Little Rocket Man' Kim Jong-un," https://www.youtube.com/watch?v=ETNKAQGq8Ts. For the DMZ meeting, see Josh Lederman and Hans Nichols, "Trump Meets Kim Jong Un, Becomes First Sitting U.S. President to Step into North Korea," June 29, 2019, NBC News, https://www.nbcnews.com/politics/donald-trump/trump-kim-jong-un-meet-dmz-n1025041.

11. Lise Morjé Howard, "Sources of Change in United States-United Nations Relations," *Global Governance* 16, no. 4 (October-December 2010): 485–503.

Teaching Women and US Foreign Policy

Hillary Rodham Clinton and Women's Rights as Human Rights

ALLIDA BLACK AND
KATE WECKESSER ENGLISH

Why Teach This Lesson?

"Women's rights are human rights." Several, if not most, of your students will have seen this mantra emblazoned across T-shirts, sweatshirts, mugs, posters, bumper stickers, and such. Yet few will know the backstory of this saying—much less its impact on the United Nations and US foreign policy. Even fewer understand the intrinsic connection the status of women has with a nation's peace, security, and economic development. And very few will grasp the role Hillary Rodham Clinton had in defining, promoting, and implementing this fundamental principle. In short, while this phrase has entered our national political lexicon, it has not entered most survey courses. Hillary Rodham Clinton was not the first person to make this declaration—but her choice of venue, audience, and language placed it before the world in unavoidable ways. Her clarion call turned a small movement into a global force, shaped UN Security Council resolutions, and made women, peace, and security key principles of the foreign policy of the presidential administration of Barack Obama. It also placed her in a very public maelstrom over women's roles in US politics, China's dismissal of human rights, and whether women's rights were a form of Western cultural imperialism.

In addition to the historical significance of Hillary Rodham Clinton's work across two presidential administrations and the connections between the "national" and "international" that are the focus of this chapter, it also centers the work of women in the crafting of US and transnational history, which may help you connect this lesson to themes of women's advancement that you have covered throughout the course. Finally, the lesson plan connected to this essay gives students the opportunity to develop and practice historical empathy and to apply the ideas developed by Clinton to their present circumstances and the news of the day.

Introduction

In 2009, during Secretary Clinton's leadership of the US State Department, I coordinated a conference in Geneva, Switzerland, for one hundred women from fifty conflict-nations for the State Department, the United Nations High Commissioner for Human Rights, the International Labour Organization, and the Eleanor Roosevelt Papers Project (of which I was the founder, executive editor, and principal investigator). The goal was to use Roosevelt's plain-spoken enunciation of rights to encourage the women to find their own words to use in supporting the rights they prioritized in their home countries. Secretary Clinton was the lynchpin to this conversation. I saw the force of her Beijing declaration up close and personal—how these women ravaged by war and famine took courage from her vision and made it their own. When she addressed the Geneva gathering—even though it was over a live satellite feed—some wept, some grasped their hands to their chests, some held their seatmate's hand, and others stood in silent attention. Two years later State sent me to Argentina to discuss women's human rights with women lawyers and with the Mothers of the Murdered. The reaction was the same. In 2017, I urged Secretary Clinton to document her archival record in ways that could help students look past easy stereotypes and have the public grapple with the complex realities of a world in which women's economic, political, and physical rights are often subject to social and political whimsy. This chapter is part of that effort.[1]

The Road to Beijing: The United Nations and Women's Rights

From its inception in 1945, the United Nations endorsed women's equality. Its Charter reaffirmed "faith in fundamental human rights, in the dignity and worth of the human person, [and] in the equal rights of men and women and of nations large and small."[2] Article 1 of the 1948 Universal Declaration of Human Rights (UDHR) similarly proclaimed "all human beings are born free and equal in dignity and in rights. They are endowed with reason and conscience and should act towards one another in a spirit of brotherhood."[3] Yet, it took decades to translate those words into action.[4] Thirty years of Cold War politics hardened national stances on social, economic, and cultural rights. Meanwhile, the US civil rights movement and global anticolonial revolutions challenged assumptions about race and authority. Moreover, although women began to speak out against the discrimination they faced, women were far from united over what their roles, priorities, and actions should be.

In short, it took thirty-one years of pressure by the UN Commission on the Status of Women, dozens of nongovernmental organizations, thousands of women activists, and the first World Conference on Women in 1975 to pressure the United Nations and its member states to act. One of the first steps in that direction was the declaration of 1975–1985 as the UN Decade for Women. Then, in 1979, on International Human Rights Day, the United Nations' General Assembly adopted the Convention to End all forms of Discrimination Against Women (CEDAW) by a vote of 130 to none, with 10 abstentions.[5] CEDAW eventually became "a global norm" and established "the moral, civic, and political equality of women; women's right to be free from discrimination and violence; and the responsibility of governments to take positive action to achieve these goals."[6]

The US delegation to the UN General Assembly voted for it. President Jimmy Carter, who had made human rights a hallmark of his foreign policy, signed the Convention the following year and sent it to the United States Senate, where it has languished for forty years — trapped by deep divisions within and between the political parties, an intractable alliance of social and fiscal conservatives, and a persistent unwillingness to consider women's status as a key indicator of a nation's stability.[7] Ironically, CEDAW arrived at the Senate at the exact moment that the fragile feminist consensus that had passed the Equal Rights Amendment in thirty-five states had frayed, leaving it three states short of ratification, and that Carter's human rights–centered foreign policy was under siege.

Undeterred by US congressional intransigence toward CEDAW, American women's and human rights nongovernmental groups had worked in the intervening years to convert CEDAW's goals into policy and started to forge the links between women's rights and human rights. This was not an easy task. Racial, religious, and ethnic differences had threatened to derail the first two UN World Conferences on Women in 1975 and 1980. So as organizers planned the third UN World Conference on Women, they realized that a new frame of reference was essential if the delegates were to influence their governments, moving from global resolutions to real changes at home. They found their focus within the UN Charter and CEDAW, both of which emphasized "equality, development, and peace." In July 1985, as the UN Decade for Women drew to a close, 31,000 activists representing 157 nations gathered in Nairobi, Kenya, for the third UN Women's Conference and debated how best to advance women's security. The action plan they issued introduced three overarching principles:

- Women's economic security did not just depend upon eliminating discriminatory policies and customs that targeted women. Programs must *advance* women's economic security and assess how nationality, region, class, and race reinforce discrimination.
- Violence against women—whether inflicted and supported by custom (female genital mutilation), used as a weapon of war (rape), or promoted as a business venture (trafficking and sexual slavery)— undermined any effort toward peace; and,
- For women to achieve full equality, governments must not only mainstream women's concerns but also establish "high-level institutional mechanisms to monitor and implement progress towards equality in all sectors."[8]

But the "official" vocabulary did not yet exist to connect women's rights to human rights in the same way that virulent racial discrimination was already identified as a fundamental obstacle to achieving human rights.

Six years after Nairobi, the UN announced it would hold a conference on human rights in Vienna in 1993—but it left women's rights off the agenda. In response, the Center for Women's Global Leadership launched the Global Campaign for Women's Rights to insist that the UN's Vienna Conference "comprehensively address women's human rights at every level" and recognize "gender violence, a universal phenomenon which takes many forms across culture, race and class, as a violation of human rights requiring immediate action." By December

1991, more than a half-million women, representing a thousand organizations in 124 countries, had signed the petition.[9] In 1992, women secured their space on the agenda. The day the delegates assembled in Vienna, Geraldine Ferraro (the 1984 Democratic Party vice presidential candidate), who chaired the US delegation to the conference, wrote,

> Several years ago, women's rights advocates worldwide began to turn up at the same conventions. . . . As they talked, the women made a global connection: these weren't scattered "women's problems," not "minor" abuses. . . . These women recognized that gender-based violence was a matter of fundamental human rights.[10]

Later that year, Bill Clinton was elected president of the United States, and hopes for CEDAW were revived. The Reagan administration had opposed it, and the Bush administration straddled the debate, refusing to make it a congressional priority. President Clinton, however, supported CEDAW, and sixty-eight senators sent him a letter supporting its ratification. As a result, Congress again held hearings, but the issue of reproductive rights once more sidelined CEDAW's adoption. In 1994, when the Senate Foreign Relations Committee finally voted CEDAW out of committee, two Republican senators put a hold on the bill. By the summer of 1995, CEDAW had become a cudgel in the Republican-controlled House to condemn the upcoming fourth UN Conference on Women in Beijing, China, with First Lady Hillary Rodham Clinton heading the US delegation.[11]

The Road to Beijing: Hillary Rodham Clinton and Women's Rights

Hillary Rodham Clinton's early life had prepared her for this leadership role. Raised to stand up for herself and educated to believe her voice mattered, she challenged convention at a young age. Her mother's journey from abandoned child to self-supporting teenager and then to "an affectionate and levelheaded" wife and mother taught a young Hillary Rodham both how perilous life can be and the courage and determination it often required. When her Yale Law School classmates pursued more lucrative and traditional careers, she chose family law — studying child trauma at the Yale Child Study Center. She then joined the Children's Defense Fund, where she uncovered how

Massachusetts public schools excluded poor children with disabilities; documented the discriminatory admissions practices that governed Alabama's private white "academies"; and convinced South Carolina jailors that juvenile offenders should not be incarcerated alongside adult prisoners.[12]

Clinton continued to use the law to improve lives after moving to Arkansas in August 1974 as the newest member of the University of Arkansas Law School faculty. She taught criminal procedure and trial advocacy, managed the school's prison project, built its legal aid program, and cofounded the state's first rape crisis hotline. Three years later, President Jimmy Carter appointed her to the Legal Services Corporation board, where—for the next four years, two as board chair— she helped fund, direct, and protect legal aid bureaus across the nation. In 1978, convinced that children needed an "independent force" to help parents and children shape relevant state policies, she founded Arkansas Advocates for Children and Families. That same year, she began her eleven-year tenure on the Children's Defense Fund (CDF) board, helping CDF develop and promote national and state policies addressing child exploitation, poverty, health, domestic violence, and education.[13] In November 1978, Bill Clinton was elected governor of Arkansas. The First Lady of Arkansas—also a partner in the Rose Law Firm—divided her activism between nongovernmental organizations and government and public health institutions. Her public role, however, only underscored her commitment to issues of access and inclusion. She chaired the governor's Advisory Commission on Rural Health; worked with Dr. Joycelyn Elders and other minority medical personnel to bring public health services to counties that had none; and after learning that children had to be driven to Memphis, Tennessee, or Dallas, Texas, for critical care, played a lead role in creating Arkansas Children's Hospital, on whose board she served until she moved to the White House in 1993.[14]

In 1980, as women's rights advocates prepared to address global inequities in employment, health, and education at the UN Conference on Women in Copenhagen, Clinton also focused on addressing systemic obstacles to women's health, safety, and employment and the racial and rural educational divides in Arkansas. In 1983–84, she led the fight to reform the state's public education system—a system that lacked instruction in the lab sciences and high-level math outside the state's few cities—and increase the salaries of the state's public school teachers. The evidence she collected, the support she marshaled, and the testimony she delivered convinced the state legislature to change the funding allocations, raise teacher salaries, and offer all phases of a comprehensive curriculum across the state.

This work had just as profound a personal impact on Clinton. As she met with teachers, parents, and children across the state's seventy-five counties, the contrast with her own public school experience in the Chicago suburb of Park Ridge, Illinois, could not have been more pronounced. Many of the young parents she met could barely read or did not know how to read to their children or prepare them for school. In 1985, when she learned of an Israel-based program that helped young, illiterate parents become their children's first teachers, she brought the leader to Arkansas to help her adapt the methodology to work across the state. Women typically ignored by the state—young, illiterate, married or single, unemployed or underemployed, Black, Latinx, and white mothers in cities, towns, and tiny rural communities—gained the skills and the confidence to read to their children, continue their own education, and reenter the job market. Her program, the Home Instruction Program for Preschool Youngsters—nicknamed HIPPY, quickly went national.[15] The international connection between Israel and Arkansas behind this success was a seed that continued to germinate in Clinton's mind. Since graduating from Wellesley, Clinton had kept up a steady correspondence with her college classmate Jan Piercy, an economist focused on impact investing and development who shared Clinton's commitment to developing public policies to combat inequality. As Clinton built HIPPY, Piercy returned from four years in Bangladesh, where she had followed Muhammad Yunus's work to develop ways poor women could access credit. In 1986, Clinton brought Yunus to Arkansas, supported the creation of the Good Faith Fund, and played a significant role in raising its investment capital and guiding its development.[16]

The American Bar Association (ABA) took notice of Clinton's leadership and innovation on issues that greatly impacted women's lives. In 1989, facing pressure from its women members to address their concerns, the ABA created the Committee on Women in the Legal Profession and tapped Clinton to chair it. She held hearings around the nation, documented the discrimination and challenges women attorneys faced, submitted detailed analyses and recommendations to the ABA's executive committee, and persuaded her reluctant colleagues to acknowledge and address the impact their attitudes had on women attorneys.

Clinton herself knew the challenges of being a female attorney first-hand. Although she had made partner at the Rose Law Firm—the first woman to do so—her time there was fraught with the pressure of balancing the firm's goals with her many public service commitments and the expectations that came with being the governor's wife. All of this out-of-the-ordinary work came with exacting costs. Teachers unions, long-entrenched local bankers, segregationists, and Arkansans steeped in cultural traditions lampooned her. Political opponents ridiculed her feminism, her hairstyle, her clothes, her investments, her accent, and her continued use of her maiden name: Hillary *Rodham* Clinton. She became the lightning rod for those Arkansans discomforted by the challenges she posed to their social views, their personal values, and their vision for the state. Many saw her as a dangerous northern woman threatening to destroy the southern way of life. Highly personal criticisms, reinforced by rumor and speculation, intensified as her work progressed.

In short, by the time Clinton entered the White House in 1993, she, like the women pressuring the United Nations, straddled the lines between insider and challenger and confronted the intense public ridicule and unbridled expectations that accompanied such untraditional action. When Clinton had addressed her Wellesley graduating class in 1969, she insisted that "politics is the art of making the impossible possible." She spent the next twenty-two years striving to master that art—with mixed success but increased focus and expertise. She addressed discrimination on multiple fronts—child exploitation; sexual violence; unequal access to education, health care, and capital; and gendered workplaces. Rather than stick to one lane, she used multiple avenues to combat it—the state and federal governments, the courts, legal clinics, professional associations, advocacy organizations, and private hospitals.[17]

By April 1993, three months after she became First Lady, Clinton's sense of human dignity and the policy work required to advance it became national news. Decrying America's inequality and its refusal to recognize all its citizens as one community, in an April 1993 address at the University of Texas, she called for all to "recognize the signs of alienation and despair and hopelessness that are all too common and cannot be ignored." Major press outlets pounced, lampooning her as Saint Hillary, while the left took credit for her remarks. Conservatives pounced: Who was she to speak for America and for its women?[18]

Two months later, men—and the few women who insisted upon being included—gathered in Vienna for the World Conference on Human

Rights. Expectations for the gathering, the first global discussion on human rights since the collapse of the Soviet Union, ran high. But women were worried, fearful that their human rights would be sidelined. However, after two weeks of deliberation, the UN human rights community embraced their demands. "The human rights of women and of the girl-child," Section 18 of the Vienna Declaration and Programme of Action proclaimed, "are an inalienable, integral and indivisible part of universal human rights." The mainstream US press paid scant attention to the proclamations coming from Vienna.[19]

Planning began for a Fourth UN Conference on Women. Three months later Clinton testified before multiple congressional committees on the importance of health-care reform, the first First Lady since Eleanor Roosevelt to testify before the House and Senate. Both initiatives required bold action and persistent engagement. Clinton, who had great interest in the conference and hoped that it could produce concrete results, instructed her staff to monitor its development.[20]

Beijing: "Women's Rights Are Human Rights, Once and for All"

In 1994, powerful forces had converged to circumscribe women's human rights and to caricature Hillary Rodham Clinton as she advocated for national health-care reform. Well-financed advertising campaigns accused Clinton of proposing "death panels," increasing health-care costs, and imposing socialized medicine. As she traveled the country holding public hearings, death threats escalated, and armed crowds often greeted her. In September 1994, the International Conference on Population and Development held in Cairo, Egypt, turned into such a televised quarrel between American Catholic bishops and birth control advocates that Vice President Al Gore (despite having just torn his Achilles tendon) was sent to assure all that the United States was not "pro-abortion."[21] That same week Congress rejected a watered-down version of the Clinton health-care plan. Two months later in the 1994 midterm elections, Republicans gained majorities in both the House of Representatives and the Senate for the first time since 1954. As the year ended, Clinton—scapegoated, threatened, and keenly aware of the attacks on single women with children and on women's rights at home and abroad—decided to address her critics, speak out for vulnerable children, attend the World Conference on Social Development in Copenhagen, Denmark, and accept the State Department's request that she visit five South Asian nations (Pakistan, India, Nepal, Bangladesh, and Sri Lanka) to reiterate American support for their troubled democracies.[22]

By March 1995, casting aside Secret Service concerns, Clinton had added her own additional priority for the South Asia trip: "to meet rural as well as urban women, to jettison the predictable itineraries and get into the villages where most people lived."[23] As she toured Pakistan, her conversations centered on "women's choices." The Rajiv Gandhi Foundation had asked her to give a major address on women's rights, but as she traveled to India, she had not yet finished writing her speech. Each draft seemed inadequate. Then a high school student gave Clinton a copy of a poem she had written:

> We seek only to give words
> to those who cannot speak
> (too many women
> in too many countries)
> I see only to forget
> The sorrows of my grandmother's
> Silence.

The poem gave Clinton the framework for her talk and the vocabulary she sought "to convey [her] belief that issues affecting women and girls should not be dismissed as 'soft' . . . but should be fully integrated into domestic and foreign policy decisions."[24]

By the time Clinton had come to India, she realized that she had been listening to women's voices since childhood, that they had played a huge role in her policy work for the CDF, Arkansas, the ABA, and the White House. Now she thought of "the billions of women around the world who were silenced every day" and the high cost women paid for breaking their silence.[25] Before returning to the White House, she met with Benazir Bhutto (the first female prime minister of Pakistan), Mother Teresa (famed humanitarian serving the poor of Calcutta, India), and pioneering financier Muhammad Yunus (of Bangladesh) as well as market women, rural women, college women, businesswomen, and, most especially, the women of the Self-Employed Women's Association of India, who serenaded her with "We Shall Overcome" in their native language of Gujarati. These experiences and Clinton's own history "now all came together." She connected human rights with women's rights in an indivisible way. America had not.[26]

Events during the summer of 1995 threatened to derail US participation in the UN's Fourth World Conference on Women. Congress was divided, and critics on the airwaves cited a variety of reasons for opposing US engagement, including China's human rights record, US engagement in the Balkan conflict, the volatile debate over gays in the military ("Don't Ask, Don't Tell"), and President Clinton's commitment to a more globalized trade policy. China, which had lobbied to hold the conference, realized that the focus would be on human rights and as a result blocked delegates' visas and separated governmental delegates in Beijing from the nongovernmental organization delegations in Huairou (an hour's drive to the north). Then Harry Wu (a Chinese American human rights activist from Milpitas, California, known for his detention in and investigation of Chinese labor camps) was arrested in early July, as he tried to reenter China with forged credentials. Capitol Hill, human rights organizations, and the national press insisted that the US boycott the conference and were particularly adamant that Clinton not attend, despite her UN invitation to address the gathering. US Representative Nancy Pelosi, whose district abutted Wu's, was particularly opposed, and Wu's wife insisted Clinton stay home. The White House grew increasingly leery, and pressure increased on her not to attend. Clinton, as the debate intensified, threatened to attend as a private citizen and instructed her staff to use her personal credit card to book her travel. The State Department grew more anxious. Only on August 24, when Wu left China after having been sentenced to exile by the Chinese government, did the White House relent.[27]

Clinton had thought deeply about her speech as the debate over her attendance escalated. She had worked with her speechwriter, Lissa Muscatine, for weeks, writing and rewriting it. When UN Ambassador Madeleine Albright, who headed the US delegation, asked Clinton what she wanted to say, Clinton replied that she wanted "to push the envelope as far as I can for women and girls." As they flew to Beijing, she, Muscatine, and senior foreign policy advisers continued revisiting the speech in Clinton's cabin.[28] Clinton was aware of the real-world impact it could have on women around the globe, not to mention the immense criticism she would have to bear if the speech bombed. A leading US senator had already labeled the gathering "an unsanctioned festival of anti-family, anti-American sentiment." Clinton also knew that a Republican victory in the 1996 presidential election would send her back to Arkansas.[29]

The speech could have been a clarion call for dignity—aspirational in tone, reflective of the UDHR and the moral imperative CEDAW embodied. Instead, it directly confronted those who questioned why the world should focus on the basic human rights of women and girls: "Let them listen to the voices of women in their homes, neighborhoods, and workplaces." To those who questioned women's political and economic contributions, Clinton insisted, "Let them look at the women gathered here and at Huairou." To those who doubted the gathering's import, she countered, "It is conferences like this that compel governments and peoples everywhere to listen, look and face the world's most pressing problems . . . to give voice to women everywhere whose experiences go unnoticed, whose words go unheard."[30]

Compel. Listen. Look. Face. Give voice. With those "bold, accessible, and unambiguous" verbs, Clinton stated simple facts with a clarity and scope that had been absent from the world stage. "There is no formula for how women should lead their lives." The Vienna Conference had enshrined women's rights; however, "women will never gain full dignity until their human rights are respected and protected." "It is time," she believed, "to break our silence," to call out the human rights abuses that women encountered around the globe. "It is time for us to say here in Beijing, and the world to hear, that it is no longer acceptable to discuss women's rights as separate from human rights." She then listed— with stark, graphic clarity, in language no government representative had uttered—the violent customs, individual acts, and government policies that violated women and that targeted women who dissented and strove to organize, work toward, and claim a more just life. "Now it is time to act on behalf of women everywhere," Clinton concluded. "If there is one message that echoes forth from this conference, it is that human rights are women's rights. . . . And women's rights are human rights, once and for all."[31]

Clinton and others have recalled their anxiety as the translation delayed response to her remarks. Muscatine initially feared their work had failed. Then the audience erupted, creating such a roar that the leader of her advance team thought there had been an explosion in the hall and rushed with the Secret Service to rescue her. Women grabbed at her and mobbed her as she exited, while some, who could not enter the crowded hall, simply wept.[32] The speech defined the conference. Its clarion call for action reverberated around the globe, galvanizing women, giving them the vocabulary they needed—delivered by a woman of international stature—to articulate and defend their positions. They quoted the speech for the next twenty-five years and beyond.[33]

The Beijing Platform for Action that the 189 delegations negotiated after Clinton's speech similarly defined the global policy agenda for women for decades. It held governments accountable for advancing and defending women's human rights in twelve areas, including combating poverty and sexual violence; ensuring access to education, health care, and wages; and involving women in the political process and all institutions that governed these areas. The platform also undergirded the creation of UNWomen and the priorities it addresses and informed subsequent investigations of the UN High Commission on Human Rights. And, due in no small part to Clinton's insistence, the principles enunciated at Beijing were integrated into US foreign policy.

Clinton returned home to unexpected rave reviews, including from those in Congress, the press, and the White House who had most objected initially to her attendance. The *New York Times* editorialized, "Making good use of her prestige and eloquence . . . Mrs. Clinton demonstrated that a clear and forthright speech makes a far more powerful point than staying home in sullen protest."[34] Suddenly, the White House, which was in the throes of planning Bill Clinton's re-election campaign, saw her as an asset rather than as a ticking time bomb. The Clinton reelection effort even produced large dramatic red campaign buttons linking Hillary Clinton's work in Beijing with Eleanor Roosevelt's work on the Universal Declaration of Human Rights.

Clinton quickly capitalized on this resurgent support. After a 1996 trip to Thailand, where she met with women who had been captured and forced to work in slave-like conditions, she shepherded the drafting and adoption of the landmark Victims of Trafficking and Violence Protection Act. Similarly, in 1997, after meeting with Bosnian women of all ethnicities who told her how they had been targeted and raped by enemy soldiers during the conflict that raged in the former Yugoslavia, she worked with 320 leaders from thirty-six nations to develop strategies and action plans to prevent such future atrocities. When Clinton returned to the White House, she and her chief of staff, Melanne Verveer, worked with the State Department to establish an office addressing women's human rights. In 2000, careful not to overshadow other leaders, Clinton worked behind the scenes to support adoption of UN Security

Council Resolution 1325—the first time the Security Council recognized women as a specific group and mandated government action to secure women's human rights in conflict and post-conflict zones.[35]

When she became secretary of state in 2009, Hillary Clinton created the Office of Global Women's Issues, appointed Verveer as global ambassador at large for women's issues, and persuaded the Obama administration to make it a permanent entity. As secretary of state, she told the Senate Foreign Relations Committee that issues related to women's peace and security must be folded into all State Department and USAID initiatives. She then monitored the drafting of the *Quadrennial Diplomacy and Development Review (QDDR)*—the blueprint detailing the State Department's and USAID's priorities for the next five years—to make certain that issues related to women and girls were prioritized as a cornerstone of US foreign policy.

Implementing this work was as difficult as it was challenging. Some senior foreign service officers interpreted diplomacy in extremely traditional ways—resolving wars, negotiating treaties, and securing flyover rights. They actively opposed women's participation in peace and reconciliation processes and refused to see the connection between gender-based violence and women's economic empowerment to the creation of stronger states. They dismissed those who advocated for Clinton's "full participation agenda" as merely indulging the secretary by working on her "pet project" and assumed that work would disappear when her tenure as secretary ended.

In December 2010, Clinton and her team unveiled the *QDDR*. The legacy of Beijing was found throughout its benchmarks and assessments. State and USAID must "ensure that women are integrated into our efforts to prevent conflict" and "focus on gender equality and elevate investment in women and girls . . . as a way to maximize results across the board."[36] The following year, guided by Clinton, the United States issued its first National Action Plan on Women, Peace, and Security, which was accompanied by President Obama's Executive Order 15395 and committed the nation "to ensure that women participate equally in preventing conflict and building peace in countries threatened and affected by war, violence, and insecurity."[37]

One legacy of Clinton's work is that the foreign policy team of the Biden-Harris administration has a demonstrable record in advancing women's human rights in development, defense, and governance. Another heritage comes in the form of UN Security Council Resolutions 1325, 1880, and 1888, which specifically address women's human rights in war and reconciliation. Yet, how US foreign policy and the United Nations will work to advance Clinton's clarion call to action remains to be seen. As of this writing, the Violence Against Women Act lingers in reauthorization purgatory, and Afghan women who defied traditions to claim their right to education, the vote, employment, and property are at particular risk following the withdrawal of US troops and the end of "America's longest war." Whether Secretary of State Tony Blinken follows the precedent set by the *QDDR* remains to be seen. What is clear is that the gauntlet has been laid at the feet of the United Nations and the United States.

Lesson Plan: Become a Speechwriter

In this chapter, we see the importance that Hillary Clinton placed on the speeches that she delivered and the long-lasting impact of her speech in Beijing. Now students will have the opportunity to test their own speech-writing skills as well as to apply what they have learned about human rights, women's rights, and Clinton's legacy to issues they see in their own lives.

Overview and Background

Students live in a world where the roles of women are in a fragile state of flux. During the COVID-19 pandemic, for example, job losses for women heavily outnumbered those for men, in spite of prior gains in representation in the workforce. This reality reverberated through families, communities, and cultures. The experiences of women directly impact broader society. They are not siloed or separate from humanity as a whole.

As Mrs. Clinton lays out in her speech in Beijing, when women flourish, families flourish, "and when families flourish, communities and nations will flourish. That is why every woman, every man, every child, every family, and every nation on our planet has a stake in the discussion that takes place here." Students of all genders need a deeper understanding of evolving perceptions, experiences, and contributions of women in human rights and security and of how women are a stabilizing force in these spheres.

This lesson is intended to build upon students' reading of the preceding content (likely as homework), which will give them the historical background and context for their work in this lesson. Also, if students have not previously been introduced to the definition of "human rights" as laid out in Universal Declaration of Human Rights (UDHR), you may want to utilize the class period before by having students read the UDHR in class and summarize the key points (see Document A in the "Supporting Resources" section below). Then to segue into what they will be reading for homework and doing in class the next day, show the twenty-minute video of Clinton's Beijing speech (listed in "Supporting Resources") and distribute a written copy of the speech (Document B in "Supporting Resources"). Have students identify which of the "human rights" listed in the UDHR Clinton mentions and what additional rights she includes; you may have students identify the former by underlining them in the text of the speech and by circling the additional rights. This exercise will help students better understand the application of human rights described in the UDHR and how women fit within that construct as well as the impact of Hillary Rodham Clinton's Beijing speech on the course of both US foreign policy and global history. It will also fully equip students to engage in a close reading of the first part of this chapter as homework.

In the next class period, students will put themselves in the role of a speechwriter addressing the topic "Women and Human Rights Today." Students can determine the identity of the speaker as well as the venue and audience for the speech they write; they also may begin preliminary research to gather information and data for their speeches. As a final assessment, students will write the speech that they have brainstormed and planned during the class period, potentially doing more light research based on the additional resources listed at the end of this chapter.

Goals for Student Understanding

According to the National Council for the Social Studies C3 Framework, "active and responsible citizens are able to identify and analyze public problems, deliberate with other people about how to define and address issues, take constructive action together, reflect on their actions, create and sustain groups, and influence institutions both large and small."[38] In order for historic events to resonate with students, establishing relevance is essential. By considering how to translate the issues illustrated in the chapter of women's rights and human rights into a contemporary setting, students will connect with issues from the past to make meaning from events surrounding them today. Specifically,

- Students will develop a deeper understanding of the changing historical definitions and contexts of "human rights."
- Students will consider how women fit into the broader recognition of human rights.
- Students will reflect on the impact Hillary Rodham Clinton had on women's human rights and their integration into US foreign policy.
- Students will develop historical empathy by considering events of the past on their own terms and by trying to develop a speech in the tradition of Hillary Rodham Clinton's.
- Students will reflect on the potential impact of compelling rhetoric and their own capacity to effect change.

What Students Will Do to Build Their Understanding

- Students will analyze the chapter's text to cite specific detail relevant to historic events and their context.
- Students will identify a contemporary figure to address issues for women and human rights that still exist today.
- Students will write persuasively for an audience and venue of their choosing, thereby instilling a sense of ownership of the material and its relevance, specifically addressing the rationale, strategies, context, and impact of a speech on the status of women and human rights today.

Supporting Resources

Document A: The Universal Declaration of Human Rights: https://www .un.org/en/universal-declaration-human-rights/. The Universal Declaration of Human Rights (UDHR) is a milestone document in the history of human rights. Drafted by representatives from different legal and cultural backgrounds from all regions of the world, the Declaration was proclaimed by the UN General Assembly in Paris, France, on December 10, 1948, as a common standard of achievements for all peoples and all nations. It set out, for the first time, fundamental human rights to be universally protected.

Document B: Text of First Lady Hillary Rodham Clinton's Remarks to the Fourth Women's Conference in Beijing, China: https://www.un .org/esa/gopher-data/conf/fwcw/conf/gov/950905175653.txt. The electronic version of this document was prepared at the Fourth World Conference on Women by the United Nations Development Programme (UNDP) in collaboration with the United Nations Fourth World Conference on Women Secretariat. It appears here as written.

Video: First Lady Hillary Rodham Clinton's Remarks to the Fourth Women's Conference in Beijing, China: https://www.youtube.com/watch ?v=xXM4E23Efvk (20:19 long). This particular copy of the material is public domain, as it is a work prepared by an officer or employee of the US government as part of that person's official duties. As referred to here specifically, it is recorded without markings retrieved from a staff file from the First Lady's Office records. Any usage must receive the credit "Courtesy: William J. Clinton Presidential Library."

Lesson Narrative:
Creating a Contemporary Call to Action

Homework Activity: Students engage in a close reading of the narrative at the beginning of this chapter (a Word version of the text is available on the companion website [http://GoldbergSeries.org/UTContemporary USHistory]).

Step 1: Students brainstorm in small groups or as a whole class on what has changed since the speech in 1995, when First Lady Hillary Rodham Clinton spoke of "the billions of women around the world who [are] silenced every day" and the cost of breaking that silence. They should consider the following questions as they brainstorm:

- What work remains undone?
- Were there unintended consequences of equating women's rights and human rights?
- What women remain consigned to silence?
- Whose voices do we need to hear today?
- Have we met the challenge First Lady Hillary Rodham Clinton laid out in 1994?
- How do we guarantee that the issues of women and girls are fully integrated into both domestic and foreign policy in this country?

Step 2: Students place themselves in the role of a speech writer; they may do this individually or in small groups. They must select the person for whom they are writing and consider the following questions:

- Why is this person ideally suited for this moment?
- How does their experience inform the message?

Step 3: Students chose the venue and audience for the speech and consider the following questions:

- Why does this audience need to hear this message?
- What action do you wish to inspire?

Step 4: Students identify communication strategies for their persuasive message and consider the following questions:

- What specific details and qualitative data do you need to make a persuasive argument?
- What quantitative data can you draw on to support your points?
- How can you create a sense of unity and inclusivity to convince your audience to take the action you are seeking?

The instructor may wish to draw their attention to the "Additional Suggested Resources" section at the end of the chapter as sources for this data.

Step 5: Students begin to draft their speeches as well as the contextual section that identifies the students' rationale for their choice of speaker, audience, and venue. Completing, revising, editing, and publishing the speeches for assessment will likely happen following this class period.

Assessment

Students will be assessed on the creation of an effective persuasive speech based on the criteria outlined above. Students will reflect on how the process of creating their speech may have altered their perception of women in human rights and security, the potential impact of compelling rhetoric, and their own capacity to effect change.

319

Additional Suggested Resources

Educators know their students, classrooms, and community best. Below are reputable resources for research on contemporary history, women's history, and history of diverse populations. As with any resource, be sure to review and determine which resources best serve your specific circumstances.

- BBC Teach, https://www.bbc.co.uk/teach
- GLBT Historical Society Museum and Archives: Research Guides, https://www.glbthistory.org/research-guides
- InfoPlease News and Events Year by Year, https://www.infoplease.com/yearbyyear
- Library of Congress, https://www.loc.gov/
- National Archives, https://www.archives.gov/
- National Women's History Museum: *Where Are the Women? A Report of the Status of Women in United States Social Studies Standards*, 2017, https://www.womenshistory.org/social-studies-standards
- PBS Learning Media: Social Studies, https://www.pbslearningmedia.org/subjects/social-studies/
- Pulitzer Center: Education, Programs for K–12 Teachers and Students, https://pulitzercenter.org/education
- Smithsonian Asian Pacific American Center, https://smithsonianapa.org/
- Smithsonian National Museum of African American History and Culture: NMAAHC Digital Resource Guide, https://nmaahc.si.edu/explore/nmaahc-digital-resource-guide
- Smithsonian National Museum of American History: Latino History, https://americanhistory.si.edu/topics/latino-history
- Smithsonian National Museum of the American Indian: Native American Women, https://americanindian.si.edu/online-resources/native-american-women
- US Holocaust Memorial Museum's Center for the Prevention of Genocide: Country Case Studies, https://www.ushmm.org/genocide-prevention/countries

NOTES

1. Publisher's note: Allida Black is the current codirector of the Hillary Rodham Clinton Oral History Project and was the cofounder and chair of Ready for Hillary from 2013 to 2015.

2. United Nations, "United Nations Charter (Full Text)," June 26, 1945, https://www.un.org/en/about-us/un-charter/full-text.

3. United Nations, "Universal Declaration of Human Rights," December 10, 1948, https://www.un.org/sites/un2.un.org/files/udhr.pdf.

4. For a thorough discussion of the events, debates, and covenants leading to CEDAW and the Fourth UN Conference on Women, see Allida Black, "Are Women 'Human'? The UN and the Struggle to Recognize Women's Rights as Human Rights," in *The Human Rights Revolution: An International History*, ed. Akira Iriye, Petra Goedde, and William I. Hitchcock (Oxford: Oxford University Press, 2012), 133–56.

5. UN Women, "Short History of CEDAW Convention," https://www.un.org/womenwatch/daw/cedaw/history.htm (accessed December 3, 2020).

6. Lisa Baldez, *Defying Convention: US Resistance to the UN Treaty on Women's Rights* (New York: Cambridge University Press, 2014), 1.

7. Ibid., 152–54.

8. Black, "Are Women 'Human'?"

9. "Women Bring Concern about Rights to UN," *New York Times*, March 14, 1992, https://www.nytimes.com/1992/03/14/world/women-bring-concern-about-rights-to-un.html.

10. Geraldine Ferraro, "Human Rights for Women," *New York Times*, June 10, 1993, https://www.nytimes.com/1993/068/10/opinion/human-rights-for-women.html.

11. Baldez, *Defying Convention*, 167–72.

12. Hillary Rodham Clinton, *Living History* (New York: Simon & Schuster, 2003), 63; "At Yale, Hillary Clinton Known for Work with New Haven Children," *New Haven Register*, August 6, 2016, https://www.nhregister.com/connecticut/article/At-Yale-Hillary-Clinton-known-for-work-with-New-11326980.php; Penn Rhodeen, interviewed by Allida Black, September 2015.

13. Al Witte, interviewed by Allida Black, August 18, 2015; Don Hollingsworth, interviewed by Allida Black, August 19, 2015; Pat Lile, interviewed by Allida Black, August 15, 2015; Arkansas Advocates for Children & Families, "About Us," https://www.aradvocates.org/about-us/ (accessed December 29, 2020).

14. Ernie Dumas, "Men & Women of Distinction: Dr. Joycelyn Elders," Arkansas PBS, https://www.myarkansaspbs.org/programs/menandwomenofdistinction/joycelynelders (accessed May 31, 2022); Scott Gordon, interviewed by Allida Black, August 17, 2015.

15. HIPPY, the Home Instruction Program for Preschool Youngsters, soon spread across the nation, with programs in every state. Gordon interview; Annette Dove, interviewed by Allida Black, August 17, 2015.

16. Jan Piercy, interviewed by Allida Black, December 17, 2020.

17. Hillary Rodham Clinton, "1969 Student Commencement Address," Wellesley College, https://www.wellesley.edu/events/commencement/archives/1969commencement/studentspeech.

18. Hillary Rodham Clinton, "Remarks by the First Lady Hillary Rodham Clinton, University of Texas," April 7, 1993, https://clintonwhitehouse3.archives.gov/WH/EOP/First_Lady/html/generalspeeches/1993/19930407.html; Michael Kelly, "Saint Hillary," *New York Times Magazine*, May 23, 1993, 22, https://www.nytimes.com/1993/05/23/magazine/saint-hillary.html.

19. United Nations Human Rights, Office of the High Commissioner, "Vienna Declaration and Programme of Action," June 25, 1993, https://www.ohchr.org/en/professionalinterest/pages/vienna.aspx.

20. Lissa Muscatine, interviewed by Allida Black, January 22, 2021.

21. Articles 10 and 16 of the Convention to End Discrimination Against Women (CEDAW), adopted in 1979, clearly assert that women have unassailable rights "to reproductive health care services, goods and facilities that are: (a) available in adequate numbers; (b) accessible physically and economically; (c) accessible without discrimination; and (d) of good quality." As discussed earlier in this chapter, despite endorsement by the Carter and Clinton administrations, the Senate refused to ratify the conventions. As abortion politics morphed into a partisan and evangelical rallying cry, it became the convenient reason to avoid ratifying CEDAW. As women's deaths from abortion increased and the polarization increased, the anti-abortion leadership argued that "family planning" was synonymous with abortion. As delegates from around the world gathered in Cairo in 1994 to address issues related to population and development, critics pounced, accusing the conference of being a world summit on the right to abortion. The states attending the conference "recognized unsafe abortion as a major public health concern, and pledged their commitment to reducing the need for abortion through expanded and improved family planning services, while at the same time recognizing that, in circumstances where not against the law, abortion should be safe." For abortion's impact on American politics see Marjorie Spruill, *Divided We Stand: The Battle over Women's Rights and Family Values That Polarized American Politics* (New York: Bloomsbury, 2017). For UN actions, see United Nations Human Rights, Office of the High Commissioner, "Sexual and Reproductive Rights," https://www.ohchr.org/EN/Issues/Women/WRGS/Pages/HealthRights.aspx.

22. Clinton, *Living History*, 268–80. Melanne Verveer Oral History, September 16, 2004, https://millercenter.org/the-presidency/presidential-oral-histories/melanne-verveer-oral-history.

23. Clinton, *Living History*, 270.

24. As quoted in Clinton, *Living History*, 278; Verveer oral history.

25. Clinton, email to Allida Black, December 21, 2020.

26. Clinton, *Living History*, 281; Piercy interview.

27. Lissa Muscatine, interviewed by Allida Black, August 3, 2015; Verveer oral history; Hillary Rodham Clinton, "Power Shortage," *The Atlantic*, October 2020, https://www.theatlantic.com/magazine/archive/2020/10/hillary-clinton-womens-rights/615463/.

28. Clinton, "Power Shortage"; Muscatine interview; Verveer oral history.

29. R. W. Apple Jr., "An Obstacle Removed; China's Ouster of Wu Helps Make Route to Better Relations a Little Less Bumpy," *New York Times*, August 25, 1995, https://www.nytimes.com/1995/08/25/world/obstacle-removed-china-s-ouster-wu-helps-make-route-better-relations-little-less.html.

30. Hillary Rodham Clinton, "Remarks for the United Nations Fourth World Conference on Women, Beijing, China," September 5, 1995, https://www.un.org/esa/gopher-data/conf/fwcw/conf/gov/950905175653.txt.

31. Ibid.

32. Rick Jasculca, interviewed by Allida Black, September 1995; Piercy interview.

33. Valerie Hudson and Patricia Leidl, *The Hillary Doctrine* (New York: Columbia University Press, 2015), 7–9.

34. "Opinion: Mrs. Clinton's Unwavering Words," *New York Times*, September 6, 1995, https://www.nytimes.com/1995/09/06/opinion/mrs-clinton-s-unwavering-words.html.

35. Hudson and Leidl, *Hillary Doctrine*, 25–28.

36. US Department of State, *Leading through Civilian Power: The First Quadrennial Diplomacy and Development Review*, 2010, https://2009-2017.state.gov/documents/organization/153108.pdf.

37. US Department of State, "US Commitment to Women, Peace, and Security," https://2009-2017.state.gov/s/gwi/wps/index.htm#:~:text=The%20United%20States'%20first%2Dever,affected%20by%20war%2C%20violence%2C%20and.

38. National Council for the Social Studies, "College, Career, and Civic Life (C3) Framework for Social Studies State Standards: Guidance for Enhancing the Rigor of K–12 Civics, Economics, Geography, and History," June 2017, https://www.socialstudies.org/standards/c3.

Contributors

ALLIDA BLACK is Research Professor of History and International Affairs at the George Washington University and the managing director of the Allenswood Group LLC. She has extensive experience advising presidential candidates, conducting presidential oral histories, and designing and managing archives of renowned women political leaders. She serves on the board of the Women's Campaign School at Yale and the Ellen Johnson Sirleaf Presidential Foundation.

MONICA L. BUTLER is an assistant professor of history at Motlow State Community College. Since earning her PhD in history at Arizona State University in 2008, she has taught in the humanities and social sciences at open access institutions in the urban and rural South. Her research explores modern Indigenous and African American history with an emphasis on political representations in popular culture.

JOSH CERRETTI is an associate professor of history and women, gender, and sexuality studies at Western Washington University. His book *Abuses of the Erotic: Militarizing Sexuality in the Post–Cold War United States* was published in 2019, and his work has also appeared in *Radical History Review* and *Gender and History*. He is a former graduate assistant for LGBTQ Wellness Outreach at the State University of New York at Buffalo and currently serves on the board of the Whatcom Peace and Justice Center as well as a delegate to the Northwest Washington Central Labor Council.

LORI CLUNE is a full professor of history at California State University, Fresno, where she teaches undergraduate and graduate courses on the modern United States, Latin America, Southeast Asia, and US diplomatic history. A former high school history teacher, she is also a faculty member with the Smittcamp Family Honors College and regularly team-teaches a US-Cuba upper-division class. Through her research, she analyzes the intersection of politics, diplomacy, propaganda, soft power, communism, and espionage. She is the author of *Executing the Rosenbergs: Death and Diplomacy in a Cold War World* (2016).

KATE WECKESSER ENGLISH is executive director of the Educators' Institute for Human Rights, a collaborative, global human rights education nonprofit NGO based in Washington, DC. An award-winning, eighteen-year classroom veteran educator, Kate holds bachelor's and master's degrees from the University of Connecticut, a graduate certificate in educational leadership from George Mason University, and an executive certificate in nonprofit management from Georgetown University. She serves as a museum teacher fellow for the United States Holocaust Memorial Museum and an ambassador for the Institute for Economics and Peace. International education experience includes work in Ukraine, Bosnia and Herzegovina, Rwanda, Poland, and Cambodia.

HAL M. FRIEDMAN is chair of history and professor of modern history in the History Program of the Department of Social Sciences, part of the School of Liberal Arts at Henry Ford College in Dearborn, Michigan. He is both the recording secretary and the Midwest regional coordinator for the Society for Military History. He has published a trilogy on US national security policy in the immediate postwar Pacific and a trilogy on the transition of the US Naval War College from the Pacific War to the Cold War in the Pacific in the same time period. He is now working on a trilogy about American naval planning for the defense and administration of the immediate postwar Pacific.

LAURA KRENICKI teaches global studies at William J. Johnston Middle School in Colchester, Connecticut. She served on the board of directors for the Connecticut Council for the Social Studies and was a teacher consultant for the Connecticut Geographic Alliance. She has consulted for National Geographic, the *Hartford Courant*, and the UN Global Educators Network and was an adjunct faculty member at the University of New Haven and Eastern Connecticut State

University. She has published inquiry lessons for the Connecticut Humanities TeachItCT.org, Yale University's Programs in International Educational Resources, Connecticut Indian Mariners Project, and the Mystic Seaport Museum Educators' Community, including "Life at Sea" and "Global Perceptions of Whaling."

JEREMY M. MCKENZIE is a retired Coast Guard officer. His last military assignment was at the US Coast Guard Academy's Center for Arctic Study and Policy, where he was a researcher. Jeremy is a member of the Pacific Council on International Policy. He has been conducting research in the Arctic for the past seven years and speaks frequently in schools on climate change issues. Jeremy has presented his research in Moscow at the United Nations House; at the Ministry of Foreign Affairs in Svalbard, Norway; at the first Arctic Safety Conference; and at a meeting of the Arctic Coast Guard Forum.

KATHRYN MCLAIN is a PhD candidate in history at Montana State University, where her research focuses on the history of illicit drug controls in the United States. Her background includes over ten years of work experience with the federal government on domestic and international counter-narcotics and crime prevention programs. Katie works as a consultant with local communities to build and fund substance use prevention and justice sector programs.

NATALIE MENDOZA is an assistant professor of history at the University of Colorado, Boulder. She is a historian of the United States who specializes in Mexican American and Chicanx history, US Latinx history, and the history of race and racism in the United States. In addition to studying the past, Natalie has an active research agenda in the Scholarship of Teaching and Learning in History (History SoTL), a body of literature that uses theoretical and evidence-based research to examine the discipline-specific problems in the teaching and learning of history. Natalie relies upon her training as a historian and her expertise in HistorySoTL to improve history education at multiple levels, including her work on the History Teaching & Learning Project at CU-Boulder, as a consultant for K–12 social studies teachers, and in a pedagogy course she developed and teaches at the graduate level.

Benjamin C. Montoya is an assistant professor of history at Schreiner University in Kerrville, Texas. His research and publications focus on the intersection of immigration and diplomatic history, especially regarding US-Mexican relations. He teaches courses on United States history, Mexican history, US-Latin American diplomatic history, the Vietnam War, and foreign relations between the United States and the Global South after 1945.

Matthew R. Pembleton is a writer and historian of twentieth-century America, US public health and safety, and the US in the world. He teaches at American University and is the author of *Containing Addiction: The Federal Bureau of Narcotics and the Origins of America's Global Drug War* (2017).

Andrew R. Polk is an associate professor of history at Middle Tennessee State University. He is an award-winning teacher and a scholar of American religious history who has published articles and essays in numerous academic journals, including *Church History* and *Presidential Studies Quarterly*, among many others. He is the author of *Faith in Freedom: Propaganda, Presidential Politics, and the Making of an American Religion* (2021), which explores the midcentury political origins of Christian nationalism and America's civil religion.

Kimber M. Quinney is an associate professor of history at California State University, San Marcos, and serves as the adviser and coordinator of the history–social science major, designed for students who want to become K–12 teachers. Her research explores the convergence of ethnicity, immigration, and domestic politics on the making of US foreign policy. Her publications include "Teaching the History of the Cold War through the Lens of Immigration" (*The History Teacher*, 2018) and, most recently, "Less Poletti More Spaghetti" (*Occupied Italy—Rivista di storia dell'Italia occupata*, 2021). She has served as chair of the teaching committee for the Pacific Coast Branch of the American Historical Association and for the Society for Historians of American Foreign Relations.

Amy L. Sayward is a professor of history at Middle Tennessee State University, where she teaches surveys of US and Tennessee history as well as upper-division courses, especially for history majors who want to be middle and high school teachers. Her research has focused on the United Nations in *The Birth of Development: How the World Bank, Food and Agriculture Organization, and World Health Organization Changed the World, 1945–1965* (2006) and *The United Nations in International History* (2018). She has also coedited two books on Tennessee's history: *Tennessee's New Abolitionists: The Fight against the Death Penalty in the Volunteer State* (2010) and *Tennessee Histories* (2016), which is the e-text used for MTSU's Tennessee history courses.

AARON TREADWELL is an assistant professor of history at Middle Tennessee State University, an assistant to the historiographer of the African Methodist Episcopal (AME) Church, and the head archivist for the AME-Archives digital database. His areas of expertise are Black spirituality with an emphasis on the AME Church; US history with an emphasis on sociopolitical activism; and African American history. He has also taught history and religion at Florida Agricultural and Mechanical University, Howard University, Howard Divinity School, and Edward Waters College.

LEAH VALLELY is a professor of history at Calhoun Community College, where she teaches surveys of US and world history. She earned a PhD in public history from Middle Tennessee State University, a master's degree in special education from Western Carolina University, and a master's degree in secondary history education from Auburn University at Montgomery. Her current research focuses on local consequences of the Cold War and the scholarship of teaching and learning.

CARL P. WATTS is the former director of online history and political science and the former chair of the Department of Social Studies in the College of Education at Baker College, Michigan. In 2021, he was appointed assistant professor of national security studies in the US Air Force Global College of Graduate Professional Military Education. He is the author of *Rhodesia's Unilateral Declaration of Independence: An International History* (2012). He has been a fellow of the Royal Historical Society since 2008.

Index

Bush, George W., 23–24; Arctic policy, 243–44; Bush Doctrine, 273; domestic surveillance policy, 114–15; drug enforcement policy, 92–93; environmental conservation and sustainability policy, 244; Executive Order 12333, 111–12, 114, 117; Executive Order 13284, 114; Executive Order 13470, 114; foreign policy efforts outside the UN framework, 286; Help Americans Vote Act, 45; Mexican immigration policy, 180–81; National Security Directive 66, 240; No Child Left Behind Act (2002), 155; President's Surveillance Program (Stellar Wind), 115; Supreme Court nominations, 75
Butter Battle Book, The (Dr. Seuss), 269–70
buttons, use of in historical thinking exercises, 272
Byrd, James, Jr., 64

C-SPAN, 23
caging, as a disenfranchisement policy, 43
Cali Cartel (Colombia), 90
California, undocumented migration policy, 178–80
Camarena, Enrique, murder of, 89
Campus Crusade for Christ, 160
Carter, Jimmy: and the Cold War, 268–69; domestic surveillance policy, 110–11; military spending, 219; USSR foreign policy, 220–21
Carver, George Washington, 5
cause-and-effect relationships, 9
Center for Strategic and International Studies, 248
Central Intelligence Agency (CIA): presence in Colombia, 92;

surveillance of citizens, 109–10; surveillance powers, 114
Cesar Chavez Service Employees International Union, 60
change and continuity in history, 7, 9, 11, 72–76
charter schools, 156–57
chattel slavery, and sex slavery, 37–38
Chernobyl nuclear accident, 270
China, influence in Arctic region, 250
Christmas, Michael, 107
chronology, importance of, 9
Church, Frank, 109
Church Committee, 109–10, 116
citizenship, critical thinking on, 26
Civicus (organization), 47
civil liberties: and national security, 105, 108–21; presidential interpretations of, 22–23
Civil Rights Act (1964), 22, 42
Civil Rights Restoration Act (CRRA, 1987), 21–23
climate change: environmental cost *vs.* security and economic benefits in policymaking, 251; study of based presidential policy on the Arctic, 239–51. *See also terms beginning with Arctic*
Clinton, Bill, 23; Antiterrorism and Death Penalty Act (1996), 113; Arctic policy, 243; drug enforcement policy, 91; efforts to build a post–Cold War consensus, 286; expansion of NATO, 224; foreign policy efforts re: Sudan and Rwanda, 286; Goals 2000: Educate America Act (2000), 155; impeachment of, 8; LGBTQ+ policy, 61; NAFTA, 176–78; "Plan Colombia" program, 92; support of CEDAW, 305
Clipper chips, 113

Dewey, John, 5
digital technology, and privacy, 106
Director of National Intelligence
 (DNI), 112; creation of, 114; partisan appointments to, 114
disenfranchisement: felon, 45–46;
 policies toward African Americans,
 38–47. *See also* voter suppression
"dissident" (term), 109
documentaries, 157
documents: analysis and interpretation of, 12; identification of, 175;
 "sourcing" of, 9
domestic policy, links to foreign
 policy, 105
Don't Ask, Don't Tell policy (1993),
 23, 55–57, 65, 223, 311
Dorman, Gerald, 153
drag queens, 62
Dreier, David, 44
Drug Abuse Policy Office, creation
 of, 87
Drug Abuse Resistance Education
 (D.A.R.E.) program, 89
drug czar, 87
Drug Enforcement Agency (DEA):
 "kingpin strategy," 85, 89; Special
 Investigative Unit, 94
drug policy, 83–86
drug trafficking, 112–13
Due Process Clause, 19–27
Durand, Jorge, 184–85

education: accountability in, 155; and
 citizenship, 154; and the decline of
 intergenerational economic gain,
 152; as an engine of national competitiveness, 152; entrepreneurialism in, 155; and national identity,
 158; and national power, 150–54;
 secularization of, 158; as a vehicle
 for economic improvement, 152

educational performance, US international standing, 153
educational policy: controversial, 147;
 and cultural wars, 158–60; debates
 on performance, 146–47; and federalism, 147, 154–57; federal reforms
 limited by constitution, 160; and
 national identity, 146–60; reform
 via external and domestic considerations, 160; sources for teaching,
 149–50; US concern about China
 and India, 160
educational reform, based on free
 market principles, 152
educational standards, and technological progress, 152
Education Freedom Scholarships, 156
eight-box law, 41
Eisenhower, Dwight, Supreme Court
 nominations, 76
Elementary and Secondary Education Act (ESEA, 1965), 151
El Paso border sweeps, 176
Endara, Guillermo, 221
Engel v. Vitale (1962), 160
Escobar, Pablo, 90
espionage, US citizens found guilty
 of, 107
Espionage Act (1917), 108, 117
Every Student Succeeds Act (ESSA,
 2015), 156

facts *vs.* opinions and conjecture, 130
Fair Fight (organization), 46–47
Fair Vote (organization), 47
"fake news," and public opinion, 8
Fate of the Earth, The (Schell), 266–67
Federal Bureau of Investigation (FBI):
 Hostage Rescue Team, 131–32;
 racial profiling, 119–20; surveil-
 lance of citizens, 109; surveillance
 powers, 114–15, 117

The Harvey Goldberg Series
for Understanding and Teaching History

Understanding and Teaching the Modern Middle East
Edited by Omnia El Shakry

Understanding and Teaching the Holocaust
Edited by Laura J. Hilton and Avinoam Patt

Understanding and Teaching American Slavery
Edited by Bethany Jay and Cynthia Lynn Lyerly

Understanding and Teaching the Civil Rights Movement
Edited by Hasan Kwame Jeffries

Understanding and Teaching the Age of Revolutions
Edited by Ben Marsh and Mike Rapport

Understanding and Teaching the Cold War
Edited by Matthew Masur

Understanding and Teaching Contemporary US History since Reagan
Edited by Kimber M. Quinney and Amy L. Sayward

Understanding and Teaching Native American History
Edited by Kristofer Ray and Brady DeSanti

*Understanding and Teaching US Lesbian, Gay, Bisexual, and
Transgender History, second edition*
Edited by Leila J. Rupp and Susan K. Freeman

Understanding and Teaching the Vietnam War
Edited by John Day Tully, Matthew Masur, and Brad Austin